THE ORTHODOX BIBLE S
SERIES

THE GOSPEL
OF MATTHEW

TORAH FOR THE CHURCH

by Fr. Lawrence R. Farley

Conciliar Press
Ben Lomond, California

Dedicated to
The Very Rev. Terry and Mrs. Wendy Wiebe,
for the gift of unfailing friendship

Table of Contents and Outline

℃ Introduction to the Series ℈

A Word about Scholarship and Translation

This commentary was written for your grandmother. And for your plumber, your banker, your next-door neighbor, and the girl who serves you French fries at the nearby McDonald's. That is, it was written for the average layman, for the nonprofessional who feels a bit intimidated by the presence of copious footnotes, long bibliographies, and all those other things which so enrich the lives of academics. It is written for the pious Orthodox layman who is mystified by such things as Source Criticism, but who nonetheless wants to know what the Scriptures mean.

Therefore, it is unlike many other commentaries, which are written as contributions to the ongoing endeavor of scholarship and as parts of a continuous dialogue among scholars. That endeavor and dialogue is indeed worthwhile, but the present commentary forms no part of it. For it assumes, without argument, a certain point of view, and asserts it without defense, believing it to be consistent with the presuppositions of the Fathers and therefore consistent with Orthodox Tradition. It has but one aim: to be the sort of book a busy parish priest might put in the hands of an interested parishioner who says to him over coffee hour after Liturgy, "Father, I'm not sure I really get what St. Paul is saying in the Epistles. What does it all mean?" This commentary tries to tell the perplexed parishioner what the writers of the New Testament mean.

Regarding the translation used herein, an Italian proverb says, "All translators are traitors." (The proverb proves its own point, for it sounds better in Italian!) The point of the proverb, of course, is that no translation, however careful, can bring out all the nuances and meanings of the original, since no language can be the mathematical equivalent of another. The English translator is faced, it would seem, with a choice: either he can make the translation something of a rough paraphrase of the original and render it into flowing sonorous English; or he can attempt to make a fairly literal, word-for-word translation from the original with the resultant English being stilted, wooden, and clumsy.

These two basic and different approaches to translation correspond to two basic and different activities in the Church. The Church needs a translation of the Scriptures for use in worship. This should be in good, grammatical, and flowing English, as elegant as possible and suited to its function in the majestic worship of the Liturgy. The Church also needs a translation of the Scriptures for private study and for group Bible study. Here the elegance of its English is of lesser concern. What is of greater concern here is the bringing out of all the nuances found in the original. Thus this approach will tend to sacrifice elegance for literality and, wherever possible, seek a word-for-word correspondence with the Greek. Also, because the student will want to see how the biblical authors use a particular word (especially St. Paul, who has many works included in the canon), a consistency of translation will be sought and the same Greek word will be translated, wherever possible, by the same English word or by its cognate.

The present work does not pretend to be anything other than a translation for private Bible study. It seeks to achieve, as much as possible, a literal, word-for-word correspondence with the Greek. The aim has been to present a translation from which one could jump back into the Greek original with the aid of an interlinear New Testament. Where a single Greek word has been used in the original, I have tried to find (or invent!) a single English word.

The result, of course, is a translation so literally rendered from the Greek that it represents an English spoken nowhere on the planet! That is, it represents a kind of "study Bible English" and not an actual vernacular. It was never intended for use outside the present commentaries, much less in the worship of the Church. The task of producing a flowing, elegant translation that nonetheless preserves the integrity and nuances of the original I cheerfully leave to hands more competent than mine.

Key to the Format of This Work:

- The translated text is first presented in boldface type. Italics within these biblical text sections represent words required by English syntax that are not actually present in the Greek. Each translated text section is set within a shaded grey box.

> ৵ঌ ৵ঌ ৵ঌ ৵ঌ ৵ঌ
>
> **18 Now the birth of Jesus Christ was thus: when His mother Mary had been betrothed to Joseph, before they came together she was found having *a child* in the womb from the Holy Spirit.**

- In the commentary sections, citations from the portion of text being commented upon are given in boldface type.

When His mother Mary had been betrothed to Joseph, before they came together in marriage and cohabitation, **she was found having *a child* in the womb**. Betrothal in those days was a legal reality, making the couple actually husband and wife.

- In the commentary sections, citations from other locations in Scripture are given in quotation marks with a reference; any reference not including a book name refers to the book under discussion.

Matthew's list diverges significantly from Luke's: Matthew mentions Solomon after David (2:6), whereas Luke mentions Nathan (Luke 3:31).

- In the commentary sections, italics are used in the ordinary way—for emphasis, foreign words, etc.

After so many instances of the active voice of the verb **begot** (Gr. *gennao*), there comes at last a single instance of the passive voice of the same verb.

❧ Introduction ❧

The Characteristics of Matthew's Gospel

The New Testament is a Jewish book, and no part of it is more Jewish than the Gospel of Matthew. In it, Jesus comes to Israel as Messiah and is hailed as the Son of David, the long-expected messianic King (9:27; 15:22; 20:30; 21:9). The Twelve, as leaders of the renewed and messianic Israel, are called to rule Israel in the age to come (19:28). Matthew's Gospel is the story of how God fulfilled His word to Israel and sent them His Messiah, who in turn carried out the work of redemption. It is like the Christian Torah, the record of God's words and deeds through Christ. Matthew's Gospel is, accordingly, the *most Jewish of the four Gospels*.

Jesus' genealogy is traced to Abraham, the father of the Jewish people (1:1f), and not (as in Luke) to Adam, the father of the human race (Luke 3:38).

Also, Jewish expressions are used without further explanation, as if the writer expects his readers to be familiar with such usage. Thus, for example, in Matthew Jesus speaks of "the Kingdom *of heaven*," and not (as in Mark and Luke) "the Kingdom *of God*," for Matthew has retained Jesus' actual Jewish phrase. (The Jews had a reluctance to use the Name of God in everyday speech, and so often employed such circumlocutions—"Heaven bless you," rather than "God bless you"; compare Peter's use of "the Excellent Glory" in 2 Peter 1:17). Matthew also retains such Jewish expressions as "the abomination of desolation standing in the holy place" (24:15), familiar to Jews from such references as Daniel 11:31 and 1 Maccabees 1:54, but incomprehensible to Gentiles (so that Luke substitutes the phrase "Jerusalem encircled by armies," Luke 21:20). Further, Matthew retains Christ's reference to "phylacteries" (23:5) with no further word of explanation, for Jews would know what they were.

It is in Matthew's Gospel alone that we read that Jesus was sent only to the lost sheep of the house of Israel (15:24), and that the Twelve too were to go (at first) only to those lost sheep, avoiding the cities of the Gentiles and the Samaritans (10:5–6).

The Law is affirmed as eternally valid (5:18f), and the disciples were to keep its commandments if they would find life (19:17; 23:23). They were called to be Christ's scribes (13:52; 23:34), and were even to keep the just rulings of those trained in the Law, who sat on Moses' seat (23:1–3). Like all pious Jews, they were to fast, pray, and give alms (6:1f), and their offerings in the Temple were expected as a matter of course (5:23). Also, Sabbath observance was taken for granted (24:20). All of this indicates a Jewish life situation in this Gospel.

Matthew's Gospel also *stresses the Church*, since it is the true Israel, the holy remnant (Eph. 2:12; Gal. 6:16; Rom. 11:5), whose message is to be taken to Jews (and Gentiles) everywhere. The very word "church" (Gr. *ekklesia*) is found only in Matthew's Gospel, and not in the other three. Matthew alone mentions Christ's founding of the Church upon Peter (16:18); he alone records Christ's words about the Church's role in binding and loosing and excluding the sinner (18:15–19). It is in Matthew's Gospel that we have the classic ecclesial promise that Christ will be present among His disciples when they gather in His Name, even if they be merely two or three (18:20).

The embodiment of this Church is Peter, the Confessor of the Faith, and so Matthew focuses on him especially. Thus Matthew alone records that Peter came to Jesus when He walked on the water (14:28; compare Mark 6:45f; John 6:16f). Matthew alone records that Peter received the keys of the Kingdom of heaven when he confessed Jesus to be the Messiah (16:17–19; compare Mark 8:29; Luke 9:20). When Matthew records the apostles' names, he refers to Peter as "the first" (10:2). He alone records that Christ paid the Temple tax for Peter and Himself (17:27). In all this, the focus is not on Peter as a private individual but on Peter as the image of the Church, the voice of the true Israel.

The Writing of Matthew's Gospel

How did Matthew's Gospel come to be written? History contains several puzzles.

Early in the second century, a bishop of Hierapolis in Asia Minor named Papias wrote *The Sayings of the Lord Explained* in five books. (These are no longer extant, but are quoted by Eusebius in his *Church History*, 3,39.) Regarding Matthew, Papias wrote, "Matthew compiled *the Sayings* [of Jesus] in the Hebrew dialect and everyone interpreted them according to the ability of each." Granted the reliability of this tradition (Papias is very early), what does it mean?

It is possible that it means Matthew wrote his Gospel first of all in Aramaic, and that what we have today is a translation of that into Greek. Certainly, there is a consistent tradition that Matthew wrote in Hebrew (i.e. Aramaic).

Irenaeus (d. ca. 202) wrote that "Matthew published a written Gospel for the Hebrews while Peter and Paul were preaching the Gospel in Rome" (quoted by Eusebius, *Church History*, 5,8). Origen (d. ca. 250) also wrote that Matthew's Gospel was "published for believers of Jewish origin, and was composed in Hebrew" (quoted in *Church History*, 6,25).

The problem with assuming that by "*the Sayings* [of Jesus]," Papias meant the Gospel as we know it, is that Matthew's Gospel reads as if it was composed in Greek, not translated from Aramaic. In fact in many places it looks like an expansion of Mark's Gospel, which it seems to have used as one of its sources. And by saying "everyone interpreted [*the Sayings*] according to the ability of each," Papias cannot mean the other Gospel writers translated it for their own Gospels. Papias himself acknowledged in his work that the Gospel of Mark is the record of the reminiscences of Peter (quoted in *Church History*, 2,15), and not a translated abridgment of Matthew.

I would suggest the following: Papias (and the other Fathers quoted after him) received a reliable tradition that Matthew committed to writing in Aramaic the original sayings and deeds of Jesus. This was *not* our present Gospel, but probably a collection of Christ's teachings and miracles, set down in writing to be circulated among the Jewish churches of Palestine where Matthew worked. This work was translated into Greek by other anonymous writers who wanted to circulate the Christian message beyond Palestine—probably by the very writers mentioned by Luke in 1:1, where he speaks of "many having set their hand to compile a description" of the first events.

This work has not survived, but was superseded by a Greek work (our present Gospel of Matthew), which made use of the original Aramaic work of Matthew (or its Greek translation), as well as the Gospel of Mark. Mark was making notes for his Gospel throughout the sixties, based on the words of Peter in Rome, and I suggest that Matthew had access to this Markan material. (We recall the tradition mentioned by Irenaeus that the Gospel of Matthew was written "while Peter and Paul were preaching the Gospel in Rome.")

I suggest that it was written by a Christian scribe in Matthew's community, probably in Palestine, and that is why it came out under Matthew's name. (The reference to *Levi* the tax-collector in Mark 2:14 and Luke 5:27f is changed to *Matthew* the tax-collector in Matt. 9:9, and this would seem to be a "tip of the hat" to Matthew, the head of the community.) I would suggest that it was written in the late sixties or early seventies, when the Jewish-Christian tension was at its height.

The ascription of the Gospel to Matthew would therefore not be unlike the ascription of the Liturgy of St. James of Jerusalem to St. James. The Liturgy was not written by St. James himself, but represented the liturgy of the Church of Jerusalem, of which St. James was the head. It is of course possible that the Gospel here was written by Matthew himself, but it seems devoid of the eyewitness touches one would expect if written by one of the Twelve. I suggest rather that it was fittingly called "the Gospel according to Matthew" because it came out of his community, with his blessing and spiritual imprimatur. Throughout this commentary, however, the author will be called "Matthew" for purposes of convenience.

Why was the Gospel written? It seems clear that it has a polemical component. The unbelieving non-Christian Jews of Palestine were arguing with their Christian brothers, and the battle was becoming hot. References to the Pharisees (the dominant opposition to Jesus and His movement) as "hypocrites" abound (e.g. 6:2, 5, 16; 7:5).

There is an entire long denunciation of their hypocritical practices (23:1–33) in which they are called "sons of Gehenna," "blind guides," "serpents," and a "brood of vipers" (23:15, 16, 33).

The battle lines had clearly been drawn, as Matthew speaks of the synagogues as *their* synagogues" (4:23; 9:35; 12:9; 13:54), indicating that the Christians by his time were already less than welcome there. The Gospel of Matthew is meant to give the Jewish Christians ammunition to prove to their Jewish countrymen that Jesus of Nazareth is indeed the Christ, the fulfillment of their Scriptures, and that the Pharisees who oppose Him are not reliable guides, but hypocrites. This is why the Pharisees come in for such blistering denunciation—Matthew is firing upon the main enemy in the Jewish-Christian dispute.

This polemical purpose is also the reason Matthew refers time and again to Jesus' fulfillment of the ancient prophecies (1:23; 2:5, 15, 17, 23; 4:14f; 8:17; 12:17f; 13:14f; 13:35f; 21:4–5; 27:9). Matthew's constant refrain is, "this took place that what was spoken in the Scriptures might be fulfilled," for Jesus' constant fulfillment of the Scriptures is evidence for the Jew that Jesus is indeed the Messiah.

That is also why Matthew records so much of Jesus' pro-Law teaching (e.g. 5:17–20), for he means to refute the accusation that Jesus was an impious Lawbreaker. He records large amounts of His ethical teaching (e.g. chs. 5—7), much of it focusing on His interpretation of the Law (e.g. 5:21f), to clear Jesus of the Pharisees' charge that He was lax about the righteousness God required.

The Gospel of St. Matthew was aimed at a primarily Jewish audience. It was written in Greek because Matthew was appealing beyond the boundaries of Palestine (within which Aramaic would have been sufficient). By the time of his writing, the Gospel had long since spread beyond Palestine and had gone out among "all the nations" (28:19). Though thinking primarily of his Jewish countrymen, Matthew writes with an eye on all the world.

Matthew's Gospel is crafted with great artistry. It contains five separate discourses of Christ (possibly corresponding to the five books of Moses, and comprising a sort of Christian Torah). Within these discourses, Christ's sayings are grouped together according to theme, with Discourse 1 (for example) containing Christ's ethical teaching, Discourse 2 His teaching on mission, Discourse 3 His parables, etc.

In these arrangements, it seems that Matthew has less regard for strict chronology than for thematic presentation. That is, in each of these five discourses Matthew collects material from throughout Christ's ministry to present it according to its theme. Thus, for example, in the section on prayer in Discourse 1, the Sermon on the Mount, in 6:9–15, Matthew presents teaching about prayer that Christ gave in response to His disciples' questions (compare Luke 11:14). In 6:25–33, he presents teaching about freedom from worry that Christ gave in response to a request to act as arbiter (compare Luke 12:13–31). In 23:37–39, in Discourse 5, he records Christ's lament over Jerusalem's hardness of heart, though the lament was made prior to Christ's entry into Jerusalem (compare Luke 13:34–35).

St. Matthew is not as concerned to present a strict chronology of when Christ uttered this or that teaching as he is to offer the systematic body of Christ's teaching. It is possible that he was motivated to do this out of catechetical concern, so that teachers of the Church (the Christian scribes) might have easy access to what Christ said on a particular subject.

❦ I ❧

THE INFANCY AND CHILDHOOD OF CHRIST
(1:1—2:23)

§I.1. Genealogy

> ❧ ❧ ❧ ❧ ❧
>
> **1** 1   The book of the birth of Jesus Christ, son of
> David, son of Abraham.

The phrase **the book of the birth** (Gr. *biblos geneseos*) hearkens back to Genesis 5:1 (LXX) with its genealogical lists, and refers here to the record of the genealogy of Jesus in verses 2–17. Jesus is called **son of David, son of Abraham** because He fulfills the promise God made to David to bring forth the Messiah from his line (2 Sam. 7:12–13), and the promise made to Abraham to make his seed a blessing to all the earth (Gen. 22:17–18). In Jesus, all the promises God made to Israel throughout its sacred history will be fulfilled.

> ❧ ❧ ❧ ❧ ❧
>
> 2   Abraham begot Isaac, and Isaac begot Jacob,
> and Jacob begot Judah and his brothers;
> 3   and Judah begot Perez and Zerah by Tamar;
> and Perez begot Hezron; and Hezron begot
> Ram;
> 4   and Ram begot Amminadab; and Amminadab
> begot Nahshon; and Nahshon begot Salmon;
> 5   and Salmon begot Boaz by Rahab; and Boaz
> begot Obed by Ruth; and Obed begot Jesse;

> 6   and Jesse begot David the king. And David begot Solomon by *her who was the wife* of Uriah;
>
> 7   and Solomon begot Rehoboam; and Rehoboam begot Abijah; and Abijah begot Asa;
>
> 8   and Asa begot Jehoshaphat; and Jehoshaphat begot Joram; and Joram begot Uzziah;
>
> 9   and Uzziah begot Jotham; and Jotham begot Ahaz; and Ahaz begot Hezekiah;
>
> 10 and Hezekiah begot Manasseh; and Manasseh begot Amon; and Amon begot Josiah;
>
> 11 and Josiah begot Jeconiah and his brothers, at *the time* of the deportation to Babylon.
>
> 12 And after the deportation to Babylon, Jeconiah begot Shealtiel; and Shealtiel begot Zerubbabel;
>
> 13 and Zerubbabel begot Abihud; and Abihud begot Eliakim; and Eliakim begot Azor;
>
> 14 and Azor begot Zadok; and Zadok begot Achim; and Achim begot Eliud;
>
> 15 and Eliud begot Eleazar; and Eleazar begot Matthan; and Matthan begot Jacob;
>
> 16 and Jacob begot Joseph the husband of Mary, of whom was born Jesus, who is called Christ.
>
> 17 Therefore all the generations from Abraham until David are fourteen generations; and from David until the deportation to Babylon, fourteen generations; and from the deportation to Babylon until the Christ, fourteen generations.

Matthew then selects certain persons from Jesus' ancestors, arranging them in three groups of fourteen. As with many such Jewish genealogical lists, no attempt is made here to be complete, nor to list every single ancestor. The verb **begot** does not necessarily mean "produced a son," for it can equally well refer to a grandson, or even a great-grandson. This in itself may go far in accounting for differences in this list from the one given in Luke 3:23–38.

There are several things to be noted in Matthew's list.

Firstly, there are several women mentioned in the list, a somewhat unusual feature. **Tamar** is mentioned (v. 3), as are **Rahab** and **Ruth** (v. 5), as well as Bathsheba in verse 6 (referred to as *her who was the wife* of Uriah). Why were these women singled out? Most likely because they were probably all Gentiles—Tamar was a local girl (that is, almost certainly a Canaanite; Gen. 38:2f). Rahab, the famous harlot, was a pagan from Jericho (Josh. 2:1f). The gentle Ruth was a Moabite woman (Ruth 1:4), and Bathsheba was probably a Hittite like her husband (2 Sam. 11:3). (It would seem that she is left unnamed and referred to only as *the wife* of Uriah to stress the unrighteousness of her union with David.)

Matthew is concerned to show how the messianic redemption, though beginning in Israel, will spread to all the Gentiles (28:19), and so he focuses upon these pagan women in Israel's sacred history. By doing so, he shows that concern for the Gentiles (a feature in the Christian movement he is defending) is not ignoble, but that such Gentiles had their place in God's plan ever since the days of the Patriarchs. Certainly God's use of these women was surprising—much as His use of Mary, found to be pregnant before marriage, was surprising to many.

Secondly, after David, Matthew's list diverges significantly from Luke's: Matthew mentions Solomon after David (2:6), whereas Luke mentions Nathan (Luke 3:31). The variations are possibly due to levirate marriage (that is, a man marrying two women, both his first wife and then the wife of his deceased brother). I would suggest, though, that the variations are due to differences of approach. Luke gives Christ's biological descent, whereas Matthew concentrates on legal descent, naming the members of the family who were in line for the Davidic throne.

Thirdly, after so many instances of the active voice of the verb **begot** (Gr. *gennao*), there comes at last a single instance of the passive voice of the same verb, used to describe the conception of Jesus from Mary (v. 16). That is, after so many times hearing that "So-and-so begot So-and-so," we expect to see the climax as "Joseph begot Jesus of Mary," but this is not what we read. Rather, Joseph is described as **the husband of Mary**, and then the spotlight shifts to her, **of whom was born Jesus**. Such sudden shifting of pattern is unexpected—just as the Virgin Birth of Jesus was in its day unexpected. Up until then, men took the active part, but now they are passive. God has now taken the active role in the saving history of His people.

Fourthly, it is significant that the names are arranged into three groups, and especially so since the groups are not of equal chronological length. From **Abraham until David** is about 750 years; **from David until the deportation to Babylon** is about 400 years; and **from the deportation to Babylon until the Christ** is about 600 years. Matthew is not dividing the names up equally; he is marking signposts along the way of redemption. From Abraham to David, history was marked by God's fidelity to His covenant with the patriarch, and stood under the shadow of that great promise. From David to the Babylonian exile, history centered on God's covenant with the house of David and was marked by the rise and fall of its fortunes. After the exile, the focus was on God's coming restoration, when He would fulfill all His promises to the struggling postexilic community and "raise up God's servant David," the Davidic Messiah, "to feed Israel and to be their shepherd" (Ezek. 34:23). By arranging Israel's history in this manner, Matthew shows how Jesus Christ came right on time, to fulfill all of history's hopes.

Finally, why does Matthew pick fourteen generations, since he could have picked more (or less)? And aren't we missing a generation "from the deportation to Babylon until the Christ"?

Regarding the thirteen names on the list from the exile to Christ, it would seem that (as both St. John Chrysostom and Blessed Theophylact suggest) the deportation to Babylon itself is counted as one generation. Certainly St. Matthew focuses on this event in his reckoning of the generations in verse 17. He stresses the event of the exile (rather than a person living at that time) because, as was said above, his aim is to mark off the epochs throughout history. Israel lived in the shadow of the promises to Abraham, and to David, and then in the shadow of the Exile, expecting the postexilic restoration.

It was the Exile that determined Israel's future hope, not anyone living at that time.

And why pick **fourteen generations** (however counted)? It was a memory device, of course, but twelve or fifteen generations would have worked just as well. I suggest that the number fourteen was chosen because Matthew is using a typically Jewish bit of teaching. The numerical value of the name "David" in Hebrew is fourteen, and Matthew was stressing how the Davidic Messiah arose from Israel's history. Admittedly his Gospel was written in Greek, not Hebrew. But it was written to Jews familiar with Hebrew, and he expects his readers to be able to work their way back to their Hebrew roots. (See the reference in 1:21, in which the Hebrew meaning of the name Jesus/Yeshua is expected to be understood, and the play on words mentioned in 2:23—a play on words present only in the Hebrew version of the Scripture cited.)

§I.2. The Birth of Christ

෴ ෴ ෴ ෴ ෴

18 Now the birth of Jesus Christ was thus: when His Mother Mary had been betrothed to Joseph, before they came together she was found having *a child* in the womb from the Holy Spirit.

19 And Joseph her husband, being righteous, and not wanting to disgrace her, intended to dismiss her covertly.

20 But *while* he was reflecting on these things, behold! an angel of the Lord appeared to him in a dream, saying, "Joseph, son of David! Do not be afraid to take Mary your wife, for that which is begotten in her is from the Holy Spirit.

21 "And she will give birth to a son, and you will call His Name Jesus, for He *Himself* will save His people from their sins."

> 22 Now this whole *thing* happened that what was spoken by the Lord through the prophet might be fulfilled, saying,
> 23 "Behold, the virgin will have *a child* in the womb, and will give birth to a son, and they will call His Name Emmanuel," which translated is, "God *is* with us."
> 24 And Joseph, being raised from sleep, did as the angel of the Lord commanded him and took his wife,
> 25 and he was not knowing her until she gave birth to a son, and he called His Name Jesus.

The **birth of Jesus Christ** is now described as happening **thus**: **When His Mother Mary had been betrothed to Joseph, before they came together** in marriage and cohabitation, **she was found having *a child* in the womb**. Betrothal in those days was a legal reality, making the couple actually husband and wife (compare the references to Mary as Joseph's wife in vv. 20, 24), and such a union could only be broken by actual divorce. The couple was betrothed (usually when the girl was no more than about fourteen years old) and then went to live conjugally a year later, after the actual marriage. It was during this time between the betrothal and the actual marriage to Joseph that Mary was found to be pregnant. This was not due to any sexual encounter, but was entirely **from the Holy Spirit**.

Joseph, her legal **husband**, was a **righteous** man, and as such refused to marry a woman who (he had no choice but to assume) had been involved in an immoral liaison. Nonetheless, as a compassionate man, he was **not wanting to disgrace her** by open and public denunciation for fornication (which brought with it, technically, the penalty of stoning; see Deut. 22:23–24), and so **intended to dismiss** and divorce **her covertly**. No open denunciation was required; only the presence of two witnesses who could testify to the fact of the divorce.

It was *while* he was **reflecting on these things** and trying to arrange the time and place for it that **behold** (the word indicates a

surprising event), **an angel of the Lord appeared to him in a dream.**
Dreams, though quite properly held in suspicion by the spirituality
of the desert fathers (for usually such dreams mean nothing, or else
can be used by the enemy), were used by God to communicate with
His chosen instruments, such as Jacob and Daniel (Gen. 28:12f;
Dan. 2:19). In this case, God sent His angel to communicate with
Joseph as the Lord's foster-father.

Joseph is addressed as **son of David**, for it is through his legal
lineage that Jesus is the messianic Son of David and heir to the
promises made to David's house. Joseph is admonished to **not be
afraid to take Mary** his **wife** home to live as his legal spouse. He
is not to continue with his plans to divorce her, **for that which is
begotten in her is from the Holy Spirit**, as she (perhaps) said to
Joseph. **She will give birth to a son** (not a daughter) and Joseph
is to **call His Name Jesus**, for it is **He** *Himself* (the pronoun is
emphatic) who **will save His people from their sins**. Through
the boy Jesus, Israel will find forgiveness of sins and the blessing
from God which flows from this. Matthew adds that **this whole
thing happened that what was spoken by the Lord through the
prophet** Isaiah **might be fulfilled, saying, "Behold, the virgin
will have *a child* in the womb, and will give birth to a son, and
they will call His Name Emmanuel"** (Is. 7:14). Matthew adds
for his Gentile readers the explanation that this is **translated** as
"God *is* with us."

After this, **Joseph** was **raised** by God **from** his **sleep**, and (not
unnaturally) he **did as the angel of the Lord commanded him.**
That is, he **took his wife** home with him after a decent period
of betrothal, breaking off his plans for divorce. Matthew stresses
that throughout this period of betrothal he **was not knowing her**
sexually, even up to the very time when **she gave birth to a son.**
Matthew says this to stress that Joseph could not therefore be the
child's father. After the birth (a son, not a daughter, confirming the
word of the angel about the Child's significance), **he called His
Name Jesus** on the day of His circumcision, when names were
customarily bestowed.

In saying Joseph **was not knowing** Mary **until she gave birth to**

a son, Matthew does not imply that after the birth he *was* knowing her sexually. The word "until" is ambiguous. It can indicate such a change, but not necessarily. Whether or not any change of state is demanded is determined entirely by the context. Thus in Isaiah 46:3, Yahweh declares to Israel, "You have been carried by Me from your birth until your old age." This use of "until" does not imply that after Israel's old age Yahweh will no longer be with them. Similarly, in 28:20, Jesus declares that He will be with His Church even "until the consummation of the age"; this does not mean that after the consummation of the age Jesus will no longer be with them. In the same way, this verse does not mean that after Jesus' birth Joseph *was* knowing Mary. Matthew's only concern is to stress that prior to the birth of Jesus there were no conjugal relations between Joseph and Mary, so that Jesus' birth was truly virginal.

In fact, Jewish thought of that day made it impossible for a pious man to approach conjugally a woman who had been the object of the Spirit's power. Jewish *midrash* (or Bible commentary) from that time, speaking about Eldad and Medad (who received the Holy Spirit in power; see Num. 11:26), lamented, "How sad for the wives of those men!" because such closeness to God meant they were now pledged to celibacy. Joseph, pious man that he was, would have shared such sentiments, which were general in his day, and would not have approached Mary conjugally after she had received the fullness of the Spirit and conceived her Son (Luke 1:35). Taking her home meant therefore that he lived with her as her protector and as the foster-father of her Son.

In this regard, it is perhaps significant that Joseph is later told not to "take your wife and her child and flee," but rather to "take the Child and His mother and flee" (2:13)—Mary was not Joseph's wife so much as the mother of her Child. Later tradition suggests that Joseph was much older than Mary, and that this was not his first marriage. If Joseph was an older widower when he married Mary, it would also explain his conspicuous absence from the later Gospel narratives: He would have died of old age before Jesus reached His thirtieth year.

ॐ EXCURSUS
On the Prophecy of Isaiah 7:14

The prophecy of Isaiah 7:14 does not, strictly speaking, predict a virgin birth for the Messiah, and Jews of Jesus' time were not expecting their Messiah to be born of a virgin. Matthew (and Luke) report such a thing, not because it was a part of the customary Jewish expectation, but simply because it was historically true.

In the Hebrew of Isaiah 7:14, Isaiah says that a young woman (Heb. *almah*) will conceive. An *almah* was a young woman of marriageable age—usually a virgin (if she were righteous), but not necessarily so. The accent is on her age, not her biologically virginal status. In Isaiah 7, the thought is as follows. Ahaz, the king of Judah, is exhorted not to rely upon Assyria for help against Syria and the northern kingdom of Israel, but upon God. He is invited to ask God for a sign that He will help him (7:10). Ahaz wants to trust Assyria for help rather than God, and so declines the sign (7:12). God then declares that He will give Ahaz a sign anyway, and the sign is this: that an *almah* will conceive and give birth to a son (7:14), presumably in the usual way, following marriage and sexual conception. This boy will eat curds and honey, the fruit of a desolate and unfarmed land, before he is old enough to refuse evil and choose good (7:15). Indeed, before the boy is old enough to know good from bad, or to say "papa" or "mama" (7:16; 8:4), the kings of Syria and Israel will be swept away before the king of Assyria, and Judah will be desolate. That is, within a few years, the feared Syrian threat will be removed. This boy and the timing of his birth will thus be a sign that God is with His People (Heb. *Emmanuel*, "God is with us"; 7:14; 8:10), and that He will yet save them.

Obviously, the primary reference of the prophecy is to

the events in the days of Ahaz, many centuries before Christ, and these words are not a direct prediction of Jesus' virgin birth. Nonetheless, Matthew is not incorrect in seeing that the ultimate fulfillment of Isaiah's words lies with Jesus, not with a child (probably Isaiah's son) born in the time of Ahaz. For the ultimate way in which God was with His people (Heb. *Emmanuel*) was through Jesus. Thus this prophecy is a true foreshadowing of Christ, the Child that was to be born, the Son that was to be given (Is. 9:6). The sign of the *almah* (Gr. *parthenos*, an actual virgin) is the sign of Jesus' birth. For Matthew, the virgin birth of Christ meant that Isaiah's words could be no coincidence, but a providential sign pointing to Jesus as the Christ.

ॐ   ॐ   ॐ   ॐ   ॐ

2 1 Now after Jesus had been born in Bethlehem of Judea in the days of Herod the king, behold! Magi from the east arrived in Jerusalem, saying,

2 "Where is he who has been born King of the Jews? For we saw His star at its rising, and have come to worship him."

3 And when Herod the king heard it, he was shaken, and all Jerusalem with him.

4 And assembling all the chief-priests and scribes of the people, he was inquiring of them where the Christ was to be born.

5 And they said to him, "In Bethlehem of Judea, for thus it has been written through the prophet,

6 "'And you, Bethlehem, *in the* land of Judah, are by no means least among the leaders of Judah, for from you will come forth *one* leading, who will shepherd My people Israel.'"

After the story of the annunciation to Joseph, Matthew relates another story, that of the visit of the **magi** after the birth of Christ. The magi (Gr. *magos*) were originally members of the Persian priestly class, skilled in ancient sciences such as astrology. By the first century, the term had come to mean often simply a fortuneteller, a cheap charlatan (thus Elymas the *magos* in Acts 13:6). These magi, however, were venerable men, seekers after eternal and universal truth. In every land God has those who seek Him, though He may be concealed under a variety of names, and these magi were such seekers. Their number is not given. Chrysostom and Augustine supposed there were twelve, while others (because of three kinds of gifts listed) supposed there were three.

They dwelt in **the east**, though exactly where in the east is also not stated. Some thought Persia (because of their historical origins there), and others, Arabia. There was a large Jewish population in Babylon, from whom the magi could have learned messianic ideas, and this is perhaps the best guess as to their land of origin.

Wherever they first dwelt, they saw a great wonder in the heavens, a star (that is, a heavenly light), and they naturally assumed that such a heavenly wonder was a portent of a corresponding earthly one. Just as a great star was born in the sky, so a great king must have been born on the earth. In those days, expectation was widespread of a coming golden age brought by a mighty king. Perhaps it was because Jewish ideas about Messiah had spread into the surrounding cultures, but (as the Roman historian Suetonius wrote in his *Life of Vespasian*), "There had spread over all the east an established belief that it was fated for men coming from Judea to rule the world." When the magi saw the star and thought it to be the natal star of a great king, it was natural for their eyes to turn to Judea.

We may ask what this "star" was. Some have thought it a special angelic manifestation, appearing in the form of a star. This is possible, but it is notable that about 7 BC there was a conjunction of Saturn and Jupiter, joined a year later by Mars, making a brilliant spectacle in the night sky. I would suggest that this was the "star" the magi saw.

Whatever heavenly light they saw, they took it to mean the birth of a great king, and so they **arrived in Jerusalem, saying, "Where is he who has been born King of the Jews? For we saw His star at its rising, and have come to worship him."** Thinking that the world-ruler from Judea had been born, they naturally supposed him to be born to the Jewish royal family, the ruling house of Herod, and so they went first to Jerusalem, where Herod was. Their intention was to pay the respects appropriate for the newborn sovereign, prostrating themselves before him with the homage due a king, and to see this sight for themselves. (The word rendered *worship*, Gr. *proskuneo*, here means not the adoration due to God, but the homage given to any exalted person; compare Jacob's deferential prostration to Esau in Gen. 33:3.)

As soon as they entered the city and the news of their local inquiries reached Herod, he **was shaken, and all Jerusalem with him**. The city was bubbling with anticipation (compare 21:10), and Herod himself (famous for his murderous paranoia) was troubled at the thought of a rival. Herod accordingly summoned **all the chief-priests** (that is, the ruling families of the capital) **and scribes** to a hastily called conference. There he began **inquiring of them where the Christ was to be born**. The reported questions of the magi about the King of the Jews could mean only one thing—that Messiah had been born—and *not* to the family of Herod! Where *was* this rival to the power of his house?

Jewish tradition was clear: Messiah, as the descendant of King David, was to be born in David's hometown, **Bethlehem of Judea**. In Micah 5:2, the prophet had written, **"And you, Bethlehem, *in the* land of Judah, are by no means least among the leaders of Judah, for from you will come forth *one* leading, who will shepherd My people Israel."**

It is interesting to look carefully at Matthew's citation of this verse. Both the Hebrew text and the Greek Septuagint speak of Bethlehem as being "least among the leaders of Judah," but in Matthew's citation Bethlehem is spoken of as "*by no means* least." It is possible that some versions of that prophecy had the reading as cited by Matthew (which in Hebrew would involve simply the addition of a single letter). I would suggest, however, that Matthew gives an interpretive translation of his own: Bethlehem, a small and insignificant town, for now may be least among the other cities of the region, but it will prove itself to be by no means least of them, for Messiah will be born in her.

ॐ॰ ॐ॰ ॐ॰ ॐ॰ ॐ॰

7   Then Herod covertly called the magi, and from them *learned* exactly the time of appearing of the star.

8   And he sent them to Bethlehem and said, "Go and inquire exactly about the Child, and when you have found Him, declare *it* to me, that I *myself* also may come and worship Him."

9   And having heard the king, they went away, and behold! The star which they had seen at its rising went before them, until it came and stood *still* over where the Child was.

10 And when they saw the star, they rejoiced exceedingly with great joy.

11 And they came into the house and saw the Child with Mary His Mother, and they fell *down* and worshipped Him; and opening their treasures, they offered up to Him gifts of gold and frankincense and myrrh.

12 And having been warned in a dream not to turn back to Herod, they withdrew to their own region by another way.

Learning that a rival king was born in Bethlehem, Herod needed to know when the Child had been born and precisely where He was now. He therefore **covertly called the magi** to visit him in his palace. Entertaining his foreign guests with royal hospitality and feigning Jewish piety, **from them he *learned* exactly the time of appearing of the star**—and therefore the age of the Child. (It took a year or so for the magi to prepare for travel and to make the journey from their land to Palestine.) Herod therefore asked them to

go and inquire exactly about the Child, checking with the locals of Bethlehem to discover His present whereabouts, and when they **had found Him**, they were to return to Herod and **declare** *it* to him, that he himself **also may come and worship Him**, paying his pious respects. Whether Herod's reputation for treachery and cruelty was known to the magi is unclear. They had, we may think, no reason to doubt Herod. Certainly they were at his mercy, and it was not safe to openly defy him.

When they left Herod, they **went away**, intent on making the short five-mile journey south to Bethlehem. It appears that it was evening when they left, and **behold** (the word indicates a surprising event), **the star which they had seen at its rising went before them, until it came and stood** *still* **over where the Child was**. This event is described according to the experience of the magi, for stars like this do not properly move, nor stand in a location with such precision as to indicate a particular house. I suggest that the magi saw the star before them in the sky as they faced Bethlehem, perhaps newly visible after a time of cloudiness when it could not be seen, and that they took this sudden reappearance as a divine confirmation that what they had been told about Bethlehem was true. **When they saw the star**, they knew that their goal was at hand, and **they rejoiced exceedingly with great joy**.

It would seem that after the journey of Joseph and Mary from Nazareth to Bethlehem for the birth of Christ (Luke 2:1–7) they stayed in Bethlehem, obtaining a house there. (Mary's tarnished reputation would have added no incentive to return to Nazareth.) After the visitation of the angels to the shepherds and the shepherds' telling their tale to all who would listen (Luke 2:8–20), the Holy Family would possess a certain local notoriety, and their location would not be hard to discover.

The magi therefore found the Holy Family and **came into the house** where they were staying. They **saw the Child with Mary His Mother, and they fell** *down* **and worshipped Him** as they had planned. **Opening their treasures** from chests they had carried, **they offered up to Him gifts of gold and frankincense and myrrh**. Legend has adorned these gifts with mystical significance, seeing in the gold a sign of Christ's royalty, in the frankincense evidence of His deity, and in the myrrh (used for burials) a sign of His saving death. Wonderful and insightful as these interpretations are, they were likely not in the mind of the magi. For them these gifts represented simply precious festive tokens, fit to offer a king. **Gold** was always worthy for a king (compare Ps. 72:15), as was **frankincense** (Is. 60:6), and **myrrh**, along with aloes and cassia, was used as a fragrant perfume (Ps. 45:8). (What the Holy Family actually used the gifts for, we do not know. I suspect they were sold for the expenses of relocating to Egypt and returning.)

The magi, after their visit to the Child and His Mother, **in a dream** were **warned** by God (Gr. *chrematizo*, used of a divine pronouncement or divine oracle) that they should not **turn back to Herod**. God, who had communicated to Joseph in a dream (1:20), now spoke to these Gentiles in the same way. Obediently **they withdrew to their own region by another way**, not returning to declare the Child's location to Herod as he had asked them to do.

Why does Matthew spend so much time reporting the visit of the magi? For one thing, it affords him the opportunity to show how that visit and its aftermath fulfilled prophecy (2:5–6, 15, 17, 23). But also, St. Matthew is concerned to demonstrate the universality of the gospel. Though thoroughly Jewish, the gospel is meant for all the nations (28:19). In the magi, God first reveals His love for the Gentiles, allowing them too to hear His voice, using such methods of revelation as they would listen to. The magi themselves may have intended not adoration for the Child, but only royal homage. Matthew, however, sees in their prostrations a prophecy and promise of the day when all the Gentiles will fall down before Christ in true adoration and worship. The magi therefore are presented as the firstfruits from among the nations, a sign that all the world will one day hail the King of the Jews as their own King and Lord.

A final word may be added about the significance of the star. The Fathers are emphatic that the natal star of Bethlehem does not justify pagan astrology, or the idea that the stars in heaven rule the fortunes of men on earth. Rather, the star represented God's condescension in speaking to the Gentiles in a language they could understand. This was a special star, a unique occurrence. God used the star (or conjunction of planets, or whatever it was) to accomplish His purposes, even as Christ used spit and mud as the instruments of healing for the blind man (John 9:6). By itself such an astrological conjunction has no more significance than spit and mud.

§I.3. Flight into Egypt and Return

ॐ ॐ ॐ ॐ ॐ

13 Now when they had withdrawn, behold! An angel of the Lord appeared to Joseph in a dream, saying, "Arise and take the Child and His Mother and flee into Egypt, and be there until I tell you, for Herod is about to seek for the Child to destroy Him."

14 And he arose and took the Child and His Mother by night, and withdrew into Egypt,

15 and was there until the death of Herod, that what was spoken by the Lord through the prophet might be fulfilled, saying, "From Egypt I have called My Son."

16 Then when Herod saw that he had been mocked by the magi, he became very indignant, and sent and destroyed all the *male* children who were in Bethlehem, and in all its areas, from two years old and under, according to the time which he had *learned* exactly from the magi.

17 Then what was spoken through Jeremiah the prophet was fulfilled, saying,

18 "A voice in Ramah was heard, crying and great mourning—Rachel weeping for her children; and she would not be comforted, because they were not."

After the visit of the magi, St. Matthew next relates the flight of the Holy Family into Egypt. Some time after the magi had **withdrawn** to their own country, **behold** (the word again indicates a startling development), **an angel of the Lord appeared to Joseph in a dream**, as he had before (1:20f). The angel said to him, **"Arise and take the Child and His Mother and flee into Egypt, and be there until I tell you, for Herod is about to seek for the Child to destroy Him."** Herod may have thought that his cunning and murderous plans would go undetected and unhindered, but he had counted only on the possible opposition of men, not on opposition from the all-seeing Lord of hosts. In our own lives too we may often be blindsided by disasters and setbacks, but our God is not blindsided. He knows all that will befall us—and takes care to preserve us.

God therefore warned Joseph of the impending search-and-destroy mission while Herod was yet preparing for it. Joseph was bidden to take refuge in **Egypt**, the place of refuge for Jews for many centuries (see 1 Kings 11:40; 2 Kings 25:26). At this time there was a large Jewish community in Egypt, and the Holy Family could find refuge there. Joseph lost no time in fleeing, even leaving **by night** so as not to attract attention or let the direction of his flight be known. They were all to remain there **until the death of Herod**, when it would be safe to return. Where in Egypt they settled is not said, though there was a sizable Jewish diaspora in Alexandria.

This, St. Matthew says, **fulfilled** the word **spoken by the Lord through the prophet** (Hos. 11:1), **"From Egypt I have called My Son."** (Matthew's citation in the Greek agrees more with the Hebrew version than it does with the Septuagint; the Septuagint speaks of calling "Israel's children," whereas the Hebrew speaks of calling "My Son." Though Matthew would use the Greek Septuagint for its international appeal, it seems his heart was in the original Hebrew.)

In its original context (both Hebrew and Greek), this Hosea passage speaks primarily about God's care for His People Israel. Hosea says that God loved Israel even from the youth of the nation, when they were slaves in Egypt, and showed His love for them by calling them out of Egypt at the Exodus under Moses. What does this have to do with Jesus and His flight into Egypt?

Matthew looks at his Scripture as a true Jew, seeing in each minute part of it a hidden depth of meaning. For Hosea's prophecies did not originate with Hosea, but with God, who spoke *through* the prophet. God was the true author of the Scriptures—and God knew when He spoke through Hosea that He would one day bring His Son Christ out of Egypt. Prophecies such as this are thus deliberate foreshadowings—God (as it were) tipping His hand in secret revelation of what was to come later. Jesus, as Israel's true King, summed up and embodied in Himself the whole history of Israel, and thus He left Egypt even as His people did. Matthew calls his readers' attention to this foreshadowing to show that Jesus is indeed the true Messiah and King of Israel. To a Jew deliberating and debating within himself whether Jesus was the true Christ, such a verse as this provided confirmation that He was, for it was (Matthew was suggesting) too much to be a coincidence.

After Herod learned that the magi had not returned to him as instructed, he felt that he had been **mocked by the magi** and treated like a fool. Play a trick on him, would they? Think to frustrate his intentions, did they? Herod (always a little paranoid) felt that all were laughing at him. They would see that Herod was not one to be thwarted! He **became very indignant** (Gr. *thumao*, cognate with *thumos*, indignant rage), and **sent** orders and **destroyed all the *male* children** in the area.

Herod did not know which child in Bethlehem and its environs was the feared rival, but he would kill them all to make sure he got the right one. In order to make certain of success, he not only destroyed all the male infants **who were in Bethlehem**, but also **in all its areas** around it, just in case the Child now resided a bit outside of town. And he sent his soldiers to slay all the males **from two years old and under, according to the time which he had *learned* exactly from the magi** that the star first appeared. I suggest that even here Herod was leaving himself a margin. If the star appeared when Christ was born, the traveling arrangements and time for the journey might have taken perhaps just over a year. By slaying the infants **from two years old and under**, Herod was again making sure (he thought) that he was killing his rival. Perhaps his soldiers were bad judges of age!

How many infants died in this first group of martyrs, those dying (had they but known it) for Christ? The Church in its calendar deals with the figure symbolically, speaking of the 14,000 infants of Bethlehem. (That this is a symbolic number denoting the immensity of the outrage, and not a strictly statistical number, is apparent from the way the calendar uses numbers elsewhere: for example, the feast of December 28 speaks of 20,000 martyrs burnt at Nicomedia.) The Western Church historically used the same symbolism, identifying the infants with the 144,000 of Revelation 14:3. In actual fact the population of Bethlehem and its environs was probably about 1000, so that the number of infants killed (allowing for infant mortality) was likely about 20 or so. Herod was quite capable of this act (which was statistically insignificant enough to go unremarked by the historians of the day, given Herod's other acts of brutality). Herod had his wife Mariamne and his own sons Alexander and Aristobulus killed, and gave orders that all his family would be killed upon his death. (The orders were not carried out.) He would not have scrupled at the killing of a few infants.

Once again, St. Matthew refers the event to a word of prophecy. **Jeremiah the prophet** wrote of **"a voice in Ramah"** that **"was heard, crying and great mourning—Rachel weeping for her children; and she would not be comforted, because they were not"** (Jer. 31:15). In its primary context, the passage refers to the outpouring of wrath upon Israel at the time of the Assyrian captivity. Rachel, the wife of the patriarch Jacob, was buried in Ramah, near Bethlehem (Gen. 35:19), and Jeremiah portrays her as mourning over her lost children, her descendants going to death and exile in Assyria. What does this have to do with the slaughter of the innocents?

The passage from Jeremiah must be seen in context. Jeremiah is speaking of the loss of the children of the Northern Kingdom of Israel as part of his announcing of salvation. Rachel is poetically told to "restrain her voice from weeping," for all Israel will be restored. Indeed, the days are coming when God will "make a new covenant with the house of Israel and the house of Judah" (Jer. 31:31)—a new covenant fulfilled in the coming of Messiah. The sufferings of Israel are thus portrayed as the portent of coming salvation, and this is the point St. Matthew is making. Sufferings and wrath attended Jesus' birth, but these sufferings were a sign that messianic deliverance was now at hand. The death of Bethlehem's innocents set the seal on all the long suffering of Israel. A new day was about to dawn.

ॐ ॐ ॐ ॐ ॐ

19 But when Herod had died, behold! An angel of the Lord appears in a dream to Joseph in Egypt, saying,

20 "Arise and take the Child and His Mother and go into the land of Israel, for those who sought the Child's life have died."

21 And he arose and took the Child and His Mother, and entered into the land of Israel.

22 But when he heard that Archelaus reigns over Judea instead of his father Herod, he was afraid to go there. And being warned in a dream, he withdrew into the regions of Galilee,

23 and came and dwelt in a city called Nazareth, that what was spoken through the prophets might be fulfilled, "He will be called a Nazarene."

At length, **Herod died** (around 4 BC, according to modern dating—the modern dividing line between BC and AD was drawn up by a scholar working much later, and he was out by a few years). **An angel of the Lord appears in a dream to Joseph, saying, "Arise and take the Child and His Mother and go into the land of Israel."** (St. Matthew marks the unexpected element in the appearance with the word **behold**.) The angel's appearance is narrated in the historic present for greater vividness. Joseph is told that it is now safe to return, **"for those who sought the Child's life have died."** He obediently did as he was told and returned to the Holy Land.

But returning to the land of Israel did not mean returning to Bethlehem. Joseph heard that **Archelaus reigns over Judea instead of his father Herod**, and **he was afraid to go there** to settle, for Archelaus shared much of his father's brutal character. It was much safer to settle elsewhere. God did not leave Joseph without guidance even here, but continued His divine protection of His Son. Joseph was once again **warned in a dream** of the danger of settling in Judea, so that he **withdrew into the regions of Galilee** in the north, which was under the rulership of Herod Antipas. Though Antipas was not kind and benevolent, he was nonetheless more tolerant than Archelaus (who was removed by the Romans in AD 6 for his harsh rule).

In particular, Joseph brought his family to dwell **in a city called Nazareth**. Matthew again declares that this also was a fulfillment of **what was spoken through the prophets**, namely, **"He will be called a Nazarene."**

The source of these words has caused some puzzlement, for it does not correspond to any known text. It seems that it is not cited as an actual quote, for the word "saying" does not precede it, as it does the previous two prophecies cited (vv. 15, 17).

It would appear that Matthew is again dealing with the text in a very Jewish way, and working from the Hebrew. In Isaiah 11:1, it is said that "a shoot will come from the stump of Jesse and a branch [Heb. *nezer*] will grow from his roots."

In this prophecy of Isaiah, the prophet is talking about the future hopes of the now humbled house of David. Just as a tree can be cut down and yet still a small branch or twig can grow from its stump, so the house of David (or Jesse), though now humbled, will yet produce the great messianic King. It is upon Him that the Spirit of the Lord will rest, and He will judge the afflicted of the earth with righteousness (Is. 11:2–4). It is a prophecy of the coming Messiah, compared here to a humble branch (Heb. *nezer*). This image is found in other prophets as well (Jer. 23:5; Zech. 3:8), although they use a different Hebrew word for "branch" (*semah*).

Matthew compares this *nezer*/branch with Nazareth (which has the same letters in Hebrew, a consonantal language). Nazareth was a despised town (so much so that it would be said, "Can any good thing come out of Nazareth?"; John 1:46). It was small and unpromising—just like the small and humble twig that grew from the felled stump of Jesse. It is not simply that the letters of the words "branch" and "Nazareth" were similar; the characters of the two were similar too, and the coincidence of letters reflected this similarity in humble estate.

Matthew, reading the prophecy of Isaiah about the humble but messianic *nezer*, saw this reflected in Christ's humble hometown of Nazareth. Once again, this coincidence was part of the providence of God. Hebrew prophecy abounds in such wordplays (e.g. Amos 8:1–2; Micah 1:10–14), and Matthew finds another one here. The use of this concept of the messianic Branch by other prophets as well (Jer. 23:5; Zech. 3:8) accounts for Matthew's reference to **what was spoken by the prophets** (plural), even though they use a different Hebrew word.

ᏋᏋ II ᏋᏋ

PREPARATION FOR CHRIST'S MINISTRY
(3:1—4:25)

§II.1. Ministry of John the Forerunner

ᏋᏋ ᏋᏋ ᏋᏋ ᏋᏋ ᏋᏋ

3 1 Now in those days John the Baptizer arrives, heralding in the wilderness of Judea, saying,

2 "Repent, for the Kingdom of the heavens draws near!"

3 For this is the one spoken of through Isaiah the prophet, saying, "A voice shouting in the wilderness, 'Prepare the way of *the* Lord, make straight His paths!'"

4 Now John himself had clothing of camel's hair, and a leather belt around his waist, and his food was locusts and wild honey.

5 Then there came out to him Jerusalem, and all Judea and all the surrounding-country of the Jordan;

6 and they were being baptized by him in the Jordan River, confessing their sins.

7 But when he saw many of the Pharisees and Sadducees coming to his baptism, he said to them, "Offspring of vipers, who directed you to flee from the coming wrath?

8 "Therefore make fruit worthy of repentance,

9 "and do not think to say within yourselves, 'We

> have Abraham *for our* father,' for I say to you
> that God is able from these stones to raise up
> children to Abraham.
> 10 "And the ax is already laid at the root of the
> trees; every tree therefore that does not make
> good fruit is cut down and cast into the fire.

John's ministry is introduced with the phrase **in those days**—a very general temporal reference, but one which has echoes of the prophets of old (compare Is. 10:20; Zech. 12:3–4). Dramatically, Matthew says that John **arrives** on the scene (using the historic present, for greater vividness). His function is that of a herald of the coming Kingdom, and he comes **heralding in the wilderness of Judea**, bringing God's prophetic Word to all who will hear. His message is simple: **"Repent, for the Kingdom of the heavens draws near!"** (Matthew reproduces the original Jewish phraseology, in which **the heavens** is a circumlocution for God. Consistent with Hebrew usage, the abode of God is conceived of in the plural, "heavens.") The messianic reign of God over Israel is at hand, yet Israel is not ready to receive the Messiah. Messiah is to judge sin and reward the righteous, and if He appears now, when Israel languishes in a state of spiritual laxity, He will come only for judgment and destruction. Let Israel therefore **repent** in preparation for the Kingdom. Only then can they hope to be blessed when Messiah appears.

St. Matthew reveals John's place in the divine plan with a citation from Isaiah the prophet (Is. 40:3)—John is the **voice shouting in the wilderness, "Prepare the way of *the* Lord, make straight His paths!"** In ancient days, roads were not kept up as they are now. If a king was intending to use a road, the local people were required to prepare that way, clearing debris, filling in potholes, making it usable. In Isaiah's prophecy, one would arise and prepare the way the Lord would use to come to His people in the final restoration. John, shouting aloud in the wilderness of Judea, is that voice. His presence in Judea confirms for Israel that the true Messiah is at hand.

John himself appeared like Elijah of old, for he had **clothing of**

camel's hair, and a leather belt around his waist (2 Kings 1:8). He ate the food of the desert, **locusts and wild honey.** As a desert-dweller, he depended on God for his food and life.

His ministry reached far and wide, for **there came out to him Jerusalem, and all Judea and all the surrounding-country of the Jordan.** As the sign that they accepted his teaching and repented of their sins, **they were being baptized by him in the Jordan River, confessing their sins.**

This baptism was very controversial. It was based, almost certainly, on the practice of Jewish proselyte baptism. In those days, when a Gentile wanted to leave off his sinful ways and become a Jew, he stated his decision to the local Jewish community, promising to keep all the Law. He then was circumcised and later, upon healing, was baptized, immersing himself in water to wash away the stain of the Gentile world. Sometimes whole families would be converted in this way. By making baptism the sign of repentance, John was insisting that his hearers needed the same spiritual cleansing as did the Gentiles. This did not sit well with the religious establishment!

The site of **the Jordan River** was significant. It was not just that there was water available there. It was also that the Jordan was the historic site of Israel entering into new life. Of old they crossed the Jordan into the new life God was giving them in the Promised Land (Josh. 3f), and here again the promise of new life was being offered. If they would confess their sinfulness and forsake their old lives, they would find mercy in the coming Kingdom.

This confession was not, we may think, a detailed listing of sins such as the Orthodox penitent today tells the priest in the sacrament of confession, but rather a more general admission of sinfulness and unworthiness before God.

Not all who allied themselves with the popular movement were equally sincere, however. Many **Pharisees and Sadducees** (a diverse lot, showing John's sweeping popularity) also came in the crowds. Their reasons for coming are not stated. Perhaps they wanted to be seen by the crowds as favoring the new prophet in hopes of retaining their own popularity. Whatever their unworthy motives, John blasts their complacency when he sees them **coming to his baptism,**

45

denouncing them as **offspring of vipers**. With withering sarcasm, he asks **who directed** them **to flee from the coming wrath**. Do they think they are following *John's* divine direction by such a superficial response? Vipers may flee from the fire (see Acts 28:3), but they remain vipers nonetheless. These men also remain spiritually dangerous to men so long as their hearts remain unchanged. Let them **make fruit worthy of repentance** and truly live new lives if they would be saved.

The temptation is for them to think they will be saved when the Kingdom comes simply because they are Jewish. It was popularly thought that "all Israel had a share in the age to come," and that one could rely on being part of the chosen people to win acceptance with God. It is not so. They must **not** even **think to say within** themselves, **"We have Abraham *for our* father,"** as if this would avail them. God has indeed promised to bless the children of Abraham (Gen. 12:3; 22:18), but He will not bless them so long as they remain impenitent. God will judge them, even if He has to **raise up from these stones children to Abraham** as the objects of His promised blessing. (There is here probably a play on words in the Aramaic: God will take as Abraham's children and *sons*—Aramaic *benayya*—the very *stones* at their feet—Aramaic *abnayya*.)

There is, therefore, no time to lose. The **ax** of judgment is **already laid at the root of the trees**. Like a woodsman who lays the ax at the place he is about to strike just before swinging the first blow, so God is preparing to come in righteous judgment. Let them all repent and **make good fruit**, for **every** single **tree** which does not do so will be **cut down and cast into the fire** of that judgment.

ॐ ॐ ॐ ॐ ॐ

11 "I *myself* baptize you in water for repentance, but the One coming after me is stronger than I, and I myself am not sufficient to bear His sandals. He Himself will baptize you in the Holy Spirit and fire.

12 "And His shovel is in His hand, and He will clean out His threshing-floor, and He will

---

> gather His wheat into the barn, but He will
> burn up the chaff with unquenchable fire."

Matthew then focuses on that part of John's message of most interest to Christians—his announcement of the coming Messiah. John consistently points away from himself and toward the coming messianic Kingdom. His baptism is simply **in water**, as a sign of **repentance**. But Messiah will **come after** him soon, He who is **stronger** and more important than John. So great is Messiah and His Kingdom that John is **not sufficient** to do the work of His slave or **bear His sandals**. The loosing and bearing of sandals was commonly thought too menial even for a slave—yet John declares himself less than that! Here is a great Messiah indeed!

Messiah's power differs from John's as fire is different from water. (Compare 1 Kings 18:38, where the fire of heaven consumed the water of earth.) John **baptizes in water**, but Messiah will **baptize in the Holy Spirit and fire**, transforming men from within with the cleansing fire of the Spirit. (This prophecy is fulfilled in Christian baptism, for in it, through the laying on of hands/chrismation, men receive the fire of the Holy Spirit.)

Messiah will come to judge, and this final separation of the godly from the ungodly is compared to winnowing. In that day, the farmer would come to his threshing-floor with his winnowing-shovel and toss the threshed grain into the air, where the wind would blow away the chaff while the heavier wheat fell back to the ground, to be safely gathered into the barn. Messiah has **His shovel in His hand**, and this winnowing judgment is about to begin. The **wheat** (those who repent) will be **gathered** safely into the **barn** of the blessed age to come, whereas **the chaff** (those refusing to repent) will be **burned with** the **unquenchable fire** of hell. Let all who hear repent!

§II.2. Baptism of Christ

ॐ ॐ ॐ ॐ ॐ

13 Then Jesus arrives from Galilee at the Jordan
to John to be baptized by him.

14 But John was *entirely* forbidding Him, saying, "I *myself* have need to be baptized by You, and You *Yourself* come to me?"

15 But Jesus answering said to him, "Let *it be so* now, for thus it is proper for us to fulfill all righteousness." Then he lets Him.

16 And after being baptized, Jesus came up immediately from the water, and behold! The heavens were opened, and he saw the Spirit of God descending like a dove, coming upon Him,

17 and behold! A Voice from the heavens, saying, "This One is My beloved Son, in whom I am well-pleased."

As the climax of John's ministry, Matthew then relates the baptism of Jesus. (John's ministry continued after the baptism of Jesus, but Matthew ends his focus on John here.) Just as Matthew dramatically narrated that "John the Baptizer arrives" (3:1), so here he dramatically says, **Jesus arrives**. (St. Matthew is concerned to show the parallelism of John and Jesus, that all may see Jesus as the fulfillment of John's work; compare their identical messages in 3:2 and 4:17.) He comes to **the Jordan to John**, as many others have done, **to be baptized by him**.

John, though not recognizing Jesus as the Messiah (see John 1:31–33), did know Him from before. Indeed, John's mother Elizabeth and Jesus' mother Mary were relatives and friends, and Elizabeth recognized Mary's unborn Child as key in the coming Kingdom (Luke 1:39–56). It is not necessary to assume that Elizabeth recognized at the time of Mary's visitation the full significance of Mary's Son. She spoke then as a prophet (Luke 1:41), and even the prophets of old did not immediately know the full significance of their words (1 Peter 1:10f). Nonetheless, she knew Mary's Son was marked by God for great things. John would have known from childhood that his relative Jesus was special, possibly hearing from his mother and also knowing Him somewhat himself.

So it is that when Jesus presents Himself among the crowds seeking a baptism of repentance, **John was *entirely* forbidding Him**. (The verb rendered *entirely forbidding* is *diakoluo*, a more intensive form of *koluo*, "to forbid, prevent.") That is, John protests strenuously that such is not proper. In fact, it would be more proper for John himself **to be baptized** by Jesus (both the pronouns are emphatic). As a holy man, John can see that Jesus is even holier than he.

Jesus, however, insists on receiving John's baptism. He says that **thus it is proper** for them both **to fulfill all righteousness**.

What does this reply mean? What is this **righteousness**? The word in Greek is *dikaiosune*, and it is the same word used in Psalm 98:2 (LXX), where the RSV translates it "vindication." The thought here is of God vindicating His people, giving them victory, bringing in His Kingdom. Jesus is saying that *this* is the way the Kingdom of God will come—by Him humbly identifying Himself with sinners and condescending to them in lowliness. Men may think the Messiah is above such things, and that He comes only to exert His authority and to rule. God's Kingdom will not come like that. Messiah comes not to be served but to serve. He is coming in humility, not pride, not to exert His authority over men, but to die at the hands of sinners. The waters of baptism are but the first step downward to the Cross.

It is doubtful that John took all this in. But he knows that Jesus is insistent, and so **he lets Him** be baptized (the historic present is used). With trembling heart, the servant baptizes the Master.

Matthew next relates the vision John had **after** Jesus was **baptized**. When Jesus **came up immediately from the water** of the Jordan and was standing on the shore (Luke adds that He was praying; Luke 3:21), John **saw the heavens opened**, and **the Spirit of God descending like a dove, coming upon** Jesus. He then hears the divine **Voice from the heavens, saying, "This One is My beloved Son, in whom I am well-pleased."** (Matthew prefaces both the vision itself and the Voice in it with his characteristic **behold!** to show how unexpected it all is.) In this way, Jesus is confirmed by John, himself a true prophet, as the Messiah of God.

All the details of the vision are important. The **heavens opened**, for God is to speak to men again in Self-revelation. When **the Spirit of God** comes upon Jesus, He comes **descending like a dove**. The dove is an image of purity and innocence (compare 10:16), and so its Presence singles out Jesus as the One innocent of sin. Among the sinners, here is the Sinless One.

Finally, John hears the **Voice** of the Father, who, with the Holy Spirit descending on the Son, reveals the fullness of the Trinity (as the Theophany troparion says). Probably John *over*heard the Father speaking to the Son, saying to Him, "*You are* My beloved Son," as in Mark 1:11 and Luke 3:22. Matthew, however, is concerned with how this unmistakably identifies Jesus as the Son of God, and so he paraphrases the utterance as "***This One is* My beloved Son,**" as if spoken to John. Matthew is concerned not so much with verbatim exactitude as he is with the testimony of John. John knew Jesus to be the Messiah because He heard it from God Himself.

§II.3. Temptation of Christ

Matthew narrates the temptation of Christ in the wilderness not just as a biographical fact, but also as a paradigm for Christians. The Holy Spirit descended on Jesus after His baptism, even as the Holy Spirit descended on the Christians at the time of their post-baptismal laying on of hands/chrismation (as narrated in Acts 19:5–6). As Christ's experience of baptism and the Holy Spirit was followed by a time of temptation and testing by the devil, so it will be for Christ's disciples. After their baptismal initiation into the Church, they too must endure a time of conflict with the devil in the world. By showing how Christ triumphed over the devil, St. Matthew provides a model for how Christians can do the same.

ॐ ॐ ॐ ॐ ॐ

4 1 Then Jesus was led up into the wilderness by the Spirit to be tested by the devil.

After His baptism, Christ did not immediately begin His ministry, but was first **tested by the devil**. This was no overthrow of the will of God, but was allowed by Him. In the same way, the war waged on the Christians by the devil and the world does not mean that God has abandoned the Christians. Rather, God sovereignly uses the devil to fulfill His own purposes—in this case, the strengthening of Christ and His people. For just as the blade must first be tested before it is used in battle, so Christ is tested before He begins His battle against the forces of darkness.

So Christ is **led up into the wilderness by the Spirit**. These were days of prayer and preparation for Christ, as He sought the will of His Father for His future ministry. As Moses communed with God on Mount Horeb for forty days (Deut. 9:9), so Christ communed with the Father throughout the time of His wilderness retreat. The devil sought in vain to disrupt this harmony, **testing** and tempting Christ all that time (the word translated *tested* is the Gr. *peirazo*, which means both to test and to tempt).

Why was this necessary for Christ? Because Christ took upon Himself the fullness of our human condition, and so it was necessary for Him to face demonic temptation in all its power, just as we do. Thus the apostolic writer says that Christ had to be made like His brothers in all things, and that it was because He Himself was tested that He is able to help us, who are similarly tested (Heb. 2:17–18). Christ faced temptation for the same reason as He faced death—to triumph over it for our sakes.

ॐ ॐ ॐ ॐ ॐ

2 And having fasted forty days and forty nights, He then was hungry.

3 And the tempter came to *Him* and said to Him, "If You are the Son of God, tell these stones to become breads."

4 But He answered and said, "It is written, 'Man shall not live by bread alone, but by every word that proceeds through the mouth of God.'"

In the first temptation, the devil appeals to Christ's sense of His own authority. At the end of the **forty days and forty nights**, Jesus is especially **hungry**, and it is this hunger which the enemy uses as the basis of his temptation.

If Jesus is **the Son of God**, then He has authority over nature itself. The many stones which littered the ground of Judea looked very much like small loaves of bread (especially to one who was hungry). Let Christ use His authority to satisfy His own needs, and **tell these stones** at His feet **to become** so many **breads**. The temptation is to use His power for His own sake and to let His appetites set the agenda for Him. It is a temptation we all endure as well—the temptation to be ruled by our passions and desires more than by God's will.

Christ responds by citing the divine Scripture (as He does in all the temptations), thereby setting an example for His disciples. The Scripture was given by God as a lamp in darkness to direct our feet and show us the safe way to walk (Ps. 119:105). The devil may try to misdirect our steps and lead us over the precipice, but what is written will show the right way.

It is significant too that all Christ's citations of Scripture during His temptations are from Deuteronomy. Israel was led in the wilderness for forty years and tested (Gr. *peirazo*) to see whether or not they would keep God's commandments (Deut. 8:2 LXX); Deuteronomy was the scriptural testimony to that time of testing. Christ uses the Scripture given during that time of wilderness testing in His own time of trial. Lifting up the Word of God like a shield, Jesus **answered** the devil, **"It is written, 'Man shall not live by bread alone, but by every word that proceeds through the mouth of God'"** (Deut. 8:3).

In the original context, God fed the Israelites in the wilderness by daily rations of manna, to teach them to rely on Him and to show them that true life does not come from earthly food alone. The provisions of manna showed that true life comes as we trust God and refer everything to Him. In the same way, Jesus clings to the will of God and His commands as His sole reference point. He will not eat in obedience to His bodily hunger, but only as instructed

by the Father. If the Father tells Him to eat, then and only then
will He eat. Bodily desires are subordinated to humble obedience
to the Father.

ॐ ॐ ॐ ॐ ॐ

5 Then the devil takes Him into the holy city, and
stood Him upon the pinnacle of the Temple,
6 and says to Him, "If You are the Son of God,
cast Yourself down, for it is written, 'He will
command His angels about you,' and 'Upon
their hands they will take you up, lest you strike
your foot against a stone.'"
7 Jesus said to him, "Again it is written, 'You shall
not test-out the Lord your God.'"

In the second temptation, the devil **takes** Christ **into the holy
city**. With a presence invisible to mortal eyes, Satan leads Jesus and
stands Him upon the pinnacle of the Temple. This was probably
the royal porch on the south side of the outer court. According to
contemporary witnesses, such a height was high enough to cause
giddiness if one looked down into the deep Kidron ravine below.

If Jesus is **the Son of God**, He can expect special protection
from God. Let Jesus prove this, and thereby have the psychological
security of knowing that He is invincible. Then He will not have to
fear the future, but will know in advance that He is safe. Let Him
cast Himself **down** and have God miraculously catch Him, so that
He will float serenely to the ground below. God will not mind! Has
not God Himself **written** by the hand of the Psalmist that **He will
command His angels** about the righteous man (Ps. 91:11)? Such a
result is doubly sure, for another Scripture says, **"Upon their hands
they will take you up, lest you strike your foot against a stone"**
(Ps. 91:12). If this is true of the righteous man in general, how much
more is it true of God's Messiah?

This is the temptation to find security against life's suffering *in
advance*, and to be spared the uncertainty that comes from walking with God by faith. It is the perennial temptation to presume

on God's care and to bend His will to ours. Such a presumption is especially common in religious folk—hence Satan's subtle (and lying) use of Scripture.

Christ does not argue with the devil about Scripture, nor point out how he is distorting its meaning. (This Scripture verse promises God's help to those who obediently follow Him, not to those who proudly presume on His care.) Rather than debating about the meaning of these verses, Christ simply responds with another Scripture, saying, **"It is written, 'You shall not test-out the Lord your God'"** (Deut. 6:16). (The word translated *test-out* is the Gr. *ekpeirazo*, a more intensive form of the verb *peirazo*, "to test.")

That is, one shall not try to make God prove Himself. Rather, one should trust that God will direct our steps as He knows best, and not presume on His unconditional protection. In obedience to this Scripture, Christ refuses to put God to the test by leaping from the Temple's pinnacle.

By doing so, Christ calls us also to walk with God by faith and to take whatever comes from His hand, confident that God's love knows what is best for us. We must not seek to bend God's will to our own.

ॐ   ॐ   ॐ   ॐ   ॐ

8   Again, the devil takes Him to a very high mountain, and shows Him all the kingdoms of the world and the glory of them,

9   and he said to Him, "All these things will I give to You, if You fall *down* and worship me."

10   Then Jesus says to him, "Go away, Satan! For it is written, 'You shall worship the Lord your God, and serve Him only.'"

11   Then the devil leaves Him, and behold! Angels came to *Him* and were serving Him.

In the third temptation, **the devil takes** Jesus **to a very high mountain, and shows Him all the kingdoms of the world and the glory of them**. This final temptation begins with the devil displaying

all the kingdoms of the world along with **the glory of them,** using his supernatural power to make them pass before Christ's gaze. The devil states that it is to Christ that he will **give** them, so that Jesus will stand as the ruler of all the world.

This was within Satan's power, for having usurped the rule from Adam and Eve when they fell, he was now the god of this age and its ruler (2 Cor. 4:4), and the whole world lay in his authority (1 John 5:19). As it was then, he could give it to whom he would (and be the power behind the throne!)

Jesus can rule the whole earth. All He has to do is a simple act of obeisance, unseen by any mortal eyes. All He has to do is **fall *down* and worship** the devil (Gr. *proskuneo,* to bow down in obeisance) and **all these things** will be His. This is the timeless temptation to compromise one's allegiance to God for the sake of worldly gain. It is a temptation to compromise moral and spiritual integrity which comes time and time again to the children of men in their quest for success.

At this arrogant and blasphemous suggestion, Christ banishes the devil from His holy Presence. With a word He drives him off, saying, **"Go away, Satan!"** Christ utterly repudiates Satan's offer, responding with the word from Deuteronomy 6:13: **"It is written, 'You shall worship the Lord your God, and serve Him only.'"** The words rendered *worship* and *serve* are the Greek words *proskuneo* and *latreuo.* The verb *proskuneo* (as said above) means "to bow down," and in this context, to bow down in total submission. The verb *latreuo* means "to serve" in the sense of performing religious duties, especially liturgical ones; in these commentaries it is usually translated as "to worship." This command in Deuteronomy 6:13 means that ultimate homage and allegiance is given to God alone, and any other act which threatens this is forbidden. With this offer, Satan has gone too far, and Christ drives him away.

Faced with Christ's sovereign command, **the devil leaves Him,** having been completely defeated. Then, just as once "the tempter came to Him" with his cunning, so now **angels came to *Him*** with their devotion. (The same Greek verb, *proserxomai,* is used both for the tempter in v. 3 and the angels here in v. 11.) The suddenness of their appearance is indicated by Matthew's **behold!** The nature of their service is not stated. Mark 1:13 mentions the service of the angels, and also says that Jesus was with the wild beasts there. Possibly the angels offered divine protection in fending them off, fulfilling the Scripture mentioned in 4:6. St. Matthew stresses their presence to show that Jesus is the true Messiah, He who is **served** by angels on earth even as God is served by them in heaven.

§II.4. Christict Settles in Galilee

࿋ ࿋ ࿋ ࿋ ࿋

12 Now when He heard that John had been delivered up, He withdrew into Galilee,

13 and leaving behind Nazareth, He came and dwelt in Capernaum, which is beside the sea, in the area of Zebulun and Naphtali,

14 to fulfill what was spoken through Isaiah the prophet, saying,

15 "Land of Zebulun and land of Naphtali, way of the sea, beyond the Jordan, Galilee of the Gentiles—

16 "the people sitting in darkness saw a great light, and those sitting in the land and shadow of death, upon them a light rose."

After narrating the temptation in the wilderness, Matthew leaps ahead to a time after **John had been delivered up** and imprisoned. (The actual arrest is not narrated until 14:3–5, but Matthew assumes that his Jewish readers are aware of this famous historical incident.) In so doing, like Mark, Matthew omits the early acts of Christ narrated in John 1—3. He now focuses on the time when Christ came into His own. After John's arrest, Jesus **withdrew into Galilee**.

This was prudent, especially since Jesus was considered by many at that time to be simply a part of John's movement. John and Jesus were both baptizing in Judea (John 3:22–23), and Judea was now becoming unsafe for those identified with John. The Baptizer was imprisoned for rebuking Herod for his sins, and Herod feared that the people would take such a public rebuke as a clarion call to rebellion. Would Jesus, a high-profile part of John's movement (as He was seen), be the next one arrested? The withdrawal from Judea to the safety of Galilee was strategically prudent.

From Matthew's reference to Christ **leaving behind Nazareth**, it would appear that Christ first went to His hometown after He left Judea. From Luke's Gospel we learn that He preached in the synagogue there, only to suffer rejection (Luke 4:16–30). Matthew, however, does not focus on this, but on His final location in **Capernaum** some ways to the north. It was here, in the heart of Galilee, that Christ made His base of operations.

Galilee at this time had quite a mixed population, with many Gentiles in the area; hence **Galilee of the Gentiles**. It might be thought that such an area was unlikely to produce the Messiah, and indeed, later on Christ's foes were quite sure of Galilee's lack of credentials. Confidently they challenged anyone to search the Scriptures and see for themselves that no prophet arises from Galilee (John 7:52). It is partly to counteract such an attitude that St. Matthew quotes **what was spoken through Isaiah the prophet** as part of Isaiah's messianic oracle (Is. 9:1–2).

Isaiah had spoken of the land in the north of Israel, the **land of Zebulun and** the **land of Naphtali**. Israel was always invaded from the north, and those northern tribes were always the first to suffer destruction from any foreign foes. They dwelt in the darkness of fear and the shadow of their powerful enemies, always dreading invasion. But, Isaiah prophesied, light would dawn on them at last. God would set upon the throne of David His righteous King, who would bring peace (Is. 9:6–7).

For St. Matthew, Christ's settling in Galilee was no mere accident, but a fulfillment of these ancient prophecies. In their original context, Isaiah's prophecies spoke of death at the hands of invading foes, but Matthew had his eye on a more powerful and universal foe—the devil, who had the power of death (Heb. 2:14). It was not just the northern tribes who were **sitting in darkness**, powerless before sin and death, but all the people of Israel, and indeed the whole world. Like the sun rising triumphantly in the sky at dawn and banishing the shades of night, **a light rose** upon all the children of men—Christ, the Sun of Righteousness. By settling in Capernaum and thus identifying Himself with Galilee, Christ revealed Himself as the **great light** foreseen by Isaiah.

§II.5. Christt Begins to Preach and to Call Disciples

ॐ ॐ ॐ ॐ ॐ

17 From then Jesus began to herald and say, "Repent, for the Kingdom of the heavens draws near!"

18 And walking beside the Sea of Galilee, He saw two brothers, Simon who was called Peter, and Andrew his brother, casting a circle-net into the sea, for they were fishermen.

19 And He says to them, "Come after Me, and I will make you fishers of men."

20 And immediately leaving the nets, they followed Him.

Matthew has but a few more things to relate as he describes the beginning of Christ's ministry. **From then** on, after settling in Capernaum, **Jesus began to herald** the proclamation of God **and say, "Repent, for the Kingdom of the heavens draws near!"** St. Matthew summarizes Jesus' message using the same words used to describe the message of John (3:2), for both Jesus and John were sent by the same Father—Jesus as the Father's eternal Son and Messiah, and John as His Forerunner.

Walking beside the Sea of Galilee, Jesus **saw two brothers, Simon** (later **called Peter** by the Church) and **Andrew his brother.** At that time they were standing in the shallow waters, **casting a circle-net into the sea**, as one would expect from **fishermen.** This **circle-net** was a small net, weighted on the edges, thrown into the waters near the shore. They had spent all that night fishing in deeper waters with a dragnet and had caught nothing (Luke 5:5), and perhaps hoped to salvage something of an otherwise fruitless time. This was not the first time that Simon and Andrew met Jesus. They had known Him from the time of their following John the Baptizer (John 1:5–42) and had spent much time with Him (John 2). Matthew omits this prehistory. Instead, he focuses on the climactic drama of their final decision to follow Him. Jesus says to them, **"Come after Me, and I will make you fishers of men."**

This call came after a miraculous catch of fish, related in Luke 5:1–11. Christ called them away from throwing the circle-net and used their boat to preach to the crowds. Afterwards, despite their protest that it was obviously not a good time to fish, Christ bade them let down their nets, with the result that they took an over-whelming catch. It was in response to this manifestation of divine power that Simon and his brother decided to **leave the nets** and their old ways and **follow Him**. Matthew omits the surrounding circumstances to better focus on the vividness of their renunciation of their old life.

> ॐ ॐ ॐ ॐ ॐ
>
> 21 And going on from there He saw two other brothers, James *the son* of Zebedee and John his brother, in the boat with Zebedee their father, restoring their nets, and He called them.
> 22 And immediately leaving the boat and their father, they followed Him.

It is the same with the call of **two other brothers, James *the son* of Zebedee and John his brother**. Like Simon and Andrew, they had known Jesus before. As Jesus had called Simon and Andrew that morning, so He called James and John. While Simon and Andrew were circle-casting in the shallows, James and John were **in the boat with Zebedee their father, restoring their nets** after the night's work. **He called them** too, and after the miraculous catch of fish, they also **left the boat and their father** and their whole way of life and **followed Him**.

St. Matthew relates the story of the call of these men as dramatically as possible to provide a paradigm of conversion for all. Faith in Christ requires a dramatic renunciation of the old ways, a willingness to abandon family and business. The world may denounce such commitment as sudden, drastic, and reckless, but that is the only path of true discipleship.

ॐ ॐ ॐ ॐ ॐ

23 And He was going about in all Galilee, teaching in their synagogues and heralding the Good News of the Kingdom, and healing every disease and every malady among the people.

24 And the report about Him went out into all Syria, and they brought to Him all who were sick *with* various diseases and distressed with torments, demon-possessed and epileptics, paralytics, and He healed them.

25 And many crowds followed Him from Galilee and Decapolis and Jerusalem and Judea and beyond the Jordan.

Matthew concludes his summary of the beginning of Christ's ministry by reporting Christ's astounding success. **He was going about in all Galilee,** finding a welcome everywhere. He was **teaching in their synagogues,** telling parables and instructing them about what God really wanted from His people. He was **heralding the Good News of the Kingdom,** proclaiming that the Kingdom was at hand. He was **healing every disease and every malady among the people,** for no kind of affliction was beyond His saving reach.

Not surprisingly, **the report about Him went out** everywhere—even beyond Israel's borders, **into all** the Roman province of **Syria.** He was able to cure **all who were sick *with* various diseases**—even such difficult cases as the **demon-possessed and epileptics** (Gr. *seleniazomai,* lit., "moonstruck"—i.e. those subject to seizures), and **paralytics.** No case was too difficult, but rather **He healed them** all. No wonder **many crowds followed Him,** not only from **Galilee**, but also from **Decapolis** east of Jordan and from **Jerusalem** and **Judea** and the rest of the area **beyond the Jordan**. St. Matthew offers this success as evidence of Christ's divine power, obvious to all Israel.

FIRST DISCOURSE—THE SERMON ON THE MOUNT
(5:1—7:29)

℅ ℅ ℅ ℅ ℅

5 1 And when He saw the crowds, He went up to the mountain, and after He sat, His disciples came to Him.
2 And opening His mouth, He was teaching them, saying,

From a comparison with Mark 3:13–14 and Luke 6:12f, we learn that Christ **went up to the mountain** to escape **the crowds** that thronged Him below, and to be alone for the purpose of prayer. After this time of prayer, He summoned **His disciples,** who **came to Him**, and from these He selected twelve as a special inner core. It is possible that He spent a few hours instructing them privately before descending to a place lower on the mountainside where He could address the larger crowd.

St. Matthew arranges his material artistically, and he omits this detail of prayer and the selection of the Twelve. (He will deal with the charge given to the Twelve in the next discourse.) By omitting mention of Christ's selection of the Twelve and His partial descent to a place lower down the slopes, Matthew is able to focus more vividly on the mountain locale of Christ's sermon. In particular, he focuses on the parallel between Christ's instruction and that given on Mount Sinai: As God spoke from the mountain in Moses' time, so now He speaks from the mountain in Christ.

Christ **sat** after His disciples came to Him because sitting was the classical posture for **teaching** (compare 23:2). Matthew prefaces the teaching with a characteristically Semitic phrase, **opening His mouth**, thereby giving the utterances that follow greater weight (compare Job 3:1; Dan. 10:16). The Teacher was about to expound His divine Torah!

§III.1. The Beatitudes

Just as the Ten Commandments stand at the head of the Mosaic instruction (Ex. 20—23), so the Beatitudes stand at the head of the Sermon on the Mount. The Ten Commandments come first in those initial instructions to Israel, followed by the rest of Exodus 20—23, which delineates more fully how Israel should live. Similarly, the Beatitudes reveal the blessedness of discipleship to Christ, while the rest of the sermon reveals what that life of discipleship consists of. Christ's disciples are blessed—and here is how they must behave.

The Beatitudes therefore, like the rest of the sermon, are not moralistic maxims for the world at large, but are promises to Christ's disciples. They were never meant to be seized on by the world as bits of Christian folk-wisdom, as if they could be applied apart from saving faith in the Lord.

And like everything else in Matthew's Gospel, they need to be placed in their Palestinian context to be fully appreciated. Christ's disciples were thought to be deluded fools by the Pharisees (compare John 7:47–49)—not least because His teaching differed so radically from theirs and contradicted it on many important points (such as how to keep the Sabbath; see 12:1–8). This rival practice of the Pharisees must be kept in mind as the background to much of the sermon, for Christ explicitly contrasts His teaching with the popularly received teaching of the Pharisees (e.g. 5:20; 6:1f).

The despised state of His disciples forms the background to the Beatitudes. The Pharisees denounced Jesus' followers as the most hapless and pathetic of men. Against this, Christ proclaims that those who have chosen to follow Him are **blessed** (Gr. *makarios*, a word used in classical Greek to describe the happiness of the gods).

In the Beatitudes, Jesus' disciples are described in these many ways—as being poor in spirit, as being those who mourn, as the meek. These nine Beatitudes do not describe nine different types of people, but are a ninefold description of His true followers.

The basic thought behind all the nine Beatitudes is that of the great reversal which will take place for Christ's followers in the age to come. Here in this age, they are poor, despised, and hungry. The world is a vale of tears for them, and they live meekly as those who cannot answer back the proud. In all this they refuse to retaliate, but extend mercy to all, striving for reconciliation with those who hurt them—and are thought fools for it. They are persecuted and reproached and universally reviled. But how fortunate they are!—for all will be theirs in the coming Kingdom.

The Beatitudes then are not commendations for certain virtues or states of mind. Christ is not commending certain forms of behavior (such as being gentle or merciful). The thought here is not *ethical* but *eschatological*. Christ focuses not on the virtue of His followers, but on the fact that they are downtrodden, and says that all this will be reversed in the age to come (compare Luke 6:20–26, with its woes to those who despise His followers).

࿐ ࿐ ࿐ ࿐ ࿐

3   "Blessed *are* the poor in spirit, for theirs is the Kingdom of the heavens.

4   "Blessed *are* those who mourn, for they will be comforted.

5   "Blessed *are* the meek, for they will inherit the earth.

6   "Blessed *are* those who hunger and thirst for righteousness, for they will be fed *to the full*.

7   "Blessed *are* the merciful, for they will *be shown* mercy.

8   "Blessed *are* the clean of heart, for they will see God.

9   "Blessed are the peacemakers, for they will be called sons of God.

> 10 "Blessed *are* those who have been persecuted for righteousness' sake, for theirs is the Kingdom of the heavens.
> 11 "Blessed are you when they reproach you, and persecute *you*, and say all *kinds of* evil against you falsely, for My sake.
> 12 "Rejoice and exult, for your reward in the heavens *is* great, for thus they persecuted the prophets before you.

First of all, Christ says, **"Blessed *are* the poor in spirit."** The thought here is of material poverty, for the poor must rely on God for everything. It is not poverty itself that brings the blessing, however, but this reliance on God (hence Christ speaks not just of being poor, but poor **in spirit**). The image in the Psalter of the oppressed but righteous poor man who belongs to God (e.g. Ps. 34:6; 72:2) finds its fulfillment in them. In this world they may be destitute, but in the age to come they will be rich, **for theirs is the Kingdom of the heavens**, and even now they have the promise of their final triumph (note the present tense of the verb **is**).

Next Christ says, **"Blessed *are* those who mourn."** Mourning is the fate of those who suffer in this age as Jesus' disciples. The primary thought here is not mourning over one's sins (though this cannot be excluded), but of weeping over the hardness of the world, for the world opposes the way of love and grinds the face of the poor (compare Luke 6:21, "Blessed are you who weep now"). The hard and wicked world will one day pass away, and the gentle mourners **will be comforted** by God in the world to come.

Thirdly, Christ says, **"Blessed *are* the meek."** The word here translated *meek* is the Greek *praus*, and it indicates not so much mildness and servility as humility. Jesus' followers are characterized here as "meek" not because they all have mild tempers (James and John obviously did not!—see Luke 9:54), but because they all are powerless in this world. The world thinks them of no account; it thinks it safe to run roughshod over them, and that they are helpless to prevent it. And so they are. But such tyrants will not rule forever. Eventually, the meek will **inherit the earth**, and humility will receive its reward.

In the next beatitude, Christ says, **"Blessed *are* those who hunger and thirst for righteousness."** As with the first beatitude, which spoke of the poor in spirit, so with this one. In Luke 6:20 it is the poor who are pronounced blessed, while Matthew speaks of them as "the poor in spirit" to bring out the inner significance of the beatitude. It is the same here. In Luke 6:21 a blessing is pronounced on those who are hungry, and Matthew here speaks about "those who hunger and thirst for righteousness." The hungry have to rely on God for their basic necessities, trusting Him to vindicate their trust and care for them. This is the **righteousness** spoken of here—the righteousness of God whereby He gives justice to His elect (see Luke 18:7). He will vindicate those who look to Him, and they will **be fed *to the full*,** feasting in the age to come. (The word rendered *fed to the full* is the Gr. *chortazo*, meaning "to gorge"—a true vindication indeed!)

Next Christ says, **"Blessed *are* the merciful."** In this age, strength alone is valued, as all compete against one another for the survival of the fittest. Mercy is not valued, but is often seen as a sign of weakness. When one has one's enemy by the throat, one should strike! It is against the background of such worldly philosophy that Christ pronounces the blessedness of those who are **merciful** to others. The world has shown them no mercy, but they refuse to retaliate in kind. In the day of judgment, they too **will *be shown* mercy** by the final Judge.

Christ then says, **"Blessed *are* the clean of heart."** Once again, the contrast is between His disciples and the world. In the world, religion had to do with ritual purity—being in a state of ceremonial cleanness, offering the correct sacrifices in the correct way, through a correct priesthood. Externalism was the ruling principle in all the religions of the world. Jesus' disciples, however, walk a different path, and the ruling principle is an internal one. What matters ultimately is purity of the heart. This is consistent with the intuitions of the prophets and sages (see Ps. 15:1f; 50:16, 23). In this beatitude, Christ promises that His disciples, though judged by the religious of His day as hopelessly lax (15:2), would one day **see God** in His glory. They will be ushered with joy into His eternal Presence at the last day, when other religious folk are denied that saving access.

Next Christ says, **"Blessed are the peacemakers."** The thought here is not so much of third-party diplomacy as it is of those who strive for reconciliation, even with those who hate them and hurt them. The world considers such love of peace to be a sign of naiveté and foolishness. Sensible men aim at the destruction of their enemies, not harmony and brotherhood with them! (The Zealots of Palestine would have agreed.) Christ says that His people, however, will offer love in return for animosity, good in return for evil, and by this strive to make peace with their foes. Such a course of action will win the divine reward in the coming age, for such peacemakers will **be called sons of God** then. God will acknowledge them openly as His sons and heirs.

Christ also says, **"Blessed *are* those who have been persecuted for righteousness' sake."** This **righteousness** is no abstract ethical uprightness, but the divine dispensation, the plan of God for the salvation of the world (as in 3:15). An ethical component, of course, is not wholly lacking here, for Jesus' disciples live ethically upright lives. But the main thought is of those who are persecuted by the world because they live as followers of Christ. The synagogue rulers may denounce them as renegades and apostates, but **theirs is the Kingdom of the heavens** nonetheless. Even now, they possess the promise of eternal life. (See the first beatitude in v. 3.)

Building on this, Christ offers a final beatitude, addressing His disciples directly: **"Blessed are you when they reproach you, and persecute *you*, and say all *kinds of* evil against you falsely, for My sake."** Face-to-face reproaches and insults, direct and tangible persecution and social exclusion, the spreading of slanders—all this might be thought a reason to lament. Not so, says the Lord. Instead, one should **rejoice and exult** at such a happy result, for the **reward** kept for them **in the heavens** is **great**. Such disciples stand in a venerable line of prophets, **for thus**, in the same way, the same religious establishment as persecutes them also **persecuted the prophets** before them. Those prophets are now recognized as blessed and fortunate, and so will His disciples be in the age to come.

ॐ ॐ ॐ ॐ ॐ

13 "You *yourselves* are the salt of the earth, but if the salt has become foolish, with what will it be made salty? It is good for nothing any longer, but to be cast outside and trampled on by men.

14 "You *yourselves* are the light of the world. A city is not able to be hidden atop a mountain.

15 "Nor do they kindle a lamp, and put it under the measure, but upon the lampstand, and it shines on all those in the house.

16 "Thus let your light shine before men that they may see your good works and glorify your Father in the heavens.

Continuing from His commendation of His followers as the successors of the prophets, Jesus further commends them, insisting that they (the pronoun is emphatic) are **the salt of the earth**. In those days, salt was precious. It was used for preserving food, and without it, food would become rotten. God said that He would spare sinful Sodom if but a few righteous could be found there (Gen. 18:32), and in the same way the presence of Jesus' followers within the sinful world also preserves it from destruction.

But let His followers preserve their righteousness, and not fall back into the ways of the world! **If the salt** used to season food has become insipid, **with what will it be made salty** again? Such salt **is good for nothing any longer**. It is fit only **to be cast outside and trampled on by men** as something utterly contemptible. It is the same with His disciples if they become foolish and apostate. On the last day, they also will **be cast outside** (the phrase has an eschatological feel to it; compare 8:12) as utterly worthless.

The word translated *become foolish* is the Gr. *moraino*, and it is so translated in Rom. 1:22 and 1 Cor. 1:20. Yet how can salt **become foolish**? From the reference to **making it salty** again, it is apparent that the salt is thought of as becoming unsalty, not foolish. The original Aramaic probably involves a wordplay. The Hebrew root *tpl* has a double meaning. The word *tapel* means "insipid things" (see Job 6:6), while the word *tiplah* means "folly" (see Job 1:22). Just as salt that loses its savor becomes insipid and useless, so the disciple who becomes foolish is also useless. Matthew chooses the second meaning of the Semitic word to apply this wordplay to his hearers.

The Lord also commends His followers as **the light of the world** (once again the pronoun **you** is emphatic). If the thought of the previous commendation is the power of the disciples' presence to preserve the world, the thought here is of their power to illumine it. By their proclamation of Jesus, they bring light to a world that would otherwise languish in darkness, for Jesus is the only light the world knows.

Jesus compares the disciples to **a city atop a mountain**. Such a city **is not able to be hidden**, but light from within shines in the night, guiding all weary travelers to safety within its walls. The Church, the City of God, is the same, and its function is to illumine the world. In this it resembles **a lamp** burning in a house. The family does not **kindle** such **a lamp** and then **put it under** a **measure** (or basket) so that its light is not seen. The whole point of lighting the lamp is so that it might be **put upon the lampstand** and may **shine on all those in the house**.

In the same way, the function of the disciples is to shine on the whole world, illumining all men and guiding them home. They therefore must **thus** (that is, openly) **let** their **light shine before men**, fearlessly living as open disciples of Jesus. (The word **thus** refers to the universal shining of the light in the previous verses.) Only then can the world **see** their **good works and glorify** their **Father in the heavens**. In this saying, Jesus is not telling His disciples to *do their good works* openly, in order to be seen by men. Indeed, He blames the Pharisees for doing just that (6:1f), and commands His disciples to do the opposite. Rather, He is telling His disciples to *confess their commitment to Him* openly, for only so can their love for men redound to the glory of God in Christ.

§III.2. Christi and the Law

ॐ ॐ ॐ ॐ ॐ

17 "Do not suppose that I came to tear down the Law or the Prophets; I did not come to tear down, but to fulfill.

18 "For amen I say to you, until heaven and earth pass away, one iota or one horn *of a letter* will never pass away from the Law, until all happens.

19 "Whoever therefore looses one of the least of these commandments and thus teaches men will be called least in the Kingdom of the heavens; but whoever does and teaches *them*, this one will be called great in the Kingdom of the heavens.

20 "For I say to you that unless your righteousness surpasses that of the scribes and Pharisees, you will never enter into the Kingdom of the heavens.

As mentioned above, all the Sermon on the Mount is to be read against the background of opposition from the Pharisees. The Pharisees denounced Jesus as a Sabbath-breaker, as one who was lax in the demands of piety (12:1f; 15:1f). Thus Matthew is concerned to show to his Jewish audience how Christ's interpretation of the Law, though different from that of the Pharisees, nonetheless fulfills the inner and true demands of God's Law. In fact it was the Pharisees whose interpretation of the Law made it void (compare 15:3).

Christ therefore denies the accusation that He **came to tear down** or abolish the demands of **the Law or the Prophets**. On the contrary, He came **to fulfill** them, to reveal by His deeds and words what God truly wants from His people. The heart of the Law and the Prophets is love of God and neighbor (22:37–40), and Christ shows how these demands are to be met.

He is far from suggesting that the true demands of the Scriptures can be set aside. He solemnly assures them (prefacing His word with His customary solemn oath, **"Amen I say to you"**) that **until heaven and earth pass away, one iota or one horn** *of a letter* from the Law **will never pass away until all** it speaks of **happens**. The Scriptures (that is, the whole of the Law, not just the Pentateuch) speak of God's will and His coming Kingdom, and until all that will is done and that Kingdom comes, the divine Law will remain, living and active in all its parts. While **heaven and earth** remain, God's Word will abide.

In speaking of the totality of God's Word, Christ speaks of every single **iota** and **horn** *of a letter* in **the Law**. This *iota* is the Greek letter "i", the Greek equivalent of the Hebrew letter *yodh*, the smallest letter of the Hebrew alphabet. The **horn** *of a letter* is the projection of a letter which differentiates one Hebrew letter from another. Christ is saying that the Scriptures are authoritative and divine down to the least part of each letter.

Therefore, one's greatness before God in the Kingdom may be determined by one's attitude towards these Scriptures. **Whoever looses** (that is, annuls) even a single one of **these command-ments**—even the **least** of them—and by his example **thus teaches men**, that one will be **called least in the Kingdom**. God's will is reflected in *all* His commandments—who is man to say which part of God's will can be disobeyed? Such a man might try to set aside a commandment, saying it is least—but it is *he* who will prove to be least. On the other hand, **whoever** respects and **does** all God's commandments and by his example **teaches** others so, **this** very **one will be called great in the Kingdom**.

What is at stake is one's submission to what God truly wants, and the character of one's righteousness. By their interpretations of the Law, the Pharisees stressed mere outward conformity to the Law, and by so doing they ignored what God truly required. The disciples of Jesus are called to penetrate to the inner heart of the Law, and to see and do what the Law truly demands. Their **righteousness** will thus **surpass that of the scribes and Pharisees**. God demands a righteousness that touches the inner motivation, that transcends casuistic loopholes. Only by having this righteousness can men hope to **enter into the Kingdom of the heavens**.

Regarding this eternal and total validity of the Law, certain things must be clarified. This validity does not mean that Gentiles are bound by Jewish prescriptions, such as Sabbaths, circumcision, and the dietary laws. The question of whether Gentile Christians, to whom the Law was never given (Rom. 3:19), should keep the Jewish Law in its cultural expression, is never asked here. The context is Jewish throughout. When Christ teaches that every part of the Law remains in force, He is speaking to Jews of *the inner intention of the Law*. The point is that *the inner attitudes inculcated by those laws* forever remain what God requires. And even Gentiles who need not keep the cultural expression of the laws (such as, for example, circumcision) still must keep the inner value contained in them (such as, in the case of the circumcision law, covenant loyalty to God).

༈ ༈ ༈ ༈ ༈

21 "You have heard that it was said to the ancients, 'You shall not murder,' and, 'Whoever murders will be liable to the judgment.'

22 "But I *Myself* say to you that everyone angry with his brother will be liable to the judgment, and whoever will say to his brother, 'Raca!' will be liable to the Council, and whoever will say, 'Fool!' will be liable to the Gehenna of fire.

23 "Therefore if you are offering up your gift on the altar, and there remember that your brother has something against you,

24 "leave your gift there before the altar, and go away; first be reconciled to your brother, and then come offer up your gift.

25 "Be well-disposed to your opponent quickly while you are with him on the way, lest your opponent deliver you up to the judge, and the

> judge to the attendant, and you be cast into
> prison.
> 26 "Amen I say to you, you will never come out
> from there until you have rendered the last
> quadrans.

Having taught that His disciples must fulfill the inner demands
of the Law and not just conform to its outer demands (as the
Pharisees taught), Christ proceeds to give six examples of how the
Pharisaical interpretation does not go far enough.

In His first example, Christ says that they **have heard** from the
Pharisees **that it was said** by God **to the ancients, "You shall not
murder,"** and **"Whoever murders will be liable to the judgment"**
(Ex. 20:13; Deut. 19:11–12). That is, in the Pharisees' interpretation,
the act of murder is what breaks this commandment and makes one
liable and guilty before **the judgment** from human courts.

Christ, however, says on His own authority (the pronoun **I** is
emphatic) that what this Law really prohibits is murderous anger.
This refusal to express anger is what God truly values and is striving
to inculcate in His people. Now that Messiah has come, the inner
intention of the Law must be fulfilled.

Thus it is not only the outward murderer who is liable to the
judgment (v. 21), but also **everyone angry** enough to kill is **liable to
judgment.** And **whoever will say to his brother, "Raca!"** (Aramaic
for "moron") will be guilty enough to be tried before the supreme
Council; whoever will say, "Fool!" to his brother will be guilty
enough to be cast into **the Gehenna of fire.**

What is envisioned here is not casual name-calling (though this
is scarcely commendable), much less a valid denunciation of folly
(compare Christ's own words in Luke 24:25). For one thing, the
words **raca** and **fool** ring much more harshly in their original cultural
context than they do in ours, since in that culture public denunciation was incredibly insulting. What is envisioned is a contempt that
would write the other person off entirely. What Christ condemns
here is the rage that implicitly denies the personhood and dignity of
the other. Such rage tends to escalate out of control, which is why

the punishments Christ lists also increase in severity. First one is guilty of the local court's **judgment**, then of condemnation before the supreme national **Council**, and finally of the **Gehenna of fire** in the age to come. We see how dangerous rage is when it can lead to such ultimate disaster for the soul.

If one is truly guided by the Law, therefore, one will take care to eliminate angry grudges from one's life. (We note in passing that Christ deals here not with the *emotion of anger*, but with *the willing acceptance of it in one's life*. It is the long-standing grudge, not the feeling of irritation, which is in view.)

Thus, Christ teaches, if **you are offering up your gift on the altar**, and are in the very act of sacrifice, and **there remember that your brother has something against you**, you should stop dead in your tracks. Better to leave your gift before the altar and go away (however strange onlookers may think you) and **first be reconciled to your brother**. Only **then** should you **come offer up your gift**. Nursing angry grudges with men blocks open communion with God, and makes true worship impossible. (This is one reason the Church exchanged the Peace before offering the eucharistic sacrifice in the anaphora.)

Quarrels must be quickly resolved (if at all possible). Christ then tells a parable to illustrate this. If a man were **on the way** to court with his **opponent**, it would be wise to become **well-disposed** to him **quickly** before reaching the court. Otherwise, the man might lose the case, and his **opponent** would **deliver** him **up to the judge, and the judge to the attendant, and** he **be cast into prison**.

This is an image of the final Judgment of God upon those who refuse to let go of angry grudges and who refuse to forgive their neighbor. Such will be cast into the eternal prison by God, and (Christ solemnly assures His hearers with His **Amen I say to you**), they **will never come out from there** until the demands of divine justice are fully satisfied, even down to the smallest offense, **the last quadrans**. A *quadrans* was a small coin, equal to one sixty-fourth of a day's wage for a laborer. In saying that the debt must be **rendered** down to **the last quadrans**, Christ is not saying that such imprison-ment will be lengthy but limited, or that the imprisoned will one day pay his debt and emerge from prison. He is saying that the full demands of justice will be exacted. The Gehenna threatening the angry sinner is eternal (v. 22).

ૐ ૐ ૐ ૐ ૐ

27 "You have heard that it was said, 'You shall not commit adultery';

28 "But I *Myself* say to you that everyone looking on a woman to desire her has already committed adultery with her in his heart.

29 "And if your right eye makes you stumble, tear it out, and cast *it* from you; for it is advantageous for you that one of your members perish, and your whole body not be cast into Gehenna.

30 "And if your right hand makes you stumble, cut it off, and cast *it* from you; for it is advantageous for you that one of your members perish, and your whole body not to go into Gehenna.

In the second example, Christ refers to the ancient commandment, **"You shall not commit adultery."** Once again Jesus penetrates past the surface of this commandment to reveal the inner value of purity it enshrines. To keep this commandment fully, one must not simply avoid the act of adultery, but also the consuming lust in the heart that precedes the act. Thus, **everyone looking on a woman to desire her** has **already** broken the commandment **in his heart**.

Christ is here not referring to simple sexual temptation, or to the fact that men find certain women desirable. This act of **looking** is not the casual glance, but the sustained and obsessive watching, the act of a man who cannot tear himself away from the object of his desire. Christ is focusing on the inner intention, the lust that consumes and obsesses, whether or not it is acted on. If a person **looking on a woman to desire her** is only deterred from acting on his desire for fear of retribution from the woman's husband, such a man is still guilty. In this commandment God wants not only abstinence from the act, but also internal purity of heart.

The disciple of Christ must act ruthlessly towards lust if he finds it has taken root in him, and energetically oppose its working within him. In so doing he may find that it is like cutting away something basic to his very self. But this must still be done, and Christ tells a parable to reveal the necessity for it.

If a man found that even his **right eye** (the more precious of the two) was causing him to **stumble** into sin and separation from God, he should **tear it out, and cast** *it* away from him, throwing the offending member as far as possible from him. For it would be **advantageous** overall for him to have **one of** his **members perish**, rather than for his **whole body** to **be cast into Gehenna**. It would be the same if his **right hand** (again the more precious of the two in a right-handed society) was bringing him to ruin. In a choice between losing one member now and losing all his members later in the age to come, it is only sensible to sacrifice one member to save oneself. In the same way the disciple must cut off the offending habit, even if it feels like the amputation of his inner and most precious self.

ॐ ॐ ॐ ॐ ॐ

31 "And it was said, 'Whoever dismisses his wife, let him give a *writ* of divorce to her.'

32 "But I *Myself* say to you that everyone dismissing his wife, except for cause of fornication, makes her commit adultery; and whoever marries a dismissed woman commits adultery.

In His third example, Christ speaks of the commandment regarding a man who **dismisses** and divorces **his wife**. The Law specified that he must not dismiss her and reclaim her at will, as if she were mere chattel. If she was dismissed, the man could not reclaim her again on a whim at a later time. As proof that such a dismissal had taken place, he must **give a *writ* of divorce to her** (Deut. 24:1–4). The goal of this law is not to mandate divorce (which was already presupposed in that culture, even before the Law was given). Rather the goal is to protect the woman from being handed about from man to man.

Christ again penetrates further into the divine intention behind this commandment. In ancient days God had spoken to limit the harm done by divorce and remarriage; now that the Kingdom is at hand, He calls His followers to shun divorce entirely. A rabbinical interpretation of this passage (made popular by Rabbi Hillel) allowed a man to dismiss his wife for any reason whatever. Jesus, however, declares that **everyone dismissing his wife makes her commit adultery**, and that **whoever marries** such **a dismissed woman commits adultery** as well.

Marriage establishes an organic union between husband and wife which persists even though the wife is unjustly sent away. Any man who divorces his wife (thereby forcing her, in that culture, to marry someone else) forces her into adultery, for the marriage bond between the first two remains intact even when the wife of necessity marries another man. (We may think, however, that the *guilt* for such adultery lies principally with the husband who unjustly divorced his innocent wife—who otherwise would not have divorced her husband—and not with the woman and her new husband themselves.)

Thus, for two followers of Jesus, divorce is not an option. The exception to this is **for cause of fornication** (Gr. *porneia*). What exactly is involved in this exception? It cannot be simply adultery on the part of the wife after marriage, for this is the grounds for divorce allowed by Rabbi Shammai (Rabbi Hillel's rival). If Christ were simply siding with Rabbi Shammai, the reaction of shock His teaching provoked would be hard to explain (compare 19:10). The omission of this significant exception in the Gospels of Mark and Luke would be hard to explain as well (compare Mark 10:11–12; Luke 16:18).

I suggest that Christ refers here to fornication on the part of the woman during the betrothal period, so that it does not form a true exception to the prohibition of divorce among those actually married. Thus if the man discovered that his betrothed had a sexual liaison with someone else prior to the actual wedding, such a dismissal or divorce was permitted. This was consistent with His insistence that conjugal union made the two people involved into one flesh: the betrothed husband ought not to marry the woman in such a case, since she was already one flesh with someone else. The marital agreement must be terminated. In Jewish terms, this was not a mere breaking off of the engagement (as with us today), but a true divorce (compare Joseph's intended divorce of Mary prior to their wedding in 1:19).

℘ EXCURSUS
On the Term "Gehenna"

The term "Gehenna" indicates the place of final punishment for the unrighteous who experience God's wrath. It is derived from the Hebrew *ge hinnom*, the valley of Hinnom, a valley west of Jerusalem. In the days of King Manasseh (ca. 680 BC) it was used for the abominable rites of child sacrifice (2 Chr. 28:3). The place was thought of as unclean and later used as a garbage dump. The fires for incinerating this garbage were perpetually burning, and so the site became an apt image for the eternal fires of punishment in the age to come (and so it was described in the Jewish apocalyptic literature around the time of Christ).

Christ's teaching is consistent with this Jewish usage. In His teaching, Gehenna is the place of eternal punishment, where the "worm does not die and the fire is not quenched" (Mark 9:48)—that is, where destruction and pain do not cease. It is the fate reserved for those who consciously reject God's light, the place of horror and agony to which they are banished after the final judgment, the outer darkness of those rejected by God, where there is only weeping and gnashing of teeth (8:12; 22:13). It was never prepared for men (for God made man for joy), but for the devil and his angels (25:41), and it is only when man turns from God and

---

becomes His enemy that he is denied by God and assigned a place with His foes (7:23; 25:11–12).

Christ's teaching on Gehenna is echoed by St. Paul (e.g. Rom. 2:8–9; 1 Cor. 3:17; 2 Thess. 2:8–10), by the author of the Epistle to the Hebrews (10:26–31), by St. James (5:1–6), by St. Peter (2 Peter 2:3–10), by St. Jude (Jude 13), and by St. John of the Apocalypse (Rev. 14:9–11; 20:10, 14–15). Modern squeamishness notwithstanding, it must be faced that this is an integral part of the Christian worldview.

ॐ ॐ ॐ ॐ ॐ

33 "Again, you have heard that it was said to the ancients, 'You shall not break oaths, but shall render your oaths to the Lord.'

34 "But I *Myself* say to you, do not swear at all, either by heaven, for it is the throne of God,

35 "or by the earth, for it is the footstool of His feet, or by Jerusalem, for it is the City of the great King.

36 "Nor shall you swear by your head, for you are not able to make one hair white or black.

37 "But let your word be, 'Yes, yes'; 'No, no'; and anything surpassing these is from the evil one.

The fourth example involves the taking of oaths. Jesus' hearers **have heard** from the Pharisees that **it was said to the ancients** by God, **"You shall not break oaths, but shall render your oaths to the Lord"** (Lev. 19:12; Num. 30:2; Deut. 23:21–23). The temptation in those days was to promise something under oath, and then afterwards to renege on the promise and thus break the oath. This was forbidden by the Law, which said that truthfulness must prevail. If one promised something, to God or to anyone else, one must do it.

There were a variety of oaths possible. One could swear by God

Himself, or by His Temple, or by the gold of the Temple (23:16). One could swear **by heaven**, or **by the earth**, or **by Jerusalem**, the holy city. One could swear by one's head, offering in effect to suffer decapitation if one failed in the oath. The rabbinic thought of that day held that certain of these oaths were more binding than others.

Again Christ cuts to the heart of the Law's intention. What God values here is truth-telling, and therefore one must live with such integrity that oaths are not necessary.

This prohibition applies to all kinds of oaths. Men might argue that the oath they swore was of a minor kind and was not sufficiently binding. Christ shows that all oaths are significant and binding, since they involve God Himself in the transaction. If one swears **by heaven**, then one swears by God, for heaven is **the throne of God**; if one swears by **the earth**, one also swears by God, for earth is **the footstool of His feet** (Is. 66:1). If one swears **by Jerusalem**, even then one swears by God, for it is His city, **the City of the great King**, as Scripture also says (Ps. 48:2). Even swearing **by** one's **head** involves God, for God rules that as well. He alone has the power to make the **hair** on it **white or black**. All oaths therefore involve God, and the breaking of any oath is sacrilege against Him.

In fact, the whole machinery of oath-taking implies that one's word itself is not binding, but only becomes binding when an oath is added. Therefore, disciples of Jesus should **not swear at all**, but should simply say, **Yes** and mean **yes** or **No** and mean **no**, and consider the words themselves sufficiently binding. **Anything surpassing these** and any further casuistry is **from the evil one**, for he is the father of lies (John 8:44), and he always pushes men away from truth-telling and integrity. The casuistry which says, "I said 'yes' but did not add an oath and therefore I am free from obligation," comes from the devil. Oath-taking is to form no part of the lives of His disciples.

꧁ ꧁ ꧁ ꧁ ꧁

38 "You have heard that it was said, 'An eye for an
eye, and a tooth for a tooth.'**

> 39 "But I Myself say to you, do not withstand the
> evil one; but whoever slaps you on your right
> cheek, turn to him the other also.
> 40 "And to him wanting to have you judged and to
> take your shirt, leave him your garment also,
> 41 "and whoever will conscript you one mile, go
> with him two.
> 42 "Give to him who asks of you, and do not turn
> away him who wants to borrow from you.

In His fifth example, Christ quotes the precept, **"An eye for an eye, and a tooth for a tooth"** (Ex. 21:24). In its original context, this law was intended to limit the amount of vengeance an aggrieved family could inflict on another family. The blood-feuds customary in those days tended to escalate, as one family would avenge one crime by exacting a penalty disproportionate to the crime avenged. Thus the loss of an eye might be avenged by killing the perpetrator. Against such a background, the Law insists that such escalation of violence must cease, and **an eye** could only be avenged by the loss of **an eye**, and **a tooth** with the loss of **a tooth**.

Now that the Kingdom of God is at hand, Christ pushes this limitation of retaliation even further, saying that His disciples must **not withstand the evil one** who insults them. One might think that consciousness of one's social dignity demanded one should indeed withstand and resist such acts, by pushing back when one is pushed and returning insult for insult. But Christ forbids His followers to be that concerned with their dignity. If one **slaps** them—even on the **right cheek** (that is, by backhanding them across the face, a greater insult than striking them with the open palm upon the left cheek, assuming the striker is right-handed)—they must still not retaliate in kind. Instead, they must **turn** to that one **the other** cheek **also**—that is, they must continue to remain vulnerable by not striking back.

If a quarrel with the neighbor turns to a civil suit, and the evil neighbor wants to have the disciple **judged** and condemned in court and thus to **take** his **shirt** from him, even then there must be no revenge or countersuit. Let the neighbor have your shirt—and **leave him** the outer **garment** or coat **also**. The gift of the outer coat will testify to the evil neighbor of the disciple's refusal to hate.

This applies not only to one's Jewish neighbor, but also to the occupying Gentile Roman army. Such military men could **conscript** the locals to help carry loads (compare Simon of Cyrene being so conscripted in 27:32), compelling them to carry a burden up to **one mile**. Christ says that His disciple must not withstand even these hated foreigners, but must offer to **go with him two** miles.

A neighbor might ask the disciple to give him money in time of need, or might ask to **borrow** his goods. Christ tells His disciples to have open and generous hearts to all, and therefore to **give to him who asks** and **not turn away** the one making his request.

These counsels are parabolic utterances, aimed at the heart that is tempted to be hard. They are not laws which can be codified and applied indiscriminately. The Church is still called to exercise discernment to weed out the conman. The *Didache*, for example (a first-century church manual), tells the local church to "beware" of sponging "false prophets" who "ask for money," and to give only to those who are not "trafficking upon Christ" (chapters 11, 12). Christ is here not counseling a soft head, but a soft heart. The presence of evil men might tempt the disciple to let his love grow cold (compare 24:12), but he is to maintain a generous attitude nonetheless.

Also, it must be recognized that Christ's examples here have to do with personal insults and quarrels, not with criminal acts. The slap in the face mentioned in verse 39 is intended as an affront, not a felonious assault. These counsels contain no prohibition against calling the police after being assaulted, only against harboring hatred in the heart as a result of it.

ॐ ॐ ॐ ॐ ॐ

43 "You have heard that it was said, 'You shall love your neighbor, and you shall hate your enemy.'

44 "But I *Myself* say to you, love your enemies, and pray for those who persecute you,

45 "that you may become sons of your Father in the heavens; for He makes His sun to rise upon the evil and the good, and rains upon the righteous and the unrighteous.

46 "For if you love those who love you, what reward have you? Do not even the tax-collectors do the same?

47 "And if you greet your brothers only, what surpassing *thing* do you do? Do not even the Gentiles do the same?

48 "Therefore you *yourselves* are to be perfect, as your heavenly Father is perfect.

The final example is drawn from the commandments that would have the Jew love his neighbor and hate only his foreign enemy. That is, hatred and harsh dealing were reserved for those not part of the holy community. (Hatred, here as elsewhere in the New Testament, means the act of rejection, not the emotion of anger. To hate someone is to reject him.)

Thus Jews may not charge interest to fellow-Jews, but may charge interest to Gentiles (Deut. 23:19–20). Thus Jews may enter into the assembly of the Lord, but not foreigners such as the Ammonite or the Moabite (Deut. 23:3). These were rejected from enjoying the same benefits as Jews. The precept **you shall love your neighbor** is a quote from Leviticus 19:18; the precept **you shall hate your enemy** is the articulation of its unspoken corollary. In its original context, this was meant to forbid hatred of one's Jewish neighbor. All fellow Jews were to be treated compassionately—even slaves, even the poor, for all were redeemed by God.

Christ takes this commandment and extends it even to enemies. Now that the universal Kingdom is being revealed, love must have no limits, no boundaries. His disciples must **love** their **enemies** and **pray for those who persecute** them. Only by so doing can they **become sons of** their **Father in the heavens**. For God extends His love to all, even to His enemies, who hate Him and refuse to walk in His Law. **He makes His sun to rise upon the evil** as well as **the good**, giving warmth and light to them both alike. **He rains upon the righteous** who keep His Law and upon **the unrighteous** who flout it, sending showers of blessing upon all. Christ's disciples must show the same family resemblance to their heavenly Father if they hope to be acknowledged by Him in the coming age as His sons and heirs.

Thus they too must make no discrimination between those neighbors and friends who do them good, and the pagans and enemies who abuse them. The righteous Jew and the Roman centurion alike must be objects of their love. Both the kind and faithful friend as well as the ungrateful user are to be embraced. For if they **love** and help only **those who love** them, **what reward** could they expect to **have? Even the tax-collectors** (notorious for their impiety) **do** that—and no one expected a tax-collector to receive any reward from God. (As always, "love" here indicates an action of help for those in need, not a warm fuzzy feeling.) If they **greet** and bless their **brothers only, what surpassing** great deed is that? Should they expect a great reward for it? Even the godless **Gentiles** greet their friends! (This greeting is no quick formality, as with us, but involves a long exchange of blessings as between friends; compare Ruth 2:4; Ps. 128:8; Luke 10:4). Jesus' followers must extend love and brotherly care to all, even to those who have hurt them.

In short, they must **be perfect**, in the same way as their **heavenly Father is perfect**. The word translated *perfect* is the Greek *teleios*. It means not so much "sinless" as it does "whole, having integrity, blameless." It corresponds to the Hebrew *tamim* (sometimes translated "blameless"). Noah is said to be *tamim* (Gen. 6:9), and the children of Israel are told to "be *tamim* before the Lord their God" (Deut. 18:13)—this last verse being translated "be *teleios*" by the Greek Septuagint. The thought here therefore is of Christ's disciples being blameless before God, manifesting the same love to men as God does, lacking nothing in mercy. St. Luke's version of this command is for the disciples to "be compassionate just as your Father is compassionate" (Luke 6:36).

§III.3. Piety: Alms, Prayer, Fasting

ॐ ॐ ॐ ॐ ॐ

6 1   "Beware of doing your righteousness before men to be beheld by them; otherwise you have no reward with your Father in the heavens.

Next Christ counsels His disciples about their piety. All pious people in Israel gave alms, said their daily prayers, and fasted (generally twice a week). Christ's followers will do the same, but they must **beware of doing** such acts of **righteousness before men** in order **to be beheld by them**. If they flout their piety publicly to win the applause of the world, they will have that applause. But that is all they will have. **Men** on earth might be impressed, but not their **Father in the heavens**. He sees into the inner heart and judges the secret motivation. If their works of piety are done mostly for men, He will know that and will render accordingly—their works of piety will **have no reward** from Him. One can expect a reward from God in return for almsgiving, prayer, and fasting.

ॐ ॐ ॐ ॐ ॐ

2   "Whenever therefore you do alms, do not *sound* a trumpet before you, as the hypocrites do in the synagogues and in the lanes, so that they may be glorified by men. Amen I say to you, they are receiving in full their reward.

3   "But when you *yourself* do alms, do not let your left *hand* know what your right *hand* is doing,

4   "so that your alms are in secret; and your Father who sees in secret will render you *your reward*.

Christ then gives three examples of such works of righteousness. As with the Sermon on the Mount generally, the practices of the

Pharisees form the background to these counsels, offering a negative example which Christ's followers must avoid.

Whenever therefore His followers **do alms,** they must **not** *sound* **a trumpet** before them **as the** Pharisaical **hypocrites do** when giving alms **in the synagogues and in the lanes.** When they gave alms, either inside the synagogue or out in the open streets, they would *sound* **a trumpet before** them, that their almsgiving might be observed by all and they **be glorified by men** as paragons of piety. In saying that the Pharisees "sounded a trumpet before them" before they gave alms, Jesus is almost certainly speaking ironically. That is, the Pharisees made such a loud verbal announcement of the alms they were about to give that it was as if they were blowing a trumpet. The Lord means to show how ridiculous are such ostentatious displays.

It is all self-serving, and He assures His disciples that when the Pharisees give alms to the applause of men, they are **receiving in full their reward**—the reward of public acclaim is the only reward they will get. Their almsgiving, which would normally receive a great reward from God (see Sir. 3:30; 29:12), will avail them nothing.

Note the present tense of the verb **are receiving** in verse 4, repeated in verses 5 and 16. This indicates that at the moment of receiving honors from men the Pharisees are also receiving all that they will get. God sees their inner hypocrisy and how little they care for Him, and He will give them nothing more.

Against the background of such display, the disciples are told to give their alms unobtrusively, as if their **left** *hand* did **not know** that their **right** *hand* was giving alms. They must care so little for public recognition that their almsgiving is almost a secret act, known only to the recipient. When their alms are given thus **in secret,** their heavenly **Father who sees in secret** will **render** them their reward.

The word rendered *secret* is the Greek *krupto*, a word usually rendered "hidden" (compare its use in 13:44; Col. 3:3). The image here is of God observing the disciples' deeds from His hiding place where He remains, unseen by men. Men may not see God, but He sees them, and their hidden acts of piety are observed by Him—and rewarded.

ॐ ॐ ॐ ॐ ॐ

5 "And whenever you pray, you are not to be as the hypocrites, for they love to stand and pray in the synagogues and in the corners of the streets, so that they may appear to men. Amen I say to you, they are receiving in full their reward.

6 "But whenever you *yourself* pray, enter into your storeroom, and having shut your door, pray to your Father who is in secret, and your Father who sees in secret will render you *your reward.*

In this second example of righteous acts, Christ speaks of how His disciples should offer their personal prayers. (Public worship, such as at synagogue or Temple, is not here in view.) **Whenever they pray, they are not to be as the hypocrites.** The Pharisees **love to stand** (Gr. *estotes*, the perfect tense, indicating that they self-consciously take their stand) **in the synagogues and in the corners of the streets** (a very public place!), **so that they may appear to men** in all their holy glory. Prayer in those days was always done aloud, with upraised hands and eyes, and everyone around the Pharisees would know about their prayers. As with their almsgiving, Christ assures His disciples that those Pharisees **are receiving in full their reward.** The honor they receive from men at that time is all they will get.

It must be otherwise with Jesus' followers. When *they* say their personal prayers (the pronoun **you** is emphatic), they must **enter into** the **storeroom** of their house—the inner room, often used for storage, where no one else was likely to be found. **Having shut** the **door** to prevent interruption and to make sure they cannot be heard, there they are to **pray to** their **Father who is in secret,** and He will **render** them their reward.

The image of entering into the inner storeroom is somewhat hyperbolic; Christ is not hereby forbidding His followers to say their prayers, for example, in an open field or in the forest. The image of shutting the door to the storeroom and praying in there is an image of determination to make one's prayers private and unobtrusive. Far from being done to garner public acclaim, Christian devotions must be offered hidden from the public eye.

ॐ   ॐ   ॐ   ॐ   ॐ

7 "And when you pray, do not babble, as the Gentiles, for they think that they will be heard for their wordiness.

8 "Therefore do not be like them; for your Father knows what you have need of before you ask Him.

Christ not only counsels His disciples about the motivation for their prayers, but also about the content of them. The temptation was to think that they would **be heard for their wordiness** (Gr. *polulogia*, literally "many words"). Indeed, it was said in Israel that "whoever is long in prayer is heard." Christ condemns this idea as fit only for **the Gentiles**. Their prayers were mere **babbling** (Gr. *battalogeo*, an onomatopoeic word imitating a person's stammering), for as pagans they did not know the true God.

Jesus is not here condemning repetition in prayers (Ps. 136, for example, has much repetition, with the phrase "for His love is eternal" repeated 26 times). Rather He condemns the idea that the length and eloquence of the prayer by themselves will impress God and secure a reward. This unworthy conception of God might be expected to be found among the Gentiles, but His disciples should know better. The true God does not need to be cajoled by eloquence, nor can His mind be changed by the length of a prayer. In fact, He **knows** what His children **have need of before** they even **ask Him**. The Father does not need us to inform Him about the state of His world, nor to tell Him what we need. Prayer is the communion of the heart with God. It is not to change *God*, but rather *us*. Prayer allows us to commune with God and to align our lives with His will.

ॐ ॐ ॐ ॐ ॐ

9 "You, therefore, pray thus: 'Our Father in the heavens, let Your Name be sanctified.

10 "Let Your Kingdom come. Let Your will be done, as in heaven, *so* also upon earth.

11 "Give us today our bread for the following *day*,

12 "And forgive us our debts, as we *ourselves* also have forgiven our debtors.

13 "And do not lead us into testing, but rescue us from the evil one.'*

Christ therefore gives His disciples a model prayer. (The giving of this prayer came in response to the disciples' request that Jesus teach them to pray—see Luke 11:1–4; it is included here by St. Matthew as part of his collection of material about prayer.) Jesus therefore tells His disciples (the **you** is emphatic in the Greek) to **pray thus**.

In the opening invocation, God is addressed as **Our Father in the heavens**. Though God is transcendent, **in the heavens**, far above earthly limitations, He is still the **Father** of Jesus' disciples. Almost certainly the Aramaic original of this was *Abba*, a close and familiar term for one's father, like our "papa." Thus Jesus shares His sonship with His disciples—He calls God His *Abba* (being the eternal Son by nature), and His disciples are to call God their *Abba* also (being His sons by adoption and grace).

The first petition is not for human need, but is concerned with God's honor. Of first importance to Jesus is that God's **Name be sanctified** in the earth. God's Name is not simply His verbal label, but His manifested power. In Psalm 54:1 and 20:1, God's "Name"

---

* The doxology "For Yours is the Kingdom, and the power and glory, to the ages. Amen," is not in the best manuscripts. It does not form a part of the original prayer, probably because Christ assumes that His disciples will conclude the prayer with a doxology of this kind without being told. A Jewish prayer would not likely end with the words, "the evil one," but with an ascription of praise to God (compare 1 Chr. 29:11).

is the open manifestation of His strength ("Save me, O God, by Your Name . . . May the Name of the God of Jacob protect you . . ."), and for God's Name to be sanctified is for men to acknowledge God as holy when they behold His power. Presently the world does not honor God, and Christ would have us pray that men would do so.

The second petition is for God's **Kingdom** to **come**. The Kingdom will come finally and fully at the Second Coming, when the kingdom of the world becomes the Kingdom of the Lord God and of His Christ (Rev. 11:15); it is to this consummation that we are to look. It is true that the Kingdom also is present now through the Church, existing sacramentally on earth throughout this age (see Luke 17:21). This petition, however, looks to the fullness of the Kingdom, when the earth will be full of the knowledge of the Lord as the waters cover the sea (Is. 11:9).

This petition finds expansion in the words that follow, **"Let Your will be done, as in heaven,** *so* **also upon earth."** It refers to the same eschatological reality as the prayer for the Kingdom to come, and is therefore omitted by Luke in his rendering of the Lord's Prayer in Luke 11:2–4. God's will is now done perfectly by the angels in heaven; we are bidden to pray for the Kingdom to come and overturn the established order here that it may be done perfectly on earth also. As a prayer in the Didache (ca. AD 100) says, "Let grace come, and let this world pass away!" These words therefore are not so much an expression of submission to God's will (though they may be used that way; 26:39), as a cry of rebellion against the world-forces of this age.

The third petition asks that God **give us today our bread for the following** *day*. By "bread" is meant all our daily needs (though in an affluent society we are tempted to think we need more than we actually do). As St. Paul teaches, "If we have nourishment and shelter, with these we will be satisfied" (1 Tim. 6:8). The phrase translated "for the following day" is the Greek word *epiousios*, which is notoriously difficult to translate. Some (such as Origen in the third century) have suggested that it means "necessary for existence"—i.e. the bread we need. Some suggest that it is related to the word *epiousa* as found in Acts 16:11, where it is translated "the following day," and that is the meaning adopted here. Christ therefore tells us to pray each day for the needs of the morrow, taking our life one day at a time.

The fourth petition is for God to **forgive us our** spiritual **debts, as we *ourselves* also have forgiven our debtors**. The thought here is of sin being a debt owed to God. Every day we sin against God, and every day need to ask His forgiveness (which presupposes a daily examination of conscience). But divine forgiveness is only offered on the basis of our extending that same undeserved forgiveness to those who have sinned against us.

The final petition is that God may **not lead us into testing, but rescue us from the evil one**. (Once again, the words **rescue us from the evil one** seem to be an expansion of the thought of not being led into testing, since the prayer for rescue is omitted in Luke's version of this same prayer.) The word translated *testing* is the Greek *peirasmos*, sometimes translated "trial" or "temptation." This is not a petition to be spared the experience of being tempted to sin, for this is scarcely possible in this age. Rather, by **testing** Christ here means the experience of succumbing to the attacks of the evil one. It was this testing that Christ told His disciples in the Garden of Gethsemane they should pray to avoid (26:41), for the evil one was going to attack them with special ferocity (Luke 22:31). This petition is a prayer that we may emerge victorious from any assault and hold firm to our faith.

❧ EXCURSUS
ON THE TERM "THE HEAVENS"

The Gospel of Matthew, being the most Jewish of the four Gospels, preserves certain Hebraicisms in its language, one of which is the Jewish plural term "the heavens." Thus Matthew preserves the Lord's original term "the Kingdom of the heavens" (see for example 4:17). We see this usage reflected also in the opening petition of the Lord's Prayer, where the prayer begins, "Our Father in the heavens." The word "heaven," however, is not always used in the plural in Matthew's Gospel, for later on in the same Lord's Prayer, the prayer speaks of God's will being done "as in heaven [singular], so also upon earth." What are we to make of these usages?

Some have suggested that the concept of there being seven heavens underlies this usage, and that St. Paul himself made use of this concept when he spoke of being "caught up to the third heaven" in 2 Corinthians 12:2. This is most unlikely. Nowhere in the New Testament do any of its writers speak of seven heavens, though the concept is found in Zoroastrianism and in some rabbinical teaching. (The concept appears to be rooted in the idea that the earth is the center of the universe and is surrounded by seven ascending planets.) St. Paul certainly does not endorse the idea in 2 Corinthians 12:2; when he speaks of being caught up to the third heaven, he does not mean that he got less than halfway to the top. Rather, he clearly means that he ascended to the uttermost heights, to the dwelling of God Himself. For St. Paul, the third heaven was the ultimate height.

Rather, I suggest that Matthew's plural term "heavens" is rooted in the Hebrew word for "heavens," *shamayim*, which is dual in form. Why dual? When the ancient Jew looked up, he not only saw the sky immediately above him, but he saw the clouds, "the waters that are above the heavens" (Ps. 148:4), and he saw that there was still more sky beyond those clouds. I suggest that it was this observation of sky both above and below the clouds that accounted for the dual form of the word "heaven" or "sky," Hebrew *shamayim*. This dual form in the Hebrew is literally rendered in the Greek of Matthew's Gospel as a plural—as we look up, we see God and His Kingdom ruling from the most exalted of heights, in the highest of the heavens.

Thus, the opening address of the Lord's Prayer

(v. 9) speaks of God "in the heavens" because it reflects His transcendence above us all. But heaven is spoken of in the singular later in the prayer, in verse 10 ("may Your will be done on earth as it is *in heaven*"), because heaven there represents the abode of God, His home, His dwelling-place. That is, in verse 10 heaven is viewed *from God's perspective*, not ours; it is His place, and so is spoken of in the singular. In verse 9, we look up to see God above all the heavens; in verse 10, we speak of heaven as God's house, where His will is perfectly done. This change of perspective, I suggest, is the reason for the change of nouns from plural to singular.

ॐ ॐ ॐ ॐ ॐ

14 "For if you forgive men for their offenses, your heavenly Father will also forgive you.

15 "But if you do not forgive men, neither will your Father forgive your offenses.

Matthew adds to his collection of Christ's teaching on prayer His warning about the necessity of forgiveness (though this was probably originally spoken on another occasion; compare Mark 11:20–25). Whenever the disciples were praying, they must **forgive men for their offenses** against them, for only so will their **heavenly Father also forgive** the offenses of the disciples and grant their prayers. Indeed, **if** they **do not forgive men, neither will** their Father **forgive**. Being a disciple of Christ presupposes that one is committed to living in peace with all men, and the forgiveness of sin Christ offers to His followers presupposes that they are living as His true disciples.

ॐ ॐ ॐ ॐ ॐ

16 "And whenever you fast, do not become as the gloomy hypocrites, for they make their faces

> disappear that they may appear to men *to be* fasting. Amen I say to you, they are receiving in full their reward.
>
> 17 "But when you *yourself* fast, anoint your head, and wash your face,
>
> 18 "so that you may not appear to men *to be* fasting, but to our Father who is in secret, and your Father who sees in secret will render you *your reward*.

In His final example of righteous practices, Christ focuses on the practice of fasting. The Pharisees fasted twice a week (on Mondays and Thursdays; compare Luke 18:12 and the *Didache,* chapter 8), even though the Law mandated fasting only on the Day of Atonement. Such twice-weekly fasting forms the background to the Lord's counsels to His disciples. Christ does not reprove the *frequency* of fasting (in fact, the *Didache* counsels fasting twice a week too, though on different days), but rather the *manner* of it.

Whenever the disciples of Jesus **fast**, they must **not become as the gloomy hypocrites**, the Pharisees. As well as leaving their hair unkempt and wearing a gloomy expression, it was the practice of the Pharisees to smear ashes on their faces as a sign of mourning (compare 2 Sam. 13:19; Est. 4:1 for the practice), and thus to **make their faces disappear** behind the layer of ashes. There is an ironic play on words here—the Pharisees **make their faces disappear** (Gr. *aphanizo*) in order to **appear** (Gr. *phaino*) before **men** in all their afflicted splendor. The irony is intended to show them up as the ridiculous posers they are.

The disciples must not imitate the methods of the Pharisees, but, as with all their other pious practices, do their fasting as secretly as they can. Thus the disciple must **anoint** his **head** with the oil used on festive days (and specifically avoided when fasting and mourning; compare Dan. 10:2), and must **wash** his **face** with special care, to remove any sign that might suggest the ashes of fasting. When his fasting is apparent only to the **Father who sees in secret**, then He will **render** the reward, for such fasting is truly only for Him.

A note may be added here about the nature of this counsel. The twice-weekly fasts of the Pharisees were voluntary and individual fasts, and Christ here counsels His disciples about such individual and voluntary acts of piety. The corporate and Church-mandated fasting of Great Lent (and the other Church fasts) falls somewhat outside this counsel, in that everyone in the Church knows that the others are fasting. The principle of not flaunting one's fasting piety remains, however, in that the Christian should take care not to flaunt his fasting before the world of outsiders.

§III.4. Trust in God, Not Wealth

> ৯৭ ৯৭ ৯৭ ৯৭ ৯৭
>
> 19 "Do not treasure up for yourselves treasures upon the earth, where moth and rust make them disappear, and where thieves break in and thieve.
>
> 20 "But treasure up for yourselves treasures in heaven, where neither moth nor rust make disappear, and where thieves do not break in or thieve;
>
> 21 "for where your treasure is, there will your heart be also.

St. Matthew then collects a series of Christ's teachings about trusting in God and not in one's wealth. First of all, Christ commands His followers to **not treasure up** for themselves **treasures upon the earth**. Earth is a most insecure hiding place for treasures, for it is the place **where moth and rust** can **make** their rich garments **disappear** in corrosion, and even **where thieves** can **break in** (by digging through the mud-brick walls usual in Palestinian homes) **and thieve** to their hearts' content.

Rather, His followers ought to **treasure up** for themselves **treasures in heaven**, where their riches will be immune to such dangers. It is human nature to worry about whether or not one's treasures are safe—if those treasures are one's heavenly rewards, then one's heart will dwell in heaven, high above all earthly anxiety, **for where** their **treasure is, there will** their **heart be also.**

ॐ ॐ ॐ ॐ ॐ

22 "The lamp of the body is the eye; if therefore your eye is simple, your whole body will be *full of* light.

23 "But if your eye is evil, your whole body will be *full of* darkness. If therefore the light in you is darkness, how great *is* the darkness!

In speaking about one's **eye** (or attitude), Christ is making a play on words. The word for the healthy eye rendered *simple* is *aplous*, which can mean not only "sound, healthy" but also "sincere, single-hearted," with connotations of generosity. And the phrase "an **evil eye**" can mean not only evil in the sense of "unhealthy, diseased," but also "grudging, envious, greedy" (compare Sir. 14:9; Tobit 4:7). Just as the diseased eye results in blindness for the body, so a stingy attitude results in spiritual blindness for the whole life. Spiritual health is characterized by generosity.

ॐ ॐ ॐ ॐ ॐ

24 "No one is able to serve *as slave to* two lords; for either he will hate the one and love the other; or he will give attention to one and despise the other. You are not able to serve *as slave to* God and mammon.

Money is addictive and makes demands imperious as those of any master or lord. Like a master, its demands are total. **Mammon** (an Aramaic word for wealth) will demand that one devote all one's energies to getting it, preserving it, and multiplying it. God, our true Lord, also makes total demands on our hearts, and we must choose which of the two we will serve. Just as **no one is able to serve *as slave*** (Gr. *douleuo*; cognate with *doulos*, "slave") **to two lords**, so it is with us.

A slave cannot belong totally to two different masters. **Either he will hate the one and love the other** (that is, choose one as his master and reject the other), or at the very least **give attention** to one's orders and **despise the other** by ignoring his orders. But a choice has to be made, both for the slave and for us, for we are **not able to serve** *as slave to* **God and mammon** simultaneously. Choosing not to serve mammon means that we will give it away in the service of God, thus treasuring up wealth in heaven instead of on the earth.

ॐ ॐ ॐ ॐ ॐ

25 "Therefore I say to you, do not worry *about* your life, what you will eat, or what you will drink, nor *about* your body, with what you will clothe yourselves. Is not life more than food, and the body than clothing?

26 "Look at the birds of heaven—they do not sow, neither do they harvest, nor gather into barns, and your heavenly Father feeds them! Are you *yourselves* much more valuable than they?

27 "And which of you by worrying is able to add a cubit to his *allotted* age?

28 "And why worry about clothing? Learn well from how the lilies of the field grow—they neither toil nor spin,

29 "but I say to you that Solomon in all his glory did not clothe himself like one of these!

30 "But if God thus clothes the grass of the field, which is today and tomorrow is cast into an oven, *will He* not much more *clothe* you, O you of little faith?

31 "Do not be worried, therefore, saying, 'What will we eat?' or 'What will we drink?' or 'With what will we clothe ourselves?'

32 "For all these things the Gentiles seek after; for

> your heavenly Father knows that you need all
> these things.
> 33 "But seek first His Kingdom and His righ-
> teousness; and all these things will be added
> to you.
> 34 "Therefore do not worry about tomorrow, for
> tomorrow will worry about itself. Sufficient for
> the day is the trouble of it.

Such refusal to store up money on earth does not mean that the disciples will be left to starve in this age. God will care for them. Trusting in this care, they are **not** to **worry** *about* their **life. Life** is about doing the will of God, and that is what they must be concerned with. Let them leave these lesser things to God. He can be trusted to look after them.

Let the disciples **look at the birds of heaven—they do not sow, neither do they harvest, nor gather into barns.** They are entirely unconcerned with how they will eat, in that they do not take these elaborate preparations to ensure they will be fed, and yet the **heavenly Father feeds them** all the same! The birds simply look every day for their daily food, and receive it from God. Are not the disciples of Christ **much more valuable** than the birds?

It is plain, therefore, that there is no need to worry about the future. For **which** of them **by worrying** can **add** even **a cubit to his** *allotted* **age?** God made everyone's days to consist of a certain number of such handbreadths (Ps. 39:5)—if worry cannot increase the number by even a single measure, it is useless indeed.

And **why worry about** having enough **clothing** to stay warm? Let them **learn well from how the lilies of the field grow—they neither toil** to gather wool **nor spin** it into fabric for clothing. But they are clothed by God in their own garments of beauty nonetheless—so much so that **Solomon in all his glory did not clothe himself like one of these.** (The reference is probably to the scarlet poppies and purple anemones, whose color suggests the royal robes of fabled Solomon.) **If God thus** lavishly **clothes** even **the grass of the field,** so transient that it **is today and tomorrow is cast into** a baking **oven** as fuel, how much more will He take care to warmly clothe the disciples? Do they think that God would lavish such care on the grass, and yet neglect the disciples of Christ? Of what **little faith** they are!

In fact their fretting about tomorrow, with their constant woeful cries of **"What will we eat?"** and **"What will we drink?"** and **"With what will we clothe ourselves?"** is unworthy of them. All these earthly concerns **the** pagan **Gentiles seek after** (Gr. *epizeteo*, not just "to seek," but to "seek after, to earnestly seek" with obsessive attention). Do they, as good Jews, want to be like the Gentiles? Their **heavenly Father knows** of their needs, and they can leave such lesser concerns with Him.

For their part, they must **seek first**, before anything else, God's **Kingdom and His righteousness**, making their abiding focus doing what He commands, and then **all these** lesser and earthly **things will be added** to them as well.

Christ ends His teaching about wealth with a typically Jewish piece of humor—a command to **not worry about tomorrow, for tomorrow will worry about itself**. The image is of the disciples thinking that tomorrow will not arrive without their worry and their anxious help. They can relax—tomorrow knows how to fend for itself! Let them not dwell and spend sleepless nights about the coming day, but trust in God to care for them, even without their wealth. Let them leave tomorrow alone—it is not as if each **day** itself did not have **sufficient trouble** in it, but needed to borrow trouble from the coming day!

§III.5. Mercy for One's Neighbor

ॐ ॐ ॐ ॐ ॐ

7 1   "Do not judge lest you be judged.
    2   "For with what judgment you judge, you will be judged; and with what measure you measure, it will be measured to you.
    3   "And why do you look at the chip that is in

> your brother's eye, but do not consider the log
> that is in your eye?
> 4 "Or how will you say to your brother, 'Let me
>   cast out the chip from your eye,' and behold!
>   the log *is* in your own eye?
> 5 "Hypocrite! First cast out the log from your
>   eye, and then you will see *clearly* to cast out
>   the chip from your brother's eye.
> 6 "Do not give holy *things* to dogs, and do not
>   cast your pearls before pigs, lest they trample on
>   them with their feet, and turn *and* tear you.

In this next section of the Sermon, Matthew presents Christ's teaching about mercy and forgiveness. The person in view is someone who has been insulted and wronged. When the disciple of Jesus is wronged, he must **not judge** his enemy or refuse to forgive him. Instead, he must extend mercy to his enemy, knowing that only thus will God have mercy on himself. For **with** the **judgment that** he **judges**, he **will be judged** by God on the last day, and with the **measure** he **measures** to others, it **will be measured** by God to him. If the disciple uses the measure of mercy in dealing with those who hurt him, he can expect that same measure of mercy from God.

Jesus then offers another parable: that of two men, one with a small chip of wood in his eye and the other with an entire log in his eye, sticking out of his head for all the world to see. It is meant to be a cartoonish image and not an actual life situation. The Pharisees (the unnamed rival **hypocrite** in this passage) can **look at the chip in** their **brother's eye**, but they fail to **consider the log that is in** their **own eye**. They are quick to say to their neighbor, **"Brother, let me cast out the chip from your eye!"** when **behold!** there is **a log** in their **own eye**! The absurdity of the image is meant to reveal the depth of the Pharisees' folly.

The followers of Jesus must take another path. They must avoid the ways of judgmentalism and refusal to forgive, and instead focus upon the task of **first casting out** whatever **log** might be in their own **eye**.

They may be tempted to argue with the Pharisees about this (or other matters). Let them give it up and leave the Pharisees alone (see 15:14). It is not fitting to **give** the **holy *things*** sacrificed to God (Ex. 29:33) **to dogs** for them to eat, for holy sacrificial food is only for those fit to receive it. And it is not fit to **cast** their precious **pearls before pigs**. The pigs cannot appreciate the beauty of pearls, but will **trample on them with their feet**, and then **turn *and* tear** the well-meaning pearl-donor to pieces.

It is the same with giving Christ's holy teaching to the Pharisees and trying to argue with them. Like the dogs and the pigs, they will not profit from the teachings, and will only use the proffered gift as an opportunity to attack the disciples. (The Church would later apply this same principle in its contacts with unbelievers, and refuse to give sacramental gifts to those not yet initiated.)

One final note may be added. It is important to see that in forbidding the disciple to judge, Christ is not calling for the suspension of the moral faculty. Christ is not saying that the disciple may not pronounce another's actions to be morally wrong—for how can one pardon a man if one does not recognize that there is something to pardon? Rather, Christ is forbidding His disciple to "write off" his foe and to refuse forgiveness. The disciple is here bidden always to extend mercy.

§III.6. God's Generosity—and Ours

7   "Ask, and it will be given to you; seek, and you will find; knock, and it will be opened to you.

8   "For everyone who asks, receives, and he who seeks finds, and to him who knocks it will be opened.

9   "Or what man is there among you, if his son will ask him for bread, will give him a stone?

10 "Or even *if* he will ask for a fish, will he give him a serpent?

11 "If you *yourselves* therefore, being evil, know how to give good gifts to your children, how much more will your Father from heaven give good *things* to those who ask Him!

12 "Therefore, all that you want men to do for you, thus you *yourselves* also do for them, for this is the Law and the Prophets.

St. Matthew next includes Christ's teaching on God's generous responses to our prayers. (This teaching originally seems to have been given in response to the disciples' request that Jesus teach them to pray; see Luke 11:1–12). Christ encourages them to boldly **ask** God for whatever they need, to **seek** from Him what they require, to **knock** on the door of heaven with their petitions. If they do so, they will find their Father will hearken to them. (The verbs *ask, seek,* and *knock* are all in the present tense, perhaps indicating that one must ask and keep on asking, even if the answer is not immediate.) For not just those then listening, but **everyone** of His disciples **who asks**, **receives**, and **he who seeks finds**, and to everyone **who knocks it will be opened**. This is not a hit-or-miss thing, but the privilege given to all the disciples of Jesus now that the Kingdom is at hand.

Do they find it incredible that God would respond with such generosity? Then let them look at human generosity and compare. **What man is there among** them, **if his son will ask him** for a loaf of **bread, will give him a stone?** A round loaf of bread common in those days might resemble a stone somewhat, but no father would ever respond by giving a stone for bread. **Or even** if the boy **will ask for a fish** (a larger gift), would the father respond by **giving him a serpent?** Obviously not! Even though the fathers might be sinners, **evil** and selfish as all men are, they still **know how to give good gifts** to their **children**. Would the **Father from** His throne in **heaven** do any less? Would He not rather **give** the **good** *things* of the Kingdom to those who ask Him?

As children of such a generous heavenly Father, the disciples of Jesus must be generous themselves. **All that** they **want men to do**

for them, **thus**, in the same way, they must **also do for** others. Do they want to be treated kindly? Then let them treat men kindly. Do they want to be forgiven when they hurt their neighbor? Then let them forgive too. Such reciprocity is the embodiment of all **the Law and the Prophets**, the heart and summary of all the Scriptures required of God's people.

§III.7. Warning against False Teaching

৵ঌ ৵ঌ ৵ঌ ৵ঌ ৵ঌ

13 "Enter through the narrow gate, for the gate *is* wide, and the way spacious leading to destruction, and many are those entering through it.

14 "How narrow *is* the gate, and constricted the way leading to life, and few are those finding it!

15 "Beware of the false prophets, who come to you in sheep's clothing, but within are ravenous wolves.

16 "By their fruits you will recognize them. Are grapes picked from thorns, or figs from thistles?

17 "Thus every good tree makes fine fruits, but the decayed tree makes evil fruits.

18 "A good tree is not able to make evil fruits, nor *is* a decayed tree *able* to make fine fruits.

19 "Every tree not making fine fruit is cut down and cast into fire.

20 "So then, by their fruits you will recognize them.

21 "Not everyone saying to Me, 'Lord, Lord,' will enter into the Kingdom of the heavens, but the one doing the will of My Father in the heavens.

22 "Many will say to Me on that day, 'Lord, Lord, did we not prophesy in Your Name, and in Your

Name cast out demons, and in Your Name do
many works of power?'
23 "And then I will confess to them, 'I never knew
you; leave Me, those working lawlessness!'

Christ then urges His followers to **enter through the narrow gate**, even though it is **narrow** and **constricted** and thus difficult to squeeze through. Through it alone is **the way leading to life**. They must avoid the temptation to enter through the **wide** gate, even though the way through it is **spacious**, for it is the way **leading to destruction**. Matthew includes this saying here, though it was uttered on the way to Jerusalem in response to someone's question, "Lord, are there just a few who are being saved?" (Luke 13:22–24). What does this question mean, and why is its answer included here?

The question was not asked out of theological curiosity, but out of perplexity at the stiff opposition Jesus was receiving. If Jesus was truly the Messiah, shouldn't all Israel be gathering to Him? There was a proverb which said, "All Israel has a share in the age to come"—and yet all Israel was not accepting Him. What did this mean? Were there just a few who were being saved? Could one reject Jesus (as the Pharisees were doing) and still be saved?

Christ answers by telling all who would be saved to **enter through the narrow gate** of discipleship to Him. Opposition from the Pharisees may make it **narrow** and **constricted** and so fraught with difficulties that **few are those finding it**, but it **leads to life**. Those who reject Him, choosing popularity over truth and wealth over poverty, may find it easier in this age. Indeed, that **way** is **spacious** and easy to travel, and the **gate** is **wide** and easy to enter, and for this reason **many are those entering through it**. Yet, for all that, it **leads to destruction**.

Matthew includes this question and response here because it forms a fitting introduction to Jesus' warning against the false prophets, the Pharisaical teachers, which follows it. Let those who would be saved enter by the narrow gate, and pay no attention to the words of the Pharisees! They lead men astray, as did the **false**

prophets of old. (From comparing the parallel in Luke 6:39–44, which is concerned with the Pharisees, the "hypocrite" of Luke 6:42, we see that the Pharisees are the subject of this passage in Matt. 7:15–20 also, and that the "false prophets" of 7:15 refers to them.) The Pharisees' teaching might sound pious enough, but it leads to spiritual death in the end. Inwardly their teaching makes them as dangerous as **ravenous wolves**, even though they **come to you in sheep's clothing**, using their piety to mask their true nature.

How can one discern the true guide from the false? It is **by their fruits** that one can **recognize them** (Gr. *epiginosko*, a more intensive form of *ginosko*, "know"). What fruit can one see in the lives of the Pharisees? Does their way of life bring joy to them—or to others? No, in fact their legalism makes for burdens too heavy to lift (23:4; Acts 15:10).

Anyone can know that the Pharisees are not true guides, for they know that **grapes** are not **picked from thorns, or figs from thistles**. Grapes are gathered from grapevines, not from thorn bushes. From thorn bushes one can expect only thorns. **Every good tree makes fine fruits** even as **the decayed tree** (eaten by disease and insects) **makes** only **evil fruits**. The evil fruit of frustration and joylessness proclaims the Pharisee a decayed tree—one that is destined to be **cut down** by the judgment of God and **cast into fire**.

True guides—the disciples of Jesus—can be recognized as such **by their fruits**. For it is not mere outward identification as His disciple that saves. There are many listening to Him who address Him with great deference as **"Lord, Lord"** (Gr. *Kurie*, like our English "sir"). Such outward deference is insufficient. Keeping His teaching and **doing the will of** His **Father** is what matters. Merely identifying oneself with Jesus and using His Name is not enough.

Thus, Jesus says, when it is time to **enter into the Kingdom of the heavens, many will say** to Him, **"Lord, Lord, did we not prophesy in Your Name, and in Your Name cast out demons, and in Your Name do many works of power?"** (Note the emphasis on the **Name** of Jesus, which stands at the head of each of the three claims.) Many who in this age say, **"Lord, Lord"** (v. 21) will say, **"Lord, Lord"** on the last day (v. 22). They will claim to be His true disciples, offering as proof that His Name enabled them to do many miracles.

In this parable, Jesus says that even if a person can do miracles in His Name, it is not enough if the person doing them spent his life **working lawlessness**. The parable comes to a horrifying climax as Jesus tells the astonished so-called disciple to leave Him and depart to the outer darkness. Jesus **will confess** the truth before all the angels of God at that judgment—the fact is, He **never knew** that person at all. The bearing of good fruits of righteousness is required from all.

(It may be added that this parable does not address the question of whether one who is not truly saved may nonetheless do genuine miracles. For purposes of parabolic drama, that scenario is advanced. But its purpose is not to teach the Church about miracles, but to add to the horrified astonishment of the one in the parable who is lost. Christ's point is simply that *absolutely nothing* can be a substitute for doing the will of the Father.)

§III.8. Warning to Heed Christ's Teaching

ॐ ॐ ॐ ॐ ॐ

24 "Therefore everyone who hears these words of Mine and does them may be likened to a prudent man who built his house upon the rock.

25 "And the rain descended and the rivers came, and the winds blew and fell against that house, and it did not fall, for it had been founded upon the rock.

26 "And everyone who hears these words of Mine and does not do them will be likened to a foolish man who built his house upon the sand.

27 "And the rain descended, and the rivers came, and the winds blew and struck against that house, and it fell, and the fall of it was great."

St. Matthew concludes the Sermon on the Mount with a final exhortation to heed all the teaching Christ has given. Christ tells a parable about two men, one **a prudent man who built his house upon the rock**, and the other **a foolish man who built his house upon the sand**. Both men encountered identical storms in life—for both of them, **the rain descended, and the rivers** and floods **came, and the winds blew**, battering their houses. But for the one who **built his house upon the rock**, his house did **not fall**, and his life remained secure. For the one who **built his house upon the sand**, however, his house **fell, and the fall of it was great**. One's safety, therefore, depends on what one uses as one's foundation.

It is the same for **everyone who hears** Christ's **words**. To hear and obey His teaching is to be **a prudent man** and to build one's life on a solid foundation. Such a one will be safe when the storm of the final judgment comes. To hear and to fail to obey is to build on the sand. Such a one will not survive when the final storm of judgment comes to try the quality of his life. Such a **foolish man** will **fall** to disaster on the last day—and **great** will be his fall.

§III.9. Conclusion of the Discourse

ॐ ॐ ॐ ॐ ॐ

28 And it happened that when Jesus finished these words, the crowds were thunderstruck at His teaching,

29 for He was teaching them as *one* having authority, and not as their scribes.

The reference to Jesus having **finished these words** refers to the entire Sermon on the Mount, begun in 5:2. (The phrase about having "finished" these words is Matthew's standard way of concluding each of the five discourses; compare 11:1; 13:53; 19:1; 26:1.) The **crowds** that gathered to hear Him after He descended to a place somewhat lower down the mountainside (see 5:1 and commentary there) **were thunderstruck at His teaching, for He was teaching them as *one* having authority, and not as their scribes**. The normal way for the scribes to teach was not to claim any authority for themselves, but to cite the opinions of other teachers. Jesus, however, put forward His own teaching as authoritative. He did not offer another interpretation, nor did He defer to the wisdom of others, but taught with the very authority of God. The assertion, "I Myself say to you," characterized all His teaching (see 5:22, 28, 32, etc.). Thus it was impossible to accept His teaching without thereby also accepting His claims of personal authority.

✃ IV ✄

MINISTRY IN GALILEE
(8:1—9:34)

§IV.1. Cleansing the Leper

> ঞ্চ ঞ্চ ঞ্চ ঞ্চ ঞ্চ
>
> **8** 1 And when He had descended from the mountain, many crowds followed Him.
> 2 And behold! a leper came to Him *and* worshipped Him, saying, "Lord, if You are willing, You can cleanse me."
> 3 And He stretched out His hand and touched him, saying, "I am willing; be cleansed." And immediately his leprosy was cleansed.
> 4 And Jesus says to him, "See that you tell no one; but go, show yourself to the priest, and offer the gift that Moses commanded for a witness to them."

Matthew then offers a series of stories and sayings of Jesus, illustrating His early Galilean ministry. He places this miracle in the context of His interaction with the **many crowds** that **followed Him** after He had chosen the Twelve, addressed the people, and then **descended from the mountain** again to continue His ministry.

The suddenness of the leper's approach is signaled by the word **behold!** The term "leprosy" included a number of infectious skin diseases, but all of them meant disaster for the sufferer, for the leper was driven from common society to face a life of isolation and poverty, far from human warmth and family, cut off from the worship of Temple and synagogue.

The leper had heard of Jesus' miraculous power and boldly **came to Him** (we may imagine the crowd made way for him and stood well back!) *and* **worshipped Him, saying, "Lord, if You are willing, You can cleanse me."** The word *worship* (Gr. *proskuneo*) here means simply "bow down to," as the man knelt and then prostrated himself in utter humility and desperation before his only hope of healing. The man had no doubt that Jesus *could* heal him—the only question was whether or not Jesus was *willing*. Christ was moved by the man's faith and assured him, saying, **"I am willing; be cleansed."** In saying this **He stretched out His hand and touched** him, laying His healing hand upon him. And **immediately his leprosy was cleansed**.

The significance of this touch should not be missed, for most men shrank from touching a leper for fear of contagion. Christ, however, was stronger than the living death that gripped the poor leper, and His power caused the dread disease instantly to withdraw.

Christ wanted the least possible notoriety for His miraculous power, for the resulting crowds would make it impossible for Him to even enter a city (Mark 1:45); and so He commanded the man to **tell no one** of the miracle. He should, however, **go, show** himself **to the priest, and offer the gift that Moses commanded** to be offered when a leper was cleansed (Lev. 14:2f). This obedience to the Law of Moses was not necessary because the Law was supreme, but was simply **for a witness to them**, that all those around the man might know that he was truly cleansed and could reenter their society.

§IV.2. Healing the Centurion's Slave

> ॐ ॐ ॐ ॐ ॐ
>
> 5   And when He had entered into Capernaum, a centurion came to Him, urging Him,

6   and saying, "Lord, my servant is lying *in bed* paralyzed at the house, tormented terribly."

7   And He says to him, "I *Myself* will come *and* heal him."

8   But the centurion answered and said, "Lord, I am not sufficient that You should enter under my roof, but only say in a word, and my servant will be cured.

9   "For I *myself* also am a man under authority, with soldiers under me; and I say to this one, 'Go!' and he goes, and to another, 'Come!' and he comes, and to my slave, 'Do this!' and he does *it*."

10 Now when Jesus heard, He marveled, and said to those following, "Amen I say to you, with no one have I found such great faith in Israel!

11 "And I say to you that many will come from east and west, and recline with Abraham and Isaac and Jacob in the Kingdom of the heavens;

12 "but the sons of the Kingdom will be cast out into the outer darkness; in that place there will be weeping and gnashing of teeth."

13 And Jesus said to the centurion, "Go your way; let it be to you as you have believed." And the servant was cured that hour.

After **He had entered into Capernaum, a centurion came to Him**. Though Roman forces were not stationed in Galilee generally until AD 44, Capernaum was on a major route, and Roman soldiers may well have been there earlier. This centurion was in great distress because his **servant was lying** in bed paralyzed at his house, **tormented terribly**. We do not know the nature of the affliction, but from the parallel account in Luke 7:2, we know that the servant was about to die. So it is that the Gentile officer **came to** Jesus with his urgent entreaty. (Matthew's account, here as generally, is concise and abbreviated; he omits the detail, present in Luke 7:3f, that the Gentile's message came to Jesus through the Jewish friends he sent—he did not come himself.)

The Lord instantly began to journey through town to the house of the centurion, saying, **"I *Myself* will come *and* heal him."** This was an extraordinary act, in defiance of all Jewish custom. The homes of pagans were thought by the Jews to be unclean, and no pious Jew would enter there lest he be ritually defiled. When the centurion saw this (Luke adds that this happened when he saw Jesus actually approaching his home, and sent yet another delegation; Luke 7:6f), he protested that this was not necessary, nor did he presume to ask Jesus for this favor. He acknowledged that he, as a Gentile, was **not sufficient** (Gr. *ikanos*, "fit, adequate") to have Christ **enter under** his **roof**.

The centurion knew all about the Jewish reluctance to enter pagan houses and would not ask Christ to do this. Christ need only **say in a word**, utter a single command, and his **servant will be cured**. For as **a man under authority** himself, the centurion knew all about authority and how it worked. As one under the authority of Rome, **with soldiers under** him, he need only **say to this one, "Go!" and he goes, and to another, "Come!" and he comes**. He did not need to see the subordinate carry out his order to know that it would be fulfilled. In the same way, he knew that Jesus, having authority from God, did not need to come to his house to see that His order was carried out. He could heal at a distance.

Here was amazing faith, and **when Jesus heard** the man's words, **He marveled**. Turning to the Jewish crowd **following**, He assured them solemnly that **with no one had** He **found such great faith**, even **in** all **Israel**. Here was a wonder—and a sign of greater wonders to come. For this Gentile's faith was a sign that other Gentiles would yet come to put their trust in the Jewish Messiah. Indeed, **many** pagans would **come from east and west, and recline** at table **with Abraham and Isaac and Jacob in the Kingdom of the heavens**, feasting at the messianic banquet. And more shocking than this, many Jews, **the sons of the Kingdom** who would have been expected to have places at the head table with the patriarchs, will be excluded from that banquet and **be cast out into the outer darkness. In that**

place there will be no feasting or joy, but **weeping and gnashing of teeth** in helpless rage at their exclusion. This centurion was a sign that a great reversal was to come at the last day.

The Lord at last gave His word to the centurion: **"Let it be to you as you have believed."** The man's faith in Jesus was vindicated, and his **servant was cured that** very **hour**.

§IV.3. Healing All in Capernaum

ꕶ ꕶ ꕶ ꕶ ꕶ

14 And when Jesus had come into Peter's house, He saw his mother-in-law lying *in bed, having* a fever.

15 And He touched her hand, and the fever left her; and she arose and was serving Him.

16 And evening having come, they brought to Him many who were demon-possessed; and He cast out the spirits with a word, and healed all who were sick,

17 that what was spoken through Isaiah the prophet might be fulfilled, saying, "He Himself took our ailments and bore our diseases."

Matthew next mentions a healing that took place **when Jesus had come into Peter's house**. From Mark 1:29, we learn that this was when they had come from the local synagogue, returning for the main meal of the Sabbath day. Peter's **mother-in-law** was **lying** *in bed, having* a **fever** (the cause of the fever is not stated). Christ **touched her hand** (possibly taking her hand as she reached up to Him; Mark 1:31 speaks of Christ *seizing* her by the hand) and the **fever left her**. So completely was she healed that **she arose and** began **serving Him**, joining the other women of the house in the serving of the festive Sabbath meal.

When the evening had come (and the Sabbath was over so that work such as carrying the sick could be done), all in Capernaum brought to Him many who were demon-possessed; and He cast out the spirits with only a word. Indeed, He healed all who were sick, so that none who came to Him in faith went away disappointed. For St. Matthew, this also fulfilled the word that was spoken through Isaiah the prophet in which he said, "He Himself took our ailments and bore our diseases" (Is. 53:4). Messiah was to bring healing to Israel and carry away all that afflicted them. Christ's ministry of universal healing revealed Him as being this Messiah.

§IV.4. Christ's Claims on His Disciples

> ॐ ॐ ॐ ॐ ॐ
>
> 18 Now when Jesus saw a crowd around Him, He ordered *them* to go to the other *side*.
> 19 And one scribe came to *Him* and said to Him, "Teacher, I will follow You wherever You go."
> 20 And Jesus says to him, "The foxes have dens, and the birds of the heaven have dwellings; but the Son of man does not have *a place* to lay *His* head."
> 21 And another of the disciples said to Him, "Lord, allow me first to go and bury my father."
> 22 But Jesus says to him, "Follow Me; and leave the dead to bury their own dead."

During one of the days Jesus was preaching by the Sea of Galilee, He saw a crowd around Him. Possibly He and His disciples were exhausted, and to find some rest, He ordered *them* to go to the other *side* of the lake, where they could escape the press. As they prepared to embark, one scribe came to *Him* and said to Him, "Teacher, I will follow You wherever You go." That is, he offered to become His disciple. Christ does not refuse the man's offer, but challenges him to count the cost. Is the man really willing to follow Jesus and share His homelessness? For Jesus is unique in His humility. Even the wild animals, untended by man, have their homes: the

foxes have their **dens, the birds of the heaven** have their **dwellings** and nests, **but the Son of man does not have** *a place* **to lay** *His* **head**. Unlike even the humblest animals, He has to wander from place to place, dependent on the kindness of men. Is the potential disciple willing to embrace such hardship?

Matthew relates another saying. Jesus challenges another disciple to follow Him and accompany Him on His journeys from town to town (Luke 9:59), but the man balks. He will do so, but not right away. He has family obligations he feels he must fulfill **first**, including caring for his aged father. After his father has died and he has **buried** him, then he will obey His Lord's summons. (It is apparent that the father has not yet died, for burials were held on the day of death, and the man would not be speaking to Christ during this time.)

Christ's reply is uncompromising. The man claims to be His disciple, and yet puts other obligations before his commitment to the Kingdom. He must **leave the dead to bury their own dead** and carry out such duties. The one whom Christ has called is like one alive from the dead (John 5:25); he belongs no longer to this age. Christ's call thus takes precedence over all earthly duties, however sacred and important they seem to be.

◌ EXCURSUS
ON THE TITLE "SON OF MAN"

The title "Son of man" was the Lord's preferred self-designation, for it identified Him as the Messiah without actually using that word. (The title "Messiah" was too politically charged in those days, and inevitably brought with it connotations of military and earthly kingship that Jesus was anxious to avoid.)

The phrase "son of man" in itself means no more than "human being," and it has connotations of weakness. Thus the psalmist cries out to God, "What is man that You think of him, and the son of man, that You care for him?"

(Ps. 8:4). Human beings in all their weakness and frailty—what are they that God should favor them so highly? The prophet Ezekiel also is addressed by God as "son of man" (e.g. Ezek. 2:1)—that is, as a mere creature of dust and ashes, one who is overwhelmed at the vision of God's majesty (Ezek. 1:28).

It is in the context of such a use of the term that Daniel sees his vision of four beasts and a son of man in Daniel 7. The four beasts are images of the bestial and brutal kingdoms of this world, but their rule is succeeded by the rule of a human being, a son of man. By these images, Daniel is shown that the Kingdom of God is a Kingdom of nobility and peace, and differs from the kingdoms of this world even as man differs from the beasts. The son of man being given the kingdom (Dan. 7:13–14) is an image for the saints of God receiving the kingdom (Dan. 7:18, 27).

By the first century, Jewish apocalyptic literature had taken up this image of the son of man and used it in a different way. It was understood that a single individual, the Messiah, would arise to bring in this Kingdom; the phrase "the Son of man" was one of His titles. (He was also called "the Chosen One.")

Thus the Book of Enoch refers to the Messiah as "the Son of man" in chapter 69: "And He sat on the throne of His glory, and the sum of judgment was given unto the Son of man, and he caused the sinners to pass away and be destroyed from off the face of the earth." And also in chapter 70: "And so there shall be length of days with that Son of man and the righteous shall have peace and an upright way, in the Name of the Lord of Spirits to ages of ages."

When Jesus used the title "Son of man" to describe Himself, He was using a familiar messianic title, one that would identify Him as the Chosen of God, but without the military connotations surrounding the use of the actual title "Messiah."

§IV.5. Christ's Authority over the Violence of Nature

ॐ   ॐ   ॐ   ॐ   ॐ

23 And when He got into the boat, His disciples
followed Him.

24 And behold! a great shaking happened on
the sea, so that the boat was covered with the
waves; but He Himself was sleeping.

25 And they came to *Him*, and rouse Him, saying,
"Save, Lord! We are perishing!"

26 And He says to them, "Why are you cowardly, you of little faith?" Then He arose, and
rebuked the winds and the sea; and a great calm
happened.

27 And the men marveled, saying, "What kind of
man is this, that even the winds and the sea
obey Him?"

After speaking with the inquirer of 8:18f, Christ **got into the boat** to go to the other side of the Sea of Galilee. He was greatly exhausted from the labors of the day (for it was evening when they departed; Mark 4:35), and He quickly fell asleep. The Sea of Galilee was known for its sudden storms. Unexpectedly (Matthew uses his customary **behold!** to indicate how unexpected it was), **a great shaking** of the sea's surface from one of those storms **happened on the sea, so that the boat was covered with the waves.** Despite this, Christ remained sleeping, even as the waves washed over the boat. (His exhaustion must have been extreme.)

The disciples, experienced fishermen though some of them were, were terrified, as they thought the boat would capsize and they would all be drowned. **They came to** Jesus **and rouse Him** (the historic present is used, so that we can almost see them shaking Him), **saying, "Save, Lord! We are perishing!"**

At last, with the terrified shouting of the disciples, Christ is awakened. He rebukes them for being **cowardly** and **of little faith.**

Did they really suppose that God would allow His Son to drown in the lake with His disciples? Jesus **arose**, standing upright in the tossing boat, **and rebuked the winds and the sea**, commanding their unruly behavior to cease. Immediately **a great calm happened**, and the disciples, being mere **men**, **marveled** at the divine power. No one but God could tame the untamable power of the sea (see Job 38:8–11), but Jesus calmed its fury with a simple word. They whispered among themselves (perhaps after Jesus returned to His interrupted sleep), **"What kind of *man* is this, that even the winds and the sea obey Him?"** They knew in their hearts that He was God's chosen instrument, but were still stunned by such a display of power.

§IV.6. Christ's Authority over Demons

૱ ૱ ૱ ૱ ૱

28 And when He had come to the other *side* into the region of the Gadarenes, two demon-possessed *men* met Him as they were coming out of the tombs, so exceedingly dangerous that no one was strong enough to pass by that way.

29 And behold! they cried out, saying, "What are we to You, Son of God? Have You come here to torture us before the time?"

30 Now there was at a distance from them a herd of many pigs feeding.

31 And the demons were urging Him, saying, "If You cast us out, send us into the herd of pigs."

32 And He said to them, "Go away!" And they came out and went away into the pigs, and behold! all the herd rushed down the slope into the sea and perished in the waters.

33 And the ones feeding *them* fled and went into the city, and reported everything, and *about* the demon-possessed.

> 34 And behold, all the city came out to a meeting
> with Jesus, and when they saw Him, they urged
> Him to move on from their area.

After they arrived that night (for they left in the evening; Mark 4:35), they came **into the region of the Gadarenes**. Though some manuscripts read "Gergesenes" instead of "Gadarenes," the reading of **Gadarenes** is probably correct. The nearest town was what is now modern Kersa, a mile or so to the south (hence the reading "Gerasenes" in Mark 5:1 and Luke 8:26). The city of Gadara was about five miles southeast from the lake, though it was the capital of the area around it, and seems here to have given its name to the **region**.

As Jesus and His disciples emerged from the boat, **two demon-possessed** *men* **met Him**. One of them was something of a local sensation, for he had often been bound with fetters and chains, which he smashed to pieces and ran off to the cave tombs near the town of Kersa not far from the lake (Mark 5:2–5). He was joined by another poor demon-possessed wretch, and the two of them met Jesus as **they were coming out of the tombs** in which they had taken shelter. These men were **exceedingly dangerous** and would attack anyone who got near them (especially those who they thought were coming near them to bind them), so that **no one was strong enough to pass by that way**. Here were two men entirely dominated by the demonic spirits of evil.

When the demons within the men saw Jesus, they recognized their Judge and feared that the final torture of Gehenna was at hand. Therefore **they cried out, saying, "What are we to You, Son of God? Have You come here to torture us before the time?"** Despite their great strength, their power was no match for the Son of God, and the demons recognized that they would have to vacate the two men who had been their prey.

There was **at a distance from them a herd of many pigs feeding** on the mountain hillside, for they were in Gentile territory. Fearing to be sent into the final abyss, **the demons were urging Him, saying, "If You cast us out, send us into the herd of pigs."**

If the Lord had expelled the demons against their will, no doubt the cost to the poor demoniacs would have been very great. When the Lord forcibly expelled a single demon from a boy, that demon convulsed the boy so badly that the child nearly died (Mark 9:26). Perhaps therefore it was out of compassion for the afflicted men that Christ allowed the demons to leave voluntarily, telling them to **go away** from the men (a sovereign single word in the Greek, *upagete*) and **into the pigs**.

The herd reacted unexpectedly. They panicked and **rushed down the slope into the sea and perished in the waters**. The pig-herders in charge of the swine **fled and went into the city** (of nearby Kersa probably), and **reported everything** about the pigs, and also *about the demon-possessed* men. At daybreak, **all the city came out to a meeting with Jesus** to see for themselves. **When they saw Him** and learned of His great power, they thought Him too dangerous to be in their midst, and **urged Him to move on from their area**.

Matthew ends his account on this note of fear. Christ's naked power had been shown on the sea, and again on land in the region of Gadara. So great was that power that it caused His disciples to marvel and pagans to tremble in fear. Who was this who wielded such power, if not God's Messiah?

❧ EXCURSUS
ON THE DOUBLES IN MATTHEW'S GOSPEL

Matthew makes a point of mentioning whenever there are doubles. Thus he mentions that there were two demoniacs in this story, whereas both Mark and Luke focus on the one who was the main speaker and the local sensation (Mark 5:2; Luke 8:27). In 20:29 Matthew mentions that there were two blind men healed as Jesus approached Jerusalem, whereas both Mark and Luke focus on one of them (Mark 10:46; Luke 18:35). In 9:27, Matthew stresses that there were again two blind men healed. In relating the story of Christ's Triumphal Entry into Jerusalem in 21:2f, he even stresses the fact that there were two animals used, though Mark and

Luke mention only the one animal Christ sat on (Mark 11:2; Luke 19:30). Why this concern with doubles?

Once again Matthew thinks and writes like a Jew. For a Jew, two witnesses confirmed a testimony (compare Deut. 19:15; Matt. 18:16), and these doubles confirmed the testimony that Jesus was the Messiah. In all the stories in which these doubles appear, Jesus is confirmed as the Son of God (8:29) and as the messianic Son of David (9:27; 20:30), even the Son of David who comes in the Name of the Lord (21:9). By stressing the dual witness attending these confessions, Matthew brings forward sure testimony that Jesus is the divine Son of David, the Messiah who comes in the Lord's Name.

§IV.7. Opposition from the Pharisees

§IV.7.i. Forgiving the Sins of the Paralytic

ॐ ॐ ॐ ॐ ॐ

9 1 And getting into a boat, He crossed over and came into His own city.

2 And behold! they were bringing to Him a paralytic, lying upon a bed; and Jesus, seeing their faith, said to the paralytic, "Have courage, child, your sins are forgiven."

3 And behold, some of the scribes said among themselves, "This one blasphemes."

4 And Jesus, knowing their thoughts, said, "Why are you thinking evil *things* in your hearts?

5 "For which is easier, to say, 'Your sins are forgiven,' or to say, 'Arise and walk'?

6 "But that you may know that the Son of man has authority upon the earth to forgive sins"—then He says to the paralytic, "Rise, take

> up your bed, and go away to your house."
> 7 And he arose and went to his house.
> 8 But when the crowds saw it, they were afraid
> and glorified God, who had given such author-
> ity to men.

St. Matthew locates the next story after Christ had **crossed over** the Sea of Galilee and again **came into His own city** of Capernaum. He prefaces it with his customary **behold!** to indicate a surprising event—namely that **they were bringing to Him a paralytic, lying upon a bed** (that is, a pallet or light mattress). This in itself was not surprising, for doubtless many paralytics were brought to Jesus. The surprise here (as Mark 2:3–12; Luke 5:17–26 make clear) is that in order to bypass the crowd, the paralytic's friends had to carry him up to the flat rooftop, remove some of the roof, and let the paralytic down with ropes in front of Jesus. Matthew omits these details (perhaps because he assumes his readers have some familiarity with the stories he tells?).

When **Jesus saw the faith** of the small group, He **said to the paralytic, "Have courage, child, your sins are forgiven."** The words *are forgiven* are in the present tense (lit., "are being forgiven"), so that the thought is not that the man has already been forgiven, but rather that Jesus was forgiving the man's sins on the spot.

Why did the Lord first speak this word of forgiveness, when the obvious request was for healing? Healing for the body is bound up with forgiveness for the soul, since man is a single compound of both. It may not be the case in every instance that a specific sickness is caused by a specific sin. But in this case the Lord knew that this man needed forgiveness, and that this was at the root of his sickness.

Some of the scribes began whispering **among themselves, "This one blasphemes."** They were horrified by Jesus' claim to have the authority to forgive sins. Jesus was actually claiming to render divine judgment, so that God would not require an accounting of this man's sins on the last day. How could a man on earth speak for God in heaven?

Jesus knew what they were about. He did not regard theirs as a legitimate question, but as **thinking evil *things* in** their **hearts**, for the miracles they had seen were enough to convince a true and open heart that there was something special about Jesus, and that He could speak for His Father.

He responded by asking them a question: **"Which is easier, to say 'Your sins are forgiven,' or to say** to the crippled man, **'Arise and walk'?"** They would have to admit that both were impossible for mere men, for a mere man could not forgive sins—but neither could he make a cripple walk simply by telling him to do so. **"But that you may know,"** He said, **"that the Son of man has authority upon the earth to forgive sins—"** (here He turns to the paralytic lying before Him and **says** to him), **"Rise, take up your bed, and go away to your house."** And obediently, the crippled man **arose and went to his house.**

The effect of such a mighty act on the crowds was immediate. They were afraid (even as the Gadarene crowd had been; 8:34), and could not but **glorify God, who had** evidently **given such authority to men.** God was in the heavens, but here was One on earth who exercised His power and authority.

§IV.7.ii. Call of Matthew the Tax-collector

ॐ ॐ ॐ ॐ ॐ

9   And as Jesus passed on from there, He saw a man, called Matthew, sitting in the tax-office; and He says to him, "Follow Me!" And he arose and followed Him.

10   And it happened that as He was reclining in the house, behold, many tax-collectors and sinners came and were co-reclining with Jesus and His disciples.

11   And when the Pharisees saw it, they said to His disciples, "Why is your Teacher eating with the tax-collectors and sinners?"

> 12 But when He heard *this*, He said, "The strong
> ones have no need of a physician, but those who
> are sick.
> 13 "But go and learn what this is, 'I want mercy
> and not sacrifice,' for I have not come to call
> the righteous, but sinners."

Next is related the call of Matthew the tax-collector. (As mentioned in the Introduction, I suggest that this Gospel was written by a member of Matthew's community, and not by Matthew himself. Thus, Matthew is not here writing about himself in the third person.) Matthew was also known as Levi (Mark 2:14; Luke 5:27), and it would seem that Matthew was the name he was known by in the wider Church (perhaps as Saul was also known by the name Paul; Acts 13:9). As is usual in this Gospel, his call is related with but a few words. Jesus saw **Matthew, sitting in the tax-office; and He says to him, "Follow Me!" And he arose and followed Him**.

Such tax-collectors were familiar sights, for they sat at their tax-tables at such conspicuous places as crossroads and bridges, where they could exact custom and duty from travelers. They were heartily hated by the common folk, not only because they seemed to be collaborators with the Romans, but because of their reputation for exacting more tax than was fair.

Matthew had undoubtedly heard about Jesus before. As a tax-collector, Matthew would have taken it for granted that respectable people like Jesus would have nothing to do with him. Yet here Jesus was, accepting him and calling him to a new life. Matthew jumped at the chance. **He arose**, leaving his tax-table, and **followed** Jesus as one of His disciples.

The narrative continues with its economy of words, the narrator evidently assuming that his hearers had heard the story before. For the narrative continues that as Jesus **was reclining** at a banquet **in the house, behold, many tax-collectors and sinners came and were co-reclining with** Him. (Banquets were eaten while reclining on couches in the Roman manner.) We are meant to understand (and the parallel in Luke confirms it) that this banquet was given by Matthew himself, to celebrate his relationship with his new Friend and to introduce his tax-collector and sinner friends to Him. (The term *sinner* here means one who was openly irreligious and scandalous.)

The Pharisees who saw it were scandalized. Pious rabbis took great care to avoid such rabble—and here was Jesus accepting them and socializing with them! At some point (perhaps the next day—it is unthinkable that the Pharisees would have been at the banquet themselves)—they challenged Jesus' disciples, asking, **"Why is your Teacher eating with the tax-collectors and sinners?"** Though perhaps this was said behind the hand as a private question to the disciples, Jesus **heard *this*** and answered for them. He replied that **the strong** and healthy **ones have no need of a physician, but** rather **those who are sick**. The tax-collectors and sinners were indeed sick—that was why Jesus went to them. A physician obviously did not confine himself to the homes of the healthy.

Then Jesus had a task for the Pharisees. They claimed to be so adept in understanding the Law. Let them **go**, then, **and learn what this** Scripture's meaning **is, "I want mercy, and not sacrifice,"** for if they knew this, they would not be scandalized at God's mercy extended to the sinner.

The citation is from Hosea 6:6, in which God was threatening judgment against His People, saying that what He wanted from Israel was mercy, true devotion, covenant loyalty (Heb. *hesed*), and all they had offered Him was cultic sacrifice coupled with disobedience to His Law. In the absence of such warm and true hearts, sacrifice itself was useless. Christ applies this insight to His day. The Pharisees had no mercy in their cold hearts, no true knowledge of God, no love for their fellow man. Their religion was reduced to outward conformity to rules, and this was not what God wanted. God wanted the devotion of the human heart, and Christ was pursuing this devotion, even in the home of Matthew the tax-collector. That was why He had **not come to call the righteous** only, **but sinners** as well.

§IV.7.iii. Conflict with Pharisees over Fasting

ॐ ॐ ॐ ॐ ॐ

14 Then the disciples of John come to Him, saying, "Why do we *ourselves* and the Pharisees fast, but Your disciples do not fast?"

15 And Jesus said to them, "Can the sons of the bridal-chamber mourn as long as the bridegroom is with them? But days will come when the bridegroom is taken away from them, and then they will fast.

16 "But no one puts a patch of unshrunk cloth on an old garment, for the patch pulls away from the garment, and a worse split occurs.

17 "Nor do they put new wine into old skins; otherwise the skins are torn, and the wine pours out, and the skins are destroyed; but they put new wine into fresh skins, and both are kept."

The respectable people there that day had another complaint as well. **The disciples of John** (who continued to follow his teaching, even after he had been arrested) came to join the discussion, saying, **"Why do we *ourselves* and the Pharisees fast, but Your disciples do not fast?"** The pious in Israel fasted twice a week, on Mondays and Thursdays, eating nothing until evening, and the followers of John could be expected to be ascetic like their teacher. True piety seemed impossible without such fasting, and yet here Jesus' disciples, at Matthew's banquet, were eating and drinking even though it was on one of those fast days. To the people who asked this question, rules were rules and were utterly inflexible. On Mondays and Thursdays, the pious should fast!

In response, Jesus asks a question of His own: **"Can the sons of the bridal-chamber mourn as long as the bridegroom is with them?"** In those days, wedding banquets would continue for days—even though it be a Monday or a Thursday, and **the sons of the**

bridal-chamber (the technical term for the wedding guests) could not **mourn** and fast during this time. Such would be an unthinkable insult to the groom and bride who invited them. Sharing the joy of the bridegroom meant suspending their fasting for a time. And if this was the case for normal weddings, how much more for the Son of man! The joy of having Jesus in their midst means that the customary fasting rules must be suspended.

The Lord then speaks with grim irony, not understood at that time. He adds that days will come when the bridegroom is taken away from them, and then they will fast. In terms of the parabolic image, this means simply that the guests cannot fast until the party ends. But in light of the Cross, the Lord means that the days of joy and celebration will end with His death—and there will be plenty of time for His disciples to fast then.

He then tells another parable to show that the new ways of the Kingdom cannot be combined with the old ways of legalism, but require greater flexibility. To attempt to combine the new Kingdom with the old patterns of piety is like one who **puts a patch of unshrunk cloth on an old garment**. Everyone knows the result of such folly: **the patch pulls away from the garment, and a worse split occurs**, for the old garment has already been shrunk through washing, but the new patch will shrink and tear away. The result of such attempted combination is that the garment becomes useless and torn.

Or consider the folly of putting **new wine into old skins**. Old wineskins are tough and leathery, with no stretchable "give" to them. If one puts freshly fermented new wine into those skins, the wine will expand too much for the skins and burst them. The new **wine** will **pour out** and be lost, and the skins too will be **destroyed**. The combination of new with old serves neither well. The new wine of the Kingdom requires fresh skins, new and flexible ways of thinking and living. Only so will **both** the wine and the skins be **kept** and preserved. To drink the wine which makes glad the heart of man (Ps. 104:15) one must adapt to the new ways.

What does this mean for the Orthodox practice of fasting? It does not mean that we need not fast (indeed, Christ assumed His disciples would; compare 6:16f). Rather it means that our fasting is not done in a legalistic spirit, and that it is never an end in itself. Our fasting is done to bring us closer to the Lord of love, and that means that sometimes our fasting must be suspended to meet the demands of love. Thus the Desert Fathers would sometimes break their fast if they were entertaining guests, for love and hospitality demanded that they share a meal together. When one such guest apologized to his Desert Father host for making him break his rule of fasting, the Father replied, "My rule is to take care of you and send you away in peace."

§IV.8. Christ's Authority over Sickness and Death

ॐ ॐ ॐ ॐ ॐ

18 While He was speaking these things to them, behold, one ruler came *and* worshipped Him, saying, "My daughter has just died; but come and put Your hand on her, and she will live."

19 And Jesus arose and was following him, and His disciples *did also.*

20 And behold! a woman who was hemorrhaging for twelve years came up behind Him and touched the fringe of His garment;

21 for she was saying in herself, "If I only touch His garment, I will be saved."

22 But Jesus turning and seeing her said, "Have courage, daughter, your faith has saved you." And the woman was saved from that hour.

23 And when Jesus came into the ruler's house and saw the flute-players, and the crowd *in an* uproar,

24 He was saying, "Withdraw, for the girl has not died, but is sleeping." And they were laughing at Him.

25 But when the crowd had been cast out, He

> entered in and seized her by the hand, and the girl arose.
> 26 And this news went out into that whole land.

Matthew connects this story with the previous one, saying that it was **while He was speaking these things** to the crowd of John's disciples and the Pharisees that a man **came and worshipped Him** (that is, fell down in humility before Him as one would before one's social superior). The man was a **ruler** of the local synagogue, who shared the task of taking care of the building itself and of arranging for the services.

The man's plight was urgent, for when he left his little daughter to find Jesus, the girl was at the point of death—and by now she must surely be dead. Matthew records the man saying, **"My daughter has just died,"** for he telescopes the man's initial request for the dying girl with his despair later when he hears that his daughter has indeed just died (see Mark 5:35f). The man's actual words are not recorded, as all three Synoptic evangelists report only the gist of his request. We may imagine that the man babbled in his panicked distress, perhaps telling Jesus that He must hurry, for by now his daughter must surely be dead. Whatever the father's exact words, he has no doubt that if Jesus will just come to his house and **put** His **hand** on the girl, **she will live**.

Immediately **Jesus arose** from where He was sitting and discussing fasting with His critics and **was following** the man with great difficulty through the dense crowd, accompanied by **His disciples** (mentioned here perhaps because of their role when they reach the man's house; compare Mark 5:37). As they made their laborious way, another surprising event awaited them: **a woman who was hemorrhaging for twelve years came up behind Him and touched the fringe of His garment**.

She had decided to touch the fringe that adorned the garments of all Jews (see Num. 15:39) and obtain healing that way, rather than by asking for Him to heal her, because her ceaseless hidden hemorrhage made her ritually unclean. She could not tell Jesus what her affliction was without also revealing that she had been spreading that ceremonial uncleanness to all in the crowd with whom she had contact. But she had faith that such was the power of Jesus that mere contact with Him was enough to bring her healing.

Jesus turning and seeing her said, "Have courage, daughter, your faith has saved you." Well might He tell her to have courage, for when she touched His garment, He perceived that power went forth from Him, and He stopped His progress through the crowd until He could discover who it was that touched Him (see Mark 5:30f). Doubtless the woman was expecting a rebuke for subjecting Jesus to ceremonial defilement, but Jesus set her heart at peace. He had no concern for such ritual uncleanness. He assured her that all was well, and that her **faith** in Him had **saved** her from her affliction.

Matthew next narrates Jesus' arrival at the ruler's house, omitting the detail of the arrival of the delegation informing Him of the girl's death. **When Jesus came into the ruler's house** to find the girl, He **saw the flute-players** who played at the time of death and at funerals. Custom dictated that even a poor man must provide for two flute-players and one professional mourner for the death of such a loved one, so we may think that the ruler, a comparatively rich man, had many such flute-players in the house waiting for the girl to die. With the mourners, **the crowd** in the house was **_in an uproar_**, wailing loudly as they were wont to do.

All the noise hit the father like so many blows into his poor anguished heart, and Jesus therefore told them all to **withdraw, for the girl has not died, but is sleeping**. The crowd began **laughing at Him** (Gr. _katagelao_, "laugh to scorn," a more intensive form of "to laugh," _gelao_). But Jesus **cast** them **out** and **entered in** the room where the dead girl lay. He **seized her by the hand, and the girl arose**.

Once again Matthew's version is condensed; he omits the Lord's command to the girl to arise, the stupefaction of the parents, and the Lord's order that the child be given something to eat (Mark 5:41–43). Instead Matthew focuses on Christ taking the child firmly by the hand, raising her as if from sleep by a single action. Such was Christ's power that no long prayers were required (as in the raising of a child by Elisha, 2 Kings 4:33–35). A simple sovereign lifting up was all that was necessary. Not surprisingly, such **news went out into that whole land**.

§IV.9. Christz Heals the Blind and Mute

ॐ ॐ ॐ ॐ ॐ

27 And as Jesus passed on from there, two blind *men* followed Him, crying out and saying, "Have mercy on us, Son of David!"

28 And having come into the house, the blind *men* came up to Him, and Jesus says to them, "Do you believe that I am able to do this?" They say to Him, "Yes, Lord."

29 Then He touched their eyes, saying, "According to your faith let it happen to you."

30 And their eyes were opened. And Jesus scolded them, saying, "See *that you* let no one know!"

31 But they went out and spread the news about Him in that whole land.

32 And as they were going out, behold, they brought to Him a mute demon-possessed man.

33 And after the demon was cast out, the mute *man* spoke; and the crowds marveled, saying, "Nothing thus has ever appeared in Israel!"

34 But the Pharisees were saying, "By the ruler of the demons He casts out the demons."

Christ **passed on from there** and found **two blind *men***, who **followed Him** as He traveled down the road. They were **crying out, "Have mercy on us, Son of David!"** By addressing Jesus as the **Son of David**, they were hailing Him as the Messiah—a very dramatic move, and one calculated to attract the attention they were desperate to win before He left them behind on the road.

It was perhaps to avoid attracting any more attention as the Messiah (which had unwelcome political overtones) that Jesus and His disciples took the two men **into the house** where they were staying in Capernaum. Once they were all safely away from public eyes, the two men approached Jesus with their actual request for healing. **Jesus says to them** (the historic present is used for greater vividness), **"Do you believe that I am able to do this?"** Having received from them a confession of faith in His ability to heal, **He touched their eyes, saying, "According to your faith let it happen to you,"** and immediately **their eyes were opened**. (As stated in the Excursus above, St. Matthew stresses that *two* men were involved in order to give dual and confirmed testimony to Jesus' Messiahship.)

After this, the men were commanded to **let no one know** about the healing. The concern seems to have been to avoid in Capernaum the swelling crowds that elsewhere made it impossible for Him to enter a city (compare Mark 1:45); possibly the men's use of the political title "Son of David" contributed to this as well. The men were evidently unwilling to do as they were bidden, so that Jesus had to **scold** them (Gr. *embrimaomai*; the same word used to describe the scolding of the woman in Mark 14:5), and insist that they do as they were told. Even so, they disobeyed and **spread the news about Him in that whole land**.

St. Matthew connects the healing of the blind men with the healing of **a mute demon-possessed man**—that is, a man whose mute condition had no physical cause, but rather was the result of demonic possession. Matthew's usual economy of words does not say, but we are left to think that this demonic possession was manifest in ways other than the man's inability to speak. Doubtless he exhibited wild and violent behavior as well, which is how his friends recognized the demonic nature of his affliction. He was, we may think, something of a local sensation.

After the demon was cast out, the mute *man* spoke calmly and rationally, perhaps for the first time in many years. For this reason, **the crowds marveled, saying, "Nothing thus has ever appeared in Israel!"** Israel had seen many miracles in centuries past (such as those of Elijah and Elisha), but never such serene power over the demons, and such power to bring peace and restoration to lives destroyed by darkness. **The Pharisees**, however, refused to acknowledge such works as signs of the Kingdom of God, or of Jesus having been sent by God. They **were saying** to the crowds that it was only **by the ruler of the demons** that **He casts out the demons**.

It would seem that St. Matthew relates these two healings together in this way to contrast the faith of the blind men (which is stressed in the story) with the unbelief of the Pharisees. In so doing, he shows how perverse is that unbelief—for even blind men could see that Jesus was the Son of David. How could the Pharisees be blinder than the blind?

❧ V ❧

SECOND DISCOURSE—MISSION
(9:35—11:1)

❧ ❧ ❧ ❧ ❧

9 35 And Jesus was going about all the cities and the villages, teaching in their synagogues, and heralding the Good News of the Kingdom, and healing disease and every infirmity.

36 And seeing the crowds, He had heartfelt *love* for them, because they were harassed and thrown down like sheep not having a shepherd.

37 Then He says to His disciples, "The harvest is great, but the workers *are* few.

38 "Therefore beseech the Lord of the harvest to send out workers into His harvest."

During this phase of His ministry, **Jesus was going about all the cities and the villages** in a circuit (see Mark 6:6), probably confined to Galilee. He was busy **teaching in their synagogues, and heralding the Good News** that the **Kingdom** of God was drawing near, and was **healing every disease and every infirmity** presented to Him. When He saw the teeming **crowds**, He **had heartfelt *love* for them, because they were harassed and thrown down** or confused, **like sheep** which did **not have a shepherd** to care for them.

The word rendered *had heartfelt love* is the Greek *splagxnizomai*, cognate with *splagxna*, the innards, popularly viewed as the seat of emotion. This was no mere sympathy, but an overflowing wave of compassion Christ felt for the masses of people that thronged around Him. Sheep with no shepherd are left with no leader to protect them, and all about Jesus were a multitude of men, women, and children who similarly had no one to care for them in their poverty and pain. Jesus was doing all that He could from morning to night to care for them, but it was not enough.

This prompts Him to say to His disciples (a characteristic utterance—He was to say it again as He sent out the Seventy; Luke 10:1–2), **"The harvest is great, but the workers *are* few. Therefore beseech the Lord of the harvest to send out workers into His harvest."** The owner of a field can hire and send out more workers to reap his crop if he needs them, and in the same way God, who is the sovereign Lord over Israel, can send out more workers for the age-long missionary enterprise of reaching the masses with His love.

---

೩೯ ೩೯ ೩೯ ೩೯ ೩೯

10 1 And having called *to Him* His twelve disciples, He gave them authority over unclean spirits, to cast them out, and to heal every disease and every infirmity.

2 Now the names of the twelve apostles are these: the first, Simon, who is called Peter, and Andrew his brother; and James the *son* of Zebedee, and John his brother;

3 Philip and Bartholomew; Thomas and Matthew the tax-collector; James the *son* of Alphaeus, and Thaddaeus;

4 Simon the Cananaen, and Judas Iscariot, the one who also delivered Him *up*.

In Matthew's collection of material for this next discourse on the Church's missionary work, the saying of Christ in 9:37–38 forms the background for the mission of the Twelve. Christ had selected twelve of His disciples to be His inner circle at an earlier time (see commentary on 5:1), and here He **gave them authority over unclean spirits, to cast them out, and to heal every disease and every infirmity** which He Himself had been healing (9:35). This special bestowal of authority over demons and sickness was given so that they could do the same work that Christ was doing, and so enlarge His area of ministry as they went out on a special missionary tour.

St. Matthew then lists the names of the Twelve. They are listed in pairs, probably because they were sent out two by two (Mark 6:7). It is possible that each is paired with the one with whom he was sent out, though the slight variations between the lists in the three Synoptic Gospels make certainty about this impossible.

I would suggest that this list in Matthew preserves the true pairing, with the other Gospels producing variations for stylistic reasons. In Mark 3:16f, for example, Andrew is not paired with Simon in order that Simon, James, and John may be listed together, since they form the innermost circle. In Luke 6:14ff, Judas the son of James (also called "Thaddaeus") is paired with Judas Iscariot rather than with James the son of Alphaeus, probably to group the two Judases together at the end of the list.

Simon, who is called Peter is called **the first**, for he was the leader of the apostolic band. The name **Peter** translates the Aramaic *Kepha*, meaning "rock," the nickname alluding to Simon's rocklike fidelity (or rocklike stubbornness?). Peter was the name by which Simon was known by the later Church. Paired with him is **Andrew his brother**, his partner in fishing—for men as well as for fish (4:18–19).

The next pair is **James the *son* of Zebedee, and John his brother**. They also were partners with Peter and Andrew (Luke 5:10). Along with Simon, James and John formed a special inner core within the Twelve (see 26:37).

Next were mentioned **Philip and Bartholomew**. Bartholomew is likely the Nathanael of John's Gospel. If this is so, Philip and Bartholomew were the Lord's disciples from the earliest days (John 1:43–45). It is possible that Nathanael was the name by which Bartholomew was known in the wider Church.

Thomas and Matthew the tax-collector are mentioned next. Matthew is certainly the name the tax-collector was known by in the wider Church, since even the Gospels of Mark and Luke (which refer to him as "Levi the tax-collector") call him Matthew in the listing of the Twelve (Mark 2:14; 3:38; Luke 5:27; 6:15).

James the *son* of Alphaeus, and Thaddaeus are listed next. Thaddaeus is called "Judas the son of James" in Luke 6:16. It is possible that Judas was his name and Thaddaeus his preferred nickname (from the Greek name Theudas?).

Finally come **Simon the Cananaen, and Judas Iscariot**. The term **Cananaen** is a transliteration of the Aramaic *Qanna*, or "zealous," and is translated in Luke 6:15 as "the Zealot." The Zealots were a group dedicated to the liberation of Israel by military means. It is possible that these last two are paired because Judas Iscariot had some sympathy for the Zealots, though this can be no more than a guess. Whatever Judas' other motivations may have been, he comes to be defined entirely by his final act of betrayal—he is mentioned simply as **the one who also delivered Him *up*.**

ॐ ॐ ॐ ॐ ॐ

5 These Twelve Jesus sent out, ordering them, saying, "Do not go in the way of the Gentiles, and do not enter into a city of the Samaritans;

6 "but rather go to the lost sheep of the house of Israel.

7 "And as you go, herald, saying, 'The Kingdom of the heavens draws near!'

8 "Heal the ailing, raise the dead, cleanse the lepers, cast out demons; freely you received, freely give.

9 "Do not acquire gold, or silver, or copper for your belts,

10 "or a bag for the way, or even two shirts, or sandals, or a staff, for the worker *is* worthy of his food.

11 "And into whatever city or village you enter, inquire who is worthy in it; and remain there until you go away.

12 "And as you enter into the house, greet it.

13 "And if indeed the house is worthy, let your

> peace come upon it; but if it is not worthy, let
> your peace return to you.
> 14 "And whoever does not welcome you, nor hear
>   your words, as you go outside of that house or
>   that city, shake out the dust of your feet.
> 15 "Amen I say to you, it will be more tolerable
>   for the land of Sodom and Gomorrah in the
>   day of judgment than for that city.

The Twelve are **sent out** to tour the cities and villages, and thus
expand their Lord's ministry of teaching and healing. The apostolic
ministry is not yet universal in scope. The Lord's first priority is to
reach **the lost sheep of the house of Israel** with the word of their
God's covenant faithfulness, and so the apostles must focus all their
energies on this work. To that end, they must **not go in the way
of the Gentiles** (such as those in the Decapolis), nor **enter into a
city of the Samaritans**. The work of reaching Israel is urgent and
requires all their time and energies.

This instruction is unique to Matthew's Gospel. It appears that
Matthew records it to show how Jesus completely fulfills the promises of God to His chosen people. Eventually the time will come for
God's Word to go forth to all the nations (28:19), but that time is
not yet. Matthew is concerned to stress that Jesus is no renegade,
but a true Jew and the fulfillment of all Israel's hopes.

As the apostles go, they are to **herald** the Good News that **the
Kingdom of the heavens draws near**. God promised long ago
through the prophets that He would come and redeem His people,
and that deliverance is now at hand. As a sign that it is drawing near,
the apostles are empowered and commanded to **heal the ailing** in
the cities to which they come, **raise** those newly **dead** whose families
have faith, **cleanse the lepers** who respond to them and **cast out
demons**. They are not to charge for this holy work. **Freely** they have
received the power to do this, **freely** they must **give** it in return.
They are not the source of this power, but merely its instruments.
They must not claim anything for themselves, nor try to enrich
themselves through its exercise.

By refusing to enrich themselves, they will add credibility to their message, for they obviously are but the instruments of a greater and divine Power. As they go from city to city, they must **not acquire gold, or silver, or** even **copper** (the smallest coins) **for** their money **belt** as payment for their services.

They must not travel burdened down with supplies by acquiring a beggar's **bag for the way** to collect money, nor **even** wear **two shirts** (the extra being used for camping outdoors). They must not acquire **sandals** as they journey, fearful that the thong of the sandals they are wearing might break and need a replacement, nor take an extra **staff** before they leave. (They are, however, to take what they have at hand at the time they are sent; Mark 6:8–9.) Rather, they are to leave immediately with what they have, confident that God will supply all their needs. He will make sure they have their **food**, and that is all they need. **The worker *is* worthy** of being thus supported by his employer and can expect no more.

Their instructions are as follows: **into whatever city or village** they **enter**, they must **inquire who is worthy in it**. By *worthy*, the Lord means those who prove their worthiness of the Kingdom by welcoming His messengers. The apostles must **enter into the house** of any who seem inclined to receive them, and **greet** those there with the customary greeting of *"Shalom!"* ("peace"). This is no empty formality, but an effective bestowal of God's peace and blessing on that home. If those there **indeed** are **worthy**, they will accept this blessing and welcome the apostles as Jesus' representatives, and so the apostles' **peace** will **come upon** that house. The apostles must **remain there** until they leave the place and not move from house to house, seeking more luxurious lodgings.

If those in the house do not welcome them warmly, but rather refuse them hospitality because they reject Jesus, the apostles' **peace** will **return** to them, and that house will know no blessing from God.

It is the same with the town as a whole. Those who do **not welcome** the apostles **nor hear** their **words** with an open heart are to be prophetically and publicly denounced. If any refuse to hear them, but instead order them off, the apostles are to **go outside of**

that house or that city and **shake out the dust of** their **feet.** Pious Jews returning to Israel would shake the pagan dust from their feet as they reentered the Holy Land, and the apostles are to do the same with those who reject them. Such a house or city is no better than the pagans and will meet the same fate. Indeed, a worse fate awaits them, for it will be **more tolerable for** the notoriously pagan **land of Sodom and Gomorrah in the day of judgment than for that city.** The apostles come bearing the very Word of God to Israel, and to reject them is to reject God Himself.

☘ ☘ ☘ ☘ ☘

16 "Behold, I *Myself* send you *yourselves* out as sheep in the middle of wolves; therefore be prudent as serpents and innocent as doves.

17 "But beware of men; for they will deliver you *up* to courts and scourge you in their synagogues;

18 "and you will be brought before governors and even kings for My sake, as a witness to them and to the Gentiles.

19 "But when they deliver you *up*, do not worry how or what you will speak; for it will be given to you in that hour what you are to speak,

20 "for it is not you who speak, but the Spirit of your Father speaking in you.

21 "And brother will deliver *up* brother to death, and a father his child; and children will rise up against parents, and *have them* put to death.

22 "And you will be hated by all because of My Name, but the one who has persevered to the end, this one will be saved.

23 "But whenever they persecute you in this city, flee to the other; for amen I say to you, you will never finish the cities of Israel until the Son of man comes.

In this discourse on the Church's mission, Matthew gathers together teaching that Christ spoke on other occasions as well, such as His Olivet Discourse (see Mark 13 and Luke 21). Matthew's aim is not chronological precision, but catechetical convenience—he wants to bring together into one place as much material about the Church's mission as he can, for use by the Church's scribes and teachers. Much of the following material therefore does not apply to the immediate mission of the Twelve, but to the Church's wider mission in the days and years following the Cross and Resurrection.

Matthew begins by recording a saying of Christ when He sent out the Seventy (Luke 10:3), though He may well have said it also when He sent out the Twelve: **"I *Myself* send you *yourselves* out as sheep in the middle of wolves; therefore be prudent as serpents and innocent as doves."** It is prefaced by **"behold"** to indicate that this is a surprise. It might be expected that ambassadors of Messiah will receive a warm welcome, but this is not to be. Christ is sending them into mortal danger. They must be **prudent** and crafty as the proverbial **serpent** (Gen. 3:1), without sacrificing their **innocent** and open hearts. (Innocence here does not mean naïveté, but rather harmlessness; the Twelve are not to let the opposition they encounter turn them bitter or revengeful.) They are to go into such danger knowing Christ has sent them (the pronouns **I** and **you** are emphatic in the Greek), and thus confident of their ultimate success.

In their apostolic mission, they must therefore **beware of men** and not take their assurances of support at face value. In the days to come, men **will deliver** them *up* **to courts** (lit., "sanhedrins"), **and scourge** them **in their synagogues** (compare Mark 13:9). They will **be brought before governors** (such as Pilate and his successor Felix) **and even kings** (such as the Emperor Nero). This was fulfilled in the decades following, when Jesus' followers were disciplined by the courts of the local synagogues for their supposed heresy by being beaten with the customary 39 lashes, and when men such as St. Paul were brought before the Roman authorities. These events are not to be dreaded, for they will provide an opportunity to **witness** to their Jewish countrymen about Jesus, **and to the Gentiles** also. It is through this suffering that the Message will be heard.

Therefore, the disciples must **not worry how or what** they **will speak** in their defense in that hour. They will not need worldly rhetoric, for they are Christ's prophets to the world (compare 23:34), and as such it will not be they who **speak, but the** prophetic **Spirit of** their **Father speaking** in His children. Let them calmly speak whatever they are given in that hour.

They should not imagine, however, that such assistance means they will avoid suffering. The days of the coming age will be times of eschatological stress, the long-expected birth pangs of the new age. Thus, **brother will deliver** *up* **brother to death, and a father his child; and children will rise up against parents and** *have them* **put to death**. The most sacred and unbreakable of bonds, those of family, will be strained and broken as men turn against even their own kin because their kin are Christian. In the coming persecution, the Faith will divide even families. Indeed, the disciples will **be hated** by all the world simply because of their allegiance to the **Name** of Jesus. But they must **persevere to the end** and not renounce that holy Name, for only by such endurance can they **be saved**.

After laying out the majestic sweep of the apostolic mission, St. Matthew returns to the immediate and local mission of the Twelve, with a saying not paralleled in Mark or Luke: **"Whenever they persecute you in this city, flee to the other; for amen I say to you, you will never finish** going through **the cities of Israel until the Son of man comes."**

The image of the Son of man coming is drawn from Dan. 7:13–14, where one like a son of man comes on the clouds of heaven and is presented to the Ancient of Days to receive a kingdom from Him. In the Gospels, this "coming" represents Christ openly receiving cosmic power and kingship from the Father, either at His Ascension (26:64) or at the Second Coming (24:3).

I would suggest that this "coming" refers to Christ's coming into His Kingdom at His Ascension. For the main thrust of this verse is not *Christ's Coming*, but *the apostles' need for haste*. That is, if they experience rejection and persecution during their immediate tour of Israel's cities, they should not stay and hope to win over their opponents. There is so much work to do that their mission is urgent (compare 9:37). If persecuted, they must simply flee to the next city and offer the Gospel there. Time is running out, for they will never finish reaching all in Israel before Christ's ministry is over, and He enters into His Kingdom after His arrest and crucifixion. And it happened as the Lord said: The work of preaching the Gospel to all in Israel was not completed when the Lord was arrested. The Church on the Day of Pentecost found that it still had work to do in Israel.

ॐ ॐ ॐ ॐ ॐ

24 "A disciple is not above his teacher, nor a slave above his lord.

25 "*It is* sufficient for the disciple that he become as his teacher, and the slave as his lord. If they have called the house-master Beelzebul, how much more his house-members!

26 "Therefore do not be afraid of them, for there is nothing covered that will not be revealed, and hidden that will not be known.

27 "What I say to you in the darkness, speak in the light; and what you hear *whispered* into the ear, herald upon the housetops.

28 "And do not be afraid of those who kill the body, but are not able to kill the soul; but rather be afraid of Him who is able to destroy both soul and body in Gehenna.

29 "Are not two sparrows sold for an assarion? And not one of them will fall upon the ground apart from your Father.

30 "But even the hairs of your head are all numbered.

31 "Therefore do not be afraid; you are more valuable *than* many sparrows.

32 "Everyone therefore who will confess Me before men, I *Myself* also will confess him before My Father in the heavens.

> 33 "But whoever will deny Me before men, I
> *Myself* also will deny him before My Father in
> the heavens.

St. Matthew returns to his practice of gathering material from a number of places into one discourse (such as the material found in Luke 12:1f; 12:51f; 9:18f; 14:25f; Mark 9:41). He begins with the Lord's oft-quoted saying, **"A disciple is not above his teacher, nor a slave above his lord"** (see Luke 6:40; John 13:16). Because of this self-evident truth, Jesus tells them, the disciples can expect at least the same persecution as their Lord received. If His foes persecuted Him, calling Him Beelzebul (that is, Satan), how much more will they persecute His followers? If a man does not scruple to insult **the house-master**, he will hardly scruple to insult **his house-members** and subordinates!

The disciples, then, must resolve **not** to **be afraid of them**. The worst their foes can do is to **kill the body**. Rather, let the disciples **be afraid** of God, the One who is **able to destroy both soul and body in Gehenna**. They have a choice of whose disapproval to fear the most—let them choose wisely and fear the disapproval of the final Judge.

They must therefore speak the truth, not fearing the slanders and lies of their opponents. On the last day, all the truth will come out and all secrets be revealed. There is **nothing covered** up that will **not be revealed** at that judgment. The Gospel must be fearlessly proclaimed to all—even as all the truth about the Gospel will later be revealed to all. The truth from Christ that they have heard privately they must **herald upon the housetops**.

It seems from Luke 12:1f that much of this teaching was given on another occasion, in connection with the hypocrisy of the Pharisees. In the Lukan passage, Christ speaks of *the fact* of the truth being openly proclaimed at the Last Judgment ("what you have spoken into the ear *will be* heralded upon the housetops"), while here in Matthew, Christ speaks of *the duty* of openly proclaiming the Gospel ("what you hear in the ear, *herald* upon the housetops"). The first is a statement; the second, a command. Assuming that Matthew

147

is using a source for this discourse, which is original? I would suggest that Luke's formulation is original, and that Matthew has here adapted it for his own didactic purposes. For Matthew, the fact of full disclosure of all truth at the end involves the necessity of the missionary Church acting a certain way now: because all truth will be spoken, we must now speak all the truth.

Christ then comforts the disciples. They all know the price of **sparrows**, sold as food to the very poor—**two** of them are **sold for an assarion**, which was one-sixteenth of a day's wage for the working man. A single sparrow, then, was incredibly cheap, and yet not even this **one** little bird will **fall upon the ground apart from** the will of their **Father**. If God's providential care extends even to such humble creatures, do the disciples of the Messiah think *their* lives will fall to the earth while their heavenly Father stands by, heedless of their suffering? God loves them so much that even **the hairs of** their **head** are all **numbered** by Him. He loves and cares for them down to the last hair.

They need not fear, therefore, but may boldly confess Jesus before men, whatever the cost. Such confessions may cost them their lives, but the stakes are worth it. For **everyone who confesses** Him **before** the jeering and hostile faces of **men** will be confessed in turn by the Messiah Himself (the pronoun **I** is emphatic) before a more august audience—the **Father in the heavens** Himself. And **whoever** bows to earthly fear and **denies** Him **before men** will later be denied by Christ in return on that final day.

ॐ ॐ ॐ ॐ ॐ

34 "Do not suppose that I came to cast peace upon the earth; I did not come to cast peace, but a sword.

35 "For I came to divide a man against his father, and a daughter against her mother, and a daughter-in-law against her mother-in-law;

36 "and the man's enemies will be his house-members.

37 "He who loves father or mother above Me is

> not worthy of Me; and he who loves son or
> daughter above Me is not worthy of Me.
> 38 "And he who does not take his cross and follow
> after Me is not worthy of Me.
> 39 "He who has found his life will lose it, and he
> who has lost his life for My sake will find it.

Christ then challenges His disciples to persevere in their mission. The disciples may suppose that the result of Messiah's coming is **to cast peace upon the earth**, so that all will be harmony and tranquility. In this age it is not to be so, but the result of Christ's coming is **a sword** of division. The truth He brings will separate the humble from the proud, those open to God from those opposed to Him. And it will divide even such formidable unities as the family, which normally nothing can divide.

Some in the family will accept Jesus as Messiah, while others will reject Him, so that **a man** will be **divided against his father**—a pair that usually stand together in close solidarity. **Daughter** will strive against **mother**, and **daughter-in-law** against **mother-in-law**, so that the household will teem with dissension, and **the man's enemies** would be **his house-members**, those closest to him.

The temptation in such situations is to choose family loyalty above loyalty to Christ—to love Christ, but to place that loyalty below family solidarity. The one who thus **loves father or mother above** Christ is rejected by Christ as **not worthy** of Him. Such a one cannot be Christ's disciple, and will be rejected by Him on the last day as an apostate. It is the same with the parent who **loves son or daughter above** Jesus, choosing the smiles of their child rather than the approval of God's Christ.

Such choices are considered by Christ as betrayals because they are but different ways of refusing to **take** the **cross and follow after** Him. This world offers joy, happiness, and fulfillment—but at a price. That price is the rejection of God's truth and the refusal to follow Christ when He calls. In a daring image, Jesus calls any who would inherit the Kingdom to **take his cross** and in this way **follow after** Him.

The image of one taking the cross was a familiar one to His hearers. They had all seen condemned criminals take up their crosses and carry them to the place of execution. To take up a cross was to count oneself as dead to this world. It is precisely this ruthless rejection of the world that Jesus demands of any who would be His disciple. The world, with its popularity, pleasures, and happiness—including the smiling approval of family members—must be rejected if it stands between the disciple and his Lord.

The one who chooses family over Christ may think that he **has found his life** and saved himself great distress. All is now peace at home! Parents, spouse, and children all hug him and congratulate him on making the right choice. But such a one **will lose** his true life and be rejected by God on the last day. It is the one who has **lost his life** for Jesus' sake, sacrificing earthly happiness and possibly even suffering martyrdom, who **will** truly **find it** and keep it to life eternal.

ॐ ॐ ॐ ॐ ॐ

40 "He who welcomes you welcomes Me, and he who welcomes Me welcomes Him who sent Me.

41 "He who welcomes a prophet for the name of a prophet will receive a prophet's reward; and he who welcomes a righteous *man* for the name of a righteous *man* will receive a righteous *man's* reward.

42 "And whoever *gives* to one of these little ones even a cup of cold water to drink for the name of a disciple, amen I say to you, he will never lose his reward."

St. Matthew concludes by recording some final encouraging words of Christ. The sacrifices referred to in verses 38–39 are worth it, for all work done for Christ will be abundantly rewarded. If one welcomes even the humblest of His disciples, it is as if such a one welcomes God Himself, for **he who welcomes** the disciple **welcomes**

Christ also, and the one who **welcomes** Christ **welcomes** the Father **who sent** Him. How could such a one not receive a great reward?

The disciples can know this from analogy. In the Old Testament, **he who welcomes a prophet for the name of a prophet** (that is, simply because that person is a prophet) **will receive a prophet's reward** (compare 1 Kings 17:9f; 2 Kings 4:9f, where those who welcomed Elijah and Elisha were abundantly rewarded). God will bless that person even as He blessed the prophet himself, simply because he welcomed the prophet. This is how God deals with those who welcome His saints.

Whoever then welcomes **one of these little ones**, the humblest of Jesus' disciples, simply because he bears **the name of** His **disciple** will **never lose his reward**. God will never forget to recompense the one who helps Jesus' disciple, even though that help be as little as **a cup of cold water**. All acts of kindness done to His disciples for His sake will have their eternal reward. How much more should the disciples themselves persevere in their faith and find their own reward?

ॐ ॐ ॐ ॐ ॐ

11 1   And it happened that when Jesus had finished ordering His twelve disciples, He moved on from there to teach and herald in their cities.

Matthew concludes the discourse, in which Jesus was **ordering His twelve disciples** prior to sending them out, by saying that Jesus then **moved on from there** to continue to **teach and herald in their cities**. The Lord did not cease His own labors after He sent out the Twelve. They did not work instead of Him, but alongside Him, both Jesus and His disciples doing the will of the Father.

❧ VI ❧

OPPOSITION TO CHRIST'S MINISTRY
(11:2—12:50)

§VI.1. The Doubts of John the Forerunner

> ❧ ❧ ❧ ❧ ❧
>
> **11** 2 Now when John in prison heard the works of Christ, he sent *a message* through his disciples
>
> 3 and said to Him, "Are You the Coming One, or will we expect another?"
>
> 4 And Jesus answered and said to them, "Go and declare to John what you hear and see:
>
> 5 "blind *people* see again, and lame *people* walk, lepers are cleansed and deaf *people* hear, and dead *people* are raised, and poor *people* have good news *brought to them.*
>
> 6 "And blessed is the one who does not stumble over Me."

St. Matthew begins this section describing the various forms of opposition to Christ with a story about a delegation sent by **John** the Baptizer **in prison**. The effects of dark confinement in the dungeon depths of the Machaerus fortress, east of the Dead Sea, have begun to tell on such a free spirit of the wilderness as John, and he begins to entertain doubts that Jesus is truly the Messiah. He has **heard** of **the works of Christ** and the rumors that He has done great wonders. John, suffering for His righteous stand against the sins of Herod, is impatient for Jesus to begin the messianic work of smiting such sinners—or at least of rebuking them. And instead of smiting notorious sinners, Jesus is eating and drinking with them! John's message, **"Are You the Coming One** (that is, the Messiah), **or will we expect another?"** is not so much a question as it is an anguished challenge from a suffering man, a call for Jesus to begin His work of messianic judgment.

John's disciples come to Jesus through the teeming crowds. Before reaching Him with their message, they wait and see all the miracles He does. Jesus' reply is not an argument about the nature of messiahship or the timing of the final judgment on sinners. It is a simple invitation for the messengers to **go and declare to John** what their own senses tell them: **blind** *people* **see again, and lame** *people* **walk, lepers are cleansed and deaf** *people* **hear, and dead** *people* **are raised, and** (as the climax of all His works) **poor** *people* **have good news** *brought to them*. The day of rescue for the down-trodden has come at last.

The Lord's words are drawn from the prophecies of Isaiah, 35:5 and 61:1. That is, Jesus is fulfilling the work the prophets said Messiah would do. Jesus does not need to defend Himself—His works, as fulfillments of ancient prophecy, are all the defense He needs.

And then Jesus adds a benediction, **"Blessed is the one who does not stumble over Me."** God will bless any who accept Jesus as He is, and do not stumble or reject Him because He does not meet their preconceived notions of what Messiah should do. This blessing is proffered to John as well as a hidden challenge. John has challenged Jesus to strike down the sinners; Jesus challenges him in return to open his mind to a wider conception of what Messiah is to do in this age.

ᠵ᠋ᢆᡉ ᠵ᠋ᢆᡉ ᠵ᠋ᢆᡉ ᠵ᠋ᢆᡉ ᠵ᠋ᢆᡉ

7   And as these were going, Jesus began to say to the crowds about John, "What did you go out into the wilderness to behold? A reed being shaken by the wind?

8   "But what did you go to see? A man clothed in soft *garments*? Behold, those wearing soft

garments are in the houses of the kings!

9 "But what did you go out to see? A prophet? Yes, I say to you, and more than a prophet.

10 "This is the one about whom it is written, 'Behold, I *Myself* send My messenger before Your face, who will prepare Your way before You.'

11 "Amen I say to you, among those born of women there has not arisen greater than John the Baptizer; yet the least in the Kingdom of the heavens is greater than he.

12 "And from the days of John the Baptizer until now, the Kingdom of the heavens *suffers* violence, and violent men snatch it.

13 "For all the prophets and the Law prophesied until John.

14 "And if you wish to welcome *it*, he himself is Elijah, the one about to come.

15 "He who has ears to hear, let him hear.

As the messengers are making their way back through the crowds, the crowds begin to debate about John and what his challenge to Jesus means. Does John's question to Jesus mean that John has fallen away, beaten down by his imprisonment? Herod is no friend of Jesus—is John starting to side with him? What will Jesus say about John, their former hero? Will Jesus denounce John for his seeming lack of support?

Jesus addresses these concerns immediately and has nothing but praise for John. Some may think that John has been worn down by his imprisonment and is vacillating, giving in to Herod like any one of Herod's flattering courtiers. Christ rejects such an idea. That is not the John they all know. **What did** they **go out into the wilderness to behold** at the beginning? Did they go to gawk at **a reed being shaken by the wind** (such as are common in the wilderness)? All can see that John is no such insubstantial reed, blown about by winds of popularity, but a man of principle, moved by no one's threats.

Christ continues His rhetorical questions as He defends His Forerunner. If not to see a reed, **what did** they **go out to see?** Perhaps **a man clothed in soft** *garments***?** Did they come all that way to admire a courtier in all his finery? Obviously not, for **those wearing soft** *garments* **are in the houses of the kings**, not in the wilderness.

So then, **what did** they **go out to see?** Perhaps in response, someone from the crowd shouts back, "A prophet!" and Jesus immediately says, "Yes, a prophet indeed—**and more than a prophet.** For John is **the one about whom it is written** by the prophets themselves, '**Behold, I** *Myself* **send My messenger before Your face, who will prepare Your way before You**'" (Mal. 3:1). John is the very Forerunner of the Messiah, the harbinger of the Kingdom of God spoken of by all the prophets that were before him.

John's significance can be measured by the greatness of the Kingdom he announces. That Kingdom is so great that, great as John is (and **among those born of women there has not arisen greater than John**), the very **least in the Kingdom is greater than he.** The greatness of the Kingdom of which he is harbinger reveals John to be greater than all the prophets.

John, in fact, is pivotal, for with his ministry the entire Old Testament era came to an end. Since **John the Baptizer** began to preach even **until now, the Kingdom** *suffers* **violence.** That is, sinners are responding to the Kingdom's call with the enthusiasm of **violent men** storming a city to **snatch** its plunder, and a host of impious people, including tax-collectors and prostitutes, are crowding into it (21:32). **All the prophets**, and indeed, the whole era of **the Law, prophesied until John.** In those previous times, there was no place for such sinners, no amnesty for the guilty, no overflowing grace. Now that era is passing, and the era of the Kingdom is at hand; and it is as if the Kingdom is being overwhelmed with the flood of sinners forcing their way into it.

The Jews of that time thought that the prophet Elijah would appear before the advent of the Kingdom (Mal. 4:5–6). Christ says that if His hearers **wish to welcome** and accept such a revolutionary idea, John himself is **Elijah, the one about to come.** Though

John is not Elijah personally, he fulfills the prophecies about Elijah's return (see Luke 1:17), and Israel should not look for any further prophetic activity to precede the Kingdom. John, though languishing in prison, has been mighty Elijah heralding the Kingdom of God. His work fulfilled all that was to precede the Kingdom, and that Kingdom has now arrived.

ॐ ॐ ॐ ॐ ॐ

16 "But to what will I liken this generation? It is like children sitting in the marketplace who call out to the others

17 "and say, 'We played *the flute* for you, and you did not dance! We bewailed, and you did not lament!'

18 "For John came neither eating nor drinking, and they say, 'He has a demon!'

19 "The Son of man came eating and drinking, and they say, 'Behold, a man *who is* a glutton and a wine-drinker! A friend of tax-collectors and sinners!' And *yet* wisdom is justified by her works."

The men of that **generation** cannot see John's significance, just as they cannot see the significance of Christ. They are, Jesus says, like **children sitting in the marketplace who call out to the others** there. Everyone has seen children playing their games in the public square. Jesus pictures one group of children wanting to play "wedding," and so pretending to **play** *the flute* for the other group of children (for flutes were played at weddings). The other children refuse to follow their orders and so do **not dance**. Then those of the first group change their minds and instead decide to play "funeral," pretending to **bewail** a funeral lament. Their playmates opposite do not follow this lead either, provoking the whining complaint that they **did not lament**.

Those who reject John and Jesus are just like those complaining children. **John came** as a true ascetic of the desert, **neither eating**

nor drinking at banquets and suppers. They wanted John to dance to their tune of feasting and flute-playing, but he would not. They denounced him, crying out, **"He has a demon!"** Such desert asceticism proves he is mad!

One would think they would like Jesus then, for **the Son of man came eating and drinking** (as John did not). But Him they denounce too, crying out, **"Behold, a man** *who is* **a glutton and a wine-drinker! A friend of** notorious **tax-collectors and sinners!"** With childish perversity they denounce both John because he did not eat, and Jesus because He does.

Nevertheless, Jesus says, **wisdom is justified by her works.** All who are truly wise acknowledge wisdom when they see it, and will recognize the divine wisdom in both John and Jesus when they see wisdom's works in them.

§VI.2. The Proud Who Reject Jesus

§VI.2.i. The Proud Cities

ॐ ॐ ॐ ॐ ॐ

20 Then He began to reproach the cities in which most of His *works of* power were done, because they did not repent.

21 "Woe to you, Chorazin! Woe to you, Bethsaida! For if the *works of* power had happened in Tyre and Sidon which happened in you, they would have repented long ago in sackcloth and ashes.

22 "But I say to you, it will be more tolerable for Tyre and Sidon in the day of judgment than for you.

23 "And you, Capernaum—will you be exalted to heaven? You will descend to Hades! For if the *works of* power had happened in Sodom which happened in you, it would have remained until today.

> **24** "But I say to you that it will be more tolerable
> for the land of Sodom in the day of judgment
> than for you."

St. Matthew then records Christ's denunciation of the **cities in which most of His *works of* power were done**. These lamentations over the hard hearts of those cities were made toward the end of Christ's work in Galilee, as He sent out the Seventy for another tour (Luke 10:1f). Matthew records those words here as a part of his thematic collection in 11:2—12:50 of stories of opposition to Christ.

At the time of Christ's denunciations, He had spent a lot of time in Galilean cities, healing and manifesting His messianic glory, and still most of the population there rejected Him and **did not repent**. Christ therefore pronounces **woe** upon the town of **Chorazin** (modern Kerazeh, two miles northeast of Capernaum), as well as upon **Bethsaida**, a town a little to the east of Chorazin. Divine judgment awaits those cities on **the day of judgment**, for the many *works of power* they have seen leave them with no excuse for their impenitent hearts. Indeed, if those same miracles had **happened in Tyre and Sidon** (proverbial for their pride; see Is. 23; Ezek. 28), even those callous cities **would have repented long ago in sackcloth and ashes**, imploring God's mercy. Thus it will be **more tolerable** even **for Tyre and Sidon** than for the cities of Galilee.

With withering scorn, Jesus turns on His own **Capernaum**, which He has made His base of operations. Do they think they will be **exalted to heaven** because He has made His residence there? They will **descend to Hades**, awaiting in the land of the dead God's final wrath. Like the ancient king of Babylon who thought he would be exalted to heaven and instead was brought low to Hades (Is. 14:13–15, 23), so Capernaum will know the judgment of God. This is just, for if the miracles they have experienced **had happened in** sinful **Sodom** (Gen. 19), even that abominable city would have repented and been spared so that **it would have remained**, even until that present day. The fiery wrath awaiting those of Capernaum is so terrible that **it will be more tolerable** even **for the land of Sodom** than for them.

§VI.2.ii. The Babes Who Find Christ

ॐ ॐ ॐ ॐ ॐ

25 At that time Jesus answered and said, "I praise You, O Father, Lord of heaven and earth, that You hid these *things* from the wise and insightful and revealed them to babes.

26 "Yes, Father, for thus it was well-pleasing in Your sight.

27 "All things have been delivered to Me by My Father; and no one really-knows the Son, but the Father; nor does anyone really-know the Father, but the Son, and anyone to whom the Son intends to reveal *Him*.

28 "Come to Me, all those who toil and are loaded-*down*; and I will *give* you rest.

29 "Take My yoke upon you and learn from Me, for I am meek and humble in heart, and you will find rest for your souls.

30 "For My yoke *is* kind, and My load is light."

As the counterpoint to the pride of those rejecting Jesus, Matthew next records Christ's exultation in those humble ones who accept Him. (The prayer dates from the time after the Seventy had returned; Luke 10:17f.)

In His prayer, Jesus shows that He is not discouraged that so many reject Him. Rather, He rejoices in the plan of God, confessing His wisdom (the verb rendered *praise* is the Greek *exomologeo*, often rendered "confess"). Christ rejoices that His **Father**, the sovereign **Lord of heaven and earth**, the One who uses all things to fulfill His will, has chosen that the truth about Christ be **hidden from the wise and insightful**, from the self-important and sophisticated, and be **revealed** only **to babes**. Thus the truth can be known by anyone, be they ever so slow and uneducated, so long as they come with humble and trusting hearts. This is God's plan, **well-pleasing**

in His **sight**—to make the riches of His Kingdom available to all who seek in humility.

Thus **all things have been delivered** to Christ **by** His **Father**, so that Christ can offer salvation to all who come to Him. As the saving Messiah, Jesus is exalted over all, and **no one really-knows** Him **but the Father** whose fullness He is. Those of Capernaum may *claim* to know Him and reject Him because of His humble origin (compare 13:54–57), but they do not truly know Him. In the same way, those who reject Him may *claim* to **really-know the Father**, but no one has true and personal knowledge of the Father's fullness **but the Son—and anyone to whom the Son intends to reveal Him**. Jesus, as the true Messiah and the fullness of the Father, can give knowledge of God to His disciples.

Because of Christ's ability to reveal the Father and to bestow salvation on any who become His disciples, He invites **all those who toil and are loaded-*down*** to **come** to Him and become His disciples rather than disciples of the Pharisees. The common man, when he looked to the Pharisees for knowledge of God, found only a burden impossible to carry (Luke 11:46). Those who **toil** and are weary, those who are **loaded-*down*** and stagger under their burdens, should leave off following the Pharisees and accept Jesus' interpretation of the Law instead. Jesus will **give** them **rest** and refresh them (Gr. *anapauo*, a verb meaning both "to rest and refresh," "to revive and give renewed strength").

The yoke of the Pharisees and the lawyers (that is, their interpretations of the Law) is hard to bear; Jesus' **yoke *is* kind** and easy to bear (the word rendered *kind* is the Gr. *chrestos*; compare the cognate noun in Rom. 2:4). His **load is light**, for He interprets the Law truly and does not load men down with burdens God never expected His children to bear. If they will **learn from** Him what God truly wants, they will **find rest** and refreshment (Gr. *anapausis*) **for** their **souls**. Unlike the proud Pharisees, Christ is **meek and humble in heart**, and as such He knows that salvation comes by taking only the loads the Father truly lays upon one, not in exalting oneself and pretending to be stronger than one is.

§VI.3. Conflict with Pharisees over the Sabbath

§VI.3.i. Picking Grain in the Fields

12 1 At that time Jesus went on *one of* the Sabbaths through the grainfields, and His disciples were hungry and began to pick the heads and to eat.

2 But when the Pharisees saw *it,* they said to Him, "Behold, Your disciples are doing what is not permitted to do on a Sabbath!"

3 But He said to them, "Have you not read what David did, when he was hungry, he and the ones with him;

4 "how he entered the House of God, and they ate the Bread of the Presentation, which was not permitted for him to eat, nor for the ones with him, but for the priests alone?

5 "Or have you not read in the Law that on the Sabbaths the priests in the Temple profane the Sabbath and are guiltless?

6 "But I say to you that *something* greater than the Temple is here.

7 "But if you had known what this is, 'I want mercy, and not sacrifice,' you would not have sentenced *as guilty* the guiltless.

8 "For the Son of man is Lord of the Sabbath."

Matthew then records a series of conflicts with the Pharisees. One of them involves a time when Jesus and His disciples **went on *one of* the Sabbaths through the grainfields**. Jesus' disciples were hungry and **began to pick the heads** of ripened grain **and to eat** them. That is, they plucked the heads, rubbed them in their palms, and blew away the chaff, eating the grain that remained in their hands. Such eating was specifically allowed by the Law (Deut. 23:25). Because this occurred on one of the Sabbaths, however, the Pharisees could see only violations of the Law. As far as they were concerned, by picking the grain, the disciples were harvesting; by rubbing it in their hands, they were threshing; and by blowing away the chaff, they were winnowing. God's Law did indeed forbid work on the Sabbath, but the Pharisees had defined work in such a way as to empty the Law of common sense.

They cannot see the great task the disciples are engaged in as they serve Jesus, nor the legitimacy of satisfying hunger as they perform this task. With all the passion of righteous indignation, they cry out to Jesus, **"Behold, Your disciples are doing what is not permitted to do on a Sabbath!"** (One imagines they are secretly delighted at finding this accusation to hurl at Jesus.)

Jesus responds by referring to the Scriptures, for they contain examples of men doing what is not technically permitted in order to meet human need, and show how keeping the Sabbath is subordinated to other worthy tasks.

Thus Jesus refers to **what David did, when he was hungry, he and the ones with him; how he entered the House of God, and they ate the Bread of the Presentation** (1 Sam. 21). This **Bread of the Presentation** was the twelve loaves of the showbread which were set out in the Holy Place, and which were, technically, not to be eaten by any **but the priests alone**. In all the Pharisees' study of the Law, **have** they **not read** that? David's hunger came before cultic details, which were to give way before human need. If David's men when in distress could eat the priestly showbread (though this was not technically permitted), how much more may the disciples of Christ, when too busy to stop for a meal, eat a few grains of wheat on the Sabbath?

Resting on the Sabbath is not the highest goal of the Law. Have not the Pharisees, for all their vaunted learning, **read in the Law that on the Sabbaths the priests in the Temple** work hard at their priestly duties, doing work which if they were not priests would **profane the Sabbath**? Yet all acknowledge that those priests are **guiltless** despite their work on the Sabbath. Obviously then, resting on the Sabbath is not an end in itself (as the Pharisees seem to imagine), but is subordinated to other worthy tasks. If the priests are guiltless because they serve the Temple, how much more guiltless are those who are serving Jesus, for His ministry is **something greater than the Temple**.

Once again (compare 9:13) they fail to understand what God really wants. If the Pharisees understood the citation from Hosea 6:6, **"I want mercy, and not sacrifice,"** they would **not have sentenced as guilty the guiltless** disciples. For this Scripture reveals that cultic rules (such as sacrifices and Sabbaths) are not ends in themselves. Rather, they point to what God really wants: mercy, devotion, and a tender heart.

As it is, the Sabbath is a means to an end, that end being the salvation of man. And because Jesus is the messianic **Son of man** and the Lord of men, He is also **Lord of the Sabbath**. That is, He has the authority to declare what is and is not allowed regarding it. Eating a few grains of wheat when hungry and rushed because of service to Messiah is allowed.

§VI.3.ii. Healing in the Synagogue

ॐ ॐ ॐ ॐ ॐ

9 And moving on from there, He came into their synagogue.

10 And behold! a man having a withered hand. And they asked Him, saying, "Is it permitted to heal on the Sabbaths?"—that they might accuse Him.

11 And He said to them, "What man will there be among you who will have one sheep, and if this *sheep* falls into a pit on the Sabbaths, will not seize it, and raise *it* up?

12 "How much more valuable therefore is a man than a sheep! So then, it is permitted to do good on the Sabbaths."

13 Then He says to the man, "Stretch out your

> hand!" And he stretched *it* out, and it was
> restored to health, like the other.
> 14 But the Pharisees went out and took counsel
> against Him, how they might destroy Him.

After this, Jesus **came into their synagogue**, probably the one in Capernaum, for the usual Sabbath service. **Behold** (Matthew's use of his favorite word indicates an unexpected event)—**a man having a withered hand**! The man seemed to have been known to the locals, perhaps because he had told them of his desire for Jesus to heal him. The man's presence in the synagogue was a standing invitation to heal him. We may think that the man never took his eyes off Jesus the whole time, but waited for Jesus to notice him and his need.

Others there noticed the man too, and could guess what Jesus' reaction would be. **They asked Him** (ostensibly asking a rabbi for a legal ruling, but actually **that they might accuse Him**), **"Is it permitted to heal on the Sabbaths?"** For the Pharisees who asked the question, the answer was self-evident: It was certainly not permitted to do anything of the kind.

They have asked for a legal ruling about what the Law permits, and Jesus obliges them, hoping to lead them to the truth. He asks them in return, **"What man will there be among you who will have one sheep, and if this *sheep* falls into a pit on the Sabbaths, will not seize it, and raise *it* up** out of the pit?" None of those present would let the sheep stay in the pit throughout the Sabbath and only rescue it the next day. Yet **how much more valuable is a man than a sheep**! The answer to their question is obvious: **it is permitted to do good on the Sabbaths**—both the rescuing of a sheep from a pit and that of a man from his suffering.

The crowd, as we learn from the parallel in Mark 3:4, was silent. Though they could not refute Christ's word, they refused to be taught. Jesus turned from them to deal with the man. He ordered him, **"Stretch out your hand!"** and **he stretched *it* out** and found that **it was restored to health, like the other**. Such a miracle should have been a cause of rejoicing for all. It was a sign of how great their blindness was that **the Pharisees went out and**

took counsel against Jesus, **how they might destroy Him**. Instead of the mighty acts of God, the Pharisees could see only violation of the Law. They projected the darkness within them onto Christ, and so could see only sin.

ॐ ॐ ॐ ॐ ॐ

15 But Jesus, knowing *this*, withdrew from there. And many followed Him, and He healed them all,

16 and warned them not to make Him manifest,

17 that what was spoken through Isaiah the prophet might be fulfilled, saying,

18 "Behold, My Servant whom I have chosen; My Beloved in whom My soul is well-pleased! I will put My Spirit upon Him, and He will declare judgment to the nations.

19 "He will not wrangle, nor clamor, nor will anyone in the streets hear His voice.

20 "A broken reed He will not crack, and a smoldering wick He will not quench, until He brings judgment to victory,

21 "and in His Name the nations will hope."

Jesus, knowing their plots, **withdrew from there**, for He had no interest in reckless and fruitless conflict for conflict's sake. **Many** sick **followed Him,** as He moved on, **and He healed them all**. He did not, however, tell them to make known abroad His miracles, nor did He seek to capitalize on the publicity. Rather, He **warned them not to make Him manifest** (compare 9:30), lest such reports inflame the crowds with messianic enthusiasm and they seek by force to make Him an earthly king (compare John 6:15).

For Matthew, this reluctance of Jesus to publicize and promote Himself was another fulfillment of prophecy, another proof that Jesus was indeed the Messiah. God had spoken **through Isaiah the prophet** (Is. 42:1–4) about His **Servant**, His **Beloved** whom He would protect and prosper. God promised that He would **put**

His **Spirit upon Him** so that **He** would **declare judgment to the nations**.

This prophecy is one of a series of Servant Songs in Isaiah (others are found in Is. 49:1–7; 50:4–11; 52:13—53:12). In its original context, this Servant of 42:1 was the king of the restored Israel. Unlike other kings of the world who ruled by violence and threatening, this king would be humble and meek. The kings who ruled before him were like men who **wrangle** and argue, **clamoring** and bellowing **in the streets**, picking fights with all around them. This King would be different. He would not be bellicose and provocative, but a man of peace. He would **not crack** off the **reed** which had been **broken**, but would straighten and try to restore it. The lamp **wick** which was **smoldering** and about to go out he would **not quench** and snuff out, but trim, set in oil, and try to keep burning. That is, he would gently try to care for the battered and nurse along the processes of peace. All the nations would not cower before him as before a tyrannical conqueror. Instead they would follow him willingly, trusting in his wisdom.

This prophecy was acknowledged by all of Jesus' contemporaries to refer to the Messiah. Matthew recognized that its description of the peaceable king found its fulfillment in Jesus, who refused to trumpet abroad His miracles lest He be taken for a military and warlike king. Like the king in the prophecy who refused to let anyone hear his threatening voice, but who trusted in God for victory, so Jesus refused to loudly promote Himself through His miracles, but trusted in His Father. In the prophetic mention of the nations (vv. 18, 21), St. Matthew means his readers to discern the Church's future ministry to Gentiles.

❦ EXCURSUS
On Zionism

The prophecy of Isaiah 42 about Israel's king was fulfilled in Christ and His Church, and in this it is typical of all the Old Testament passages about the Kingdom of God.

However, within the last century or so, a school of

---

thought has arisen (sometimes called "Dispensationalism") which sees the Old Testament prophecies of Israel's restoration fulfilled in the creation of the modern State of Israel. For this school, the "Israel" in the Old Testament prophecies refers to the Jews generally and the Zionist state in particular. Thus, when the prophets declare that Israel will return to the land (e.g. Ezek. 36:24f), this is said to have its final fulfillment not so much in the return from Babylon after the Exile as in the return of Jews to Palestine following 1948. When the prophet says that "the desert will rejoice and blossom" (Is. 35:1f), this again is referred to the irrigation projects in the Zionist state. In this scheme, the prophecy of Isaiah 42 finding fulfillment in Christ is an exception to the rule, for the Old Testament prophecies of Israel's blessing usually have nothing to do with faith in Jesus. What are Orthodox Christians to make of this new school of interpretation?

Whatever one's sympathy for the State of Israel, it must be recognized that this school of interpretation is in flat contradiction to the apostolic view of the Old Testament prophecies. Each and every time the Old Testament prophecies are quoted by the apostles, it is in connection with Christ and His Church. Thus, the prophecies of Israel being blessed are fulfilled in those Jews who accept Jesus as Messiah; the Jews who do not accept Him are not part of blessed Israel, but are considered as apostate (see Rom. 9:6). The Church, being that part of Israel which accepts the Messiah, is the true Israel (compare Gal. 6:16; Eph. 2:12), and all the Old Testament oracles that predict Israel's restoration are fulfilled spiritually in the Church.

§VI.4. Conflict with the Pharisees—Satan Casts Out Satan?

ॐ ॐ ॐ ॐ ॐ

22 Then there was brought to Him a demon-possessed *man*, blind and mute, and He healed

him, so that the mute *man was able* to speak and see.

23 And all the crowds were beside *themselves* and were saying, "Can this *one* be the Son of David?"

24 But when the Pharisees heard *this*, they said, "This one does not cast out demons but by Beelzebul, the ruler of the demons."

25 And knowing their thoughts, He said to them, "Every kingdom divided-up against itself is desolated; and every city or house divided-up against itself will not stand.

26 "And if Satan casts out Satan, he is divided-up against himself; how therefore will his kingdom stand?

27 "And if I *Myself* by Beelzebul cast out the demons, by whom do your sons cast *them* out? Therefore they *themselves* will be your judges.

28 "But if by the Spirit of God I *Myself* cast out the demons, then the Kingdom of God has reached you.

Next Matthew relates the story of a sensational exorcism and the controversy it brought. A man was brought to Jesus who was **demon-possessed**. The man was evidently well known as a hopeless case whose plight was made all the more pathetic in that his affliction involved him being both **blind and mute**. The Lord **healed him, so that the mute *man was able* to speak and see.** When **the crowds** around the man heard him crying out with joy and looking at all of them with new eyes, they **were beside *themselves*** with amazement. Some even began to wonder if **this *one*** who healed the man could possibly be the messianic **Son of David**, unlikely as it seemed. (The Greek indicates that a negative answer to the question is expected.) Certainly none of them had seen anything like this!

The Pharisees in the crowd, however, were dismissive. When they heard the crowd's wondering if Jesus were the Messiah, they said, **"This one does not cast out demons but by Beelzebul, the ruler of the demons."** They did not deny that a demon had been cast out, but they attributed Jesus' power to Satan. (The title **Beelzebul** originally derived from the Heb. *baal zebul*, "lord of the house," referring to the pagan god Baal. The title was later transformed into the derisive *baal zebub*, "lord of the flies," in 2 Kings 1:2, and at the time of Jesus it was used as a title for Satan.)

Jesus responds to them by showing the absurdity of the notion that He is in collusion with Satan, for it would mean there was a civil war in Satan's realm, with Jesus forming a kind of rebel force against His former master. This is manifest nonsense, for everyone knows that **every kingdom divided-up against itself is desolated.** No kingdom can survive civil war. Indeed, even a **city or** a **house** or family cannot stand if it is thus divided. Their suggestion that there is a civil war in the devil's realm would mean that **Satan** was **divided-up against himself** so that his **kingdom** could not **stand.** Alas, such is not the case, for Satan is as active as ever. Obviously, then, Satan is not being menaced *from within*, but *from without*. Besides, if Jesus is **casting out the demons** through the power of Satan, **by whom do** their **sons**, the Jewish exorcists of that day, **cast them** out? The examples of those Jewish exorcists prove that Jesus' exorcisms are done through divine power, for exorcism by its very nature constitutes a violent attack on Satan *from without*.

Indeed, Jesus' exorcisms, done not with long prayers and invocations (like those of the Jewish exorcists) but with a simple word of command and by **the Spirit of God**, prove that **the Kingdom of God has reached** them.

ॐ ॐ ॐ ॐ ॐ

29 "Or how is anyone able to enter into the strong *one's* house and snatch his possessions, unless he first binds the strong *one*? And then he will rob his house.

30 "He who is not with Me is against Me; and

> he who does not gather with Me scatters.
> 31 "Therefore I say to you, any sin and blasphemy will be forgiven men, but blasphemy against the Spirit will not be forgiven.
> 32 "And whoever will speak a word against the Son of man, it will be forgiven him; but whoever will speak against the Holy Spirit, it will not be forgiven him, either in this age or in the coming one.

To make this clearer still, Jesus tells a parable about a home invasion. Surely all know that a would-be robber cannot just **enter into the strong *one's* house** and plunder the well-armed man at will. The robber must **first bind the strong *one***, and only **then** can he **rob his house**. In the same way, Satan is strong and capable of keeping his demon-possessed prey captive and secure. Christ is only able to plunder Satan of his prey and liberate the demon-possessed because He has first overpowered Satan by the power of the divine Spirit.

In this matter, no neutrality is possible. One must side *with* Jesus (considering that His exorcisms are done with divine power) or *against* Him (considering Him a demonic deceiver). **He who is not with** Jesus is thus **against** Him, and if one does **not gather** other supporters as His disciple, then one is thereby **scattering**. The issue of by whom He casts out demons makes the matter of loyalty acute.

Christ sums up the issue. **Any sin and blasphemy** can be **forgiven men**, but **blasphemy against the Spirit** (such as the Pharisees are committing) will **not be forgiven**. That is, if one repents of one's sins, however heinous these sins might be, one can be forgiven. To **speak a word against the Son of man** thus can be forgiven. To opine that Jesus should not eat and drink with sinners, or that He should not heal on the Sabbath, though wrong, is forgivable. But to ascribe His exorcisms and power to the devil, and thus to **speak against the Holy Spirit**, is different. This sin can **not be forgiven, either in this age or in the coming one**, for only repentance and faith in Jesus as Messiah can cleanse it away, and as long as they reject Jesus, they can never know this forgiveness.

ॐ ॐ ॐ ॐ ॐ

33 "Either make the tree fine, and its fruit *will be* fine; or make the tree decayed, and its fruit *will be* decayed; for by its fruit the tree is known.

34 "Offspring of vipers, how are you able to speak good things, being evil? For the mouth speaks from the abundance of the heart.

35 "The good man from his good treasure brings what is good; and the evil man from his evil treasure brings what is evil.

This accusation made the choice between Christ and the Pharisees stark and inevitable. To help clarify the choice before His hearers, Christ offers the parables of the two trees and of the two treasures.

A **fine tree** produces **fine fruit**, and a **decayed tree**, eaten by disease and insects, produces **decayed fruit**. The kind of fruit gathered reveals the inner state of the tree that produced it. The Pharisees' teaching produces joyless censoriousness; Jesus' teaching and works produce joy and freedom. Obviously the Pharisees are but decayed trees, diseased and dying within, an **offspring of vipers**. How can they **speak good things** and have a true estimate of Jesus, since they are **evil**? For **the mouth speaks from the abundance of the heart**, and their heart is filled with error and blindness. How can one hope to find a sound judgment about Jesus' miracles from them?

The Pharisees have only **evil treasure** to dispense. In this second parable, Christ presents the image of two men storing up loads of different things: **The good man** stores up **good treasure** in his house, items of worth and value. **The evil man** stores up **evil treasure**, garbage and worthless junk. What each has to give reveals his inner character, for a man collects what he regards as valuable. The blindness of the Pharisees' accusations reveals how blind and worthless they really are. Let the wise man not choose them as guides for life!

🙐 🙐 🙐 🙐 🙐

36 "And I say to you that every idle word that men
will speak, they will render an account about
it in the day of judgment;

37 "For by your words you will be justified, and by
your words you will be sentenced *as guilty*."

Christ has a final warning to give. In accusing Jesus, the Pharisees
uttered hasty words—words that are **idle**. The word translated *idle*
is the Greek *argos*, meaning "unworking" (compare its use in 20:3).
The thought here is of words that are carelessly spontaneous, coming straight from the heart without any prior thought. For all such
utterances men will **render an account in the day of judgment**,
for they reveal the true state of the heart and one's inmost attitudes.
Thus **by our words** we **will be justified** and acquitted on the last
day, and by them we **will be sentenced** *as guilty*. The lesson is not
to refuse to utter idle words (for we cannot but speak spontane-
ously), but to keep our hearts pure, so that our spontaneous words
will show we are God's true children. Only thus will we be justified
and forgiven on the last day.

§VI.5. Conflict with the Pharisees—Seeking Signs

🙐 🙐 🙐 🙐 🙐

38 Then some of the scribes and Pharisees
answered Him, saying, "Teacher, we want to
see a sign from You."

39 But He answered and said to them, "An evil
and adulterous generation seeks after a sign,
and a sign will not be given to it but *only* the
sign of Jonah the prophet.

40 "For just as Jonah was three days and three
nights in the belly of the sea-monster, thus will
the Son of man be three days and three nights
in the heart of the earth.

> 41 "The men of Nineveh will stand up with this generation at the judgment and will condemn it, because they repented at the heralding of Jonah, and behold! *something* more than Jonah is here.
>
> 42 "The Queen of the South will be raised with this generation at the judgment and will condemn it, because she came from the ends of the earth to hear the wisdom of Solomon, and behold! *something* more than Solomon is here.

Then **some of the scribes and Pharisees answered** His reply about the impossibility of Satan casting out Satan (v. 25f) with a further challenge. They considered that the question of the source of His exorcistic power could only be settled by a further miracle. If Jesus was casting out demons by divine power, let Him produce another **sign**, such as an audible voice from heaven, identifying Him as a true prophet. *This* they would accept as proof of His divine mission—but nothing less!

This desire for such a sign (after all the other miracles He had done) was evidence that they were **an evil and adulterous generation**, one that was unfaithful to God in their hearts. They were unworthy of hearing God's voice, and so a **sign would not be given**. The only sign authenticating Christ's work would be **the sign of Jonah**—that of His Resurrection from the dead after three days. In the biblical story (Jon. 1—3), Jonah emerged from **the belly of the sea-monster** after three days to preach to the men of Nineveh, and Christ would likewise emerge from **the heart of the earth** after three days. (The chronological parallelism is only approximate, for Christ did not actually remain in the tomb three days and nights. He was buried on a Friday night and rose early Sunday morning, after two nights. The parallel is built on the fact that Christ arose after three days by Hebrew reckoning, which counts part of a day as a whole day.)

To say that the Resurrection was their sign was, of course, to offer no sign at all, for the Pharisees were demanding a *public* spectacle, which was explicitly denied. The Resurrection itself was seen by none, and the risen Christ appeared only privately to His own. At the time Christ spoke these words to the Pharisees, we may think His hearers did not understand their significance. It was only after the Resurrection that the Church could see the aptness of the image.

The hardness of heart on the part of that generation was unparalleled in the history of Israel. In the Jonah story, the men of Nineveh **repented at the heralding of Jonah** and his work (Jon. 3), but Jesus' generation would not repent at His preaching, although it was *something* **more than Jonah.** Thus **the men of Nineveh will stand up with** Jesus' **generation at the** final **judgment and condemn it.** Their example of repentance will show up the sinful impenitence of Jesus' audience for what it is.

It is the same with **the Queen of the South.** She **came from the ends of the earth to hear the wisdom of Solomon,** recognizing his wisdom for what it was (1 Kings 10). Assuming she came from southwestern Arabia, she made a journey of twelve hundred miles to hear the king of Israel. Jesus' hearers, however, could not recognize His message as divine wisdom, even though this was *something* **more than Solomon** and his wisdom. Thus the pagan queen **will be raised with this generation at the judgment and will condemn it.** Her recognition of Solomon's greatness will provide the yardstick against which the faithless people of Christ's generation will be measured and condemned.

꙳ꙮ ꙳ꙮ ꙳ꙮ ꙳ꙮ ꙳ꙮ

43 "Now when the unclean spirit goes out from the man, it goes through waterless places seeking rest, and does not find *it.*

44 "Then it says, 'I will return to my house from which I came out'; and when it comes, it finds it unoccupied, swept and adorned.

45 "Then it goes and takes along with itself seven other spirits more evil than itself, and they enter in and dwell there, and the last *state* of

---

> that man becomes worse than the first. Thus it will also be with this evil generation."

Christ then tells a parable to illustrate the peril of that **evil generation** if they persist in their unbelief. In the parable, a man experiences an exorcism. After the **unclean spirit** has been cast out, **it goes through waterless places seeking rest, and does not find it**. Despite its wandering through the desert, it finds no other victim to inhabit. Then it says, **"I will return to my house from which I came out,"** its former victim, and when it returns, **it finds** its former dwelling **unoccupied, swept and adorned**. A perfect place to which to return! It then gleefully goes and **takes along with itself seven other spirits more evil than itself, and they enter in and dwell there, and the last** *state* **of that man becomes worse than the first**. Better the poor wretch had never been exorcised in the first place than to come to this!

It is **thus**, Christ warns, with His hearers. They have experienced so many of His healings and exorcisms and have received so much benefit from Him. Yet better they should never have experienced it than to experience it, turn against Him as a demonic deceiver (v. 24), and finally benefit nothing, for then they will experience more wrath from God than if He had never come at all. Experiencing His power and hearing His words means that they are now responsible to live up to the light they have seen. To whom much is given, of that one much is required.

§VI.6. Opposition and Jesus' True Family

> ༄༅ ༄༅ ༄༅ ༄༅ ༄༅
>
> 46 While He was still speaking to the crowds, behold, His mother and brothers were standing outside, seeking to speak to Him.
> 47 And someone said to Him, "Behold, Your Mother and Your brothers are standing outside seeking to speak to You."
> 48 But He answered the one who was telling Him

and said, "Who is My mother and who are My brothers?"

49 And stretching out His hand towards His disciples, He said, "Behold, My mother and My brothers!

50 "For whoever does the will of My Father in the heavens, he is My brother and sister and mother."

During this exchange (which took place inside a house), **behold, His mother and brothers were standing outside, seeking to speak to Him**. As we learn from the parallel in Mark 3:21f, this delegation had come with a somewhat hostile intent (which is why St. Matthew groups it here with other stories of opposition to Jesus). His family thought He was crazy, beside Himself (Mark 3:21), and they had come to seize and take Him home. They were not patiently waiting for an audience, but sending an imperious message to Him that He cease His ministry and accompany them home.

The presence of Jesus' Mother in such a delegation requires comment. It is impossible to think that the Holy Theotokos, she who had received word from the archangel about the messianic destiny of her Son (Luke 1:35), who had virginally conceived Him, and who had heard word of angelic choirs at His birth (Luke 2:19), should entertain doubt in her holy heart. Rather, as a powerless and poor widow with no other children (the "brothers" were in fact kinsmen, not children of Mary), she was brought along with them to be used as a kind of bargaining chip. The Lord's unbelieving kinsmen hoped that her presence would add persuasiveness to their demands and make Him accompany them. The Theotokos, as a widow and a woman in a man's world, had little to say.

When this was reported to Jesus, He responded by saying, **"Who is My mother and who are My brothers?"** To answer His own rhetorical question, He **stretched out His hand towards His disciples** who were sitting around Him (Mark 3:34), saying, **"Behold, My mother and My brothers!"** All agreed that family commanded the ultimate loyalty, and Christ did not dispute this.

But He acknowledged His disciples as His true family, those who had left the world to follow Him. His loyalty lay with them, not with any biological kin. **Whoever does the will of** His **Father in the heavens**, this one was the Father's child, and therefore also Jesus' **brother and sister and mother.** Christ rejected the claims of the world and of family from having any binding authority over Him, refusing to be deflected from His divine mission. His disciples too must reject the claims of family if it meant a choice between loyalty to them and loyalty to God and Christ. Discipleship to Jesus meant being adopted into a new family.

❧ VII ❧

THIRD DISCOURSE—PARABLES
(13:1–53)

In the next discourse, St. Matthew gathers seven parables of Christ, interspersing them with a story of how the disciples asked Jesus why He used parables as His preferred method of teaching (v. 10) and an explanation of how this was a fulfillment of prophecy (vv. 34–35), concluding with a parabolic image of the trained disciples as a well-stocked householder (vv. 5–52). The sevenfold number of the parables indicates Matthew's deliberate artistry in arranging the discourse. Like the other discourses, this is a collection of material arranged for use by the Church's teachers.

§VII.1. Introduction

❧ ❧ ❧ ❧ ❧

13 1 On that day Jesus went out of the house and was sitting beside the sea.
2 And many crowds gathered together to Him, so that He got into a boat to sit down, and all the crowd was standing on the beach.

Matthew locates the first of the parables after **Jesus went out of the house** where He was teaching His disciples (12:46f). So great were the crowds that gathered together around Him that **He got into a boat to sit down** (sitting was the usual posture for teaching), leaving the **crowd standing on the beach**. This was the only way to avoid His being trampled by them, as well as allowing Him to use the natural acoustics of the place. St. Matthew stresses the huge number of people, for it was because of them that Jesus taught in parables. The masses of men were not open to putting aside their prejudices and learning the true nature of the Kingdom.

Like all Jews at that time, they thought the Kingdom would come cataclysmically and in political form. When Messiah came, they expected He would rally an army of angels and men and sweep the sinners (especially Roman sinners!) out of the land, exalting Israel to a place of political prominence in the earth. It was hard for them to accept the idea that the Kingdom Christ brought would take a different form in this age.

That is why Christ taught the masses in parables. The true and humble of heart would learn, but the unbelieving and stubborn would not. These latter would hear only interesting stories. The use of parables therefore suited the mixed nature of such a large crowd, for they would be received by everyone according to his ability.

§VII.2. First Parable: The Sower

३ॐ ३ॐ ३ॐ ३ॐ ३ॐ

3 And He spoke many *things* to them in parables, saying, "Behold, the sower went out to sow,

4 "and while sowing, some fell beside the road, and the birds came and ate them up.

5 "And others fell upon the rocky *soil*, where they did not have much earth; and immediately they sprang up, because they had no depth of earth.

6 "But after the sun had risen, they were burnt, and because they did not have a root, they withered.

7 "And others fell upon the thorns, and the thorns came up and choked them.

8 "And others fell upon the good earth and gave fruit, some a hundredfold, some sixtyfold,

and some thirtyfold.

9 "He who has ears, let him hear!"

§VII.3. Speaking in Parables

ॐ ॐ ॐ ॐ ॐ

10 And the disciples came to *Him* and said to Him, "Why are You speaking to them in parables?"

11 And He answered and said to them, "To you it has been given to know the mysteries of the Kingdom of the heavens, but to them it has not been given.

12 "For whoever has, to him will more be given, and he will have an abundance; but whoever does not have, even what he has will be taken away from him.

13 "Therefore I am speaking to them in parables; because seeing they do not see, and hearing they do not hear, nor have insight.

14 "And in them the prophecy of Isaiah is being fulfilled, saying, 'Hearing, you will hear, and will never have insight; and seeing you will see, and will never perceive;

15 "'For the heart of this people has been made dull; and with their ears they are heavy of hearing, and their eyes are closed, lest they should see with their eyes, and hear with their ears, and have insight with their heart and turn back, and I should cure them.'

16 "But blessed *are* your eyes, for they see, and your ears, for they hear.

17 "For amen I say to you, that many prophets and righteous *men* desired to see what you see, and did not see; and to hear what you hear, and did not hear.

§VII.4. Explanation of the Parable of the Sower

༄༅ ༄༅ ༄༅ ༄༅ ༄༅

18 "Hear therefore the parable of the sower.

19 "*When* anyone hears the Word of the Kingdom and does not have insight *about* it, the Evil One comes and snatches what has been sown in his heart. This is the *seed* sown beside the road.

20 "And the *seed* sown upon the rocky *places*, this is the one hearing the Word and immediately receiving it with joy;

21 "yet he has no root in himself, but is temporary, and when tribulation or persecution happens because of the Word, immediately he stumbles.

22 "And the *seed* sown among the thorns, this is the one hearing the Word, and the worry of the age and the deceitfulness of riches choke the Word, and it becomes unfruitful.

23 "And the seed sown upon the good earth, this is the one hearing the Word and having insight *about* it; who indeed bears fruit and yields, some a hundredfold, some sixtyfold, and some thirtyfold."

In the first parable, the Kingdom is presented as seed sown on the earth. Just as all seed sown does not germinate, so the Kingdom will not come equally to all in Israel. All will not be saved and enjoy the Kingdom simply because they are Jewish. Rather, it all depends on the state of the individual's heart (just as the fate of the seed depends on the quality of the ground into which it falls).

Thus, the **sower went out to sow** His seed. In those days, sowers would walk along narrow paths through the fields, throwing seed from a bag upon the wide ground. Inevitably, while most seed sown would fall into fertile earth and germinate, some would be lost.

Accordingly, **some** seed **fell beside the road, and the birds came and ate them up**. In His interpretation given later to His inquiring disciples (vv. 18f), Christ interprets this seed as the one who **hears the Word of the Kingdom**, but **does not have insight *about* it**. That is, he is unwilling to put aside His prejudices about the form the Kingdom will take and refuses to accept it. To such a person, **the Evil One comes and snatches what has been sown in his heart** (by telling lies about Jesus; compare 12:24), so that he receives no benefit from the Word.

Others fell upon the rocky *soil*, where they did not have much earth; and immediately they sprang up, because they had no depth of earth. This seed represents the one **hearing the Word** who **immediately receives it with joy**. He is delighted to become Jesus' disciple. But he **has no root in himself**, for he refuses to cultivate a sense of interiority. He is a prisoner to his own shallowness, and so **when tribulation or persecution happens** because of his discipleship to Jesus, **immediately he stumbles** and falls away.

Other seed **fell upon the thorns, and the thorns came up and choked them**. This one hears the Word of the Kingdom with his ears, but **the worry of the age and the deceitfulness of riches** that fill his life prove too much. Wealth, which promises fulfillment it cannot grant, and all the anxieties that haunt those who pursue wealth do not allow room for the message to take root, and **the Word** is **choked**.

Most of the seed, of course, fell where the sower intended—**upon the good earth**, and it **gave fruit** and produced a crop, **some a hundredfold, some sixtyfold, and some thirtyfold**. Such seed represents the one who **hears the Word** and **has insight *about* it**, humbly receiving the Lord's teaching. This one **indeed bears fruit** in his life and receives benefit from the Kingdom. Some receive more benefit than others and thus receive a greater reward, depending on the extent of their dedication. Thus, even in the saved, the power of the Kingdom depends on the state of the heart.

As mentioned above, the interpretation of the parable is given to the disciples privately (Mark 4:10). They not only want to know what the parable of the sower means, but also why Jesus **is speaking to them in parables** at all, since this form seems to hide the meaning.

Christ replies that the inner circle of the Twelve are privileged, for to them it **has been given** by the Father's will **to know the mysteries of the Kingdom of the heavens**, while to those outside **it has not been given**. Since the Twelve are to be His apostles and ambassadors, it is imperative that they know all His teaching (compare John 15:15–16). But the others receive His teaching both as illumination (for the humble) and as judgment (for the proud). Thus, to the humble one who **has, to him will more be given**. Such a humble soul already has insight into what God truly requires of him in His Law, and now he will receive further instruction about the Kingdom too. But to the one who **does not have, even what he has will be taken away**. The proud Pharisee who has no insight into what God truly wants—such a man will become blinder still (compare John 9:39).

In such proud ones **the prophecy of Isaiah is being fulfilled** before their eyes (Is. 6:9–10): They will keep on hearing but will not **hear,** nor **have insight** into what they hear. They will keep on **seeing**, but **will never perceive**. Like the proud, doomed ones of Isaiah's time, their **heart has been made dull**. They have heard so much that they can hear no more. They are no longer open to truth, nor willing to **turn back** so that God can **cure them** of their sins. The word of judgment that threatened Israel in Isaiah's day is still potent and will fall on them also.

The apostles, on the other hand, are truly **blessed**. They are given teaching in parables and miracles that **many prophets and righteous** *men* (such as Solomon and the other royal sages) **desired to see**, but did not live to see it.

The word rendered *desired* is the Greek *epithumeo*—a stronger word than that usually translated "wanted." The word *epithumeo* is sometimes translated as "to lust" or "to covet" (e.g. Rom. 7:7); in other cases simply "to greatly desire" (e.g. Luke 22:15). In all cases, a strong desire is indicated. The saints of old greatly longed to experience what the apostles are experiencing. The apostles therefore should be grateful for the privilege they are receiving!

§VII.5. Second Parable: The Tares in the Wheatfield

ॐ ॐ ॐ ॐ ॐ

24 He committed another parable to them, saying, "The Kingdom of the heavens is likened to a man who sowed good seed in his field.

25 "But while the men were sleeping, his enemy came and afterwards sowed tares in the middle of the wheat, and went away.

26 "But when the wheat sprouted and made fruit, then the tares became manifest also.

27 "And the slaves of the house-master came and said to him, 'Lord, did you not sow good seed in your field? How therefore does it have tares?'

28 "And he said to them, 'A man *who is* an enemy has done this!' And the slaves say to him, 'Do you want us, therefore, to go and pick them?'

29 "But he says, 'No, lest while you are picking the tares, you uproot the wheat with them.

30 "'Leave both to grow together until the harvest, and at the time of the harvest, I will say to the harvesters, "Pick first the tares and bind them into bundles to burn them up; but gather the wheat into my barn."'"

The second parable Matthew relates is that of the tares in the wheat field. Jesus' hearers assumed that the imminent coming of the Kingdom would separate the sinners from the righteous, the oppressors from the oppressed. This parable reveals that, in this age, the two groups will continue together. It is only at the end of the age, when lawlessness has increased and when the two groups have polarized, that they will be separated for the final judgment.

Jesus therefore tells a story of a **man who sowed good seed in his field**. He took care to plant only good wheat, with no harmful mixture of weeds. **While the men** who planted the good seed **were sleeping**, however, the farmer's **enemy came and afterwards sowed tares in the middle of the wheat, and went away** undetected.

These **tares** were a weed called bearded darnel. Though mature darnel seeds can be easily distinguished from wheat by the darnel's gray color, while it is growing darnel looks just like wheat. Moreover, darnel is bitter tasting and slightly poisonous, so that it must be laboriously separated by hand from the wheat after both have been threshed, lest the two become mixed. By sowing tares into the field, the man had committed major mischief, as the farmer later discovered when the first of **the tares became manifest**.

The farmer's **slaves** asked him if he wanted them to **go and pick them** out, removing the suspected tares while both the tares and wheat were growing. The farmer was unwilling to follow this course, lest while his slaves were **picking the tares**, they **uproot the wheat** by accident. There was only one course of action: they must **leave both to grow together until the harvest**, when the one could be distinguished from the other. Only then would the **harvesters pick the tares** from the wheat and **bind them into bundles to burn them up**. Only then could **the wheat** be safely **gathered into** the **barn**. The wheat was as precious as the tares were noxious, and both must be left to grow to maturity. The separation would have to wait until then.

§VII.6. Third Parable: The Mustard Seed

ॐ   ॐ   ॐ   ॐ   ॐ

31 He committed another parable to them, saying, "The Kingdom of the heavens is like a

> mustard seed, which a man took and sowed in his field;
>
> 32 "and this is smaller indeed than all the seeds; but when it is grown, it is larger than the shrubs and becomes a tree, so that the birds of the heaven come and nest in its branches."

§VII.7. Fourth Parable: The Leaven

> ॐ ॐ ॐ ॐ ॐ
>
> 33 He spoke another parable to them: "The Kingdom of the heavens is like leaven which a woman took and hid away in three pecks of meal, until the whole *batch* was leavened."

In this third parable, Christ speaks of **the Kingdom of the heavens** as **like a mustard seed**. The mustard seed was proverbially small, **smaller indeed than all the seeds**. Yet **when it is grown, it is larger than the** other **shrubs** planted from larger seeds and **becomes a tree**, one so large that **the birds of the heaven come and nest in its branches**. The image is drawn from such Old Testament passages as Ezekiel 17:23, which speaks of the Kingdom of God growing taller than all the other kingdoms of men, like a tree tall enough to provide shelter for the birds.

This image, with its contrast between the small beginnings and the great completion, is presented again in the fourth parable, that of the leaven. This parable tells of **a woman** who took a little **leaven** or yeast and **hid** it **away in three pecks of meal** (*peck* translating the Gr. *sata*, corresponding to about 7 quarts, and making enough bread to feed 160 people). The tiny bit of leaven, though imperceptible, was enough to leaven even this **whole *batch***.

In both of these parables, the contrast is between tiny beginnings and universal diffusion at the end. The ministry of Jesus seemed to many to be small and insignificant. He had no outward glory, no mighty army, no political connections—just a small group of twelve ordinary men. Was this the Kingdom of the heavens that would one day topple Rome from its throne and fill the universe with God's glory? But small beginnings can lead to great things—as the examples of the mustard seed and the bit of leaven make plain.

§VII.8. Parables as Fulfillment of Prophecy

ॐ ॐ ॐ ॐ ॐ

34 All these things Jesus spoke to the crowds in parables, and apart from a parable He did not speak to them,

35 that what was spoken through the prophet might be fulfilled, saying, "I will open my mouth in parables; I will utter *things* hidden from the foundation of the world."

At this point, Matthew stresses how parabolic utterances were Jesus' preferred method of mass communication, so that **apart from a parable He did not speak** to the crowds. This fulfilled the prophetic saying in Psalm 78:2 (considering Asaph, the author of the psalm, to be a prophet): **"I will open my mouth in parables; I will utter *things* hidden from the foundation of the world."**

In the original context, the psalmist was revealing the hidden significance of events in Israel's long-past history, and the parables referred to were comparisons of those events with Israel's then-contemporary situation. Thus, for example, the psalmist compared Israel's ancient rebellion against God in the desert with Israel's then-present situation, in order to encourage them not to repeat that rebellion (Ps. 78:17f).

For Matthew, mention in the Psalms of parables as the way of revealing ancient truth was too striking to be a simple coincidence, given that this was the Lord's way of revealing truth also. The words of the prophet Asaph found their final fulfillment in the ministry of Jesus, who was Himself the embodiment of the wisdom of the ancient Scriptures. Like the sages of old, Jesus came to reveal hidden truths, not to lead armed rebellion against the world forces, as many thought. He was a Teacher, not a warrior.

§VII.9. Explanation of the Parable of the Tares

ॐ ॐ ॐ ॐ ॐ

36 Then He left the crowds and came into the house. And His disciples came to Him, saying, "Explain for us the parable of the tares of the field."

37 And He answered and said, "The one sowing the good seed is the Son of man,

38 "and the field is the world, and good seed, these are the sons of the Kingdom; but the tares are the sons of the Evil One;

39 "and the enemy, the one who sowed them, is the devil, and the harvest is the consummation of the age; and the harvesters are angels.

40 "Therefore just as the tares are gathered up and burned up with fire, thus will it be at the consummation of the age:

41 "the Son of man will send out His angels, and they gather from His Kingdom all stumbling-blocks, and those doing lawlessness,

42 "and will cast them into the furnace of fire; there will be weeping and gnashing of teeth in there.

43 "Then the righteous will shine out as the sun in the Kingdom of their Father. He who has ears to hear, let him hear!"

After these parables and reflections, Matthew relates how Jesus' disciples **came to Him** privately after He had **left the crowds** with a request that He **explain** to them **the parable of the tares of the field**. (These private requests for explanation had already been intimated in v. 10f.) Christ unpacked the details of the parable, the gist of which has already been examined in the above commentary on verses 24–30.

As mentioned above, Jesus' hearers assumed that evil men would be removed from among the righteous as soon as the Kingdom had come. In this parable Jesus reveals that good and evil will be allowed to grow side by side throughout this age, so that both grow to the point where each can be unmistakably seen for what it is. It is only at the final judgment that evil will be removed from the world.

In the parable then, **the good seed** represents **the sons of the Kingdom**—those who serve Jesus and will finally inherit the Kingdom of God. They become such when they respond to the Word Jesus preaches, so that **the one sowing the good seed** (the farmer in the parable) is **the Son of man**, Jesus Himself. It is through His quiet ministry that the Kingdom is established in the earth.

The **tares are the sons of the Evil One**, those who oppose Christ. They are characterized as **stumbling-blocks** and as **those doing lawlessness**—that is, those who by their sinful lives cause others to apostatize. They are the work of **the devil** (the enemy in the parable).

It is only at **the consummation of the age** (in the parable, at the time of harvest) that all these evil ones will be **gathered from** Christ's **Kingdom**, which has been present in the world throughout the age. The **angels** will be the agents of judgment (the harvesters in the parable), and they will **cast** the enemies of God into **the furnace of fire** (in the parable, the place where the bundles of tares are burned), where there will be **weeping and gnashing of teeth**. **The righteous** who remain, however, will **shine out as the sun in the Kingdom of their Father**, blazing with uncreated light, even as does their Savior, the Sun of Righteousness (17:2f; Mal. 4:2). Now they remain oppressed and obscure, but their time will come.

The sum of all these details shows the power of the judgment to come, with the enemies of God brought to agony and ruin, and the righteous shining in radiance and triumph. But until that judgment, both will grow together. In this age, the Kingdom will include both.

§VII.10. Fifth Parable: The Treasure in the Field

> ൠ ൠ ൠ ൠ ൠ
>
> 44 "The Kingdom of the heavens is like a treasure
> hidden in the field, which a man found and hid;
> and from joy over it he goes and sells all that
> he has, and buys that field.

§VII.11. Sixth Parable: The Pearl of Great Price

> ൠ ൠ ൠ ൠ ൠ
>
> 45 "Again, the Kingdom of the heavens is like a
> merchant man seeking fine pearls.
> 46 "And having found one precious pearl, he went
> and sold all that he had, and bought it.

The fifth parable likens the Kingdom to **a treasure hidden in the field**. In those days before banks and safety deposit boxes, treasure was often buried in the ground for safekeeping, especially if the owners had to flee in time of war. Sometimes they would not be able to return (possibly dying in war), and the land would pass to someone else, who would then find treasure hidden in their field (possibly as they were plowing or digging rocks from the ground).

In this parable, the Kingdom is compared to such a hidden treasure. The **man** in the parable, a day-laborer working in the field, to his surprise **found** the treasure buried there (perhaps jewels or coins hidden in a jar). He then **hid** it, so that the owner of the land would not know it was there and refuse to sell the land at a low price. **From joy** over such a find, the man went and **sold all that he had** in order to come up with the money necessary to **buy the field**. Such selling of all that he had was worth it, for the hidden treasure was worth much more.

This is what the Kingdom of the heavens is like, Jesus says. It does not come cataclysmically to all Jews alike, simply because they are Jews. An inner dedication to God is necessary to receive the Kingdom. Just as the man in the parable had to sell all he possessed if he would obtain the treasure, so a man must give up all his stake in this world to be Jesus' disciple if he would obtain the Kingdom. Inheriting the Kingdom depends on a person's decisions about God.

The message of the sixth parable is the same—that in order to obtain the Kingdom one must become a disciple of Jesus even should it cost one everything. This parable tells the story of **a merchant man** who was **seeking fine pearls**. In the ancient world, pearls were considered things of breathtaking beauty, to be valued for their aesthetic beauty alone, and thus worthy images of the Kingdom. The merchant **found one precious pearl**, the find of his life, which somehow had gone unnoticed by all the other pearl merchants, and he knew he must have it. In order to do this, he **sold all that he had** to get the money needed and **bought it**. In obtaining it, he felt his joy was complete. In the same way, a man must be willing to sacrifice all—even his life—for the sake of following Jesus and the Kingdom of God, which is worth any sacrifice.

§VII.12. Seventh Parable: The Dragnet

> ℘ ℘ ℘ ℘ ℘
>
> 47 "Again, the Kingdom of the heavens is like a dragnet cast into the sea and gathering fish of every kind,
>
> 48 "which when it was filled, they hauled it up on the beach; and they sat down and picked the good *ones* into containers, but the decayed *ones* they cast out.
>
> 49 "Thus it will be at the consummation of the age: The angels will come out and separate the evil from the middle of the righteous,
>
> 50 "and will cast them into the furnace of fire; there will be weeping and gnashing of teeth.

The seventh parable in the collection compares the Kingdom to **a dragnet cast into the sea** that **gathers fish of every kind**, both **good *ones***, fit for eating, and **decayed *ones***, dead putrid fish, unfit for human consumption. This dragnet (or seine net as it is sometimes called) was a large cone-shaped net which was dragged behind a boat so that it collected whatever was in the water. Once filled, it was **hauled up on the beach** to be emptied and its contents sorted. The fishermen would **pick the good** fish **into containers** for sale, **but the decayed** and dead ones **they cast out**. Thus the net took in everything, while the process of sorting and separating was left until later.

This is what the Kingdom of the heavens is like. As taught in the parable of the tares in the wheat field (vv. 24f), the Kingdom in this age includes both good and bad. The process that will **separate the evil from the middle of the righteous** will not occur until **the consummation of the age**, when **the angels will come out** for judgment. It is only then that the evil oppressors and lawless men will be **cast into the furnace of fire**. Until that time, both will exist together, even as good and bad fish mix together within a dragnet.

§VII.13. The Disciples as Providers of Things New and Old

> ॐ ॐ ॐ ॐ ॐ
>
> 51 "Have you insight into all these things?" They say to Him, "Yes."
>
> 52 And He said to them, "Therefore every scribe who has become a disciple of the Kingdom of the heavens is like a man *who is* head of a household, who brings from his treasury *things* new and old."

At the end of His teaching to the disciples, Christ asks them if they **have insight into all these things** and if they understand these new principles. They reply that they do, and He concludes with a final parabolic comparison—that of the efficient and well-stocked **head of a household**, who has a storeroom full of all sorts of things. From this **treasury** he brings *things* new and old, giving to each according to need.

The disciples are like that, as indeed are all His faithful scribes or teachers. (The thought here is of those who will be teachers in His Church.) The **scribe** of Israel, once he has become **a disciple of the Kingdom** and a follower of Jesus, has a replete store of wisdom—both old wisdom and insight from the Law, and also new wisdom from Christ's parables. The Pharisees, however, do not have any new treasures and are not as well-supplied as Jesus' scribes. Thus the teaching of Christ does not replace or contradict the old wisdom of the Law, as the Pharisees allege (compare 5:17–19). Rather it illuminates and supplements it.

§VII.14. Conclusion of the Discourse

ॐ᠍ ॐ᠍ ॐ᠍ ॐ᠍ ॐ᠍

53 And it happened that when Jesus finished these parables, He went away from there.

This discourse ends according to the same pattern as the previous ones (7:28; 11:1), with the mention that Jesus **finished** His teaching. The presence of this formula marks these discourses as artistically produced collections for easy use by a scribe who has become a disciple of the Kingdom (v. 52).

❦ VIII ❧

MINISTRY IN GALILEE AND BEYOND
(13:54—16:20)

§VIII.1. Rejected at Nazareth

❧ ❧ ❧ ❧ ❧

13 54 And coming to His hometown He was teaching them in their synagogue, so that they were thunderstruck and said, "Where did this *one get* this wisdom and *works of* power?

55 "Is not this the carpenter's son? Is not His mother called Mary and His brothers James and Joseph and Simon and Judas?

56 "And His sisters, are they not all with us? Where therefore did this *one get* all these things?"

57 And they stumbled at Him. But Jesus said to them, "A prophet is not dishonored except in his hometown and in his own house."

58 And He did not do many *works of* power there because of their unbelief.

Matthew then relates how Jesus came from His base in Capernaum to **His hometown** of Nazareth. On the Sabbath (compare Mark 6:2), **He was teaching them in their synagogue**, as might be expected of an honored guest and celebrity. From the parallel passage in Luke 4:16–30, we know that He was commenting on a messianic prophecy in Isaiah 61:1–2, telling them the promised Kingdom was coming upon them as He spoke.

The people listening to Him **were thunderstruck**, both at His eloquence and **wisdom**, and also by His reputed ability to perform miraculous *works of* **power**. They could scarcely believe what all this seemed to imply—that Jesus, the very one they had known from childhood, and a mere **carpenter's son** at that, could be the Messiah. His family still lived among them, and they knew them well. Indeed, they even knew their names: **His mother** was **called Mary,** and **His brothers** were called **James and Joseph and Simon and Judas**. Even **His sisters**—less well-known than the brothers, since women in that society were less prominent—even they were known by them. **Where therefore did** the hometown boy *get* **all these things?** There is in the question a hint of suspicious malice, as if the source of these powers might be demonic.

So it was that **they stumbled at Him**, taking offense that such a One should claim such things for Himself. The Lord, however, discounts their lack of acceptance as irrelevant. He wryly observes that a true **prophet** never experiences **dishonor—except**, of course, **in his hometown and in his own house** and family. Matthew adds that **He did not do many** *works of* **power there** in Nazareth **because of their unbelief**. Finding not many receptive to His Word, He left them as they were, in their sins and sicknesses.

§VIII.2. Herod's Reaction and the Death of John

ॐ ॐ ॐ ॐ ॐ

14 1 At that time Herod the tetrarch heard the report about Jesus,

2 and said to his servants, "This *one* is John the Baptizer—he *himself* has risen from the dead, and that is why *works of* power are at work in him!"

3 For when Herod seized John, he bound him, and put him in prison because of Herodias, the wife of his brother Philip.

4 For John had been saying to him, "It is not permitted for you to have her."

5 And *although* he wanted to kill him, he feared

the crowd, because they held John *to be* a prophet.

6   But when Herod's birthday came, the daughter of Herodias danced in the middle and pleased Herod.

7   Thereupon he confessed with an oath to give her whatever she asked.

8   And having been prompted by her mother, she says, "Give me, here, on a plate—the head of John the Baptizer!"

9   And *although* he was sorrowful, the king commanded *it* to be given, because of his oaths and those reclining with him.

10 And he sent and beheaded John in the prison.

11 And his head was brought on a plate and given to the girl; and she brought *it* to her mother.

12 And his disciples came and took the corpse and buried it; and they went and declared *the news* to Jesus.

At this point Matthew narrates the story of the execution of John. It seems that it is narrated here to form the counterpoint to the rejection of Jesus at Nazareth, to show that Jesus will one day die at the hands of those who reject Him even as John died at the hands of the worldly.

The story begins with the guilty conscience of **Herod the tetrarch** (that is, one who had authority over a fourth part of the land), sparked when he **heard the report about Jesus**. The story continues by explaining how Herod came to have such a guilty conscience.

The report about the mighty *works of* power done by Jesus had reached the court of Herod, and there were many proffered explanations of this power. Some said that Jesus was Elijah returned, and that He was doing miracles now as Elijah had done during his lifetime. Others thought He was a prophet newly raised up by God, like one of the prophets of old (Mark 6:15). The explanation favored by Herod is that Jesus was **John the Baptizer**, somehow **risen from the dead**, and therefore now in possession of supernatural powers. (It would seem that Herod had not heard of Jesus before, and did not know that He and John were contemporaries.) This seemed impossible, but how else to account for Jesus' miracles? Herod's guilty conscience made such daytime impossibilities seem all the more likely during the wee hours of the morning.

Herod had cause to feel guilty. This Herod was the son of the famous Herod the Great. He had married **Herodias, the wife of his brother Philip**, even though his brother was still alive. Such a marriage was forbidden by the Jewish Law (Lev. 18:16), and **John had been saying** to Herod through his preaching, **"It is not permitted for you to have her."** John was not thereby meddling in the business of others. Israel was a theocracy, knowing no "separation of church and state." The sins of the king could bring divine judgment upon the whole land, and as a prophet John's task was to rebuke such sins.

Herod, though, had no intention of repenting. Fearing that John's public denunciations might provoke a popular rebellion against him, **Herod seized John and put him in prison**. Indeed, **he wanted to kill him**, thinking this the only politically safe thing to do (despite his personal ambivalence; compare Mark 6:20), but **he feared the crowd,** who **held John** *to be* a prophet. Such an execution, he thought, might cause even more riots. So it was that John languished in the dark prison in Machaerus, east of the Dead Sea.

This all changed when **Herod's birthday came**. During the festivities, **the daughter of Herodias danced in the middle** of the feast **and pleased Herod**. This dance was one of the lascivious, erotic dances done at that time only by prostitutes in the pagan world, and its performance by the princess caused a sensation. (It is possible that Herodias knew Herod had been lusting after the princess, and that she arranged the whole thing.) After the dance, Herod, inflamed by wine and lust, stood up and **confessed with an oath to give** the girl **whatever she asked** for as a reward. No doubt he was expecting her to respond to his promise with a request for gold or garments or perhaps a favorite property.

Herod was not prepared for her actual request. **Having been prompted by her mother** (after fleeing the room for a quick consultation with her; Mark 6:24), she returned to state her request. Her words are related by Matthew in the historic present for greater vividness (i.e. **she says**): **"Give me, here, on a plate—"** (one can almost hear the dramatic pause)—**"the head of John the Baptizer!"** The grisly reference to a plate made the guests think she was about to request some special food. Doubtless all present were horrified by the macabre dish she actually asked for.

Herod **was sorrowful** and unwilling to grant such a thing. But **because of his oaths and those reclining** at table **with him**, he felt he had no choice. He could not afford politically to be seen reneging on his word, for what other political promises might prove disposable? He sent word for the executioner to do his work and the head to be brought as requested. At a later date, John's **disciples came and took** away **the corpse** of their teacher **and buried it**. Then **they went and declared** *the news* **to Jesus**, since He was, they felt, to be John's successor.

§VIII.3. Bread in the Wilderness

ॐ ॐ ॐ ॐ ॐ

13 Now when Jesus heard *this*, He withdrew from there in a boat to a wilderness place by Himself, and when the crowds heard, they followed Him on foot from the cities.

14 And having come out, He saw a great crowd, and felt heartfelt *love* for them, and healed their infirm.

15 And when it was evening, the disciples came to Him, saying, "This is a wilderness place, and the hour is already past. Dismiss the crowds that they may go into the villages and buy food for themselves."

16 But Jesus said to them, "They have no need to go away; you *yourselves* give them *something* to eat."

17 And they say to Him, "We do not have here *anything* but five breads and two fish."

18 And He said, "Bring them here to Me."

19 And ordering the crowds to recline on the grass, He took the five breads and the two fish, and looking up to heaven, He blessed, and breaking the breads He gave them to the disciples, and the disciples *gave* to the crowds,

20 and they all ate, *even* to the full. And they picked up what was left over of the broken *pieces*, twelve full baskets.

21 And those who ate were about five thousand men, apart from women and children.

After Jesus heard of the death of John, He and His disciples **withdrew** from Capernaum **in a boat** to a lonely place on the northeastern side of the lake so that they could rest safely after all their frantic work (Mark 6:31–32). **When the crowds heard** of His plan, however, **they followed Him on foot** (the trip was not far, only about four miles), and after Jesus and His disciples **came out** from their boat, **He saw a great crowd** waiting for them. Even though He and His disciples badly needed a rest, Jesus still **felt heartfelt** *love* for them. His compassion overflowed, and He **healed their infirm** and taught them all day long (Mark 6:34).

When it was evening, the disciples came to Him wondering aloud about the mounting crisis. They said **this** was **a wilderness place**, far away from people's homes, **and the hour** was **already past** (i.e. daylight was fading). Let Jesus **dismiss the crowds that they may go** into the many **villages** around them **and buy food for themselves** (for a single village could not supply the needs of such a multitude). Capernaum itself held only about two thousand five hundred people, and here were many more, all of them hungry.

To the apostles' amazement, Jesus responds that the crowds **have**

no need to go away to find food. The apostles themselves (the pronoun **you** is emphatic) should **give them *something* to eat**. It was, of course, an invitation for them to trust in His messianic power.

The Twelve, however, failed to take this invitation to trust Him, and turned instead to their own resources. **They say to Him** (the historic present is used, to make their plaintive response all the more vivid), **"We do not have here *anything* but five breads** (or barley loaves) **and two fish,"** the lunch offered by a young lad (John 6:9). (We learn from this parallel in John's Gospel that these fish were not large fish, but small pickled fish, like sardines.) How could they be expected to feed such a multitude with this? Jesus simply responds by telling them to **bring** the food to Him and to **order the crowds to recline on the grass** where they are, ready to eat.

Jesus, **looking up to heaven** (and not to the food, as was typical in Jewish blessings over food), **blessed** God with the usual blessing, "Blessed are You, O Lord our God, King of the world, who brings forth bread from the earth," and began **breaking the breads**. He **gave them to the disciples**, who in turn gave them **to the crowds**. (St. Matthew mentions this detail, which stresses the instrumentality of the disciples, because of its parallel with the Church's Eucharist; it is through the clergy that Christ continues to feed His people with the living Bread.) Handful after handful continued to be given to the disciples until **all** the multitude **ate, *even* to the full**. Moreover, the disciples **picked up what was left over of the broken *pieces***, and found that it filled **twelve full baskets**. (The **baskets** were the little wicker carrying-baskets worn by pious Jews as part of their daily attire.) Here was true messianic abundance, a testimony that Jesus of Nazareth was indeed the Christ, for **those who ate were about five thousand men, apart from women and children**.

§VIII.4. Walking on the Sea

ॐ ॐ ॐ ॐ ॐ

22 And immediately He compelled the disciples
to embark in the boat and precede Him to the

other side, while He dismissed the crowds.

23 And having dismissed the crowds, He went up to the mountain by Himself to pray, and when evening had come, He was there alone.

24 But the boat was already many stadia distant from the land, tormented by the waves, for the wind was against *them*.

25 And in the fourth watch of the night He came to them, walking on the sea.

26 And when the disciples saw Him walking on the sea, they were shaken, saying, "It is a phantom!" And they cried out for fear.

27 But immediately Jesus spoke to them, saying, "Have courage, I *Myself* am *here*; do not be afraid!"

28 And Peter answered Him and said, "Lord, if it is You, order me to come to You on the waters."

29 And He said, "Come." And Peter got down from the boat, and walked on the waters, and came to Jesus.

30 But seeing the wind, he was afraid, and beginning to sink, he cried out, saying, "Lord, save me!"

31 And immediately Jesus stretched out His hand and took hold of him, and says to him, "O you of little faith, why did you hesitate?"

32 And when they got up into the boat, the wind ceased.

33 And those in the boat worshipped Him, saying, "Truly You are the Son of God!"

34 And when they had crossed over, they came to land at Gennesaret.

35 And when the men of that place recognized Him, they sent into the whole of that surrounding-

> country and brought to Him all who were
> sick.
> 36 And they were urging Him that they might only
> touch the fringe of His garment, and as many
> as touched it were *brought* to salvation.

After the miracle of the loaves, **immediately** Jesus **compelled the disciples to embark in the boat and precede Him to the other side** of the lake. The urgency involved is apparent from the parallel account in John 6:14–15, which reveals that the multitude was so inflamed with enthusiasm after the miracle that they were intending to come and take Jesus by force to make Him King. Christ quickly sent His disciples away lest they be swept up in the fray. They were to return to the western side of the lake while He pacified and **dismissed the crowds**. After this, **He went up to the mountain by Himself to pray**, as was His custom.

He remained praying until after three A.M. It was then that He knew His disciples needed Him, for what should have been an easy journey across the lake had become a nightmare for them. A storm had suddenly swept down on the Sea of Galilee, and the disciples' **boat was already many stadia distant from the land** (a mile or so, too far for them to turn back), and was **tormented by the waves**. The **wind was against *them***, and however hard they rowed, they could get nowhere.

In their hour of need, **in the fourth watch of the night** (that is, between three and six A.M.), Christ **came to them, walking on the sea. When** they **saw Him walking on the sea, they were shaken** to the core, for their nerves had already been stretched to the breaking point by the events of the day. The sea, for them as for all Jews, was a place of restless evil, a haunt of demons, and it seemed to the disciples that this shape moving eerily across the waves was such a demonic phantasm. They **cried out for fear**, saying, **"It is a phantom!"**

Jesus was quick to calm them. His familiar voice **immediately** called out across the howling winds, **"Have courage, I *Myself* am *here*; do not be afraid!"** Peter, however, was not so sure, for demonic phantoms could impersonate the living. He answered Christ, **"Lord, if it is You, order me to come to You on the waters,"** for only Jesus could empower the apostles to do such miracles. The request was not born out of presumption, but out of desire to avoid demonic deception, and Christ bade Him **come**.

Peter got down from the boat, resting his feet (gingerly, one foot at a time?) upon the heaving waters. Seeing that the sea would support his weight, he **walked on the waters and came to Jesus**.

For a while, all was well, and he drew near to Christ. Then Peter hesitated between faith and unbelief. He took his focus off his Lord and focused instead on the ferocity of the wind and the height of the waves, and the storm that was outside the boat entered Peter's heart as well. Though close to Jesus, he was **beginning to sink**. As the sea began to swallow him up, **he cried out, "Lord, save me!"** Once again, Christ's response was immediate; He **stretched out His hand and took hold of him**. He rebuked Peter not for trying, but for hesitating in his faith. Jesus had rejoiced at Peter's boldness and his success (as He rejoices at all our striving for Him), and He was disappointed at Peter's failure. With the sadness of a disappointed parent for his child, He says to Peter, **"O you of little faith, why did you hesitate?"** Peter was so close to success!

It seems that both Jesus and Peter were near to the boat, and that they simply turned and **got up into the boat** afterwards. As soon as they did, the stormy **wind ceased** and a great calm occurred. The disciples were amazed at such events as they had witnessed and **worshipped Him**, prostrating themselves in the crowded boat and saying, **"Truly You are the Son of God!"** Who else could tame the untamable sea?

When they came to land, they were at **Gennesaret**, on the western side of the Sea of Galilee. Jesus' divine power was recognized by the general populace as well (even though they had not seen the miracle of walking on the sea), and they **sent into the whole of that surrounding-country** to bring Him their sick. So great was His power that those who would simply **touch the fringe of His garment** in faith were *brought* **to salvation** (Gr. *diasozo*, a more intensive verb than *sozo*, "to save"). For Matthew, this fame simply confirmed that Jesus was the Son of God.

§VIII.5. Conflict with the Pharisees over Ritual Uncleanness

ॐ ॐ ॐ ॐ ॐ

15 1 Then some Pharisees and scribes come to Jesus from Jerusalem, saying,

2 "Why do Your disciples transgress the tradition of the elders? For they do not wash their hands when they eat bread."

3 And He answered and said to them, "Why do you *yourselves* also transgress the commandment of God for the sake of your tradition?

4 "For God said, 'Honor *your* father and mother,' and 'He who speaks-evil of father or mother, let him die the death.'

5 "But you *yourselves* say, 'Whoever will say to father or mother, "Given *to God* be anything of mine from which you might have been benefited,"

6 "'he is never to honor his father.' And you nullify the Word of God on account of your tradition.

7 "You hypocrites, well did Isaiah prophesy of you, saying,

8 "'This people honors Me with their lips, but their heart is removed far from Me.

9 "'They venerate Me uselessly, teaching *as* teachings the commands of men.'"

Matthew then relates how **some Pharisees and scribes** came **to Jesus from Jerusalem**. This was an official delegation, sent to check out Jesus and investigate rumors of heresy. What they noticed was that He and His disciples disregarded the customary ritual of hand-washing before meals.

This hand-washing had nothing to do with hygiene, but was purely a ceremonial matter. The Law mandated that *priests* had to wash their hands before offering sacrifice (Ex. 30:19), and the Pharisaical custom (which was increasingly popular) was for *all people* to wash before eating any food, whether sacrificial or not. This would, they reasoned, wash away any ceremonial defilement they may have contracted. The scribes considered this to be part of the oral law going back to Moses himself, and was called **the tradition of the elders**. For scribal piety, such a transgression was of immense importance, and they demanded why Jesus allowed His disciples to do this.

Jesus retorts with a question of His own: **Why** do they (the pronoun is emphatic) **transgress** not the tradition of the elders, but the very **commandment of God** Himself? For by insisting on keeping their scribal **tradition**, they are nullifying the intention of the Law they claim to reverence.

Christ gives an example. In the Law **God said, "Honor *your* father and mother"** (Ex. 20:12), and even said that **"he who speaks-evil of father or mother** (by invoking a curse on them)**, let him die the death"** and be executed (Ex. 21:17). Obviously respect for parents was important to God. But *they* say (again the pronoun is emphatic, to stress how their tradition differs from God's Law), **"Whoever will say to father or mother, 'Given *to God* be anything of mine from which you might have been benefited,' he is never to honor his father."**

This interpretation ruled that if a man pronounced a certain formula about any item of property from which his parents **might have been benefited**, saying, "This property is **given *to God*,**" then as far as the scribes were concerned, the man was positively forbidden to use this property to help his parents, even if he changed his mind. In this case the final result of their **tradition** and the scribal piety is to **nullify the Word of God**. No wonder Christ ignores such "tradition"!

For Christ, such hypocritical regulations are a part of the externalism and impiety condemned by **Isaiah** long ago. He **prophesied well** of those modern scribes, for they were included in his denunciations, since they persevered in the sins he denounced. Quoting from Isaiah 29:13, Christ denounces a **people** who **honor** God **with their lips** while **their heart is removed far from** Him. **They venerate** God **uselessly**, substituting the **commands of men** for the teaching and response God truly wants. Such are the Pharisees with their oral tradition. They claim that they apply the Law but in fact are overthrowing its true intentions.

༄ ༄ ༄ ༄ ༄

10 And after He called the crowd to Him, He said to them, "Hear and have insight!

11 "Not the thing that goes into the mouth defiles the man, but the thing that comes out of the mouth, this defiles the man."

Having dealt with the challenge from Jerusalem, Christ **called the crowd to Him** to give some positive teaching about the true nature of defilement. He declares that **not the thing that goes into the mouth** (such as bread eaten with unwashed hands) **defiles the man, but the thing that comes out of the mouth, this** is what truly **defiles the man**. It is not what goes *in*, but what comes *out*.

༄ ༄ ༄ ༄ ༄

12 Then the disciples come to Him, saying, "Do You know that the Pharisees stumbled when they heard this word?"

13 But He answered and said, "Every plant which My heavenly Father did not plant will be uprooted.

14 "Leave them; they are blind guides of the blind. And if a blind *man* guides a blind *man*, both will fall into a pit."

The disciples, though not yet understanding this parabolic utterance, understood that Christ was making powerful enemies, and that the **Pharisees stumbled** (that is, were highly offended) when they heard Christ's **word** rejecting the tradition of the elders. Shouldn't

He have been a little more conciliatory and politically wise?

Christ is unconcerned about His political popularity, and He dismisses their being offended from His consideration. They do not matter, for **every plant which** His **heavenly Father did not plant will** ultimately **be uprooted** by Him at the judgment as if it were a weed. Their disapproval therefore does not matter. The disciples should simply **leave them** alone. They are **blind guides**, incapable of providing true guidance into what God truly wants in His Law. One should not follow them or be concerned with their disapproval. Everyone knows what happens if **a blind *man*** follows **a blind *man*** as his guide—**both will fall into a pit** and meet disaster.

ॐ ॐ ॐ ॐ ॐ

15 And Peter answered and said to Him, "Explain the parable to us."

16 And He said, "Are you *yourselves* also still without insight?

17 "Do you not know that everything that goes into the mouth passes into the belly and is cast out into a latrine?

18 "But the things that come out of the mouth come out of the heart—those defile the man.

19 "For out of the heart come evil questionings, murders, adulteries, fornications, thefts, false witnessings, slanders.

20 "These are the things which defile the man; but to eat with unwashed hands does not defile the man."

The disciples still do not understand Christ's **parable** about things going in and coming out of man's mouth, and so through their spokesman **Peter**, they ask Him to **explain** it to them. In His reply, Christ stresses that no food (such as bread eaten with unwashed hands) that **goes into the mouth** can defile, for such food **passes into the belly and is cast out into a latrine**. That is, food does not enter into the heart, but simply passes through the body and out again. True defilement and uncleanness are a matter of the heart and will, and physical food remains external to the heart.

It is the wicked things that dwell and **come out of the heart**—those things that **come out of the mouth** and express themselves in words and actions—that truly **defile the man**. Such things as **evil questionings** (that is, rebellious resistance to God's will), **murders, adulteries, fornications, thefts, false witnessings, slander**—all of these things are not external but internal, and it is these that truly defile a man and render him unclean. Ceremonial uncleanness (such as might be incurred if one **eats with unwashed hands**) cannot defile anyone or render him unfit for communion with God.

§VIII.6. Healing for a Gentile

ॐ ॐ ॐ ॐ ॐ

21 And Jesus went away from there, and withdrew into the parts of Tyre and Sidon.

22 And behold! a Canaanite woman came out from those areas and was crying out, saying, "Have mercy on me, O Lord, Son of David! My daughter is severely demon-possessed."

23 But He did not answer her a word. And His disciples came to *Him* and were asking Him, saying, "Dismiss her, for she is crying out after us."

24 But He answered and said, "I was not sent *to any* but the lost sheep of the house of Israel."

25 But she came and was worshipping Him, saying, "Lord, help me!"

26 And He answered and said, "It is not good to take the children's bread and cast *it* to the *little* dogs."

27 But she said, "Yes, Lord, yet even the *little* dogs eat from the crumbs falling from their lords' table."

28 Then Jesus answered and said to her, "Woman,

> great *is* your faith! Be it done for you as you
> want." And her daughter was cured from that
> very hour.

Next **Jesus went away** from Galilee and **withdrew** to the north of Israel, to the borders of the ancient towns of **Tyre and Sidon**. His disciples badly needed a rest, which they could not find within Jewish territory, since Jesus was so popular there. Christ hoped that here, away from Jewish cities, He could find the repose His disciples needed.

It was not to be, for **a Canaanite woman came out from those areas and was crying out, saying, "Have mercy on me, O Lord, Son of David!"** She had evidently heard of Jesus' fame as a healer (compare Mark 3:8) and was desperate that He come to see her **daughter**, who was **severely demon-possessed**. The woman knew that Jesus was her only hope. (We may surmise that the woman was a widow, since it was unusual for a married woman to make such connections in public.)

The woman was asking for Jesus to come to Tyre and heal the child, which would mean more work for Christ and His disciples, for the etiquette and social customs of the day did not permit a quick visit. They would have to spend some days there, healing not only the woman's daughter but the crowds of Gentiles who would surely throng Him with their own requests for healing. Doubtless thinking also of His disciples' need for rest, Jesus **did not answer her a word**. The **disciples**, however, **were asking Him** to give her an audience and **dismiss her**, for her constant shouting was intolerable. Jesus refused to give her an audience, saying He was **not sent *to any*** but **the lost sheep of the house of Israel**. The time was not yet for a mission to a pagan city.

The woman, however, was insistent. She seems to have pushed past the disciples after they had entered a house (Mark 7:24), and came **and was worshipping** Jesus, falling down at His feet in an act of desperate obeisance, saying, **"Lord, help me!"** Jesus was still reluctant to deprive His spiritual children and disciples of their rest to accompany her on a mission to pagan Tyre. He gently responded,

"**It is not good to take the children's bread and cast** *it* **to the** *little* **dogs.**" That is, it would be as inappropriate for Him to take their anticipated rest away from the disciples to meet her need as it would be to take food prepared for the children and instead throw it on the floor for the little lapdogs to eat.

The woman did not argue with the Lord. She shrewdly agreed with Him—the children's meal need not be interrupted or pre-empted: but while the children were eating, **even the** *little* **dogs** might be allowed to **eat from the crumbs falling from their lords' table**. Let the disciples rest, and let Jesus heal the daughter here, from a distance!

No wonder Jesus exclaimed, "**Woman, great** *is* **your faith!**" Others thought Jesus had to be present to heal (compare 8:8–10), but this pagan woman believed such a healing could be done from afar. Because of her faith, He granted the request, and she went home to find that **her daughter was cured from that very hour** in which Christ spoke.

§VIII.7. Healing in Decapolis

ॐ ॐ ॐ ॐ ॐ

29 And moving on from there, Jesus came beside the Sea of Galilee, and having gone up to the mountain, He was sitting there.

30 And many crowds came to Him, having with them the lame, blind, crippled, mute, and many others, and they laid them beside His feet, and He healed them,

31 so that the crowd marveled as they saw the mute speaking, the crippled healthy, the lame walking, and the blind seeing; and they glorified the God of Israel.

After this, **Jesus came beside the Sea of Galilee** on the east, in the predominantly pagan area of the Decapolis (Mark 7:31). Here it might be expected that He could avoid the purely Jewish crowds and the work that awaited Him everywhere in Galilee. He went up on the **mountain** slopes and **was sitting there**, teaching His disciples (sitting was the posture for teaching).

In the **many crowds**, there were **lame, blind, crippled,** and **mute**, and even here in the Decapolis they **laid** their sick **beside His feet** for Him to cure. When **He healed them**, the crowds **glorified the God of Israel**. Though a full-fledged mission to pagan territory (such as in Tyre and Sidon) was not yet God's plan, the responses of this mixed Jewish-Gentile crowd prefigured the time when pagans would leave their idols and worship Israel's God in the Church.

§VIII.8. Bread in Decapolis

ॐ   ॐ   ॐ   ॐ   ॐ

32 And Jesus called His disciples to *Him*, and said, "I have heartfelt *love* for the crowd, for they have remained with me now three days and have nothing to eat, and I do not want to dismiss them fasting, lest they faint on the way."

33 And the disciples say to Him, "Where *would* we *get* so many breads in the wilderness to feed *to the full* such a crowd?"

34 And Jesus says to them, "How many breads have you?" And they said, "Seven, and a few little-fish."

35 And He ordered the crowd to recline on the earth,

36 and He took the seven breads and the fish, and giving thanks, He broke *them* and gave to the disciples, and the disciples to the crowds.

37 And they all ate, *even* to the full, and they picked up what was left over of the broken *pieces*, seven hampers full.

38 And those who ate were four thousand men, apart from women and children.

> **39 And dismissing the crowds, He got into the boat and came into the areas of Magdala.**

While Jesus was healing the many crowds that had gathered around Him in the Decapolis, a great need arose. They had **remained with** Jesus **three days** with **nothing to eat**, and if He **dismissed them fasting** to their homes, some would **faint on the way**. (The reckoning of **three days** was doubtless by the Jewish way of counting each part of a day as one day. The total time the crowds were with Jesus may have been fifty hours or so—still a long time of untiring devotion.) Christ's observation of this need is an invitation for the disciples to profit by the lesson learned the last time He multiplied the loaves for such a multitude.

The disciples, however, are slow to learn such lessons, and they respond by asking **where** they can obtain **so many breads** there **in the wilderness to feed** *to the full* such a crowd. With His customary patience for the frailties of men, Christ does not rebuke His disciples for their slowness, but simply asks **how many breads** they have with them. After being told they have **seven and a few little-fish** (Gr. *ixthudion*, the diminutive for fish, indicating small pickled fish such as were eaten for tidbits), **He ordered the crowd to recline on the earth** in preparation for the meal.

Once again Matthew recounts the miracle with words that echo the Lord's Last Supper with His disciples (compare 26:26), saying that **He took** the breads, and **giving thanks, broke** *them* **and gave to the disciples**. As with the last time Christ multiplied the loaves, Matthew again stresses the role of the disciples as Christ's instruments in feeding the people (14:19), saying that it is **the disciples** who actually give the bread **to the crowds**. The Church, reading this account, would inevitably think of their clergy as the instruments of Christ feeding His people in the Eucharist.

The crowds **ate,** *even* **to the full**. The word rendered *even to the full* is the Gr. *chortazo*, sometimes translated "to gorge" (compare such a use in Rev. 19:21)—this is no light snack, but a great feast. In fact there is so much food that after **four thousand men** have eaten (not counting the **women and children**), there are **seven hampers**

full of the **broken *pieces* left over**. And these **hampers** are not the small baskets (Gr. *kophinos*) carried as part of personal attire and mentioned in 14:20. The Greek word here is *spuris*, and these are large enough to carry a man, for Paul would be let down a city wall in such a hamper (Acts 9:25). Here is messianic bounty indeed!

It is only after He has fed the crowds that He begins dismissing them to their homes. Departing from the Decapolis, he returns to **the areas of Magdala**, probably on the west side of the Sea of Galilee.

§VIII.9. The Pharisees' Blindness and the Disciples' Blindness

🙐 🙐 🙐 🙐 🙐

16 1 And the Pharisees and Sadducees came to *Him*, testing Him, *and* asked Him to show them a sign from heaven.

2 But He answered and said to them, "When it is evening, you say, 'Fair *weather is coming*, for the heaven *is* fiery-red!'

3 "And in the morning, 'Stormy *weather* today *is coming*, for the heaven *is* red and darkened!' Do you know *how* to discern the face of heaven, but are not able *to discern* the signs of the *appointed* times?

4 "An evil and adulterous generation seeks after a sign, and a sign will not be given to it, but *only* the sign of Jonah." And He left them behind and went away.

After this second miracle of the loaves, some **Pharisees and Sadducees came** to Jesus, **testing Him, *and* asked Him to show them a sign from heaven**. This alliance of Pharisees and Sadducees was very unusual, for the two groups were usually adversaries. What they had in common was their rejection of Jesus—and their hypocrisy, for both claimed to be dedicated to doing God's will, whereas in reality their hearts were far from Him. These groups

came to Jesus confronting Him, demanding that He produce **a sign from heaven,** such as an audible voice of God designating Jesus as a true prophet. This, they say, they will accept as proof of Jesus' divine mission, but nothing less.

This Christ absolutely refuses to do, for their desire for signs does not come from hearts that truly want to know the truth. Rather, such requests are characteristic of **an evil and adulterous generation**, one that cares nothing for truth, and therefore **a sign will not be given to it**. The only authenticating sign given will be **the sign of Jonah**—which would not be a public demonstration for unbelievers, but the third-day Resurrection that would confirm the hearts of His disciples.

His adversaries' desire for a sign from heaven is ironic. They can read and **discern the face of heaven** clearly enough. **When it is evening**, they look up to heaven and say, **"Fair *weather is coming*, for the heaven *is* fiery-red!" And in the morning**, they look up and say, **"Stormy *weather* today *is coming*, for the heaven *is* red and darkened!"** They have no trouble getting messages from heaven about *the future*—how is it that they have trouble getting *the present*, and cannot read the message about **the signs of the appointed times?**

How indeed to explain such a strange inability in the readers of heaven—except to recognize that they did not *want* to know the truth about **the *appointed* times**. Any humble heart could discern that the time had come for the Kingdom to arrive, and that Jesus' miracles were signs that Messiah had come. Christ abruptly **left behind** such blind guides without giving them any further sign.

꓿꙰ꗷ   ꓿꙰ꗷ   ꓿꙰ꗷ   ꓿꙰ꗷ   ꓿꙰ꗷ

5 And the disciples came to the other *side* and had forgotten to take breads.

6 And Jesus said to them, "See *to it* and beware of the leaven of the Pharisees and Sadducees."

7 And they *began to* question among themselves, saying, "We did not take breads."

8 But Jesus, knowing *this*, said, "O you of little

> faith! Why do you question among yourselves, saying you have no breads?
>
> 9   "Do you not yet understand or remember the five breads of the five thousand, and how many baskets you took?
>
> 10 "Or the seven breads of the four thousand, and how many hampers you took?
>
> 11 "How *is it* you do not understand that I did not speak to you about breads? But beware of the leaven of the Pharisees and Sadducees."
>
> 12 Then they had insight that He did not say to beware the leaven of the breads, but of the teaching of the Pharisees and Sadducees.

Hurriedly getting in their boat to leave the Pharisees and the Sadducees (presumably without taking time to get more provisions), Jesus warned His disciples to **beware of the leaven of the Pharisees and Sadducees**. Christ was grieved at their hypocritical hardness of heart and did not want His disciples to be afflicted with the same disease.

They *began to* question among themselves, thinking His comment had to do with the fact that they **did not take breads** along with them on their journey, and that they had only one loaf with them in the boat (Mark 8:14). Each no doubt blamed the others for this oversight, in a flurry of mutual recrimination.

Christ was weary with such lack of insight. His true meaning should not have been difficult to fathom. In the original Aramaic they spoke, the words for "teaching" (Aramaic *amirah*) and for "leaven" (Aramaic *hamirah*) were homonyms—words spelled differently but alike in their pronunciation. Obviously Christ meant the leaven of **the teaching of the Pharisees and Sadducees**, their hypocritical rejection of Him, and not **the leaven of the breads** they might provide the hungry. As leaven or yeast affects the whole batch of dough, so the attitude of the Pharisees and Sadducees could corrupt one's entire life, and Jesus' disciples must take the utmost care to avoid it.

Do they really think He is warning them not to get more bread from the Pharisees? Let them **remember the five breads** and how they fed **the five thousand** and more, and **the seven breads** and how they fed **the four thousand** and more. What **little faith** they have! Do they **not yet understand** that Christ could multiply their one loaf and feed the twelve of them if He had to? Obviously He is **not speaking** to them about actual **breads**. The disciples, in their own way, are as blind as the Pharisees and Sadducees.

§VIII.10. Peter and the Apostles See that Jesus Is the Messiah

ॐ ॐ ॐ ॐ ॐ

13 Now when Jesus came into the region of Caesarea Philippi, He was asking His disciples, saying, "Who do the men say that the Son of man is?"

14 And they said, "Some *say* John the Baptizer; and others, Elijah; and others, Jeremiah, or one of the prophets."

15 He says to them, "But who do you *yourselves* say that I am?"

16 And Simon Peter answered and said, "You *Yourself* are the Christ, the Son of the living God."

17 And Jesus answered and said to him, "Blessed are you, Simon bar-Jonah, because flesh and blood did not reveal *this* to you, but My Father in the heavens.

18 "And I *Myself* also say to you that you *yourself* are Peter, and upon this rock I will build My Church, and the gates of Hades will not overpower it.

19 "I will give to you the keys of the Kingdom of the heavens, and whatever you will have bound upon the earth will have been bound in the heavens, and whatever you will have loosed

> upon the earth will have been loosed in the
> heavens."
> 20 Then He ordered the disciples that they should
> tell no one that He *Himself* was the Christ.

After relating the blindness of the disciples, Matthew then relates how the disciples, in the person of Peter their leader, came to see. This happened when **Jesus came into the region of Caesarea Philippi**, far to the north, about twenty-five miles north of Bethsaida. It was a Hellenistic city, and in taking His disciples to such a remote location, Jesus was assured of being far from any crowd that might want to make Him King by force (compare John 6:15).

In eliciting a confession of faith from His disciples, Jesus begins by **asking His disciples who the men** of Israel **say that** He, **the Son of man, is**. The disciples are delighted to relate the ignorance of the masses. **Some** people say (they relate with perhaps a laugh) that He is **John the Baptizer**, while others think He is **Elijah** come down from heaven to signal that the Kingdom is at hand. Still **others** suggest that He might be **Jeremiah or one of the prophets** of old.

Amidst this lighthearted ridicule of the masses, Christ casts His own challenge to them, cooling their easy pride. But who do *they* say that He is? The pronoun **you** is emphatic, as if to say, "Enough about them—what about *you?*" Mere men might have such opinions; but the apostles are not mere men. They have been chosen to receive mysteries denied to the masses.

Simon Peter, the spokesman for the group, gives his own answer: **"You *Yourself*** (the **You** is emphatic) **are the Christ, the Son of the living God."** Though such an answer seems self-evident to us today, in that day such an insight required a revelation from God. The popular idea of the Christ, the Messiah, then was of a military figure, one who would come on the clouds with heavenly armies to smite God's enemies and spill the blood of the Romans. The masses were only too ready to see Jesus as the one designated to fulfill such a role in the future, and that was why they wanted to make him a king by force, complete with peasant army and defiant declarations of war on Rome.

The apostles, however, knew that Jesus had no intention of waging such a war against sinners. He was one who would not wrangle, nor let His voice be heard in the streets; He would not crack the broken reed, nor quench the smoldering wick (12:19–20), but dealt gently with the sinful and weak. He walked in humility, with no military might or political connections, opposed by the powers of the world. To see in such a one the glorious Messiah could not come through the human insight of **flesh and blood** men. It could only come through divine revelation. Thus, Jesus pronounces Peter **blessed** indeed, solemnly using his full name, **Simon bar-Jonah** (i.e. son of John), for Christ's **Father in the heavens** has chosen him for such a revelation. And as the Father has blessed Peter, so Jesus **also** will bless him (the pronoun **I** is emphatic), choosing him to be the **rock** upon which He will **build** His **Church**.

When Jesus first met Simon (John 1:41–42), He gave him the nickname Peter (Aramaic *kepha*, "rock"). Now Jesus builds on that nickname, saying that He will build His Church on such a rocklike confession of faith as his.

This is more obvious in the Greek, for it involves a play on words—the name *Peter* is the Greek *Petros*, while the word *rock* is the Greek *petra*. A (perhaps inelegant) English rendering might be, "You are Rocky, and upon this rock I will build My Church." In the original Aramaic, the same word *kepha* would have been used for both Peter and the rock on which the Church was to be built—"You are *Kepha*, and upon this *kepha* I will build My Church." That is, Peter *is* the rock—not in himself, but insofar as he embodies the Church's confession. (As the Blessed Theophylact commented on this passage, "The Lord says here, 'This confession which [Peter] has made shall be the foundation of those who believe.'" St. John Chrysostom also, in his *Homily 54* on Matthew, interprets this rock as "the faith of [Peter's] confession.")

This is the first reference to the **Church** (Gr. *ekklesia*) in Matthew's Gospel. The word *ekklesia* is used in the Greek Septuagint to translate the Hebrew *qahal*, which means "gathering, assembly" (see e.g. Deut. 18:16). In its use here, Christ refers to gatherings of His disciples as they meet to form and constitute the renewed and messianic Israel. The use of the term here is not anachronistic, as some have suggested, for even in Jesus' time those who accepted His Word were becoming an identifiable group, separate from the masses and slandered by them (compare 5:11; John 9:22).

This group of disciples was built on Peter's confession, since they were all to share that saving confession. Though the group would be attacked and persecuted, Christ Himself would **build** it, so that it would withstand any such assaults. Indeed, He would fill it with His life and power, and **the gates of Hades** would **not** be able to **overpower it**. (By **gates of Hades**, Jesus means the power of death; compare Is. 38:10.) No attack of Satan—through either persecution from without or heresy arising from within—would be able to conquer Christ's Church or prevail against those assembled in His Name. The Church would stand eternally, a citadel and refuge for the world.

To Peter, as the embodiment of discipleship and leader of the apostles, Christ would **give the keys of the Kingdom of the heavens**, and **whatever** he would **have bound** or **loosed upon the earth** would be found to **have been bound** or **loosed in the heavens**. The image of receiving keys is one of stewardship (compare Is. 22:22), and Peter is being made chief steward of the Kingdom with authority to administer God's House.

The rabbis, in their discussions of what was forbidden and allowed in the Law, spoke in terms of binding and loosing. In binding an act, they declared it forbidden; in loosing an act, they declared it allowed, and this is the meaning that obtains here. Christ bestows on Peter such authority as the rabbis claimed to have—the authority to speak for God and to declare what was forbidden and allowed in the heavens. That is, he was given an effective stewardship of God's mysteries, as the chief rabbi and the authoritative scribe of the Kingdom (compare 13:52).

This promise is not so much given to Peter personally as it is given to the Church of which he is an image. It is the Church that is the pillar and buttress of the truth (1 Tim. 3:15), through which the wisdom of God is revealed (Eph. 3:10). This promise of Christ declares that the Church on earth has saving authority with God.

Pharisees and Sadducees might claim that the disciples were simply deluded fools, and to join them was to be cast out of the synagogue and to forfeit divine favor. Christ declares that His disciples, gathered in community, have power to speak with the voice of God. To join the Church is to receive the Kingdom, and to oppose it is to war against the Most High.

Finally, Christ **ordered** His **disciples** to **tell no one that He was the Christ**. Most in Israel still thought of Messiah in crudely military terms, and to spread abroad that Jesus had confessed Himself to be Messiah would be to spark rebellion against Rome. Until the Cross and Resurrection, the time for open proclamation had not yet come.

❧ EXCURSUS
ON PETER AS A SPECIAL FOCUS IN MATTHEW'S GOSPEL

Matthew's interest in Peter is characteristic of his Gospel. Mark and Luke also report Peter's confession of Jesus as the Christ at Caesarea Philippi, but Matthew alone records Christ's promise to Peter that He would build His Church upon the rock of his confession, and give him the keys of the Kingdom. Similarly, Mark records the miracle of Christ walking on the waters, but Matthew alone records how Peter also walked on the waters when bidden by Christ. Matthew, it would seem, had a particular interest in the apostle Peter.

Since the Gospel of Matthew is the most Jewish of the Synoptic Gospels and was produced (as suggested in the Introduction) within a Jewish Palestinian church community, this is not surprising. The first-century churches recognized Peter as having a particular calling to coordinate Christian outreach within the Jewish circumcision, even as Paul had a particular calling to spearhead an outreach to the Gentiles (Gal. 2:7). As such, the Jewish communities of Palestine looked to Peter with special affection, and

Matthew's Gospel reflects that affection with its special focus on Peter.

Thus, Matthew focuses on Peter's role in the miracle of Christ's walking on the sea (14:28–31). This is to show that the Church is called and empowered by Christ to do His work—Christ can walk on the sea, and so therefore can Peter. Peter's participation in Christ's power over the waves is a promise that the Church, built on Peter, will also participate in His miraculous power. If the Church therefore will exercise its faith (and not falter, as the all-too-human Peter did when he began to sink; compare also his lapse in 16:22), then it will miraculously survive all the turmoil and persecution of the age. Upheld by God's power, it will not be overwhelmed by the tempests of this world.

Also, this Gospel focuses on Christ's bestowal of authority on Peter at Caesarea Philippi (16:19). This is in reality a bestowal of divine authority on *all* His Church, not just on Peter personally. That this is so is shown in 18:18, where Christ bestows this same power to bind and loose on all the Twelve. His authority does not belong to Peter alone, but to all the teachers and rulers of the Church (in later terms, to all the bishops). Once again, Peter here is an image of the Church.

Finally, and unique to Matthew's Gospel, is the story of Christ's payment of the poll-tax, due from every adult male Jew for support of the Temple (17:24f). Christ declares Himself exempt from such obligations, since as the Son of God He is superior to the Temple. Nonetheless, He chooses to pay it lest He give offense. It is significant that, after the miracle of taking a coin from the mouth of the fish, Jesus uses that coin to pay the tax for Himself *and for Peter*. That is, Peter is paired with Jesus. Christ did not have to pay the tax for Peter as well, since the original challenge and question related only to Himself. Nonetheless, Jesus chose to identify Peter with Himself in this way by paying the tax for both of them at the same time. This seemingly insignificant detail reflects Peter's importance as one who is Christ's chief representative.

In all these details that are unique to Matthew's Gospel, we see Peter's special importance. Peter is present not only as the leader and spokesman of the Twelve, but also as an image of the Church. In this sense, Peter *is* the Church, for he embodies its authority and mission, and provides for the Church its saving and eternal confession of faith. In the words of Peter, "You are the Christ, the Son of the living God," the entire Church finds its voice.

❦ IX ❧

PREPARATION OF DISCIPLES FOR JERUSALEM
(16:21—17:27)

§IX.1. First Passion Prediction: Peter's Rebuke and the Cost of Discipleship

16 21 From then Jesus began to show His disciples that it was necessary for Him to go to Jerusalem, and suffer many things from the elders and chief-priests and scribes, and be killed, and be raised on the third day.

22 And Peter took Him aside and began to rebuke Him, saying, "*God be* merciful to You, Lord! This will never happen to You!"

23 But He turned and said to Peter, "Go away after Me, Satan! You are a stumbling block to Me, for you are not minding the things of God, but the things of men."

Having received a confession of faith in Him as Messiah, Jesus then **began to show His disciples** what kind of Messiah He was. As mentioned above, the popular understanding of the Messiah was that of a conquering hero. The disciples had to learn that He must **go to Jerusalem and suffer many** indignities **from the elders and chief-priests and scribes.** He would even **be killed,** and only after this defeat would He **be raised on the third day.** This **was necessary,** for it had been preordained by God and prophesied in the Scriptures.

Peter, however, was aghast, and the thought of his beloved Lord suffering such things cut him to the heart. He **took Him aside and began to rebuke Him**, not so much in haughty anger, but in pain, saying, "*God be* **merciful to You, Lord!** (That is, God forbid!) **This will never happen to You!**"

Despite His love for His chief apostle, Christ knew how fatal such an attitude was, for this same attitude rested in the hearts of the crowds when they tried to make Him king by force (John 6:15). It was this same attitude which would eventually result in the crowd's disowning Him when they perceived He would not bring them military victory over the Romans. By **minding the things of men**, rather than **the things of God** (that is, by having such a worldly attitude), Peter had became an adversary, a **Satan** (*satan* is Hebrew for "adversary"), and **a stumbling block** for the Lord.

To protect Peter and the others from becoming God's adversaries, Jesus **turned** and rebuked Peter in the presence of all, saying to him, **"Go away after Me, Satan!"** The words *after Me* (Gr. *opiso mou*) denote walking behind and are used again in verse 24, where Jesus describes the disciple as one who "comes after Me." The Lord is telling Peter that he has become His adversary by trying to be His teacher, and must once again take up the role of a disciple; he must **go away** from *in front* of Him to take his appropriate place *behind* Him, coming **after** Him as he did before.

ॐ ॐ ॐ ॐ ॐ

24 Then Jesus said to His disciples, "If anyone wants to come after Me, let him *completely* deny himself, and take his cross and follow Me.

25 "For whoever wants to save his life will lose it, but whoever loses his life for My sake will find it.

26 "For what will a man be profited if he gains the whole world, and *experiences* the loss of his life? Or what will a man give in return for his life?

27 "For the Son of man is about to come in

> the glory of His Father with His angels, and will then render to each according to his practices.
>
> 28 "Amen I say to you, there are some of those who are standing here who will never taste death until they see the Son of man coming in His Kingdom."

Christ **then** turns His attention to the larger crowd of **disciples**, generalizing the private lesson offered to Peter and the Twelve. It is crucial for **anyone** who **wants to come after** Him not to shrink from death. Peter reacted with horror to the thought of Jesus being disgraced and killed, but such is the fate that awaits all those who refuse to compromise with the world. If one wants to be Jesus' disciple, one must be prepared for such sacrifices. Such a one must *completely* **deny himself** (Gr. *aparneomai*, a stronger verb than *arneomai*, "to deny") and **take his cross**.

The image of taking up one's cross was stunning. Crucifixion was the worst death imaginable in those days, one the Romans reserved for the worst criminals and for slaves. The man condemned to such a death was first scourged so that his back was laid open. He then took up his cross (i.e. the crossbeam) and carried it to the place of execution. Finally, his forearms would be nailed to the crossbeam and his feet to the upright stake, and he would be left there to die. It often took days. The Lord's hearers knew that to take up a cross was to embrace death and to lose the whole world. But that was the price of discipleship. One must be willing to sacrifice everything for the sake of Jesus.

It is natural to shrink from such sacrifices and to try to **save** one's **life**. But if one refuses Jesus for the sake of life's comforts, one will not truly save one's life, but will **lose it** in the age to come. Similarly, if one will **lose his life** for Jesus' sake, he will **find it** and keep it forever in the age to come. Though difficult, this is the only sensible course of action. For **what will a man be profited if he gains** even **the whole world**, with all its honor, health, and riches, and then *experiences* **the loss of his life?** In this short parable, Jesus asks

His audience to evaluate this bargain: If a man is offered the whole world in exchange for being killed, what kind of a bargain is that? For **what will a man give in return for his life?** Surely a wise man would keep his life, even if it meant forfeiting the offer of receiving the world. In the same way, Jesus says, one should follow Him and inherit eternal life, even if it means forfeiting all the pleasures and comforts in this world.

This bright and tempting world beckons alluringly enough, and while it beckons, one might think that it is the only reality there is. But the world will pass away soon enough, and when **the Son of man** will **come in the glory of His Father with His angels**, He will **then render to each according to his practices**. In this age Jesus is easily rejected by the worldly as of no account. What does He matter? He has only a few disciples with Him, no power, no connections, and only the mindless rabble follow Him! But a day will come when Jesus' true significance will be undeniably revealed to the whole quaking cosmos. In that day, He will stand as the Judge of all who so easily rejected Him, and give to each one as their deeds deserve.

That day may seem far off. But a foretaste of Christ's future glory will soon be glimpsed, as a confirmation of His messianic majesty to come. Jesus solemnly assures them that **some of those standing** there will **never taste death** until they see that glory. Most of them will indeed die and never see Jesus in His eternal power. But some, in this life, will see the glory **the Son of man** will have later when He will **come in His Kingdom** and ascend to the right hand of God.

§IX.2. The Transfiguration

The Lord's words about some of His hearers seeing in this life the glory of the Son of man coming in the Kingdom of God (16:28) are fulfilled in the Transfiguration, which follows this prediction in all three Synoptic Gospels. For the Transfiguration was a foretaste for those who saw it of the glory Christ was to receive in the Kingdom—which would finally be openly manifested on the last day.

ॐ ॐ ॐ ॐ ॐ

17 1   And six days later, Jesus takes with Him Peter
and James and John his brother, and brings
them up to a high mountain by themselves.

2   And He was transfigured before them, and
His face shone like the sun, and His garments
became white as light.

3   And behold! Moses and Elijah appeared to
them, speaking with Him.

4   And Peter answered and said to Jesus, "Lord,
it is good for us to be here; if You want, I will
make three tents here, one for You, and one for
Moses, and one for Elijah."

5   While he was still speaking, behold! a cloud
full of light overshadowed them; and behold!
a voice speaking from the cloud, "This is My
beloved Son, with whom I am well-pleased;
hear Him!"

6   And when the disciples heard *it*, they fell on
their faces and were extremely afraid.

7   And Jesus came to them and touched them and
said, "Arise, and do not be afraid."

8   And lifting up their eyes, they saw no one but
Jesus Himself alone.

This was fulfilled **six days later**. Christ had the habit of ascending a mountain to pray into the night (Mark 6:46; Luke 6:12), and
this was His practice here (Luke 9:28). With Him went the inner
circle, **Peter and James and John**. The **high mountain** to which
He took them is not named. Mount Tabor in the north, between
Nazareth and the Sea of Galilee, is the traditional site.

As He prayed into the night, His disciples slept (compare their
descent from the mountain the next day; Luke 9:37). Something
awakened them (possibly the sound of other voices, those of Moses
and Elijah?), and they saw that Jesus was **transfigured before them,**

so that **His face shone like the sun, and His garments became white as light**. The Messiah was expected to be a figure of glory and to shine with the splendor of heaven. Those who suspected Jesus might be the designated Messiah were doubtless puzzled by His ordinary appearance. This stumbling block was removed for the inner circle of Jesus' disciples when they saw their Lord resplendent with the glory proper to the Messiah.

This glory was no superadded splendor, but His own glory. As He walked among men, this glory had been veiled—though apparently the terrified demons had no trouble seeing it (compare their reaction to Him in 8:29; Mark 3:11). Now, for the apostles' sakes, this veil was removed, and they saw Christ as He was, shining with the uncreated light of divinity.

There were more surprises for Peter, James, and John: **Moses and Elijah appeared to them, speaking with** Jesus. (The word **behold!** is used three times in as many verses, reflecting the succession of unexpected occurrences that night.) Jesus did not prostrate Himself before these ancient worthies (as anyone else might have), but stood erect, conversing casually with them as with friends.

It is **Peter** who breaks the disciples' stupefied silence. It is **good** for them **to be here**, he says. They are fortunate to have seen this vision. Peter desired to prolong and repeat this time of glory, and offered to make **three tents here, one for** Jesus, **one for Moses, and one for Elijah**. As a good Jew he remembered how God's glory had appeared to this same Moses through the tent of meeting (Ex. 33:9), and he sought some way to preserve this manifested radiance. Perhaps if these tents were made, Jesus could return here, and Elijah and Moses also, each to their appointed tent! It was an odd suggestion, to say the least, and the other evangelists offer something of an apology for Peter, Mark saying that Peter was too rattled to answer properly (Mark 9:6), and Luke simply saying that Peter did not know what he was talking about (Luke 9:33).

Jesus did not have time to reply to Peter's offer, for **while** Peter **was still speaking, a cloud** *full of* **light overshadowed them,** and **a voice** speaking **from the cloud** said, **"This is My beloved Son, with whom I am well-pleased; hear Him!"** When the disciples experienced this, **they fell on their faces** in terror, for they **were extremely afraid**. Well they might be, for this **cloud** was the *Shekinah*, the divine Presence that once overshadowed tabernacle and Temple (Ex. 40:35; 1 Kings 8:10). This **voice** was the very voice of God that spoke the cosmos into existence, whose sound broke the mighty cedars of Lebanon (Gen. 1:3; Ps. 29:4–5).

As they remained on their faces, **Jesus came to them** and gently **touched them** to rouse them and banish their fear, saying, **"Arise, and do not be afraid."** They **lifted up their eyes**, looking about wildly (Mark 9:8), but all had changed. They **saw no one but Jesus Himself alone**.

What did it all mean? Why did Moses and Elijah, and not some other ancient prophet, appear to Jesus? What did their sudden departure mean? To the apostles, as men steeped in the Old Testament, the answers were clear. Moses was the great Lawgiver, and Elijah was the greatest of the prophets. Together they embodied the Law and the Prophets, the whole Old Testament dispensation.

These spoke to Jesus, then vanished. Jesus was not, as some might have supposed, simply one more prophet in a line of many prophets. He was not subordinate to Moses or the Law. Rather, Moses and the Prophets were subordinate to *Him*. When Peter suggested that three tents be erected, he failed to appreciate this, for he thought that Jesus was no more than one among three equals. Peter did not see that Moses and Elijah were simply a preparation for Jesus, destined to fade when He arrived. That is why they vanished, leaving Christ alone, for the Old Testament was to give place to the New. As the voice of the Father said, all were to **hear Him** and to focus on Jesus alone. The Old Testament dispensation was drawing to its close.

§IX.3. Descent from the Mountain and Healing of Demoniac Child

ৡ৵ ৡ৵ ৡ৵ ৡ৵ ৡ৵

9   And as they were coming down from the mountain, Jesus commanded them, saying, "Tell the

> vision to no one until the Son of man has risen from the dead."
>
> 10 And His disciples asked Him, saying, "Why therefore do the scribes say that Elijah must come first?"
>
> 11 And He answered and said, "Elijah indeed comes and will restore all things.
>
> 12 "But I say to you that Elijah already came, and they did not recognize him, but did to him whatever they wanted. Thus also the Son of man is about to suffer from them."
>
> 13 Then the disciples had insight that He had spoken to them about John the Baptizer.

The next morning, as they were **coming down from the mountain, Jesus commanded them** to **tell the vision to no one until the Son of man had risen from the dead**. Though they had not (we think) spoken of it upon rising, their hearts were full of the night's events, and they were eager to tell others. In that time, such news would spark a further fever of messianic enthusiasm that would endanger His mission. The apostles must keep it a secret therefore until Jesus' work was done.

The reference to Jesus having risen from the dead puzzled the disciples. The resurrection from the dead was something that would happen at the end of time, when all men would rise and stand before God to be judged. Was Jesus saying they were *never* to tell this news? But He seemed to be referring to a more imminent event—almost as if He were expecting to die soon.

But this could not be. In their understanding of the messianic redemption, there was no room for Messiah's death and defeat. The **scribes** had taught that **Elijah must come first**—perhaps returning to earth in his chariot of fire—and restore all things. This would usher in a time of blessing and peace. Where was there room for death?

Jesus answered that **Elijah indeed comes and will restore all things**, even as the prophecies said (Mal. 4:5). The prophesied work would fulfill its purpose in Israel. But they were to know that **Elijah already came**, and men **did not recognize him** as Elijah, **but did to him whatever** atrocities **they wanted.** The presence of Elijah restoring all things by bringing Israel to repentance did not mean that there was no place in that restoration for death. Elijah had been killed—and **thus,** in the same way, was **the Son of man about to suffer from them** also. They need not be puzzled—there was room enough for death! It was only then that the three **had insight that He had spoken to them about John the Baptizer,** who came to be Elijah to his generation—not Elijah personally returned or reincarnated, but one who came with Elijah's power to fulfill the prophecies about him.

ॐ ॐ ॐ ॐ ॐ

14 And when they came to the crowd, a man came to Him, falling on his knees *before* Him and saying,

15 "Lord, have mercy on my son, for he is an epileptic and suffers terribly; for he often falls into the fire, and often into the water.

16 "And I brought him to Your disciples, and they were not able to heal him."

17 And Jesus answered and said, "O unbelieving and perverse generation, how long will I be with you? How long will I bear with you? Bring him here to Me."

18 And Jesus rebuked it, and the demon came out of him, and the boy was healed from that hour.

19 Then the disciples came to Jesus by themselves and said, "Why were we *ourselves* not able to cast it out?"

20 And He says to them, "Because of your little faith; for amen I say to you, if you have faith as a mustard seed, you will say to this mountain, 'Move from here to there!' and it

> will move, and nothing will be impossible
> to you."*

At length they rejoined their companions at the foot of the mountain and found there a tumultuous **crowd**. From this crowd a **man came** to Jesus, **falling on his knees** *before* **Him and saying, "Lord, have mercy on my son."** The distraught father quickly told all his tale to Jesus, including how the boy was an apparent **epileptic** (Gr. *seleniazomai*, literally "moonstruck," indicating one given to seizures), who **suffered terribly, often falling into the fire and often into the water**, as the demon within tried to destroy him. The father had **brought** the boy to Jesus' **disciples** for a cure, but **they were not able to heal him**. Now the man was at his wits' end. Could Jesus possibly help him?

The Lord reacted strenuously to the father's lack of faith, for the man was part of an **unbelieving and perverse generation**—his doubts had found fertile soil in the crowd that gathered, and all were muttering about what it all meant. The disciples' inability to cure the boy reflected badly on their Master. With the wearied resignation of the God who has long endured the faithlessness of Israel (compare Jer. 2:5), Jesus rhetorically asks **how long** He will **be with** them and **bear with** them. No matter. Let them **bring** the boy **here** to Him.

What was impossible for the baffled apostles at the foot of the mountain is easy for their Lord. He **rebuked it, and the demon came out of him**, and the boy **was healed** instantly. The authority and power of the Lord are vindicated.

When it is all over and they are alone, the disciples ask why they were unable to perform the exorcism. The answer is simple—because of their **little faith**. If they would but trust God at all—even with faith as proverbially small as **a mustard seed**—they could **say to this mountain** before which they stand, **"Move from here to there!" and it** would **move**. The same little faith that hindered them in

---

* *Verse 21, which says that "this kind does not go out but by prayer and fasting," is not found in the best manuscripts of Matthew's Gospel, but is a later borrowing based on the parallel in Mark 9:29.*

the past (8:26; 14:31; 16:8) hinders their work now. Yet even in answering their question, Christ does not rebuke them in anger for their failure. Rather He simply says that given their little faith, that kind of demon (more difficult than most) could only come out by prayer and fasting (comparing Mark 9:29).

§IX.4. Second Passion Prediction

ॐ ॐ ॐ ॐ ॐ

22 And while they were gathering together in Galilee, Jesus said to them, "The Son of man is about to be delivered into the hands of men;

23 "and they will kill Him, and He will be raised on the third day." And they were extremely sorrowful.

While the crowds were milling about them **in Galilee** and rejoicing at His many miracles, Jesus continued to press upon His apostles the necessity of His being **delivered into the hands of men** who would **kill Him**. That death was imminent, and He did not want them to be overly traumatized and to fall away. As it was, **they were extremely sorrowful** at such words, even though they did not fully understand them (Mark 9:32).

§IX.5. Christ and the Poll-tax

ॐ ॐ ॐ ॐ ॐ

24 And when they had come into Capernaum, those receiving the two-drachma came to Peter and said, "Does not your Teacher pay the two-drachma?"

25 He says, "Yes." And when he came into the house, Jesus anticipated him, saying, "What do you think, Simon? From whom do the kings of the earth receive customs or poll-tax—from their sons or from the others?"

26 And upon his saying, "From the others," Jesus said to him, "Then the sons are free.

27 "But that we may not cause them to stumble, go to the sea, and cast in a fishhook, and take the first fish that comes up, and when you open its mouth, you will find a stater. Take that and give *it* to them for Me and you."

When they **had come into Capernaum** again, they met those whose task it was to **receive the two-drachma** tax. In the month of Adar (about March), every Jew over twenty years had to pay a half-shekel to support the Temple (the two-drachma piece was about equal in value to a half-shekel). To pay this tax meant that one was a loyal Jew, dedicated to the Temple and loyal to its priesthood. The Temple tax-collectors **came to Peter and said, "Does not your Teacher pay the two-drachma** tax?" The question presupposes a positive answer, though the fact that it was asked indicates perhaps a slight doubt. Surely a pious rabbi like Jesus would be loyal to the Temple of God, wouldn't He? Enough controversy swirls around Jesus that they think the question worth asking. Peter, somewhat defensive, instantly answers, **"Yes,"** though without checking first with his Master to see if this is correct.

No sooner has Peter entered his house in Capernaum where they are all staying than **Jesus anticipated him.** Jesus has supernatural knowledge of what has happened, and He speaks first before Peter has a chance to tell him of his exchange with the tax men. He begins by asking a typical rabbinical question: What is Simon's take on this—**from whom do the kings of the earth receive customs or poll-tax—from their sons or from the others?** Do pagan kings tax their families or just those subject to them?

Simon Peter gives the obvious reply: **"From the others."** Kings do not tax their children. Christ instantly replies, **"Then the sons are free"** from taxation and exempt. The lesson is obvious. As the sons of the heavenly King, the disciples of Jesus are also exempt from such Temple taxation, for they are not subordinate to the Temple. They stand on a higher plane than the other Jews, for they serve

One who is greater than the Temple (12:6). They may worship in the Temple, but Christ's authority transcends it.

Nonetheless, Jesus is concerned that they **not cause them to stumble**. Though exempt from the Temple tax in God's eyes, they will pay it anyway rather than give offense and create an unnecessary stir. Peter is told to **go to the sea** nearby **and cast in a fishhook**, which would take up but one fish (a net would take in several). **The first fish** caught by the hook would have **a stater** in its **mouth** (which it tried to eat, thinking it was food). This coin was worth two two-drachma pieces and would pay the tax for Jesus and for Peter. Peter should **take that and give *it* to them**.

The nature of the miracle is significant. Christ did not choose to acquire the stater in this miraculous way because He had no other money or because He liked performing miracles. Rather, the stater was obtained in such a way as to express the fact that He did not have to pay it, for it actually *cost Him nothing*. Moreover, the miraculous nature of the acquisition proved to Peter the truth of Christ's assertion that He and His disciples were exempt in God's eyes and were not subordinate to the Temple authorities. The miracle was thus not unnecessary, but crucial in vindicating Christ's claim.

For the Jewish Christians of the first century, this lesson was important, for it freed them from their obligation to submit to the unbelieving Temple authorities. They declared themselves loyal to the Temple (the apostles continued worshipping in the Temple until they were driven away; compare Luke 24:53). But this loyalty was a matter of social convenience, lest they give offense to the Jewish brothers and make their conversion to Christ harder. In actuality, the Christian Jews no longer needed the Temple to find access to God.

❧ X ❧

FOURTH DISCOURSE—DISCIPLESHIP
(18:1—19:2)

In this discourse, Matthew focuses on humility, righteousness, and forgiveness as the essence of Christian discipleship. The piety of the Pharisees was based on pride in their meticulous keeping of the tradition of the elders; the piety of Jesus' followers was based on imitation of Him who was "humble of heart" (11:29).

§X.1. First Place and Humility

❧ ❧ ❧ ❧ ❧

18 1 In that hour the disciples came to Jesus, saying, "Who then is the greatest in the Kingdom of the heavens?"

2 And having called a child *to Himself*, He stood him in the middle,

3 and said, "Amen I say to you, unless you turn and become as the children, you will never enter into the Kingdom of the heavens.

4 "Whoever therefore humbles himself as this child, this one is the greatest in the Kingdom of the heavens,

5 "and whoever welcomes one such child in My Name welcomes Me;

6 "but whoever makes one of these little ones who believe in Me stumble, it is more advantageous for him that a millstone *turned by* a

donkey be hung around his neck and that he be sunk in the open sea.

7   "Woe to the world because of stumbling blocks! For it is necessary that the stumbling blocks come, but woe to that man through whom the stumbling block comes!

8   "And if your hand or your foot makes you stumble, cut it off and cast *it* from you; it is good for you to enter the Life crippled or lame, than having two hands or two feet to be cast into the eternal fire.

9   "And if your eye makes you stumble, tear it out and cast *it* from you. It is good for you to enter into the Life one-eyed, than having two eyes to be cast into the Gehenna of fire.

10   "See that you do not despise one of these little ones, for I say to you that their angels in the heavens always see the face of My Father in the heavens.*

12   "What do you think? If any man has a hundred sheep, and one of them has strayed, does he not leave the ninety-nine upon the mountains and go and seek the one that is straying?

13   "And if it happens that he finds it, amen I say to you, he rejoices over it more than over the ninety-nine that have not strayed.

14   "Thus it is not the will of your Father in the heavens that one of these little ones perish.

In collecting material for this Fourth Discourse, St. Matthew draws from a number of events. In this first part of the discourse, Matthew draws from the story narrated in Mark 9:33f. This event took place in Capernaum **in that hour** (i.e. during the same time

---

* Verse 11 is not contained in most manuscripts, but seems to be borrowed from Luke 19:10.

that Christ spoke with Peter about paying the two-drachma tax; 17:24–25). Unlike Mark, Matthew passes over the detail that the disciples had a heated debate between them before they reached the house on the subject of **who is the greatest in the Kingdom of the heavens**. He also passes over the detail that they were at first reluctant to admit they had such a quarrel (Mark 9:33–34). The disciples' question came to Jesus mostly through an embarrassed silence.

Christ answers their concern by **calling a child *to Himself*** to serve as a visible object lesson to those who would be His servants. (This lesson was the more obvious to the disciples, for the word for "child" and for "servant" was the same in Aramaic.) Having **stood** the child **in the middle** of them where all could see him, Christ declares that those who are proudly concerned for their status in the world must **turn** and repent **and become as children**. Otherwise they will **never enter into the Kingdom of the heavens**. Children had no more social status than slaves in those days (see Gal. 4:1); His disciples must resign themselves to having no status in the world and to being marginalized and despised. Their concern for who would be greater than his fellows is utterly inconsistent with their discipleship.

Does any of them want to be **the greatest in the Kingdom**? Let **this one therefore humble himself** and be servant to the others, content to have no status in this world.

Christ then picks the child up to identify him with Himself (Mark 9:36). The humblest disciple, even the one with the least status, shares Christ's dignity as one beloved by the Father, so that to **welcome one such child** or disciple **in** His **Name** (that is, simply because such a one is Christ's disciple) is to **welcome** Christ Himself. *All* Christ's disciples are beloved, and **whoever makes one of these little ones**, the humblest of His disciples, to **stumble** and fall away will suffer the gravest of consequences at the last day. Indeed, it would be better for the offender to have **a millstone *turned by*** a donkey (that is, the large grinding stone used to make flour, so heavy that a donkey was used to turn it) **hung around his neck and be sunk in the** deep **open sea**. Let the disciples take care that their quarreling does not cause their weaker brothers to be offended and to forsake the fellowship of Christ's disciples!

Woe to the world, tyrannized by Satan, **because of** its **stumbling blocks!** Because of Satan's activity it is **necessary** and inevitable **that stumbling blocks** and apostasies occur, but **woe to that man through whom** they come! Each disciple should take care that his quarreling is not the cause of someone else's fall.

Each must cut off jealous pride from his heart, be it ever so dear to him. **If** the disciple's **hand or foot made** him **stumble** and sin so that he would **be cast into the eternal fire**, would he not **cut it off and cast** *it* far from him to save himself? Better **to enter the Life** of the Kingdom **crippled or lame than having two hands or two feet** to be eternally lost. Even one's precious **eye** could not be spared if it stood between oneself and salvation. Better to **tear it out and cast** *it* far away and **enter into the Life one-eyed, than having two eyes to be cast into the Gehenna of fire**. If one would even sacrifice one's bodily members to gain salvation, how much more must one's pride be sacrificed?

Each disciple, then, is valuable to God, and they should **not despise** even **one of these little ones**, the humblest of them. Each is so dear to God that their guardian **angels always see the face of** the **Father**. Not all angels have such immediate access to the King, but only those closest to the throne, such as the cherubim and seraphim. Yet the guardians of Jesus' disciples have such an important mission that they have constant access to the Father.

Surely the disciples can understand the value possessed by a single one of them? **If any man has a hundred sheep** in his flock and finds that **one of them has strayed**, will he **not leave the ninety-nine upon the** perilous **mountains?** Such a man does not say, "Oh well, it's only one sheep—I still have ninety-nine others!" No, he **goes and seeks the one that is straying**, whatever the danger to himself and his flock. And if he **finds it**, Christ assures His disciples, **he rejoices over** that one sheep **more than over the ninety-nine which have not strayed**. Just as the shepherd values that single sheep, in the same way God values each and every one of the disciples, even the least of them, so that it is **not** His **will** that even one of them

perish. In saying this, Jesus challenges His disciples to value each other as dearly as their Father values them—and cease quarreling over first place.

§X.2. Sin among the Disciples

> ৡ৾ ৡ৾ ৡ৾ ৡ৾ ৡ৾
>
> 15 "And if your brother sins, go and reprove him between you and him alone; if he hears you, you have gained your brother.
>
> 16 "But if he does not hear, take along one or two more with you, that in the mouth of two or three witnesses every word may stand.
>
> 17 "And if he refuses to hear them, tell it to the Church; and if he refuses to hear even the Church, let him be to you as the Gentile and the tax-collector.
>
> 18 "Amen I say to you, whatever you will have bound upon the earth will have been bound in heaven, and whatever you will have loosed upon the earth will have been loosed in heaven.
>
> 19 "Again I say to you that if two of you agree upon the earth about every matter whatever they ask, it will be done for them by My Father in the heavens,
>
> 20 "for where two or three have been gathered in My Name, there I am in the middle of them."

Having spoken of the necessity of humility and unity in verses 1–14, Jesus continues His discourse to the disciples, and speaks of what to do when a fellow disciple insists on breaking this unity. The scenario here supposed is that of a **brother** who **sins** by persisting in grievous sin, not simply by committing a petty offense against his fellow. (The best manuscripts say, "if your brother sins," not, "if your brother sins *against you*"; the additional words were probably added later on the basis of Peter's question in v. 21.) When you see your brother sinning, Christ says, you are to **go and reprove** the offender **between you and him alone**. The privacy of the reproof will make it easier for the offender to repent, for it will allow him to save his pride in so doing. **If he hears you** and heeds the reproof, **you have gained** and saved **your brother**.

It is unlikely that the sin here discussed is simply a personal quarrel, such as are inevitable in any relationship. In speaking of **reproving** a brother (Gr. *elegxo*), Christ echoes the counsel given in Leviticus 19:17 (where the same Greek verb is used in the Septuagint). Leviticus 19 contains a series of serious offenses to be avoided, for which a man would incur the wrath of God (such as idolatry; Lev. 19:4). Leviticus 19:17 counsels that if anyone sees his neighbor committing these sins, he must "not hate his brother in his heart" but "reprove" him that he "may not incur sin because of him." That is, to allow one's neighbor to do these sins would be to share in his sin and guilt. He must rather reprove him that he might repent. I suggest that sins of the same gravity are in view here. The sinning Christian brother is not simply committing a personal slight against another, but living in such a way as to repudiate the Gospel.

If the brother does not repent on being privately reproved, the first brother is to **take along one or two more** with him, that these may act as **witnesses** of all that follows. (This is in accordance with the spirit of Deuteronomy 19:15, which speaks of the necessity of two or three witnesses before condemning someone accused.) Such a larger delegation may move the sinning brother to repentance, as he sees the gravity of his actions. But **if he refuses to hear** even **them**, the next step is to **tell** the man's sins **to the Church**, revealing the sin to the entire local community of disciples. Then the whole community is to unite in their pleas to bring the offender back to righteousness. But **if he refuses to hear even the Church,** he has clearly hardened his heart and is a lost cause, preferring his own pride to the love of all his brethren. He is therefore to be ostracized and disowned by the Christian community, avoided as Jews avoided **the Gentile and the tax-collector**. That is, none were to acknowledge him as a brother or a fellow disciple. In later Church terms, he was to be barred from Church assembly and Eucharist.

Christ then solemnly declares that God will confirm the judgment of the Church in such matters. The authority Christ earlier gave to the Church in the person of its leader Peter (see 16:19 and commentary) is now confirmed here also. In declaring acts bound or loosed, forbidden or allowed, the Church community, guided by its apostolic leaders, spoke on behalf of God. The declaration of verse 18 is made to all the apostles (the **you** is plural), as representative of the entire Church. The erring sinner has no other earthly court of appeal once the Church has spoken.

Christ affirms this authority **again** in verse 19, for it stands at the heart of His will for His Church. **If two** of them **agree upon the earth about every matter** like this for which they **ask** God's confirmation, **it will be done** by Christ's **Father in the heavens**. What they bind or loose **upon the earth** will be confirmed in heaven also. This was certain **for** (note the causative) where even **two or three have been gathered in** Christ's **Name, there** He is **in the middle of them**.

It is important to note the context of this promise. It is not a promise that any two Christians may obtain their general requests from God so long as they can agree about it. The context here is rather the inclusion or exclusion of a sinning brother, and the Church's decision **upon the earth** about him (verses 17–18). Christ spoke in verse 16 of two (or three) witnesses who deal with the erring brother, and who constitute the witnesses in the Church's judgment, and I would suggest that the same two (or three) are in view in verses 19–20. That is, the **two** who **agree** and reach the same verdict are the minimum two who first confronted the sinner and who now constitute the Church's judges in the **matter** or legal case before them (Gr. *pragma*, compare its use in 1 Cor. 6:1). If these two ask the heavenly Father to confirm their earthly judgment, **it will be done**.

The reason it will be done is that Christ Himself will be in the middle of them, guiding them with His invisible Presence. In the

Jewish *Sayings of the Fathers*, it is said that "when two sit and there are between them words of the Law, the *Shekinah* [or Divine Presence] rests between them" (3,3). Christ gives a similar promise to His disciples, saying that when they are **gathered** together in solemn assembly as His Church, He will be present in their midst, even if that gathering be only **two or three** of them. Even if the local Church is that small, the Presence of Christ goes with it.

§X.3. Parable of the Unforgiving Servant

ॐ ॐ ॐ ॐ ॐ

21 Then Peter came *to Him* and said to Him, "Lord, how often shall my brother sin against me and I forgive him? Up to seven times?"

22 Jesus says to him, "I do not say to you, 'up to seven times,' but 'up to seventy times seven.'

23 "For this reason the Kingdom of the heavens may be likened to a man, a king who wanted to settle accounts with his slaves.

24 "And when he had begun to settle, there was brought to him one debtor *who owed* a myriad of talents.

25 "But since he did not have *the means* to repay, his lord ordered that he be sold, and his wife and children and all that he had, and *that he* be repaid.

26 "The slave therefore falling down, worshipped him, saying, 'Be patient with me, and I will repay you everything!'

27 "And the lord of that slave had heartfelt *love* and released him and forgave him the loan.

28 "But that slave went out and found one of his fellow-slaves who owed him a hundred denarii, and he seized *him* and was choking him, saying, 'Repay what you owe!'

29 "Therefore his fellow-slave fell down and was

> entreating him, saying, 'Be patient with me
> and I will repay you!'
>
> 30 "He was not willing, however, but went and
> cast him into prison until he should repay what
> was owing.
>
> 31 "When therefore his fellow-slaves saw the
> things that had happened, they were extremely
> sorrowful and came and explained to their lord
> all the things that had happened.
>
> 32 "Then having called him, his lord says to him,
> 'Evil slave, I forgave you all that debt because
> you entreated me.
>
> 33 "'Should you *yourself* not also have had mercy
> on your fellow-slave, as I *myself* also had mercy
> on you?'
>
> 34 "And his lord, *filled* with anger, delivered him
> over to the torturers until he should repay all
> that was owing.
>
> 35 "Thus will My heavenly Father also do to you,
> if each does not forgive his brother from your
> hearts."

Still smarting somewhat perhaps from the initial rebuke of their quarrel (see Mark 9:33–34), **Peter came** to Jesus with the question, **"How often shall my brother sin against me and I forgive him? Up to seven times?"** Many rabbis (possibly on the basis on Amos 1:3f, which speaks of Israel being punished for three transgressions) suggested that three was the maximum number of times a man must forgive the same offense. Peter seemingly had doubled this number and added even to that, and doubtless felt that his question showed how spiritual (and great) he truly was.

If so, he must have been shocked at his Lord's answer: **not "up to seven times," but "up to seventy times seven"**—that is, one should not keep track of such things, but forgive indefinitely. At Peter's stunned silence, Christ showed how reasonable such generosity was by telling a parable.

If the disciples would enter **the Kingdom of the heavens**, they must know by what arithmetic it is governed. This can be learned by heeding the story of **a man, a king who wanted to settle accounts with his slaves**. Early in the process, **there was brought to him one debtor** *who owed* **a myriad of talents**—that is, ten thousand talents, though the Greek *myrioi* was often used for any astronomically high number.

Each talent was worth approximately six thousand *denarii*, or six thousand days' wages for the laborer. Ten thousand talents was an extraordinary amount of money, for the total taxes collected from all Judea, Samaria, and Idumea in 4 BC equaled only six hundred talents. Even granting that the debtor in the parable is a governor of some sort, the debt is obviously unrealistic, for it amounts to billions of dollars in today's money. But Christ is not aiming at historical realism in this part of the parable. The figure is so huge because it images the debt of sin we owe to the King of heaven.

The debtor in the parable of course **did not have** *the means* **to repay** such a loan, and so **his lord** the king **ordered that he be sold**, along with **his wife and children and all that he had,** until the royal treasury **be repaid**. The practice of selling whole families into slavery to repay debts was the customary punishment in such cases.

The slave, falling down, worshipped his lord (i.e. fell down in prostrate and humble obeisance), begging him, **"Be patient with me, and I will repay you everything!"** The word **everything** comes first in the Greek ("everything I will repay"), stressing the man's promise to pay every single bit of his debt. This was ridiculous, of course, because the debt was too large, but the man spoke out of his grief and desperation. The man's tearful grief touched the heart of the king, and he **had heartfelt** *love* for him, pitying the pathetic man lying prostrate before him. He therefore **forgave him the loan**, and the man went forth owing nothing.

His heart should have been light and jubilant as he gazed at the world with new and happy eyes. One might have expected him to go to his family and friends with the good news. But he did not. Instead he **went out and found one of his fellow-slaves who owed**

him a hundred denarii (that is, just over three months' wages for the working man—a figure about 600,000 times less than that he had owed the king.) His thought was not on the king's generosity, but on what was owed him by others, and he went to find the other debtor as soon as he left the king's presence. Though the fellow-slave was not his social inferior but his equal, **he seized *him*** by the throat and began **choking him, saying, "Repay what you owe!"**

The unfortunate debtor **fell down** before him even as the first slave had fallen down before the king not long before, and entreated him using almost the identical words: **"Be patient with me and I will repay you!"** This entreaty, however, was the more reasonable, since if he had a delay, the debtor could indeed have repaid the debt; whereas the first debtor could not have repaid it no matter how long a delay was granted.

Despite the reasonableness of the request for a delay, **he was not willing, but went and cast him into prison until he should** (through the actions of his family and friends) **repay what was owing**.

This whole drama was observed by their **fellow-slaves**, and these were **extremely sorrowful** over the plight of their fellow who was thrown into prison so heartlessly. They therefore **came and explained to their lord** the king all that had occurred. The king's response was immediate—and just. He recalled the first debtor into his presence and denounced him as an **evil slave**, a wicked and worthless servant of his lord. Since the king **forgave** him **all that debt** simply because he **entreated** his lord, should he not have **had mercy** on his **fellow-slave** in the same way? He should have not only granted him the requested delay, but forgiven him the loan also! The king was *filled* **with anger** at such heartlessness and revoked his earlier remission of debt. Instead he **delivered him over to the torturers** who ran the pagan prisons of those days. He would stay there **until he should repay all that was owing**—that is, permanently, given the size of the debt.

The disciples, hearing this parable, could see the reasonableness of Christ's demand that they forgive their brother's sin seventy times seven. They had been forgiven an astronomical debt of sin by Christ's

heavenly Father—how could they not forgive the comparatively trivial debts owed to them? Christ ends His parable with a warning: in the parable, there was no mercy for the one who refused to be merciful. Neither will there be for His disciples, **if each does not** mercifully **forgive his brother** truly, **from** their **hearts**.

§X.4. Conclusion

ॐ ॐ ॐ ॐ ॐ

19 1   And it happened that when Jesus had finished these words, He departed from Galilee and came into the areas of Judea beyond the Jordan,

   2   and many crowds followed Him, and He healed them there.

Matthew concludes this discourse with the characteristic formula about Jesus having **finished these words**. In saying that **He departed from Galilee and came into the areas of Judea beyond the Jordan,** Matthew sets the stage for the final part of Christ's journey to Jerusalem (20:17). The reference to the district **beyond the Jordan** (i.e. east of the Jordan River) is probably a reference to Christ's stay in Perea (compare John 10:40) prior to the final journey to the Holy City.

Matthew adds that **many crowds followed Him, and He healed them there** to show that Christ entered Judea with the same power He displayed in Galilee. Wherever Jesus went, there was the power of God.

❧ XI ☙

MINISTRY IN JUDEA
(19:3—20:34)

§XI.1. Conflict with the Pharisees over Divorce

ৡ৶ ৡ৶ ৡ৶ ৡ৶ ৡ৶

19 3 And Pharisees came to Him, testing Him, and saying, "Is it permitted to a man to dismiss his wife for every cause?"

4 And He answered and said, "Have you not read that He who created them from the beginning made them male and female,

5 "and said, 'For this reason a man shall leave behind his father and mother, and shall be joined to his wife, and the two will be one flesh'?

6 "So they are no longer two, but one flesh. What therefore God has yoked-together, do not let man separate."

7 They say to Him, "Why therefore did Moses command to give her a booklet of divorce and dismiss her?"

8 He says to them, "Because of your hardness of heart, Moses allowed you to dismiss your wives; but from the beginning it has not been thus.

9 "And I say to you, whoever dismisses his wife, except for fornication, and marries another commits adultery."

In relating Christ's ministry in Judea, St. Matthew begins with a confrontation with some **Pharisees** on the subject of divorce. They begin by asking if it is **permitted to a man to dismiss his wife** in divorce **for every cause**. This was not so much a question as an opening gambit, for all knew that divorce was permitted under the Law, and the interpretation of Rabbi Hillel, which favored allowing divorce for any reason whatever, was the more popular. (The rival interpretation of Rabbi Shammai allowed it only in cases of adultery.) What did Jesus think of divorce? Would He side with Hillel or Shammai? In asking this, they were not seeking to be taught, but were **testing Him**, possibly trying to lure Him into making a statement about Herod's divorce, which had proven to be John the Baptizer's undoing (14:3–4), so that they could denounce Him to Herod.

Jesus responds by referring them back to the Scripture they have **read** so often, that **He who created them** at the very first said that **a man shall leave behind his father and mother, and shall be joined to his wife,** so that **the two will be one flesh** (Gen. 2:24). Jesus concludes from this part of the Law that the man and his wife are **no longer two, but one flesh**, one single organism. This represents God's primordial will for His creation, for it predates the Fall. **God** Himself **yoked-together** the two, and it is wrong for mere **man** to **separate** them through divorce, for this is to undo the work of God. Christ thus sides with neither Hillel nor Shammai, for He disallows divorce altogether.

The Pharisees focus on what Moses wrote later in the Law, in which he said that a man who wanted a divorce should **give** his wife **a booklet of divorce and dismiss her** (Deut. 24:1–3). If divorce is contrary to the will of God, **why** did **Moses command** this? Jesus does not dispute this provision, but declares that it was historically conditioned, a concession granted because of men's **hardness of heart**. The intent of the provision in Deuteronomy 24 was not to hold up divorce as good, but, assuming the reality of divorce, to prevent serial divorce and remarriage of the same woman, treating her like so much chattel. Like laws regulating war and slavery, this law presupposed an existing evil and sought only to minimize the harm.

To find God's perfect will for His people now that the Kingdom is at hand, one must return to His words about the relationship of **male and female** when God **created them from the beginning**. And these words in the early chapters of Genesis reveal that His perfect will does not include divorce, and that therefore **whoever dismisses his wife, except for fornication, and marries another commits adultery**. That is, divorcing one's wife does not alter the fact that the two are still one flesh, and so the second marriage constitutes adultery. The apparent exception to this principle is in cases of **fornication**—that is, fornication during the betrothal period (see commentary on 5:32). In such a case, the man need not go through with the marriage, but may divorce the betrothed woman. Thus this is not a true exception to the principle, for the fornicating woman has already become one flesh with someone else.

ॐ ॐ ॐ ॐ ॐ

10 The disciples say to Him, "If the case of the man with his wife is thus, it is advantageous not to marry."

11 But He said to them, "Not everyone *can* make room for this word, but those to whom it has been given.

12 "For there are eunuchs who were born thus from their mother's womb; and there are eunuchs who were made eunuchs by men; and there are eunuchs who made themselves eunuchs for the sake of the Kingdom of the heavens. He who is able to make room for *this*, let him make room."

The disciples come to Jesus privately with their perplexity over the apparent severity of Christ's response. If that is how it is, it is **advantageous not to marry**, for marriage seems to bring with it permanent obligations.

Christ acknowledges that **not everyone** can **make room** in his heart **for this word** of teaching, and that most men will find it too difficult. In the world, it is easier to regard marriage simply as a contract one can make or break at will. But **those to whom it has been given** by God to become His disciples are not of the world. They belong to the Kingdom and can, through God, do the apparently impossible (see also v. 26).

As evidence of this, He points to those who **make themselves eunuchs for the sake of the Kingdom**—that is, those who, like John the Baptizer, embrace a life of celibacy for the sake of God's work. There are eunuchs who decline marriage because they are **born thus from their mother's womb** and have a congenital impotence. There are those who are **made eunuchs by men**, castrated so as to serve as slaves in certain capacities. The involuntary nature of these eunuchs shows more clearly the amazing nature of those who voluntarily choose to be celibates, and to decline marriage so as to serve God free from the constraints of family. God can give this grace to His spiritual eunuchs, and He can give a similar grace to all Jesus' disciples to accept this more stringent view of marriage. Let the one who is **able to make room** for this view **make room** for it!

⚘ EXCURSUS
ON DIVORCE AND THE CHURCH'S PERMISSION TO REMARRY

The Church has always accepted as authoritative her Lord's declaration that all marriage (that is, sexual union) is organic, in that it makes two people into one single organism, "one flesh." That means that two married disciples of Jesus, having become one, should never divorce from each other, and that if they do, they incur guilt. From as early as St. Paul, however, the Church has recognized that this basic teaching of Jesus regarding marriage could not be equally applied to every conceivable situation—it was a norm, not a law.

Thus St. Paul wrote to the Corinthians that, although he was simply passing along the instructions of Jesus regarding married disciples (1 Cor. 7:10), he had no such detailed instructions to pass along regarding mixed marriages between believers and unbelievers, and therefore he gave his own apostolic ruling about this situation (1 Cor. 7:12). This ruling allowed for the believing partner to separate from the unbelieving one if the unbelieving one insisted on a divorce. St. Paul declared that the believer was "not enslaved in such cases," but could separate in peace (1 Cor. 7:15). In the culture of that day, freedom to separate contained within it the freedom to remarry, and it seems likely that this freedom was allowed the believing divorcee by St. Paul too.

That the Lord's teaching on divorce could not be uniformly applied to every situation was recognized by the Church of the patristic era also. Imperial laws allowed for divorce and remarriage on a number of grounds, and the Church did not denounce these laws as contrary to the Faith. Rather, the Church knew that human sin often mars the ideal, but that grace can forgive the penitent. As St. Epiphanius (+ 403) wrote in his book *Medicine Box*, "He who has separated from his wife for a valid motive, such as fornication, adultery, or another misdeed, if he takes another wife, the divine Word does not condemn him nor exclude him from the Church, but tolerates it rather on account of his weakness." And even those who divorced their spouses for invalid motives and remarried, when they repented and did the required penance of abstinence from Holy Communion, were restored to communion (see Canon 87 of the Quinisext Council).

The Lord's teaching on the permanence of the marital bond, therefore, constitutes the norm and goal for devout believers. The Church, in dealing with the complexities of life and all the permutations of sin and repentance, has directed her children toward that goal through a variety of means and paths.

§XI.2. The Rebuke of the Disciples over the Blessing of Children

ॐ ॐ ॐ ॐ ॐ

13 Then children were brought to Him that He might put His hands on them and pray; and the disciples rebuked them.
14 But Jesus said, "Let the children *come*, and do not forbid them from coming to Me; for the Kingdom of the heavens belongs to such as these."
15 And after putting His hands on them, He departed from there.

After this some **children were brought** to Jesus **that He might put His hands on them and pray** for God's blessing. It was not unusual for mothers to bring their young children to a famous rabbi that he might invoke God's blessing on their future lives. After Jesus had already spent a long and exhausting day teaching, this was what the mothers there wanted from Him.

The disciples, however, considered this request to be a trivial one, and they **rebuked them**, telling the mothers to go away and let the Master rest. When Jesus (possibly resting nearby) overheard this (possibly the mothers were protesting loudly?), He insisted that His disciples **let the children *come***. They are **not** to **forbid them from coming to** Him, as if they were insignificant. Contrary to what the world thinks of children, they have great status in the eyes of God, for **the Kingdom of the heavens belongs to such as these**. He therefore received the delegation of mothers with their children, and did not **depart from there** until He had **put His hands on them** in blessing, as requested.

What did Christ mean in saying that the Kingdom belongs to people like those children? What was it about those children that made them suitable heirs of the Kingdom? Their free and open acceptance of Jesus and His love. The children had no status on which they could rely. Unlike the proud Pharisees who were testing the Lord regarding divorce (19:3f), the children did not rely on their own righteousness, but came with open hearts and empty hands. They received the Kingdom as a gift, without trying to earn it, as must all who would receive it. The children thus were an example of true discipleship to all. It was supremely fitting that Christ receive them and bless them.

§XI.3. The Rich Young Man and the Kingdom of God

ॐ ॐ ॐ ॐ ॐ

16 And behold! one came to Him and said, "Teacher, what good *thing* shall I do that I may have eternal life?"

17 And He said to him, "Why are you asking Me about the good? *There is* One *who* is good; but if you want to enter into the Life, keep the commandments."

18 He says to him, "Which ones?" And Jesus said, "You shall not commit murder; you shall not commit adultery; you shall not steal; you shall not bear false witness;

19 "honor your father and mother; and you shall love your neighbor as yourself."

20 The young man says to Him, "All these things I have kept; what am I still lacking?"

21 Jesus said to him, "If you want to be perfect, go, sell your possessions and give to the poor, and you shall have treasure in the heavens; and come, follow Me."

22 But when the young man heard this word, he went away sorrowful; for he was *one who* had many properties.

Next Matthew relates the story of a **young man** who came to Jesus with an urgent question. In Mark 10:17, it is related that he ran up to Jesus and knelt before Him, and in Matthew's narrative

the surprise of his sudden appearance is expressed by the characteristic **behold!**

The young man addresses Jesus respectfully as **Teacher** and
asks, **"What good *thing* shall I do that I may have eternal life?"**
That is, he asks what *mitzvah*, what good deed or mighty work
he could do to secure himself a place in the age to come. His use
of the adjective **good** shows that his conception of good is superficial and inadequate. The young man thinks he can easily perform
some feat of goodness that will impress God and ensure him
eternal life.

Before answering the question, Christ first brings to the man's
attention the inadequacy of his understanding of goodness, asking,
"Why are you asking Me about the good?" For there is only **One**
who **is** truly **good**—God. If the young man is to find his way, he
must recognize that true goodness is transcendent and otherworldly,
and not be so quick to think that goodness can be easily attained.

Christ then answers the question directly. The young man knows
the commandments—if he would **enter into the Life** to come,
let him **keep** these. The young man responds by asking, **"Which
ones?"** for the Pharisees were quick to focus on the tradition of the
elders. Christ, however, means the basic commandments of the Law,
which focus on love of neighbor, for love of God can be measured
in love of neighbor. (The commandments cited are from the Ten
Commandments in Ex. 20 and the commandment to love one's
neighbor from Lev. 19:18.) If one expresses one's love for God in
such ways, one can rest assured that all will be well.

The young man assures Jesus that **all these things** he has **kept**
ever since he became a man (Mark 10:20). Yet he **still** feels that he is
lacking something. He is still tormented by a void that weighs daily
on him. Something more is needed. He is ready to do some heroic
feat for God by which he hopes he can fill the void in his heart.

Jesus does not contradict the man, nor say that he has not kept
the commandments. But He realizes that the man's perception of
something lacking is a sign that God is calling him to perfection, to
Christian discipleship. His keeping of the Law is enough for him to
inherit life in the age to come, but God is calling him to an experience

of that life right now, as a disciple of Christ. He therefore invites him to become **perfect** (Gr. *teleios*—"mature, whole"; compare 5:48), to reach the goal for which he was made. He should **go** from where he is, **sell** his **possessions,** and **give** the money **to the poor.** Then he will **have treasure in the heavens.** He should break the mold of his past life and **come, follow** Jesus in a new life. In that new life, the void of his heart will be gloriously filled.

When the young man heard this word, however, he was **sorrowful**. He was prepared to give away *some* money, but not to break the mold of his past so thoroughly. He had hoped that Jesus would give him advice that could fit into his life as he knew it. He was not prepared to bid farewell to that life completely. He liked his life, **for he was** *one who* **had many properties**. He then **went away,** spurning the Lord's offer and leaving unfulfilled the possibility of a new life.

ॐ ॐ ॐ ॐ ॐ

23 And Jesus said to His disciples, "Amen I say to you, it is difficult for a rich *man* to enter into the Kingdom of the heavens.

24 "And again I say to you, it is easier for a camel to go through the eye of a needle than for a rich *man* to enter into the Kingdom of God."

25 And when the disciples heard, they were extremely thunderstruck and said, "Then who is able to be saved?"

26 And looking at them, Jesus said to them, "With men this is impossible, but with God all things *are* possible."

As the rich man departs, Jesus solemnly declares to His disciples that it is obviously **difficult for a rich *man* to enter into the Kingdom of the heavens** in this age. The experience of this young man proves how hard it is for those who have wealth to become Jesus' true disciples. That life of discipleship involves willingness to lose wealth and popularity in this world, and to shake oneself free from the chains of Mammon. The rich are reluctant to do this, for they have much to lose. Indeed, it is **easier for a camel to go through the eye of a needle than for a rich *man* to enter into the Kingdom of God**. That is, humanly speaking, it is impossible! Such is the vulnerability of the human heart to wealth's temptations.

When the disciples heard this, **they were extremely thunderstruck**. Most assumed that wealth was the reward of God, a sign of His favor. If even the rich were to have such difficulty, **then who** was **able to be saved?** Surely there was no hope for the rest of the world!

Christ **looked at them**, staring at them, measuring the despair of their hearts (*emblepo*, a more intensive form than *blepo*, "to look"). He does have a word of assurance for them after all, though He does not revoke any of His words about the dangers of wealth. But He does say that **with God all things *are* possible**. With divine help, even the rich can find the power to renounce their pursuit of wealth and follow God in singleness of heart. With God working in the human heart, even the rich can use their wealth for God's sake (compare 1 Tim. 6:17–19).

ॐ ॐ ॐ ॐ ॐ

27 Then Peter answered and said to Him, "Behold, we *ourselves* have left everything and followed You; what then will there be for us?"

28 And Jesus said to them, "Amen I say to you, that you who have followed Me, in the regeneration when the Son of man will sit on the throne of His glory, you *yourselves* also will sit upon twelve thrones, judging the twelve tribes of Israel.

29 "And everyone who has left houses or brothers or sisters or father or mother or children or fields for My Name's sake will receive a hundredfold, and will inherit eternal life.

30 "But many *who are* first will be last; and the last *ones*, first."

Peter, speaking for the rest, was anxious for reassurance. Like the rest, he was startled by Christ's words of verses 23–24. The rich young man was not willing to leave everything behind—but the disciples had done so! With the plaintiveness of a nervous child, he reminds the Lord that *they* anyway (the pronoun **we** is emphatic) have **left everything and followed** Jesus. What will their reward be? Surely they will inherit the Kingdom?

Christ assures him that all the Twelve who have followed Him in such dedication, **in the regeneration** (the time when all the world will be born anew in the age to come), **when the Son of man will sit on the throne of His glory** and reign over Israel, will **also sit upon twelve thrones, judging the twelve tribes of Israel** on His behalf. The glory He will know will be shared by them.

And it is not just the Twelve who will be rewarded. **Everyone** in fact who has **left houses or brothers or sisters or father or mother or children or fields for** the **sake** of being His disciple will be compensated a **hundredfold**. That is, every sacrifice of earthly security will be gloriously rewarded, even in this age. (Thus would the void within the heart of the rich young man have been filled.) And in the age to come, all will **inherit eternal life** as well. But one's status in this age does not determine one's status in the age to come. **Many** *who are* **first** in this age, who are important men, will **be last** and least in the age to come, just as many who are **the last** and least in this world will occupy the **first** places in the Kingdom. Wealth and status are supremely unimportant, and all can cheerfully renounce their status for the sake of God.

§XI.4. Parable of the Workers in the Field

꣓ꣴ ꣓ꣴ ꣓ꣴ ꣓ꣴ ꣓ꣴ

20 1   "For the Kingdom of the heavens is like a man *who was* a housemaster, who went out early in the morning to hire workers for his vineyard.

2   "And having agreed with the workers for a

denarius *for* the day, he sent them into his vineyard.

3　"And having gone out about the third hour, he saw others standing idle in the marketplace;

4　"and he said to those, 'You *yourselves* also go away into the vineyard, and whatever is just I will give you.' And they went.

5　"Again he went out about the sixth and the ninth hour, and did likewise.

6　"And about the eleventh *hour* he went out, and found others standing; and he says to them, 'Why have you been standing here idle all the day?'

7　"They say to him, 'Because no one hired us.' He says to them, 'You *yourselves* also go away into the vineyard.'

8　"And when evening had come, the lord of the vineyard says to his manager, 'Call the workers and render them their wages, beginning with the last to the first.'

9　"And when those *hired* about the eleventh hour came, each one received a denarius.

10　"And when those *hired* first came, they thought that they would receive more; and they *themselves* each also received a denarius.

11　"And when they received *it*, they grumbled against the housemaster,

12　"saying, 'These last *ones* have done one hour, and you have made them equal to us who have borne the burden and the heat of the day!'

13　"But he answered and said to one of them, 'Comrade, I am not unjust; did you not agree with me for a denarius?

14　"'Take what is yours and go away, but I want to give to this last *one* as *I gave* also to you.

> 15 "'Is it not permitted me to do what I want with what is my own? Or is your eye evil because I *myself* am good?'
> 16 "Thus the last *ones* will be first, and the first *ones* last."

The Lord illustrates this principle of the last being first and the first last (19:30) by telling another parable, for **the Kingdom of the heavens** is such that it overthrows all the standards of this age. In his question of 19:27, Peter showed that he was very concerned that he be adequately rewarded for his labor, and was worried that God might unjustly overlook his sacrifices and work. Christ perceived lurking behind this question a dangerous attitude, one which, if left unchecked, might grow into a niggardly and grudging spirit. God would indeed reward the Twelve for their work. But in the Kingdom, God's response to men was still one of grace, not one of works. He would recompense the apostles for their sacrifices, but they should not conclude from this that God would give to each one no more than he deserved. That was the mistake of the Pharisees: they knew that sinners deserved punishment, not forgiveness, and they stumbled at the thought of God giving the sinner undeserved grace. In the Kingdom, God would always give more than one deserved.

In the parable, therefore, Christ presents His disciples with a **man** *who was* **a housemaster** (that is, a landowner) who **went out early in the morning to hire workers for his vineyard**. The first group of workers were hired early for the whole day's work, being promised **a denarius** for their labor, the usual wage for such a worker.

It is possible that the harvest urgently needed to be brought in, for the landowner went out several times that day to hire men. Therefore at **about the third hour** (that is, nine A.M.) he went out to the **marketplace** (the normal place to find men seeking work) to find more workers, and again at **about the sixth and the ninth hour** (that is, noon and three P.M.). At the **eleventh** *hour* (that is, five P.M.), just an hour before quitting time, **he found others standing** about idle, and asked them, **"Why have you been standing here idle all the day?"** Upon receiving the answer, **"Because no one hired us,"** he promptly hired them and sent them into the vineyard, even if it was just for an hour's work in the cool of the day.

At the end of the day, he tells his **manager** or foreman to summon the workers that they might be paid. (According to the provision of the Law in Deut. 24:15, the laborer was paid for his work at the end of each working day.) Those hired **last, at about the eleventh hour,** were the first to receive their wages, and they were paid **a denarius**—as were each of the other workers. Not surprisingly, those *hired* first and who had **borne the burden** of work and **the heat of the day** were impressed at this generosity, and thought they would receive more than the promised denarius. When they too were paid the same wage as those who worked only one hour, they **grumbled against** their employer, protesting loudly at what they considered a flagrant injustice. The **lord of the vineyard** had **made these last ones** equal to them, though they had only **done one hour's** work! Who did he think he was? What kind of pay was this?

The landowner is unimpressed by these protests. He addresses them formally and courteously as **comrade** (Gr. *etairos*, "companion, friend"), but firmly rejects their accusation of injustice. **Did** they **not agree** with him **for a denarius?** And have they not received what was promised? Let them **take** what is now theirs and **go away**—and let *him* **do what** he **wants** with what is *his*! Or do they have a problem with greed? Is their **eye evil** (that is, greedy and envious) because he is **good** and generous?

So, Jesus concludes, it will be the same at the last judgment, for there **the last ones will be first and the first ones** last (compare Luke 13:28–30). Those who had small hearts (like the Pharisees) might grudge God's generosity in the Kingdom. They had labored long and hard at righteousness. How was it that the sinners and tax-collectors, those who had not borne the heat of the day or labored at righteousness, could repent at the last minute and be offered the Kingdom too? It was not fair!

By this parable Christ reveals the unworthy and grasping nature of such complaints. The righteous were offered the Kingdom, just like the rest. What harm is it to them if God grants the Kingdom also to the unrighteous who repent? In the Kingdom, therefore, all the mathematics of the worldly are overthrown by the grace of God. For He "will accept the last even as the first; He gives rest to him who comes at the eleventh hour, even as to him who has worked from the first hour; He shows mercy upon the last and cares for the first" (Paschal Sermon of St. John Chrysostom). Peter and the others must therefore beware that their proper concern for rewards not degenerate into resentment over the grace of God given to all.

One final observation about one of the details of the parable: The dialogue between the lord of the vineyard and the unemployed workers of the eleventh hour in verses 6–7 is not necessary to the parable as a whole. Why is this detail there? I suggest that it is there because it reveals God's love for sinners and expresses His grace, which the workers from the first hour found so objectionable. Those eleventh-hour workers were idle, not because of laziness, but simply because no one had hired them despite their willingness to work. Thus the lord of the vineyard has no word of rebuke for them, but simply hires them, willing to pay them an undeserved full wage for just an hour's work. In the same way, God has no word of rebuke for sinners, but in kindness offers them the Kingdom, just for their discipleship to Jesus. The dialogue is there to show how those unemployed in righteousness are not blamed for their idleness, but given a new chance and put to work.

§XI.5. Third Passion Prediction

ॐ ॐ ॐ ॐ ॐ

17 And as Jesus was about to go up to Jerusalem, He took the Twelve by themselves, and on the way He said to them,

18 "Behold, we are going up to Jerusalem, and the Son of man will be delivered to the chief-priests and scribes, and they will condemn Him to death,

19 "and will deliver Him to the Gentiles to mock and scourge and crucify, and on the third day He will be raised."

As the final journey to **Jerusalem** grew nearer, Christ continued to prepare **the Twelve** to endure the trials they would face, lest they entirely lose their faith because of them. He told them that He would be **delivered to the chief-priests and scribes** there, who would **condemn Him to death** and **deliver Him** in turn **to the Gentiles** to be put to the most shameful of deaths. It was only after this that He would **be raised** in triumph. By recording Christ predicting His Passion these three times, Matthew makes clear that the final events were entirely voluntary. Christ was not defeated against His will, but all happened according to His exact foreknowledge and the Father's plan.

The apostles, however, did not understand these predictions of the Passion, for their minds were full of thoughts of the earthly glory that would be theirs in the coming Kingdom. They continued to view the Kingdom in worldly terms, and concluded that Christ's words about death and defeat must be some kind of metaphor or parable.

§XI.6. James and John Rebuked for Seeking First Place

20 Then the mother of the sons of Zebedee came to Him with her sons, worshipping and requesting something from Him.

21 And He said to her, "What do you want?" She says to Him, "Say that in Your Kingdom these two sons of mine may sit, one on Your right and one on the left."

22 But Jesus answered and said, "You do not know what you request. Are you able to drink the cup that I *Myself* am about to drink?" They say to Him, "We are able."

23 He says to them, "My cup indeed you will drink; but to sit on My right and on the left, this is not Mine to give, but it is for those for whom it has been prepared by My Father."

This concern for worldly glory is aptly illustrated by the attempt of James and John to secure for themselves the top two places in the new regime they thought Christ was about to establish. During what was perhaps a roadside rest on the way to Jerusalem and a more private moment, **the sons of Zebedee** got their **mother** to do the talking for them and present their request, thinking perhaps it would seem less self-serving if it came from her. They begin in a formal Eastern way, **worshipping** before Him (that is, making a prostration), and asking if they may present their **request**.

Jesus asks what this request might be, and is told she wants His promise that **in** His **Kingdom** and the new regime that is about to arrive, her **two sons** James and John might **sit, one on** His **right and one on** His **left**. That is, she is requesting that they receive the top two places of authority, on the time-honored basis of this secret "backroom" deal—cutting out Peter, who until then has occupied first place as leader of the Twelve.

Christ does not immediately rebuke this desire, even though it is entirely wrongly motivated. Rather He begins by saying that they do **not know what** they are **requesting**, for in the new Kingdom receiving glory is the reward for enduring suffering. Are they really asking for the greatest suffering? Are they **able to drink the cup** of suffering that He is **about to drink** in Jerusalem?

They quickly reply that they are **able**, and although they do not fully know to what they are agreeing, Christ takes them at their word. They will **indeed** suffer for Him (James would be beheaded, and John would be banished to Patmos). Nonetheless, the top two positions are **not** His **to give** on the basis of such requests, but are only **for those for whom it has been prepared by** His **Father**. They may have glory through suffering, but having *more glory than the others* is not something given as a personal favor. This lies with the wisdom and will of God, who orders all men and their lot as He decrees.

ॐ ॐ ॐ ॐ ॐ

24 And hearing *this*, the ten were indignant about the two brothers.

---

25 But Jesus called them to Himself and said, "You know that the rulers of the Gentiles lord it over them, and the great men exercise *tyrannous* authority over them.

26 "It will not be thus among you, but whoever wants to become great among you will be your servant,

27 "and whoever wants to be first among you will be your slave;

28 "just as the Son of man did not come to be served, but to serve, and to give His life a ransom for many."

Though this was meant to be a private conversation, word inevitably got out to the other **ten**, who were understandably **indignant about the two brothers**. This was not because they understood about humility and the true nature of rewards in the Kingdom, but rather because each of them was coveting the best position for himself. All thought of the Kingdom only in terms of glory and privilege.

Christ then deals with the inner attitude that motivated the request of James and John, and which lives within the hearts of them all. He **calls them to Himself** for a time of teaching and begins to show them the priority of humility. He appeals first to a reality they all know and detest—the example of Gentiles in authority. As Jews, they all know of the arrogance of the Romans who occupy Palestine, and how things are in the Gentile world. **The rulers of the Gentiles lord it over them** and **the great men** in the world **exercise *tyrannous* authority over them**. Yet the disciples are acting in the same way as those hated Gentiles, for they are concerned only about power and status.

It will **not be thus among** them in the coming Kingdom. Rather, **whoever wants to become great** in that Kingdom must behave like the **servant** of all (Gr. *diakonos*), and **whoever wants to be first** there must prove himself their **slave** (Gr. *doulos*). Glory and authority in the age to come will not be given to those who are self-serving, but to those whose hearts are set on serving their fellows. Christ Himself will lead the way and show them this. Though He is **the Son of man**, the Messiah, He still **came not to be served, but to serve** (Gr. *diakoneo*), putting the welfare of others before His own, as servants do. He will do this, holding nothing back—not even His own **life**, which He will **give** as **a ransom for many**.

Doubtless the Twelve did not understand this last reference to Christ giving His life, any more than they understood the repeated predictions of His Passion. This understanding would come later, when they could look back on the Cross and see that His death was not a simple execution, but a sacrifice that bought back the many millions of the world from slavery to death and sin.

§XI.7. Healing of the Blind Men

꒨ ꒨ ꒨ ꒨ ꒨

29 And as they were going out from Jericho, a large crowd followed Him.

30 And behold! two blind men sitting beside the way, hearing that Jesus was passing by, cried out, saying, "Have mercy on us, Lord, Son of David!"

31 And the crowd rebuked them, that they should be silent, but they cried out all the more, saying, "Have mercy on us, Lord, Son of David!"

32 And Jesus stood and called them, and said, "What do you want Me to do for you?"

33 They say to Him, "Lord, that our eyes be opened!"

34 And having heartfelt *love*, Jesus touched their eyes; and immediately they saw again and followed Him.

The last event narrated before Christ's entry into Jerusalem is the healing of two blind men as Christ and His disciples were **going out from Jericho** with **a large crowd**. The **two blind men** were

sitting beside the way, begging by the roadside. This account is related in Mark 10:46f and Luke 18:35f, where Luke combines it with the story of Zacchaeus of Jericho in Luke 19:1f. It would seem as if the story has undergone considerable abbreviation in all three accounts.

I would suggest the following reconstruction of events: As Jesus and His entourage entered Jericho, He met one of the beggars, Bartimaeus, one well-known to the locals (hence Mark 10:46 gives his name). Jesus enters Jericho, stays overnight at the home of Zacchaeus, and leaves the town the next morning. By then Bartimaeus has been joined by another, who had perhaps learned of Bartimaeus' plan to reposition himself and meet Jesus as He leaves Jericho. All three Synoptic writers telescope these events, with Luke mentioning Bartimaeus's original location on the way into Jericho (Luke 18:35), and Matthew and Mark mentioning their position on the way out of Jericho (20:29; Mark 10:46). Luke alone mentions the overnight stay with Zacchaeus, and Matthew alone mentions the second blind man joining Bartimaeus.

Matthew focuses on the fact that there were two blind men because of his Jewish concern with providing the legal two witnesses to Jesus' messiahship. (See the Excursus: "On the Doubles in Matthew's Gospel.") When they heard that it was the famous wonderworker **Jesus** of Nazareth who was **passing by**, they **cried out, "Have mercy on us, Lord, Son of David!"** This was a popular estimation of Jesus, as many thought He would be the designated Messiah (compare 9:27; 12:23; 15:22).

Their relentless crying was irritating to the crowd, and they **rebuked them, that they should be silent**. Perhaps it shocked them that these beggars should shout out such a controversial title, which others had only whispered privately. But the more the blind men were told to be quiet, they more they shouted.

Upon hearing them, **Jesus stood** still in the road **and called them** to Him. It was obvious what two blind men wanted, but for Jesus, these men were not two "cases," or two interruptions that must be dealt with before moving on. They were two people, and were to be treated with respect. Therefore, Jesus did not presume, but allowed them to state their request, **that** their eyes **be opened**.

Matthew records that at the pathetic sight of two wretched blind beggars trembling before Him, Jesus **had heartfelt *love*** for them, and that His heart overflowed with compassion. He **touched their eyes** in a gentle laying on of hands, and **immediately they saw again**. As the boisterous and joyful procession continued on its way to Jerusalem, the two healed men also **followed Him**, not just as joining the crowd, but as His newest disciples.

❦ XII ❧

MINISTRY IN JERUSALEM
(21:1—23:39)

§XII.1. Entry into Jerusalem

§XII.1.i. Triumphal Entry

❧ ❧ ❧ ❧ ❧

21 1 And when they had drawn near to Jerusalem and had come to Bethphage, to the Mountain of Olives, then Jesus sent two disciples,

2 saying to them, "Go into the village opposite you, and immediately you will find a donkey bound and a colt with her; loose *them* and bring *them* to Me.

3 "And if anyone says anything to you, you will say, 'The Lord has need of them,' and immediately he will send them."

4 Now this happened that what was spoken through the prophet might be fulfilled, saying,

5 "Say to the daughter of Zion, 'Behold your King comes to you, humble and mounted upon a donkey, even upon a colt, the son of a yoke-animal.'"

6 And the disciples went and did just as Jesus had directed them,

7 and brought the donkey and the colt, and laid their garments on them, and He sat on top of them.

> 8 And a large crowd spread their garments in the way, and others were cutting branches from the trees and spreading them in the way.
>
> 9 And the crowds going before Him and those who were following were crying out, saying, "Hosanna to the Son of David! Blessed is He who comes in the Name of the Lord! Hosanna in the highest!"
>
> 10 And when He had entered into Jerusalem, all the city was shaken, saying, "Who is this?"
>
> 11 And the crowds were saying, "This is the prophet Jesus, from Nazareth in Galilee!"

Matthew's narrative of Christ's final days in Jerusalem begins with His triumphal entry into the city. This had long been planned, and was to be done in such a way as to reveal what sort of Messiah Jesus was. They were staying overnight in Bethany (John 12:1f), just a mile or so from Jerusalem. The next morning, when they had **drawn near to Jerusalem** and were facing **Bethphage** (a suburb of Jerusalem, which was actually within its city limits), **Jesus sent two disciples** from Bethany to **the village** of Bethphage opposite them.

He had prearranged the use of a special animal for His entry into the city—a **colt** on which no one had ever sat (Mark 11:2). Being a young animal, it was accompanied by **a donkey**, whose presence doubtless kept it calm. The animals were bound and tethered by a door in the open street, so that the two disciples would find them as soon as they entered the village. They must **loose *them* and bring *them*** to Christ. **If anyone** was to **say anything** to them and try to stop them, they need simply **say, "The Lord has need of them,"** and they would have no problem.

Such prearrangements with passwords were necessary, for Jerusalem was still a dangerous place for Jesus, since the authorities were looking for Him to arrest Him (John 11:57). This password, "The Lord has need of them," was perfect, as it was intentionally ambiguous. The words "the Lord" could mean the owner of the animal, giving listening bystanders the idea that the owner was simply claiming his own animals, or "the Lord" could refer to Jesus. Hostile listeners would be none the wiser for overhearing the exchange, and would not be able to have Jesus arrested before a crowd of supporters gathered.

Before narrating the actual entry, St. Matthew takes a moment to explain how these arrangements were one more fulfillment of ancient prophecy. In Zechariah 9:9, **the prophet** declared that the messianic **King** would **come** to **the daughter of Zion, humble and mounted upon a donkey, even upon a colt, the son of a yoke-animal**. This was why Jesus chose to arrive on a colt—not just as the fulfillment of prophecy, but also to reveal what kind of Messiah He was. A warlike king might come riding a warhorse, but Jesus was coming in peace, and therefore rode upon a colt. In this way Jesus proclaimed to all who could see that He was not coming to conquer the Roman legions, but to witness to the truth (John 18:37).

It is not by accident that Matthew mentions both the animals involved, whereas the other evangelists mention only the colt on which Jesus actually sat. This is partly because Zechariah's prophecy mentions two animals, and as a Jew, Matthew cannot resist calling attention to the verbal coincidence of there being two animals (though actually the prophecy *means* only one animal: "a donkey, *even* a colt"). But Matthew mentions the two animals mostly because this constitutes another double witness to Jesus being the Messiah.

The **disciples did** as they were **directed**, bringing the animals to Jesus. They **laid their garments on them**, and Jesus mounted them (that is, He mounted the colt, with the donkey next to it), beginning His royal entry. Those in Jerusalem instantly grasped the royal significance of His riding into their city in this way and began to shout in joy, welcoming the Kingdom. **A large crowd spread their garments in the way**, forming a kind of carpet on the road, and **others** (perhaps not having an outer garment) **were cutting branches from trees** in the fields nearby for this purpose. All those around Him, both preceding Him into the city and **following** behind, **were crying out, "Hosanna to the Son of David! Blessed**

is He who comes in the Name of the Lord! Hosanna in the highest!" The term "hosanna" meant originally "save us"—see its use in Psalm 118:25, but by that time was used simply as an acclamation, like our "Hurray!" Though they still had a political and military understanding of the Messiah (the peaceful significance of the colt was evidently lost on them), they were correct in hailing Jesus as the coming Messiah and Son of David.

The whole city **was shaken** at the shouting of the great crowds who welcomed Him, and those who could not see past the throng asked, **"Who is this?"** For whom was all this joyful shouting? The answer came, **"This is the prophet Jesus, from Nazareth in Galilee!"** By hailing Him as a prophet, they were acknowledging that God was truly with Him (compare Luke 7:16). As His foes lamented, the whole world had gone after Him (John 12:19).

§XII.1.ii. Cleansing the Temple

ॐ ॐ ॐ ॐ ॐ

12 And Jesus entered into the Temple and cast out all those buying and selling in the Temple, and overturned the tables of the moneychangers and the seats of those selling the doves.

13 And He says to them, "It is written, 'My House will be called a House of prayer'; but you *yourselves* are making it a thieves' cave."

14 And the blind and lame came to Him in the Temple, and He healed them.

Immediately upon entering Jerusalem, He came into the Temple, and afterwards, when it was late, went out of the city to spend the night at Bethany (Mark 11:11). The next day, He again entered the Temple, intent on bringing it into divine order. Though it was the house of His Father, and was meant to be a place of prayer and spiritual healing for the world, it had become corrupted with greed.

People came to the Temple from afar to offer sacrifices (such as doves), and the only coinage accepted in the Temple for the purchase of such animals for sacrifices was Tyrian coinage. Accordingly, tables of moneychangers must be available for pilgrims to change the coinage of their homeland for that acceptable in the Temple. Tables for this purpose had been set up on the Mount of Olives nearby. More recently, however, such tables were also set up within the Temple itself, in the Court of the Gentiles. The only place the visiting Gentiles had to pray in had thus become like a noisy and worldly bazaar.

Christ was determined to end this abuse of the Father's house. The prophet Isaiah had declared that it was meant to be **a House of prayer** (Is. 56:7), but such commerce within its courts made such prayer impossible. Instead, it had become no better than **a thieves' cave**, a place where the unrighteous hid in safety, avoiding detection and punishment for their deeds (Jer. 7:11). Jesus therefore **cast out all those buying and selling in the Temple, and overturned the tables of the moneychangers and the seats of those selling the doves**. By these vigorous acts, He cleansed the Temple and returned it to what it was meant to be: a center for truth and healing. For **the blind and lame came to Him in the Temple, and He healed them** there, taking over the Temple for Himself.

ॐ ॐ ॐ ॐ ॐ

15 But when the chief-priests and the scribes saw the marvelous things that He had done, and the children who were crying out in the Temple and saying, "Hosanna to the Son of David!" they were indignant,

16 and said to Him, "Do You hear what these are saying?" And Jesus says to them, "Yes; have you never read, 'Out of the mouth of infants and nurslings You have prepared praise for Yourself'?"

17 And He left them behind and went out from the city to Bethany, and stayed there.

The chief-priests and the scribes, those who were ultimately responsible for the Temple, **saw** these **marvelous** miraculous **things**—how Christ had taken over the Temple and made it a place of teaching and healing—and they did not think it was so wonderful. Like the merchants Christ had ejected, they resented such interference in what they considered their turf. To make it worse, **children** were surrounding Jesus and **crying out** the scandalous words they had heard chanted shortly before at His triumphal entry, **"Hosanna to the Son of David!"** To suggest that Jesus of Nazareth was the messianic Son of David was an outrage—and here those children were doing it **in the Temple** itself! The masters of the Temple therefore **were indignant** and insisted that Jesus shut them up. **Did** He **not hear what these were saying?**

Christ's response is immediate: **yes**, He heard them. How can they possibly object to their words? **Have** they **never read** their own Law, and how the Psalmist prophesies that **out of the mouth of infants and nurslings** God has **prepared praise** for Himself (Ps. 8:2)? Scripture predicted that children would praise God in this way—how can they suggest that He stop it? He would not argue long with such as them, but **left them behind** at the day's end to go **to Bethany** (probably to the home of Lazarus and his sisters; John 12:1).

(We note in passing that Psalm 8:2 quoted by Christ is quoted from the Greek Septuagint version, which reads, "You have prepared praise," rather than from the Hebrew version, which reads, "You have established strength." Some have suggested that this was because the high priests spoke Greek as their first language, but it cannot be ruled out that Christ knew a Targum or Aramaic paraphrase of the psalm that rendered it the same way the Greek Septuagint did.)

§XII.1.iii. Cursing the Unfruitful Tree

ॐ ॐ ॐ ॐ ॐ

18 Now going up into the city early, He was hungry.

19 And seeing one fig tree by the way, He went up

to it and found nothing on it but leaves only;
and He says to it, "No longer will there be fruit
from you forever." And immediately the fig tree
withered.

20 And seeing it, the disciples marveled, saying,
"How did the fig tree wither immediately?"

21 And Jesus answered and said to them, "Amen I
say to you, if you have faith and do not doubt,
you will not only do *what was done* to the
fig tree, but even if you say to this mountain,
'Be taken up and cast into the sea,' it will
happen.

22 "And all things you request in prayer, having
faith, you will receive."

From the parallel in Mark 11:12–14, 20–25, we learn that Jesus first cursed the fig tree early in the morning, before entering and cleansing the Temple. It was only later, as He and His disciples left the city at day's end, that the disciples noticed that the tree had withered. With his customary flair for abbreviation, Matthew telescopes these two events into one.

Thus Matthew relates that when Christ went up **into the city early** that morning, **He was hungry** (perhaps not having eaten breakfast), and **seeing one fig tree by the way, He went up to it**. Figs ripened in mid-August to October, and since this was spring, He **found nothing on it but leaves only**. Its spectacular show of foliage served only to hide its fruitlessness beneath.

Looking upon it with a prophetic eye, Christ saw not only a fig tree, but the people of Israel and their Temple. Like the fig tree whose leaves promised food, the outward pomp and glory of the Temple promised spiritual fruit to all the world. But just as the fig tree's leaves hid its fruitlessness, so the outward glory of the Temple hid the spiritual fruitlessness of the Jews. As the prophets of old acted symbolically (Jer. 13:1f; Ezek. 4:9f), so Christ also symbolically curses the hypocrisy of Israel under the form of the lone fig tree. Israel was about to reject the Messiah, so that **no longer** would **there**

be fruit from Israel **forever**. God would leave its Temple desolate, abandoning His people to their sins.

The disciples heard this curse, and on **seeing** how **the fig tree withered immediately** (that is, over the course of a few hours), they **marveled**. Not unnaturally, they asked about such a miracle, as if such things were forever beyond them.

Christ encourages them to trust that God will work in their midst also. Not just He, but they also, if they **have faith and do not doubt**, will one day **not only do** *what was done* to the fig tree, but greater works also. Indeed, they could **say to this mountain** beside them (the Mount of Olives), **"Be taken up and cast into the sea"** (the Dead Sea, nearby and visible to them from where they stood), and it would **happen**. Let His Church **request in prayer**, and **having faith**, they will **receive** their request.

This promise is not, of course, a blank check by which each one can fulfill his own selfish will. Rather, it is an assurance that the Church, united in godly prayer, will be the instrument of God's miraculous power on the earth. Let the disciples trust in God's power, and not doubt it!

§XII.2. Jesus' Foes Challenge His Authority

§XII.2.i. Challenge of Temple Cleansing

> ৺ৄ ৺ৄ ৺ৄ ৺ৄ ৺ৄ
>
> 23 And when He had come into the Temple, the chief-priests and the elders of the people came to Him as He was teaching and said, "By what authority are You doing these things, and who gave You this authority?"
>
> 24 And Jesus answered and said to them, "I *Myself* also will ask you one word, which if you tell Me, I *Myself* will also tell you by what authority I do these things.
>
> 25 "The baptism of John—where was *it* from? From Heaven or from men?" And they were

> questioning among themselves, saying, "If we say, 'From Heaven,' He will say to us, 'Then why did you not have faith in him?'
>
> 26 "But if we say, 'From men,' we are afraid of the crowd; for all hold John as a prophet."
>
> 27 And answering Jesus, they said, "We do not know." He also said to them, "Neither will I *Myself* tell you by what authority I do these things.

Matthew now focuses on the challenges to Jesus' authority which occurred **when He had come into the Temple** after His triumphal entry. During one of the days when **He was teaching** the people there, an official delegation of **chief-priests and the elders of the people** came to put a stop to it. (From Mark 11:27, we learn that this happened when Jesus was walking, probably in the colonnade, on His way to teach the crowds.) They were furious that He had cleansed the Temple and had made it a center for His own work. Previously they had been caught off-guard by His boldness (21:16), but now they had regrouped and were better prepared.

They had been charged by God to keep order in His House. **By what authority**, they demanded, was Jesus **doing these things** (that is, cleansing the Temple and using it for His teaching), **and who gave** Him **this authority?** If He said that God gave Him authority, they would doubtless ask Him to prove it by giving a sign. If He refused to give such a sign (and they felt sure He would refuse—see 12:38; 16:1f), He would publicly lose face, and they would ask Him to leave.

To their surprise, Jesus answers with a counter-question. If they want Him to answer their question, let them first answer one of His. If they will clear up one matter (or **one word**), then He will oblige them. That matter concerns **John** the Baptizer and his **baptism**. Was this baptism **from Heaven** (that is, from God) or merely **from men?** Did John have divine authority as a true prophet, or was he falsely claiming such authority, and so was a false prophet? Jesus is not asking them to justify their verdict, but just to state their opinion.

This presents them with a problem—one that exposes their moral cowardice, thereby showing all that they have no claim to be keepers of order in God's House. Retreating from the pressing crowd, they begin **questioning among themselves** in a hurried exchange. If they say, **"From Heaven,"** Jesus will retort, **"Then why did you not have faith in him?"** If they misjudged John then, how can they claim to reliably judge Jesus now? But the other alternative, answering, **"From men,"** is equally out of the question, for all **the crowd held** that **John** was a **prophet**, and if they denounce him now as a false prophet the crowd will surely stone them.

Emerging from their huddle, they report, **"We do not know"**—in other words, "No comment!" Jesus therefore declines to answer their question, since they refuse to answer His. It is important to see that Christ's counter-question was not asked simply to avoid answering their question. Rather, He was revealing their hearts, as well as laying the foundation for any real answer. By their cowardice they proved themselves unworthy to hear the truth, for if they were not willing to recognize the authority of John, they could not recognize His either, as both came from the same source.

§XII.2.ii. Parable of the Two Children

ॐ ॐ ॐ ॐ ॐ

28 "But what do you think? A man had two children, and he came to the first and said, 'Child, go away today to work in the vineyard.'

29 "And he answered and said, 'I will not.' But later he regretted it and went.

30 "And he came to the other and said likewise. But he answered and said, 'I *myself* go, lord'—and did not go.

31 "Which of the two did the will of his father?" They say, "The first." Jesus says to them, "Amen I say to you that the tax-collectors and prostitutes are going before you into the Kingdom of God.

> 32 "For John came to you in the way of righteousness, and you did not have faith in him; but the tax-collectors and the prostitutes had faith in him, and you *yourselves*, seeing *this*, did not regret it later *so as* to have faith in him.

Christ continues His response to their question by asking for their opinion on another matter. This concerns **a man** who **had two children**, two sons (Gr. *tekna*), and a vineyard. **He came to the first and said, "Child, go away today to work in the vineyard."** Filial piety demanded that the son oblige, but this one answered brusquely, **"I will not"**—two terse words in the Greek, *ou thelo*, like our English, "no way!"). **Later**, however, **he regretted** this disobedience **and went**.

For now, though, the father was distressed at his son's refusal to help with the work, and leaving the son who disobeyed **he came to the other** to look for the needed help, **and said likewise**. This boy answered with heartwarming zeal, **"I *myself* go, lord"** (or sir). Once again in the Greek we have a brief two words, *ego, kurie*, short for *idou ego, kurie*, and answering to the Hebrew *hinneni*—"behold, I!"—the usual formula of consent. It sounded wonderful. But as it turned out, the boy **did not go**.

Christ turns to His challengers for their verdict about this situation: **Which of the two did the will of his father?** There could only be one answer: **the first**. In saying this, they condemn themselves also, and so Jesus declares, **"The tax-collectors and prostitutes are going before you into the Kingdom of God."**

For **the tax-collectors and prostitutes** (some of whom might have been in the listening crowd) were like the first son. They initially refused the Father's call to work at a life of righteousness, but since **John came** calling them back into **the way of righteousness**, they regretted their sin and turned to God, **having faith** in John. The chief-priests and elders, however, were like the second son. This boy, even after he saw his brother's repentance and subsequent obedience, still disobeyed his father's command, despite his fine words. And the chief-priests and elders, even though **seeing** sinners returning to God through John, **did not regret** their refusal to follow John *so as* **to have faith in him**. What matters in doing the will of the Father is not fine words and protestations of righteousness (which Jesus' foes had in abundance). What matters is actual obedience. The repentant tax-collectors and prostitutes had such obedience and were going into the Kingdom before the disobedient foes of Christ.

§XII.2.iii. Parable of the Vineyard

ॐ ॐ ॐ ॐ ॐ

33 "Hear another parable. There was a man *who was* a housemaster who planted a vineyard, and put a hedge around it and dug a winepress in it, and built a tower, and rented it out to farmers, and left home.

34 "And when the *appointed* time of the fruits drew near, he sent his slaves to the farmers to receive the fruits of it.

35 "And the farmers took his slaves and beat one, and killed another, and stoned another.

36 "Again he sent other slaves, more than the first ones; and they did likewise to them.

37 "But later he sent his son to them, saying, 'They will respect my son.'

38 "But when the farmers saw the son, they said among themselves, 'This is the heir; come, let us kill him and have his inheritance!'

39 "And they took him and cast him out of the vineyard, and killed him.

40 "When therefore the lord of the vineyard comes, what will he do to those farmers?"

41 They say to Him, "He will put those wretches to a wretched *end*, and will rent out the vineyard to other farmers, who render him the fruits at their appointed times."

42 Jesus says to them, "Have you never read in

the Scriptures, 'The stone which the builders rejected, this has become the head of the corner; this occurred from the Lord, and it is marvelous in our eyes'?

43 "For this reason I say to you, the Kingdom of God will be taken from you, and will be given to a nation producing the fruits of it.

44 "And he who falls on this stone will be broken *to pieces*, but on whomever it falls, it will crush him."

45 And when the chief-priests and the Pharisees heard His parables, they knew that He was speaking about them.

46 And when they were seeking to seize Him, they were afraid of the crowds, because they held Him to be a prophet.

Christ next tells them **another parable** (perhaps as soon as He reaches His destination in the Temple, where the crowds are awaiting Him). Fresh from this challenge, He tells a parable of **a man *who was* a housemaster**, or landowner. This man **planted a vineyard, and put a hedge around it and dug a winepress in it, and built a tower, and rented it out to farmers, and left home**. The details of the man's care for his vineyard echo the parable in Isaiah 5, where the vineyard is Israel, planted by God. The care lavished by the man on his vineyard shows how the owner had a moral right to some of the fruit, which he collected as rent.

When the *appointed* time of the fruits drew near, the owner **sent his slaves to the farmers to receive the fruits** as his rightful due. But instead of giving the slaves the agreed-upon produce, they **took his slaves and beat one, and killed another, and stoned another**, sending the survivors away empty-handed. With astonishing patience at this crime, the owner **sent other slaves, more than the first ones**, thinking that this larger delegation would command more respect. But to no avail, for the farmers **did likewise to them** as well.

All those listening to the parable by this time knew that it sounded all too familiar, for it was reminiscent of God's response to Israel, sending prophet after prophet to His stiff-necked people. Then the parable took an unexpected turn—the lord of the vineyard **sent his son to them**, saying to himself, **"They will respect my son."** Beating slaves was one thing, but attacking the son was something else!

Nonetheless, **when the farmers saw the son**, they did not respect him, but **said among themselves, "This is the heir."** If they killed him, the land would be legally without an owner upon the death of the father, and they would **have his inheritance** for themselves. They therefore **cast him out of the vineyard**, running him off the property, **and killed him.**

The parable held the hearers spellbound. When Christ asked the question, **"When the lord of the vineyard comes, what will he do to those farmers?"** some from the crowd shouted back, **"He will put those wretches to a wretched *end*, and will rent out the vineyard to other farmers, who render him the fruits at their appointed times."** (The words in the Greek contain a play on words: *kakous kakos apolesei autous*—"he will put those wretches to a wretched end," or "he will wreck those wreckers.")

The chief-priests and elders listening were horrified at this conclusion, for they knew only too well that they had been cast in the part of the rebellious farmers, and they doubtless reacted with a splutter of incoherent protest. But Jesus was insistent that this doom of being judged and dispossessed by God awaited those then in authority. Had they never even read in the Scriptures, **"The stone which the builders rejected, this has become the head of the corner; this occurred from the Lord, and it is marvelous in our eyes"** (Ps. 118:22)? This psalm prophesied that David's messianic descendant would be rejected, even though He had been chosen by God. Jesus' foes thought it impossible that one whom they rejected could turn out to be the Messiah, but David had prophesied exactly this.

It was **for this reason** that **the Kingdom of God** would **be taken** from them, and **be given to a nation producing the fruits of it**, one which would obey the Lord of the Vineyard and give Him His fruits at the proper time. The Kingdom would not be received by the religious leaders of Israel, the designated sons of the Kingdom to whom it was first promised (compare 8:12). Instead, another nation (Gr. *ethnos,* v. 43) would receive it—even the Gentiles, the nations (*ethnoi*) who came from afar, from the east and from the west (8:11). St. Matthew expects his Christian readers to see in this word a prophecy of the inclusion of the Gentiles, who inherit the promises forfeited by the bulk of the Jews.

Christ has a final word of judgment for His foes. The messianic Stone which the builders rejected will bring the wrath of God to those who rejected it. Echoing such passages as Isaiah 8:14–15 and Daniel 2:34–35, He declares that **he who falls on this stone will be broken *to pieces,* but on whomever** the stone **falls** it will **crush** him to dust. To reject the Son of the Vineyard's Lord is to court final disaster.

When the chief-priests and the Pharisees listening **heard** these **parables** of verses 28–44, **they knew** (as did everyone else there) **that He was speaking about them** and their opposition. They would have loved **to seize Him** on the spot, but **they were afraid of the crowds,** who **held** Jesus **to be a** true **prophet** and would not have permitted Him to be openly arrested.

§XII.2.iv. Parable of the Royal Wedding Feast

ॐ ॐ ॐ ॐ ॐ

22 1   And Jesus answered and spoke to them again in parables, saying,

2   "The Kingdom of the heavens may be likened to a man *who was* a king, who gave a wedding *feast* for his son.

3   "And he sent his slaves to call those who had been called to the wedding *feast*, and they did not want to come.

4   "Again he sent other slaves, saying, 'Tell those

who had been called, "Behold, I have prepared my dinner; my bulls and my fattened *cattle* are slaughtered, and all is prepared; come into the wedding *feast*!'"

5   "But they neglected *this* and went away, one to his own field, and another to his trading-house,

6   "and the rest seized his slaves, and abused and killed *them*.

7   "But the king was angry and sent his armies, and destroyed those murderers and set their city on fire.

8   "Then he says to his slaves, 'The wedding *feast* is indeed prepared; but those who were called were not worthy.

9   "'Go therefore to the outlets of the ways, and as many as you find, call into the wedding *feast*.'

10   "And those slaves went out into the ways and gathered all they found, both evil and good, and the wedding *hall* was filled with those who reclined.

11   "But when the king came in to behold those who reclined, he saw there a man not clothed in wedding clothes,

12   "and he says to him, 'Comrade, how did you come into here not having wedding clothes?' And he was speechless.

13   "Then the king said to the servants, 'Bind him hand and foot, and cast him into the outer darkness; there, there will be weeping and gnashing of teeth.'

14   "For many are called, but few chosen."

The Lord **answered** the chief-priests' and Pharisees' ongoing criticism of Himself by speaking to them **again in parables**. In particular, He told the parable of **a man *who was* a king, who gave a wedding *feast* for his son**. Though bearing some resemblance to the parable related in Luke 14:16f, this is a different parable, and it breathes a different atmosphere. The parable related in Luke was told while eating in the house of a Pharisee (Luke 14:1), and in that parable the offenders are punished by being deprived of the feast (Luke 14:24). This parable in Matthew was told in the Temple, and it dates from a time when the rupture with the Pharisees was all but complete (21:45–46; John 12:42). In this parable the punishment for offenders is the destruction of their city (22:7).

In this parable, **a king** called certain of his subjects to **a wedding *feast* for his son**, and (in accordance with the custom of those days) when the actual day of the feast arrived, **sent his slaves to call** the invited guests to come take their places. Astonishingly enough, **they did not want to come**, even though coming to such a royal feast was a great privilege. This astonishing refusal images the refusal of the pious in Israel (such as the chief-priests and the Pharisees) to accept the Kingdom of the heavens declared by Jesus, after having waited for it for so long.

The king patiently **again sent other slaves**, thinking perhaps that his subjects had misunderstood the first messengers. He repeated his declaration that **all was prepared**, including a magnificent table with **bulls** and **fattened *cattle***. Let them now **come into the wedding *feast*!**

Once again **they neglected** this invitation **and went away, one to his own field, and another to his trading-house**, each one pursuing his own private affairs and insulting the bounty of their king. Worse, **the rest**, the ones who stayed, traitorously **seized his slaves, and abused and killed *them***. This was not just an insult to the king, but a declaration of civil war. The behavior of those of the city was incredible—they responded to the king's generosity with hostility and treason! In this we see an image of the persecution with which the unbelieving Jews responded to Jesus and His messengers, who called them to the messianic banquet (10:17; 23:34).

The king responded to this betrayal as could only be expected: He **was angry** with the rebels and **sent his armies and destroyed**

those murderers and set their city on fire. Those reading this prophetic parable in decades to come could not fail to see a reference to the destruction of Jerusalem in AD 70 by the Roman armies, who came as the wrath of God upon the rebellious city. Zion once was *His* city, the city of the great King (Ps. 48:2), but now that it had come to house the **murderers** of Jesus and His messengers, it was simply *their* city, not the city of God. God had disowned them all and abandoned them to judgment.

Meanwhile, the bounty of the king for his son still remained to be distributed. He therefore sent his slaves **to the outlets of the ways**, to the places where the roads ran through the city and into the country, where many could be found. **As many as** they would **find**, no matter how scruffy, these they must **call into the wedding feast**, so that the king's bounty could be enjoyed. The slaves fulfilled this order—an image of the Gospel gathering all sorts of people, as both **evil and good**, both tax-collectors and righteous, responded to Jesus' word and counted themselves His followers. At last **the wedding *hall* was filled**.

The parable does not end here. It is not enough simply to respond to Jesus' word and call oneself His disciple. Such claims must be matched by true holiness of life. And so Jesus continues His parable with **the king** coming to **behold** and look over his guests just prior to taking his own place at the table. Among the multitudes, he saw one **man not clothed** in the appropriate **wedding clothes**. Instead of the finery proper to such a royal feast, he was wearing his dirty everyday work clothes. This was not simply an embarrassment, but in that culture was a serious insult to the king who invited him. (The question of where he was supposed to have gotten the proper clothes is not really relevant. Whether he was expected to have gone home first to secure them, or whether he was provided with them by the king at the feast, his appearance there without them was clearly culpable.)

The king is mild (compare his patience with those who first spurned his invitation; v. 4), and he assumes that perhaps the man has a reason for his appearance. He mildly addresses him as **comrade** (Gr. *etairos*; compare its use in 20:13) and asks the reason for this apparent insult. The man, however, has nothing to mitigate his guilt and so is **speechless**. In his guilty silence, he is an image of all confessing Christians who will stand guilty before the Last Judgment, having no robes of righteousness to clothe their naked sin (compare Rev. 3:18; 19:8). **The king said to his servants, "Bind him hand and foot, and cast him into the outer darkness; there, there will be weeping and gnashing of teeth."** In this final punishment, the king is revealed as an image of God the King, whose angelic servants will banish all evildoers to the Gehenna of fire (8:12; 13:49–50).

Christ here provides an overview of the Kingdom for His hearers and drives home the main point of the parable: **Many are called** into the Kingdom, **but few** are **chosen**. It was not enough to be Jewish, for if one spurned Christ's word, wrath would come from God. And it was also not enough simply to listen to His word—one must act on it as well, clothing oneself in the garments of obedience (compare 7:21). Many in Israel were called and invited to the feast, but comparatively few actually trod the narrow way to life (7:14). (We note in passing the play on words in the Greek: "many are *kletoi* [called], but few *eklektoi*" [chosen].)

§XII.2.v. Question about Taxes to Caesar

ॐ ॐ ॐ ॐ ॐ

15 Then the Pharisees went and took counsel how they might ensnare Him in *His* word.

16 And they send their disciples to Him, with the Herodians, saying, "Teacher, we know that You are truthful and teach the way of God in truth, and it is not a concern to You about anyone, for You do not look at men's faces.

17 "Tell us, therefore, what do You think? Is it permitted to pay a poll-tax to Caesar, or not?"

18 But Jesus knew their evil and said, "Why are you testing Me, hypocrites?

19 "Show Me the *legal* coin of the poll-tax." And they brought Him a denarius.

> 20 And He says to them, "Whose image and
> inscription is this?"
> 21 They say to Him, "Caesar's." Then He says to
> them, "Then render to Caesar the things that
> are Caesar's—and to God the things that are
> God's."
> 22 And hearing *this*, they marveled, and leaving
> Him, they went away.

In response to such teachings, **the Pharisees went and took counsel how they might ensnare Him in *His* word**. For this they turned to their old (and unlikely) alliance with **the Herodians**, the partisans of King Herod (see Mark 3:6). They hoped to provoke Jesus into saying something they could use against Him with the authorities (the Herodians were expert in such political matters).

As He is teaching, they send a delegation to Him, ostensibly wanting Him to rule on a sticky religious matter. They approach Him with great deference, calling Him **Teacher**, and with long flattery about how everyone **knows** that He is **truthful** and **teaches the way of God in truth**, and how it is **not a concern** to Him **about anyone**, for He **does not look at men's faces** to defer to the powerful before answering. He is not partial to any, but teaches about Jewish duty to God and lets the chips fall where they may. They think such a long preface necessary, for He refused to answer their question on a previous occasion (21:27). With such a flattering introduction, He can scarcely refuse to answer now!

Their question is a masterpiece of entrapment, for whichever alternative Jesus chooses, He will lose. Their question is whether it **is permitted** by God **to pay a poll-tax to Caesar or not**. The Romans collected a tribute tax from every adult Jew, as they did from all conquered peoples. The tax was thus a sign of Israel's subjugation by Rome and was heartily hated by all Jews. In particular, the Zealots, a Jewish group dedicated to the violent overthrow of Rome, said that it violated God's Law to pay the tax, for God was Israel's only true King. The Romans, for their part, considered refusal to pay the tax a kind of treason. What does Jesus think?

If Jesus answers, "We must pay the tax," then He will lose popularity, especially since John defied the authorities even at the cost of his life. How can Jesus be a true prophet like John if He is not prepared to defy the authorities also? If Jesus answers, "We must not pay the tax," then they have Him in their clutches, for this is treason, and He will be taken by the Romans.

The Lord, however, is untroubled. He **knows their evil** and their false motives. Why this charade? He asks them to **show** Him the *legal* coin of the poll-tax. (Matthew's Gospel, alone among the Synoptics, says that Jesus asked them to bring the *legal* coin—Gr. *nomisma*—a more precise word than that used by Mark and Luke. Was the influence of Matthew the tax-collector showing here?)

Holding the coin up for them to see, He asks them a question: **"Whose image and inscription is this?"** They have no choice but to state the obvious—it is **Caesar's**. The Lord then hands their coin back to them—if it is Caesar's coin, then let Caesar have his own property. They must **render to Caesar the things that are Caesar's**. Let them pay the tax—but take care to give Caesar no more than his humble due. The more important things—worship and ultimate loyalty—belong not to Caesar but to God, and they must take equal care to render **to God the things that are God's**. The Romans may tax Israel, but they can never usurp the place of God, Israel's true King.

This was a staggering answer. No wonder that upon **hearing** *this*, **they marveled** at such acuity and **went away**.

§XII.2.vi. Question about the Resurrection

ॐ ॐ ॐ ॐ ॐ

23 On that day *some* Sadducees (who say *there is* not to be a resurrection) came to Him and questioned Him,

24 saying, "Teacher, Moses said, 'If one dies, not having children, his brother shall marry his wife as next of kin, and raise up seed to his brother.'

25 "Now there were seven brothers with us, and the first married *and* died, and having no seed, left his wife to his brother;

26 "likewise also the second, and the third, until the seventh.

27 "And finally *after* all, the woman died.

28 "In the resurrection, therefore, *to* which of the seven will she be wife? For *they* all had her."

29 But Jesus answered and said to them, "You are deceived, not knowing the Scriptures, nor the power of God.

30 "For in the resurrection they neither marry, nor are given in marriage, but are like angels in heaven.

31 "But concerning the resurrection of the dead, have you not read what was spoken to you by God, saying,

32 "'I *Myself* am the God of Abraham, and the God of Isaac, and the God of Jacob'? He is not the God of the dead, but of the living."

33 And when the crowds heard *this*, they were thunderstruck at His teaching.

After this, *some* **Sadducees came to Him** with a challenge of their own. These were a sect consisting of high-priestly families and other leading aristocratic families of Jerusalem who had connections with the Temple. They were known for their many disagreements with the Pharisees, and in particular for their assertion that *there is* **not to be a final resurrection**. Also, the Sadducees accepted only the first five books of Moses as true Scripture, rejecting the rest of the Hebrew Scriptures as of merely human origin.

They approached Jesus with feigned deference, calling Him **Teacher** and requesting His rabbinical ruling on a point of Law. In their proposed scenario, **there were seven brothers** with them, **and the first married *and* died, and having no seed, left his wife to his brother**. This situation was an application of the so-called "levirate law," whereby a man dying without legal descendant would be provided with legal descendants through his brother marrying his widow. The children of this union would be counted children of the dead man, so that his ancestral inheritance would stay within his family (Deut. 25:5f).

In the scenario proposed by these Sadducees, **the second** brother **likewise** married the widow and died without leaving children, then **the third**, and all the brothers **until the seventh. Finally** *after* **all, the woman died.** That was the situation. Then came their question: **In the resurrection,** *to* **which of the seven will she be wife? For** *they* **all had her.**

The question was not simply intended to stump Jesus so that He could not answer, but was an attempt to show the incompatibility of a belief in the final resurrection with the world presupposed by the Mosaic Law. For (they argued) if one tried to combine the Mosaic worldview with a belief in the final resurrection, then such insoluble and absurd situations as this arose. One could not sensibly apply the Law to situations envisioned by the world of the resurrection, and since the Law was divine and universal in application, *that world of the resurrection did not exist.* The Sadducees were in fact arguing that the worldview presupposed by the Law was a naturalistic one.

Jesus decisively cut through their arrogance and declared that they were **deceived** about spiritual things—inevitably so, since they did **not know the Scriptures, nor the power of God.** The true meaning of the Law eluded them, and furthermore, they had too small a conception of God, for they thought it ridiculous that He would restore all the dead to life by a simple word.

In answering their question about this supposed woman, He replied that **in the resurrection they neither marry, nor are given in marriage, but are like angels in heaven.** That is, the social institutions of marriage and procreation, of agriculture and industry, have no place in that age, but are realities meant for this age only. In the age to come, the Presence of God will be the ceaseless contemplation of all, even as it now is for the angels.

But concerning the fact of **the resurrection of the dead,** they could know that even from the five books of the Law they accepted as Scripture. **Have** they **not read** over and over again **what was spoken** to them **by God** Himself in the passage about the burning bush? There God declared that He was **the God of Abraham, and the God of Isaac, and the God of Jacob** (Ex. 3:6). This must mean that the dead do not perish, as the Sadducees imagined, for to be someone's God meant to be their protector, and God declared that He was still the protector of the patriarchs. To be the protector of the dead was a contradiction in terms, and it was unworthy of the living God to be **the God of the dead.** Therefore these men must still be living—and capable of final resurrection.

When the crowds heard Jesus prove the fact of the coming resurrection from the Law, **they were thunderstruck** at the depth of **His teaching.** He had vanquished the Pharisees with the trap about the poll-tax, and now He had vanquished the Sadducees too.

§XII.2.vii. Question about the Great Commandment

> ༄ ༄ ༄ ༄ ༄
>
> 34 But when the Pharisees heard that He had muzzled the Sadducees, they gathered themselves together.
> 35 And one of them, a lawyer, asked Him, testing Him,
> 36 "Teacher, which is the great commandment in the Law?"
> 37 And He said to him, "You shall love the Lord your God with all your heart, and with all your soul, and with all your mind.
> 38 "This is the great and first commandment.
> 39 "The second is like it, 'You shall love your neighbor as yourself.'
> 40 "On these two commandments hang all the Law and the Prophets."

Now **when the Pharisees heard that He had muzzled** and silenced their adversaries **the Sadducees, they gathered themselves**

together. They were not prepared to leave the field of combat with their Sadducean rivals. **One of them, a lawyer** (that is, a scribe who taught the Mosaic Law), **asked Him** a question of his own. Though the question was not a trap as the previous questions had been, the man was still not coming as a humble disciple, seeking to learn from Jesus. Rather, he was **testing Him**, seeing how the rabbi from Galilee would measure up to the ideals of the Pharisees. (The lawyer, though aligned with the Pharisees, had not completely lost sight of what God truly wanted, and he was not far from the Kingdom of God; see Mark 12:32–34.)

The lawyer knows that some commandments in the Law are pivotal, weightier than others. According to Jesus, **which is the great commandment in the Law?** Jesus zeroes in on the passage in Deuteronomy 6:5: **"You shall love the Lord your God with all your heart, and with all your soul, and with all your mind."** This is **the first** and foundational commandment, and without being asked, Jesus also adds **the second** commandment, a corollary of the first: **"You shall love your neighbor as yourself"** (Lev. 19:18). **All the Law and the Prophets**, the entirety of the Scriptures, **hang** upon these two principles and are extended expressions of it. Love for God and love for one's neighbor are the goal of all God has spoken.

§XII.2.viii. Jesus' Reply about the Son of David

ॐ ॐ ॐ ॐ ॐ

41 Now while the Pharisees were gathered together, Jesus asked them a question,

42 saying, "What do you think about the Christ? Whose son is He?" They say to Him, "David's."

43 He says to them, "How therefore does David in the Spirit call Him 'Lord,' saying,

44 "'The Lord said to my Lord, "Sit at My right hand until I put your enemies under your feet"'?

45 "If David therefore calls Him 'Lord,' how is He *his* son?"

> **46 And no one was able to answer Him a word, nor did anyone dare from that day to ask Him any more *questions*.**

After these questions, **Jesus asked them a question** of His own: **"What do you think about the Christ? Whose son is He?"** Jesus asked this question because He wanted to correct the popular misunderstanding of the Messiah as **David's** son. In objecting to the title "the Son of David," Jesus was not denying the fact that Messiah was a lineal descendant of King David. Rather, He was objecting to the popular understanding of the Messiah as a military hero like David. The people expected the Christ to be a revolutionary, and to raise an army that would drive the Romans from Palestine and make Israel a political power in the world.

Instead, Jesus taught, the Christ was to be transcendent, and the Kingdom He was to bring was a spiritual one, not a political one. This, He said, was apparent from the words of David himself in Psalm 110:1. **David**, when **in the Spirit** (that is, under divine inspiration as God's prophet), wrote, **"The Lord said to my Lord, 'Sit at My right hand until I put your enemies under your feet.'"** The first **Lord** in this quotation was God; the second **Lord** was the Messiah. Jesus here points out that **David** himself **calls Him "Lord,"** acknowledging his messianic descendant as superior to himself and as utterly transcendent. **How** then could the Messiah be *his* **son**, his derivative and inferior? Obviously the people were wrong in supposing that the Messiah was a "chip off the old block" of David the war hero.

After such a dazzling display of wisdom and such a penetrating examination of the Scriptures, **no one was able to answer Him a word** in reply, or **dared to ask Him any more *questions*.** He was left in peace to teach in the Temple.

§XII.3 Denunciation of the Scribes and Pharisees

The other Synoptic Gospels record Christ's denunciation of the Pharisees in the Temple immediately before recording His Olivet

Discourse (Mark 12:38–40; Luke 20:45–47). Matthew expands this brief denunciation by gathering material from other places (compare Luke 11:37f; 13:34f; 20:45f), so that we have here an extended indictment of the piety of the Pharisees and of the hard-heartedness of His adversaries in general.

Unlike the other Synoptics (which relate the humble piety of the poor widow as the introductory contrast to the prediction of proud Jerusalem's destruction—Mark 12:41–44; Luke 21:1–4), in Matthew the sins of Jesus' foes form the background and introduction to the Olivet Discourse. The hard-hearted sin of Jerusalem (related in ch. 23) is the crime, and the destruction of Jerusalem (related in ch. 24) is the divine punishment.

ॐ॰ ॐ॰ ॐ॰ ॐ॰ ॐ॰

23 1   Then Jesus spoke to the crowds and to His disciples,

2   saying, "The scribes and the Pharisees have seated themselves upon the chair of Moses;

3   "therefore all that they tell you, do and keep, but do not do according to their works, for they say, and do not do.

Before Jesus begins His indictment of **the scribes and the Pharisees,** He shows how their practices are in stark contrast to their claims. He acknowledges the worthiness of their aims. They **have seated themselves upon the chair of Moses**—that is, they have inherited Moses' Law and have succeeded to his task of teaching the people God's Law. This is a worthy task, and Matthew is emphatic that Jesus as a good Jew reveres God's Law and is concerned that Israel keep it (compare 5:17–19; 19:17). **All** therefore that the scribes **tell** them when it comes to pursuing the intent of the Law, they must **do and keep.** When they exhort them to fulfill the Law, they should do it! But this is done not by imitating the scribes' and Pharisees' actual **works,** for they **say** one should truly fulfill the Law, but they **do not** actually **do** it. The scribal interpretations of what constitutes a true fulfillment of the Law are not valid interpretations.

ৡ৾ ৡ৾ ৡ৾ ৡ৾ ৡ৾

4   "And they bind weighty loads and lay them on men's shoulders; but they themselves are not willing to move them with their finger.

5   "They do all their works to be beheld by men; for they widen their phylacteries and enlarge the fringes.

6   "And they love the first-places at the suppers, and the first-seats in the synagogues,

7   "and the greetings in the marketplaces, and being called by men, 'Rabbi.'

8   "But you *yourselves* are not to be called 'Rabbi,' for one is your Teacher, and you *yourselves* are all brothers.

9   "And do not call *any* on the earth your father, for one is *such*—your heavenly Father.

10 "Nor be called instructors; for one is your Instructor—the Christ.

11 "But the greatest of you will be your servant.

12 "And whoever exalts himself will be humbled; and whoever humbles himself will be exalted.

Jesus begins His indictment of the scribes and Pharisees by calling attention to the fact that all they do is motivated by love of praise, while they are devoid of true justice, mercy, and faith. In their interpretation of the Law, **they bind weighty loads and lay them on men's shoulders**. They make rulings all but impossible to carry out. By their piling requirement on requirement, the common man could scarcely move without breaking some law, and was left like a beast of burden weighted down with an impossible load. The Pharisees, however, were not inclined to use their ingenuity to help the poor wretch find a way out, or discern what God truly wanted in His Law. They were **not willing to move** any of the load off the back, even **with** a single **finger**.

Their energies were spent elsewhere. They would **do all their works to be beheld** and admired **by men**. Pious Jews would wear phylacteries (little boxes attached with bands to the head and arm, containing Scripture verses). All Jews were required in the Law to wear fringes, or tassels on the corners of their garments, to remind them of God's Law (Num. 15:37f). The Pharisees delighted to **widen** these **phylactery** bands and to **enlarge the fringes** they must wear, so that all could see them and know how pious the wearers were. Moreover, they **loved the first-places at the suppers** (the seats nearest the host, reserved for the most important guests). They expected as their due to have **the first-seats in the synagogues** (the ones up at the front, facing the people, where all could see them). They loved **the greetings** they would receive **in the marketplaces**, where the people would stand up and bow as they passed, addressing them with the title **Rabbi**. (This term was not yet the technical term for a Jewish clergyman it later became; it literally means "my great one," and at this time was an honorific title given to any authority, including princes in a kingdom and chiefs of an army. The rabbi was a "teacher" in the sense of being the expert.)

As Jesus teaches the crowds and His disciples in the Temple, He forbids them to imitate this pride of the Pharisees. As for His disciples (the **you** is emphatic in the Greek), they are **not to be called "Rabbi."** They have **one** only who is their **Teacher**, and **all** of them are co-equal **brothers**. Similarly, they must **not call** *any* **on the earth** their **father**, for they have but **one** such—their **heavenly Father**. **Nor** must they seek to **be called instructors**, for only **one** is their true **Instructor—the Christ**. (The Greek word here rendered *instructor* is *kathegetes*, a term indicating a private tutor and personal guide.)

How are these precepts to be carried out? It is important to see that Jesus is not at all concerned about mere titles. He is not saying that "rabbi" or "instructor" must not be used as titles, nor that His followers must not look to anyone on earth as their spiritual father. In fact, St. Paul presents himself as a spiritual father, both to his churches (1 Cor. 4:15) and to individuals such as Timothy (Phil. 2:22; 1 Tim. 1:2). Rather, Christ is saying that *the model of discipleship to men propagated by the rabbis* must not be used by His disciples.

According to this rabbinic model, a man would become a disciple to his rabbi and seek to conform all his views to those of his teacher. The rabbi was not simply an interpreter of the Law; he was also the guru to his disciples, and their plumb line for truth. That was the kind of fatherhood that obtained among them, and what the title "rabbi" signified. Jesus says that, among His disciples, that kind of unconditional loyalty belongs only to their heavenly Father and to Himself, the Christ. All of the disciples are but brothers, children of the same Father, disciples of the one true Instructor, Christ. The authority one would exercise over another in the Church must not override that basic spiritual egalitarianism.

Thus, they must not seek to proudly dominate another (as the rabbis dominated their disciples). **The greatest** of them will not be the one who has disciples of his own, but the one who acts as the **servant** of all. If one seeks to **exalt himself** (such as by making himself the focus of Christian loyalty), that one will **be humbled** by God at the Last Judgment. It is the one who **humbles himself** in service to his brothers who will be finally **exalted**. (The historical practice of naming philosophies—or denominations—after individuals is perhaps relevant here.)

ॐ ॐ ॐ ॐ ॐ

13 "But woe to you, scribes and Pharisees, hypocrites! For you shut the Kingdom of the heavens before men; for you *yourselves* do not enter, nor do you let those who are entering go in.

St. Matthew then relates a series of seven Woes pronounced upon the scribes and Pharisees (seven obviously being chosen as a sacred number, indicating the fullness of woe).

In the *first woe*, Jesus castigates them because they denounce Him and His Message and thus **shut the Kingdom of the heavens before**

men, banging the door shut in their faces (as it were). Not only do they **not enter** the Kingdom themselves, but by their denunciation of Jesus they dissuade others from following Him, and thus do not **let those who are entering go in**. How great will be their doom on the last day!

ॐ ॐ ॐ ॐ ॐ

15 "Woe to you, scribes and Pharisees, hypocrites! For you go about on the sea and the dry *land* to make one proselyte; and when he becomes *one*, you make him twice as much a son of Gehenna as yourselves.*

In the *second woe,* Christ blames them for what they make of their converts. They show commendable zeal in bringing pagan Gentiles to faith in the Jewish God, even **going about on the sea and the dry *land*** for the sake of a single such conversion. But such is their blindness that all that effort is wasted, for when the former pagan becomes a proselyte (or convert), his imitation of his Pharisaical teachers makes him **twice as much a son of Gehenna** (that is, one destined for hell) as the Pharisees themselves. The new convert zealously imitates the worst things about the Pharisees, so that he was better off when he was a pagan. (Let all new converts to Orthodoxy take note!)

ॐ ॐ ॐ ॐ ॐ

16 "Woe to you, blind guides!—who say, 'Whoever swears by the sanctuary, that is nothing; but whoever swears by the gold of the sanctuary, he is obligated.'
17 "You fools and blind *ones*! Which is greater—

---

* *Verse 14 is not original to Matthew, but rather is added from its parallel in Mark 12:40. That it is not original is apparent from its absence in the best manuscripts, and from the fact that without it, Matthew records seven woes (a deliberate and sacred number), while with it, there are eight woes.*

the gold, or the sanctuary that sanctifies the gold?

18 "And 'Whoever swears by the altar, that is nothing; but whoever swears by the gift upon it, he is obligated.'

19 "You blind *ones*! For which *is* greater—the gift or the altar that sanctifies the gift?

20 "Therefore he who swears by the altar, swears by the altar and by everything on it.

21 "And he who swears by the sanctuary, swears by the sanctuary and by Him who dwells *within* it.

22 "And he who swears by heaven, swears both by the throne of God and by Him who sits upon it.

In the *third woe*, Jesus castigates the Pharisees for their casuistry, which makes them blind to holy things—such as oaths. Use of oaths was very common in the daily speech of that day, and the Pharisees distinguished between types of oaths. Thus, if one would **swear by the sanctuary** (e.g. "By the sanctuary, I will do this!"), that oath was **nothing**, and was not binding. However if one would **swear by the gold** stored in **the sanctuary** (e.g. "By the gold of the sanctuary, I will do this!"), then that oath was regarded as binding. It was similar with invoking **the altar** in the sanctuary—this oath was considered as **nothing**, whereas if one invoked **the gift upon** the altar, one was **obligated** to fulfill that oath.

For Christ, the Pharisees are **blind guides**, completely unreliable in such matters, for such distinctions reveal their complete blindness to the sanctity of *all* oaths. And these Pharisaical distinctions do not even make logical sense, for obviously the **sanctuary that sanctifies the gold** is **greater** than **the gold** itself, just as **the altar that sanctifies the gift** is **greater** than **the gift** itself. Christ sweeps away all such casuistry and declares all oaths binding, because all oaths invoke God.

Thus, if one **swears** an oath **by the altar** (a minor and non-binding oath according to the Pharisees), one is thereby swearing not only **by the altar**, but also **by everything on it**, by all the sacrificial gifts. If one swears **by the sanctuary** or **by heaven** (a fairly common oath), one is swearing by the highest possible realities: by **Him who dwells** *within* the sanctuary, and by the very **throne of God** Himself, and by **Him who sits upon it**. All oaths are equally binding, for all involve God.

ॐ ॐ ॐ ॐ ॐ

23 "Woe to you, scribes and Pharisees, hypocrites! For you tithe mint and dill and cumin, and have left the weightier *things* of the Law: justice and mercy and faith; these *things* it was necessary to do without leaving those *things*.
24 "You blind guides!—those who strain out the gnat and swallow up the camel!

The *fourth woe* blames the scribes and Pharisees for their failure to discern the truly important things in the Law. They zealously obey the Law's minute prescriptions, and **tithe** not only the prescribed crops (see Lev. 27:30), but even such garden herbs as **mint and dill and cumin,** which did not need to be tithed. But **the weightier *things* of the Law**, things like **justice** for the oppressed, **mercy** to one's fellow, and **faith** (i.e. faithfulness) to God and man alike—these are utterly **left** out of their consideration. They neglect the central values of the Law to indulge their preoccupation with its minutiae. It is not even that these minutiae can be dispensed with—it is **necessary to do these *things*** too, for all zealous obedience is commendable. It is their disregard of the matters of the heart that is the problem.

This is as ridiculous as men who, in their attempt to obey the proscription against eating winged insects in Leviticus 11:23, carefully **strain out the gnat** from their drink—and then **swallow up** an entire **camel** (also forbidden in Lev. 11:4). (The original Aramaic contained a pun—they were straining out the *qalma* and swallowing up the *gamla*.)

ॐ ॐ ॐ ॐ ॐ

25 "Woe to you, scribes and Pharisees, hypocrites! For you cleanse the outside of the cup and of the dish, but inside they are full of robbery and lack of control.

26 "You blind Pharisee, first cleanse the inside of the cup, that the outside of it may become clean also.

In the *fifth woe*, Jesus denounces them for their preoccupation with the external, to the utter neglect of the internal. They are careful to **cleanse the outside of the cup and of the dish**, observing a concern for ceremonial cleanliness that even goes beyond the demands of the Law. For when they come from the marketplace they cleanse their hands, as well as their cups and pitchers before using them, lest by accident they have contracted ceremonial defilement while away (see Mark 7:3–4). Though not mandated by the Law, such ritual purity is of great concern to the Pharisees.

This concern makes their complete neglect of inner purity all the more remarkable. On the **inside** they are **full of robbery** and greed, of **lack of control** of their appetites and self-indulgence of every passion. Let them **first cleanse the inside of the cup, that the outside of it may become clean also**. That is, if they will attend to internal matters of heart purity, then the outer matters of ritual cleanliness will thereby be taken care of too (compare Luke 11:39–41).

ॐ ॐ ॐ ॐ ॐ

27 "Woe to you, scribes and Pharisees, hypocrites! For you are like whitewashed graves, which on the outside indeed appear beautiful, but inside they are full of the bones of the dead and every *kind of* uncleanness.

28 "Thus you *yourselves* also outwardly indeed appear righteous to men, but inwardly you are full of hypocrisy and lawlessness.

The *sixth woe* again concerns the stunning contrast between their exterior appearance of righteousness and the rebelliousness that lurks in their hearts. It was the custom in Palestine to apply a coat of whitewash to the graves in order to make them conspicuous. This was to prevent people (especially pilgrims, who flooded into the country every Passover) from inadvertently coming into contact with the graves and becoming ceremonially defiled for seven days (see Num. 19:16).

The Pharisees are **like** these **whitewashed graves**, for **on the outside** they **indeed appear beautiful** and attractive with their claims to righteousness (even as the graves on the outside appear white and clean). But, like the graves, their outward brightness conceals a horror, for just as the graves are **full of the bones of the dead and every** *kind of* **uncleanness**, so they **inwardly** are **full of hypocrisy and lawlessness**. Just as contact with the graves brought ritual defilement, so following the Pharisees' teaching brings spiritual defilement, contagion, and death.

ॐ ॐ ॐ ॐ ॐ

29 "Woe to you, scribes and Pharisees, hypocrites! For you build the graves of the prophets and adorn the tombs of the righteous,

30 "and say, 'If we had been *living* in the days of our fathers, we would not have been sharers with them in the blood of the prophets.'

31 "Consequently you witness against yourselves, that you are sons of those who murdered the prophets.

32 "You also—fill the measure of your fathers!

33 "You serpents, you offspring of vipers! How *can* you flee from the judgment of Gehenna?

34 "For this reason, behold! I *Myself* send you prophets and wise *men* and scribes. Some of them you will kill and crucify, and some of them you will scourge in your synagogues and persecute from city to city,

> 35 "so that upon you may fall all the righteous blood spilt on the earth, from the blood of righteous Abel to the blood of Zechariah son of Berechiah, whom you murdered between the sanctuary and the altar.
>
> 36 "Amen I say to you, all these *things* will come upon this generation.

With the *seventh woe*, the Lord's condemnation of the Pharisees reaches its climax. Once again Jesus castigates them for their hypocrisy. The hypocrisy here involves their praise of the prophets, who were persecuted and killed for the sake of their righteousness. The **graves** of these good men were known, and the Pharisees delighted to tend their monuments and to **adorn the tombs of the righteous**. In this care for the tombs of the prophets, the Pharisees advanced their claim to be righteous and to champion the principles laid down by the prophets. Indeed, they said, **"If we had been *living* in the days of our fathers, we would not have been sharers with them in** spilling **the blood of the prophets."** They were much better than their ancestors!

Yet these are the same men who are now actively engaged in persecuting Jesus, the modern-day prophet (21:11; Mark 3:6), and even now murder is in their hearts. Jesus therefore shows how their own words **witness against** them. They refer to **those who murdered the prophets** as their **fathers**—well, that would make the Pharisees their **sons**! In Jewish thought, a son was not simply someone's biological offspring. The word also sometimes meant one who partakes of the quality of another, so that, for example, a "son of Belial" (e.g. 1 Sam. 2:12) is a Belial (or devil) himself. The Pharisees' reference to the ancient persecutors being their fathers reveals the spiritual family likeness of the two groups—like father, like son! The Pharisees are murderous as well. Let them therefore **fill the measure of** their **fathers**, and finish what their fathers started. Let them keep on their murderous way.

It is **for this reason** that Jesus Himself (the **I** is emphatic) will **send** them **prophets and wise *men* and scribes** to **kill and crucify**.

Just as His Father sent the prophets of old, so Christ will send His own prophets, whom they will **scourge in** their **synagogues** and harry **from city to city** (compare 10:17, 23). With heavy irony, Jesus says they are determined to fill up the measure of their fathers and finish their work, so here are some messengers to persecute! Israel's measure of sin and rebellion is almost full, and the persecution of Jesus' messengers in the coming decades should fill it up. Then all the accumulated judgment due from centuries past will **fall upon this generation—all the righteous blood spilt on the earth** by Israel, **from the blood of righteous Abel to the blood of Zechariah**. The Lord's words found terrible fulfillment when the Romans came in AD 70 to destroy the Temple and scatter the nation of Israel.

One final note may be added about the identity of this **Zechariah**. He is described as the one **murdered between the sanctuary and the altar**, and this identifies him as Zechariah the son of Jehoiada, whose murder is recounted in 2 Chronicles 24:21f. Dying, he said, "May Yahweh see and avenge!" This Zechariah was chosen because his is the last judicial murder recounted in the Hebrew Scriptures. In speaking of all the blood unjustly spilt from Abel to Zechariah, Christ declares a coming vengence for all the righteous blood shed by Jewish authorities throughout Israel's sacred history. The totality of the past was about to come crashing in upon the Israel of Christ's day.

It may be asked too why Christ calls this Zechariah, **son of Berechiah**, when he was in fact rather the son of Jehoiada. The prophet Zechariah was called "the son of Berechiah, son of Iddo" (Zech. 1:1), but it is impossible that he was the same Zechariah mentioned in 2 Chronicles (the prophet was post-exilic, and the martyr pre-exilic). Nonetheless, many Jews in Christ's day mixed them up, and the Palestinian Targum (or Aramaic paraphrase) renders Lamentations 2:20 as, "Should priests be slain in the sanctuary as you slew Zechariah the son of Iddo?"

Also, a Jewish tradition says that the blood of this Zechariah (who said, "May Yahweh see and avenge!") continued to bubble where it was spilt until many Jews were slain at the destruction of the Temple in 586 BC. In referring to the martyr Zechariah as **son of**

Berechiah, Christ alludes to this popular identification of the two men for the purpose of saying that the blood of His messengers also will be avenged by God by the imminent destruction of the Temple, just as the blood of martyred Zechariah was. The blood of the man popularly known as Zechariah the son of Berechiah the son of Iddo did not rest until it had been avenged by national catastrophe, and neither would the blood of those sent by Jesus rest in the coming decades until it was similarly avenged. In referring to the Zechariah of 2 Chronicles as **son of Berechiah**, Jesus was not sanctioning the popular confusion of the two men, but simply using the popular designation to bring home the reality of the coming judgment.

ॐ ॐ ॐ ॐ ॐ

37 "O Jerusalem, Jerusalem, who kills the prophets and stones those sent to her! How often I wished to gather together your children, the way a hen gathers together her brood under her wings, and you did not wish *it*!

38 "Behold, your House is left to you a wilderness!

39 "For I say to you, from now on you will never see Me until you say, 'Blessed *is* He who comes in the Name of the Lord!'"

St. Matthew concludes his collection of gathered polemic against the Pharisees with Jesus' word of judgment upon Jerusalem. It actually dates from a time prior to Jesus' entry into Jerusalem (see Luke 13:34–35), but Matthew places it here in his collection as a fitting climax to the prophecy of judgment in verses 35–36.

For all His pain at being rejected by Jerusalem, Jesus does not delight in this coming judgment. He addresses the city tenderly, calling out to her, **Jerusalem, Jerusalem!** She is the city **who kills the prophets and stones those sent to her**, yet even so Jesus always loved her. **How often**, on previous visits there, did He **wish to gather together** her **children** and citizens and keep them safe in the will of God, but they **did not wish *it***. Now there is no help for them, but their **House** is **left** to them **a wilderness**. It will be abandoned by God, since God's will has been abandoned by them, and their Temple is doomed to become desolate and deserted, torn down stone by stone. They will **never see** Jesus in blessing or know the divine protection unless they cry, **"Blessed *is* He who comes in the Name of the Lord!"** Apart from this acknowledgment of Jesus as Messiah, they will never see His maternal protection for the city.

FIFTH DISCOURSE—
JERUSALEM AND THE LAST JUDGMENT
(24:1—26:2)

In this final discourse, Matthew draws material together from a variety of places and times in the Lord's ministry (compare Luke 12:35–48; 17:22–37; 21:5–36), showing that his concern is less chronological than thematic.

§XIII.1. Judgment on Jerusalem

❧ ❧ ❧ ❧ ❧

24 1 And Jesus came out from the Temple and was going away when His disciples came to *Him* to show to Him the Temple buildings.

2 And He answered and said to them, "Do you not see all these *things*? Amen I say to you, *one* stone here will by no means be left upon *another* stone, which will not be torn down."

3 And as He sat on the Mountain of Olives, the disciples came to Him privately, saying, "Tell us, when will these *things* be, and what *will be* the sign of Your coming, and of the consummation of the age?"

It was after **Jesus came out from the Temple** during His final week of teaching there and **was going away** that **His disciples came to *Him*** to point out the impressive beauty of **the Temple buildings**. They were indeed one of the wonders of the ancient world, for the

Temple itself was made of huge white stones, ornate with gold, so that it shone with brilliance in the morning sun. Jesus, however, could see past its external splendor to the proud defiance that lurked beneath the outward glory. He knew that God would punish such rebellion by destroying that Temple. He responded to His disciples' enthusiasm by saying, **"Do you not see all these *things?* Despite their massive solidity which promises that they will last forever, *one* stone here will by no means be left upon *another* stone, which will not be torn down."**

The disciples were stunned by this reply, for like all Jews they thought this Temple would last until the world's end. Surely then Jesus must have been speaking about the end of the world, and of the Temple's destruction as part of that final conflagration. After they were safely out of earshot of the crowds, **the disciples came to Him privately**, asking, **"When will these *things* be** (i.e. the destruction of the Temple), **and what *will be* the sign of Your coming, and of the consummation of the age?"** Though Jesus had spoken only of the destruction of the Temple, they thought of the consummation of the age as accompanying it, and wanted to know what sign would herald the end.

ॐ ॐ ॐ ॐ ॐ

4   And Jesus answered and said to them, "Watch out that no one deceives you.

5   "For many will come in My Name, saying, 'I *Myself* am the Christ,' and will deceive many.

6   "And you are about to hear of wars and reports of wars; see that you are not disturbed. It is necessary that this happen, but it is not yet the end.

7   "For nation will be raised against nation, and kingdom against kingdom, and in *various* places there will be famines and earthquakes.

8   "But all these *are the* beginning of birthpangs.

Jesus begins to answer their question about the destruction of the Temple in such a way as to warn them not to expect the imminent end at that time. They must **watch out that no one deceives** them, for much uproar was about to begin. **Many** will **come in** His **Name**, claiming that they are **the Christ**, and such claims will **deceive many**. Under the influence of these false-Messiahs, many Jews will fight for Jerusalem, confident that God will deliver them and their city from the Gentiles.

Moreover, the disciples **are about to hear of wars and reports of wars**, as if the whole fabric of the world were coming unraveled, and this may seem to support the idea that the end is at hand. They must **not be disturbed** by such events. It is **necessary** and ordained by God **that this happen**, but this does not mean (as the false-Christs will claim) that it is the end, for **it is not yet the end. Nation will be raised against nation** (note the passive voice, indicating that this will happen by the hand of God), and even **kingdom against kingdom**. All stability will seem to vanish, and even the earth itself will seem affected, as **there will be famines and earthquakes**, not just in one place but **in *various* places**. But these are not harbingers of the end, but simply *the* **beginning of birth-pangs**.

In the apocalyptic vocabulary of that day, people spoke of "the birth-pangs of the Messiah"—that is, the increasing upheavals that would characterize the end of the age, leading up to the reign of the Messiah. Jesus says that these disasters are not those birth-pangs, but only *the* **beginning** of them. Birth-pangs begin slowly and are spaced far apart. When they begin, birth is not imminent. In the same way, these disasters will have to grow much worse before the end comes.

ॐ ॐ ॐ ॐ ॐ

9 "Then they will deliver you to tribulation, and will kill you, and you will be hated by all the nations because of My Name.

10 "And at that time many will stumble, and will deliver *up* one another and hate one another.

---

11 "And many false-prophets will arise and will deceive many.

12 "And because lawlessness is multiplied, the love of many will become cold.

13 "But the one who perseveres to the end, this one will be saved.

14 "And this Gospel of the Kingdom will be heralded in the whole world for a witness to all the nations, and then the end will come.

In these tumultuous days, the disciples must take care, for their Jewish adversaries will **deliver** them **to tribulation, and will** even **kill** them, and the disciples **will be hated** not just in Israel but even **by all the nations** because they invoke Jesus' **Name**. These words found fulfillment in the persecution of Christian Jews by their unbelieving countrymen in the decades following (see for example the martyrdom of Stephen and of James, and the slander against the Church by the whole world; Acts 7:58f; 8:1; 12:2f; 17:6; 28:22).

At that time of trouble, **many** of those sympathetic to the Christian cause **will stumble** (i.e. turn against Christ). Christ here speaks of the situation in Jerusalem and Palestine in the years prior to the Roman war against Jerusalem in AD 66. In those terrible days, **lawlessness** was indeed **multiplied**, as one Jewish group fought against another for control. **The love of many became cold**, with all talk of surrender ruthlessly punished. **False-prophets** did indeed **arise**, promising the final salvation of the city, and they **deceived many** into fighting on. In this context, the disciples of Jesus (who denied that God would save the city that had rejected the Messiah) must have seemed like the ultimate traitors. No wonder their compatriots **delivered** them *up* to the authorities and **hated** them.

For their part, the disciples must **persevere** in their faith **to the end**, and not renounce their loyalty to Jesus to follow a false-Messiah. **This one**, and this one only, will finally **be saved**. If they would enter into life at the last day, let them not deny their true Lord. The persecution they will undergo is not a disaster, but an opportunity to witness to their faith. And not just in Israel, but the **Gospel**

of the Kingdom they are even now preaching will **be heralded in the whole world for a witness to all the nations**. Only then, when the Faith has been proclaimed to every nation under heaven, will **the end come**. Their sufferings are not signs of the defeat of the Christian movement, but rather bring the end ever nearer.

ॐ ॐ ॐ ॐ ॐ

15 "Therefore when you see the abomination of desolation spoken of through Daniel the prophet standing in the holy place (let the reader understand),

16 "then let those in Judea flee to the mountains;

17 "let the one on the housetop not go down to take the things from his house;

18 "and let the one in the field not turn back to take his garment.

19 "But woe to the ones having *children* in *the* womb and the ones nursing *babies* in those days!

20 "But pray that your flight may not occur in the winter, or on a Sabbath;

21 "for then there will be a great tribulation, such as has not occurred since the beginning of the world until now, nor ever will occur *again*.

22 "And unless those days had been chopped, no flesh would have been saved; but because of the chosen those days will be chopped.

23 "Then if anyone says to you, 'Behold, here *is* the Christ!' or 'There *He is*!" do not have faith in *him*,

24 "for false-Christs and false-prophets will be raised up and will give great signs and wonders, so as to deceive, if possible, even the chosen.

25 "Behold, I have foretold you.

26 "If therefore they say to you, 'Behold, He is

> in the wilderness!' do not go out, or, 'Behold,
> He is in the storerooms!' do not have faith
> in *them*.
>
> 27 "For just as the lightning comes out from the
> east and appears even to the west, thus will the
> coming of the Son of man be.
>
> 28 "Where the corpse is, there the vultures will be
> gathered.

Christ then comes to answer the disciples' initial question about the destruction of Jerusalem. Their request in verse 3 for a sign (for both the destruction of Zion and the end of the world, which they incorrectly thought would coincide) is now answered. (Compare Mark 13:4: "What is the sign when all these things [i.e. the destruction of the Temple] are about to be consummated?") The sign that Zion is about to be overthrown will be the sight of **the abomination of desolation standing in the holy place**.

By comparing this with the parallel in Luke 21:20, we learn that this is a reference to Jerusalem being encircled by armies. The **holy place** is the sacred soil of Jerusalem and its environs, and the **abomination of desolation** (i.e. the desolating sacrilege) is the idolatrous military standards of the Roman armies. This was all foretold by **Daniel the prophet** (compare Dan. 9:27; 11:31), whose prophecies of Jerusalem's desolation will find a complete fulfillment in the coming events.

When the disciples see the Roman armies encircling Zion, they must recognize that God has abandoned her to her sins, and that judgment is at hand. After this time, all **those in Judea** must **flee to the mountains** (and not take refuge in the city, thinking it will provide safety in the future). They must utterly separate themselves from the world they know, and not let worldliness tie them down. They must not postpone their departure, waiting to wind up their business affairs, but must have the inner detachment that will allow **the one on the housetop** to flee without **going down to take the things from his house**. Let them flee instantly, abandoning all to save their lives!

St. Matthew adds a cryptic parenthesis, asking **the reader** of his Gospel to **understand** the reference to the desolating armies of Rome. Such caution was necessary for Christians of the first century, for they could not speak openly of Rome in such negative terms.

The Lord declares that **woe** and disaster will befall **the ones having *children* in *the* womb, and the ones nursing *babies*,** for these women will be too encumbered to flee quickly to safety. He likewise asks His disciples to **pray** that the **flight may not occur in the winter** (when swollen impassable rivers would make the flight all the more difficult), **or on a Sabbath** (when the more punctilious may refuse to travel the necessary distance, or to provide help for those so traveling). For those will be terrible days indeed, **a great tribulation**, such as the world there has never seen. So severe will be the suffering that **unless those days had been chopped** and short-ened by God, **no flesh** in Jerusalem **would be saved, but because of the chosen**, the Christians who intercede for their comrades, **those days will be chopped** and the ordeal ended the sooner.

The temptation then is to believe that God will intervene and save Zion, and in those dark days **false-Christs and false-prophets will be raised up** who will predict just such an intervention. Some-one will say, "**Behold, here *is* the Christ**, the Messiah who will save us! Join His army and be rescued!" Such Messiahs will even **give great signs and wonders** to substantiate their claims. But Jesus' disciples must **not have faith** in the one proclaiming imminent rescue for the city, for no rescue will come. The true final Coming will be different. These men will proclaim that the Messiah is hidden away, about to be revealed from His hiding place **in the wilderness**, or **in the storerooms**, the secret chambers of the city. When Jesus, the **Son of man**, does return, His Presence will not be hidden, nor His return in any doubt. Rather His **coming** will be **just as the lightning**, which **comes out from the east and appears even to the west**. One can-not miss the lightning, which flashes across the whole sky, and one will not be able to miss the return of the true Messiah.

Thus, Jerusalem will not enjoy any special protection from God, nor any immunity from judgment. **Where the corpse is, there the vultures will be gathered** to feed on the carrion. In the same way, where Jerusalem's sin is, there will come the judgment of God.

It all happened exactly as the Lord predicted. In the days leading up to AD 70, there were indeed earthquakes and famines, and as Jewish nationalism grew ever more intense, the persecution of Jesus' followers grew ever more savage. In October 66, the Roman armies under Cestius Gallus marched against Jerusalem and surrounded her. The Christians there remembered the Lord's words and fled to the mountain city of Pella. In 70, the Romans returned under Titus and laid siege to Zion again. The city put up a valiant struggle, even though starvation reduced them to cannibalism. At last the city fell, and the Temple was burned to the ground, with not one stone left upon another. (The story of Jerusalem's fall and the Christians' flight is narrated by Eusebius in his *Church History*, 5.5–8.)

§XIII.2. The Second Coming

29 "But immediately after the tribulation of those days the sun will be darkened, and the moon will not give its light, and the stars will fall from heaven, and the powers of the heavens will be shaken,

30 "and then the sign of the Son of man will appear in heaven, and then all the tribes of the earth will lament, and they will see the Son of man coming on the clouds of heaven with power and much glory.

31 "And He will send His angels with a great trumpet, and they will gather together His chosen from the four winds, from *one* end of the heavens to the *other* end.

32 "Now from the fig tree learn the parable: When its branch has already become tender and puts forth the leaves, you know the summer *is* near.

> 33 "Thus you *yourselves* also, when you see
> all these things, know that it is near, at *the*
> doors.

The disciples asked the Lord not only about the destruction of the Temple, but also about the final end, and here Christ begins to answer that part of their question. In referring to the judgment of God on Zion, He was speaking not only of an event that occurred in AD 70, but also of its effects throughout this tumultuous age. (The parallel description of that judgment in Luke 21:24 describes it as Jerusalem being "trampled by the nations until the times of nations are fulfilled" at the end of the age.) Thus Christ's reference here to **the tribulation of those days** looks beyond AD 70 to encompass all the upheavals of the present age.

Immediately after those upheavals, during the final days, **the sun will be darkened, and the moon will not give its light, and the stars will fall from heaven**. The natural order will seem to be coming apart as the very **powers of the heavens** which sustained that order are **shaken**. This description is drawn from such classic apocalyptic texts as Isaiah 13:10, Ezekiel 32:7, and Joel 2:10, but the phenomena it predicts are real enough. Luke, paraphrasing such Jewish phrases for his Gentile audience, says simply, "there will be signs in the sun and moon and stars" (Luke 21:25).

It is after a period of such cosmic upheaval that the sign of the Son of man will appear in heaven. The disciples had asked for the sign of the Temple's destruction and of the world's end (v. 3). Since these are two separate realities, Christ responds by giving the two signs: the abomination of desolation standing in the holy place as the sign of the first, and **the sign of the Son of man in heaven** as the sign of the second.

What is this sign? St. Theophylact expresses the patristic view when he says that it is "the Cross in heaven, shining more brightly than the sun." At this sight, **all the tribes of the earth will lament** their rejection of the world's true King, and then **they will see the Son of man coming on the clouds of heaven with power and**

much glory. The Second Coming is described in these few words, since it is an attempt to describe the indescribable. St. Peter says that the heavens will pass away with a roar and the elements will be destroyed with intense heat (2 Pet. 3:10). The overwhelming fullness of this reality we cannot imagine.

As part of that final Coming and cosmic transformation, Christ **will send His angels with a great trumpet, and they will gather together His chosen from the four winds**. Israel had long nurtured the hope that when Messiah came, all the Jewish exiles would be called home to the Promised Land to live in security forever (Deut. 30:4; Is. 43:6; Zech. 2:6), and this hope is fulfilled in Christ. But His **chosen** ones are not simply faithful Jews, but His faithful Christians from all nations, both Jew and Gentile. These will be brought by **His angels** at the Second Coming, when the **great trumpet** sounds, and all are **gathered together** as a single army to stand before their King, though they be scattered **from *one* end of the heavens to the *other* end** (1 Cor. 15:52; 1 Thess. 4:16).

The Lord then offers a **parable**: Let them **learn** from **the fig tree,** which they all knew. Unlike most other trees in Palestine, which blossomed in the spring, the fig tree blossomed later, in the summer. When the branches of the fig tree had **become tender and put forth the leaves**, this was a sure sign that **the summer** was **near**. One could count on summer's nearness by looking at the fig tree. In the same way, one could count on the nearness of the Kingdom by looking at **all these things** (i.e. the signs described in v. 29). Most men would look at them and tremble with fear, but the disciples should look at them and rejoice, for these were sure signs that the Kingdom was **near, at *the* very doors**, and ready to enter.

ॐ ॐ ॐ ॐ ॐ

34 "Amen I say to you, this generation will by no means pass away until all these things occur.

35 "Heaven and earth will pass away, but My words will by no means pass away.

36 "But concerning that day and hour no one

> knows, not even the angels of the heavens, nor the Son, but the Father only.

Christ then sums up His answers to the questions He was asked in verse 3, adding a word of certainty about His predictions. He promises that **this generation** (the adulterous generation then living and resisting Him—compare the use of the term in 16:4; 12:41–42, 45; 23:36) **will by no means pass away** (the negative is emphatic) **until all things occur**. That is, the entire sequence of events Christ describes will begin to happen before that generation dies out. This is not to say that all those things, including the Second Coming, will *occur* within that generation—indeed, much of the Lord's teaching here is aimed against the idea that the end is imminent. The concern here is not with *timing*, but with *certainty*: Christ says here that they will not have to wait for proof of the certainty of His words, for their fulfillment will begin within that generation.

Christ's words were indeed fulfilled, for within a generation of the time these words were spoken, Jerusalem lay in ruins. His words were not the words of men, but of God, and will therefore abide forever. **Heaven and earth** will one day **pass away, but** His **words will** never **pass away**. They remain forever and will find their speedy fulfillment.

Concerning, however, **that day and hour** when heaven will pass away at the Second Coming, **no one knows, not even the angels of the heavens** or even **the Son** Himself, **but the Father only**. In saying this, Jesus intends to close the door forever on human speculation regarding the time of the Second Coming. His disciples must not conclude from their being able to predict the destruction of Zion that they will be able to predict the end also. No one on earth has the wisdom to read all the contours of history, discern the hand of God in all things, and thus accurately calculate that day. Not even **the angels of the heavens** with their transcendent vision are wise enough for that. Indeed, even **the Son** Himself, who had emptied Himself and spoke then in His incarnate state, had access to such knowledge as was hidden in the abyss of **the Father**. The disciples therefore must rest content to live without such knowledge.

ॐ ॐ ॐ ॐ ॐ

37 "For just as the days of Noah *were*, thus will be the coming of the Son of man.

38 "For as they were in those days before the flood, eating and drinking, marrying and giving in marriage, until the day Noah entered into the ark,

39 "and they did not know until the flood came and took them all away; thus will the coming of the Son of man be.

40 "Then there will be two in the field; one is taken, and one is left.

41 "Two will be grinding at the mill; one is taken, and one is left.

42 "Therefore keep alert, for you do not know which day your Lord is coming.

43 "But know this, that if the house-master had known at which watch the thief was coming, he would have kept alert and would not have allowed his house to be broken into.

44 "For this reason you *yourselves* be prepared also; for the Son of man is coming at an hour when you do not think *He will*.

The final events will come too suddenly to allow for any change of allegiance. It will be **just as the days of Noah *were***. In those days, people were **eating and drinking, marrying and giving in marriage**, and all social intercourse continued as usual right up **until the day Noah entered the ark, and they did not know until the flood came and took them all away**. The end came without any unmistakable warning to them that they should change their lives because doom was about to engulf the world. **Thus will be the coming of the Son of man**: sudden and without a prior warning that could awaken a godless world.

On that day, only the state of one's heart will avail—sharing a common Jewishness will be of no use. Two people could share the same race and the same family, and still inherit two different fates. **Two** men will be working **in the field** at early dawn as members of the same family. **One** will be **taken** away in the flood of judgment, even as the Flood took the men of Noah's generation, and **one** will be **left** to inherit the world to come. **Two** women could arise early to do their morning chore of **grinding at the mill**, one pouring the grain and the other turning the millstone to grind their daily bread. **One** will be **taken** in judgment, and the **one left**, even as Noah and his family were left to inherit the new world. Safety will not be found in righteous company, but in being righteous.

The disciples must therefore **keep alert**, for they do **not know which day** their **Lord is coming**, and therefore they must be prepared on all days. It is like **the house-master** whose **house** the **thief** had **broken into** at night. If the lord of the house had known at **which watch** of the night the burglar was coming, he would have **kept alert** and prevented the burglary, but he did not know. In the same way, the disciples will not know at which hour **the Son of man is coming**, for He will send no advance message announcing it, and so they must be **prepared** at all hours. They must not sink into a state of unrighteousness and so be unprepared for their Lord's return.

§XIII.3. Parable of the Faithful Slave

ॐ ॐ ॐ ॐ ॐ

45 "Who therefore is the faithful and prudent slave whom his lord appointed over his household *slaves* to give them their food at the *appointed* time?

46 "Blessed *is* that slave whom his lord finds doing thus when he comes.

47 "Amen I say to you, he will appoint him over all his possessions.

48 "But if that wicked slave says in his heart, 'My lord delays,'

> 49 "and begins to strike his fellow-slaves and eat
> and drink with the drunkards,
>
> 50 "the lord of that slave will come on a day when
> he does not expect, and at an hour which he
> does not know,
>
> 51 "and will cut him in two and put *him to have*
> his part with the hypocrites; there, there will
> be weeping and gnashing of teeth.

The Lord then tells several parables about the importance of His disciples remaining righteous in preparation for His sudden return. In the first parable, Jesus pictures two possible responses on the part of the head slave to the apparent delay of his lord's return. The slave has been **appointed** by **his lord over** the other **household *slaves* to give them their food at the *appointed* time**. That is, he is to care for his fellow-slaves as a good steward of his master's bounty, mindful of his responsibilities. If the **slave** is **faithful and prudent, his lord will find** him **doing thus when he comes** back. How pleased his master will be! Indeed, he will not just promote him to a place over that household, but will **appoint him over all his possessions**, making him steward over other households also.

But if that **slave** is **wicked** and **says in his heart, "My lord delays**—here's my chance to abuse my authority!" and **begins to strike his fellow-slaves** for their supposed disrespect (even though he is a slave like them), and to **drink with the drunkards** of the town, using up his master's goods as if they were his own—then the result will be different. For **the lord of that slave**, having **come on a day when** the slave **does not expect**, will return too suddenly to allow the abusive head slave to change his ways. Having found him out, he will **cut him in two** as if he were a criminal, and **put *him to have* his part with the hypocrites**, far from any blessing or reward. In that place there will be eternal **weeping and gnashing of teeth**.

In both scenarios, the lord is perceived as delaying his return. How will his servant respond to this delay—by carrying out his last orders, or by falling into a life of unrighteousness? The disciples have this choice also, and on this choice hinges their eternal destiny. The stress of the last days may tempt them to despair of their Lord's return and to turn to worldly pleasures (Luke 21:34–35), but they must resist this if they would avoid the lot of the hypocrites.

§XIII.4. Parable of the Wise Virgins

ॐ ॐ ॐ ॐ ॐ

25 1 "Then the Kingdom of the heavens will be likened to ten virgins, who took their lamps and went out to meet the bridegroom.

2 "And five of them were foolish, and five prudent.

3 "For when the foolish took their lamps, they took no oil with them,

4 "but the prudent took oil in vessels with their lamps.

5 "Now while the bridegroom was delaying, they all became drowsy and were sleeping.

6 "But in the middle of the night a yell occurred: 'Behold, the bridegroom! Come out to meet him!'

7 "Then all those virgins rose and put their lamps in order.

8 "And the foolish said to the prudent, 'Give us *some* of your oil, for our lamps are quenching.'

9 "But the prudent answered, saying, 'Perhaps there will not be sufficient for us and you; go rather to the sellers and buy for yourselves.'

10 "And while they were going away to buy, the bridegroom came, and those who were prepared went in with him to the wedding; and the door was shut.

> 11 "And later the other virgins also came, saying,
>   'Lord, lord, open to us!'
> 12 "But he answered and said, 'Amen I say to you,
>   I do not know you.'
> 13 "Keep alert therefore, for you do not know the
>   day nor the hour.

The necessity of living a life of faithful obedience to the Lord's instructions is taught in this second parable also. If the last parable focused on the different fates of promotion for the obedient or destruction for the disobedient, this parable focuses on the joy of inclusion for the spiritually prepared and exclusion for the unprepared. Here the Lord is **likened** to a **bridegroom**, whose arrival will signal the start of the wedding feast, and His servants are likened to **ten virgins** who attended the bride.

In antiquity, weddings were always held at night. The Jewish custom was for the bridegroom to come from his home to that of the bride, collect the bride and the young girls who attended her, and take them all back to his place, where the wedding feast would last for days. In Israel, nothing was more splendid and joyful than the wedding feast, and it was a fit image for the joy of **the Kingdom of the heavens**.

In this parable, however, for some reason **the bridegroom was delaying** his expected arrival at the home of the bride, and as the evening wore on, **all** of those waiting for him **became drowsy** and began **sleeping**. Their sleep was interrupted **in the middle of the night** when **a yell occurred** which woke them with a start: **"Behold, the bridegroom! Come out to meet him!"** The men attending the bridegroom were shouting out that the bridegroom had left his house and was on his way. He would soon be there!

Of the ten young girls attending the bride, as it turned out, **five were foolish and five prudent, for when the foolish** ones **took their lamps, they took no oil with them, but the prudent** ones **took oil in vessels** along **with their lamps.** (These **lamps**— Gr. *lampas*—were probably torches, oil-soaked rags upon sticks;

compare the use of the word in John 18:3. Such rags might burn for about fifteen minutes without being replenished with oil.) Thus, when **all those virgins rose** in the middle of the night and began to **put their lamps in order** by soaking the dry rags in oil, the foolish ones found that they did not have enough oil for that. They asked their friends to **give** them *some* of their **oil**, but were answered that **perhaps there will not be sufficient** for them both. There was nothing for it but for them to **go to the sellers and buy** more oil for themselves. Buying oil that late would not be impossible in a small village where all were involved in the wedding, but the purchase would take time.

In fact, it took too much time. For **while they were going away to buy, the bridegroom came, and those who were prepared went in with him to the wedding**. When the unprepared virgins returned from the sellers, they found that **the door was shut**. It is here that the parable shades off from village experience to the age to come of which the wedding feast is a parable. (Compare a similar shading off in the previous parable, 24:50–51.) Despite their expectation of being admitted to the feast, the latecomers were denied entrance. This was surprising—after all, they were attendants of the bride, with every right to enter. They therefore hammered on the door, saying, **"Lord, lord, open to us!"** But the Bridegroom **answered** from within **and said, "Amen I say to you, I do not know you."** The light-filled feast would continue without them. They were left out in the dark, and no desperate entreaty could gain them entrance.

The words **"Amen I say to you"** identify the speaker as Christ, the heavenly Bridegroom of His Bride, the Church. No matter how well His servants feel they know Him (compare 7:22–23), He will disown them at the end if His Coming finds them spiritually unprepared—and as the foolish virgins discovered, one cannot rely on the preparedness of others to make up one's own lack (v. 9). Let His disciples **keep alert therefore**, and persevere now in obeying His commands, for He will return too suddenly and without warning to allow a lifesaving change of life.

§XIII.5. Parable of the Talents

ॐ ॐ ॐ ॐ ॐ

14 "For *it is* just like a man leaving home *who* called his own slaves and delivered to them his possessions.

15 "And to one he gave five talents, to another two, and to another one, each according to his own power, and he left home.

16 "Immediately the one who had received the five talents went and worked with them, and gained five other *talents*.

17 "Likewise the one *who had* the two *talents* gained two other *talents*.

18 "But he who received the one *talent* went away and dug in the earth, and hid his lord's money.

19 "Now after much time the lord of those slaves comes and settles accounts with them.

20 "And the one who had received the five talents came to *him and* brought five other talents, saying, 'Lord, you delivered to me five talents; see, I have gained five other talents.'

21 "His lord said to him, 'Well *done*, good and faithful slave! You were faithful over a few *things*; I will appoint you over many *things*. Enter into the joy of your lord!'

22 "The one *who had* the two talents also came to *him* and said, 'Lord, you delivered to me two talents; see, I have gained two other talents.'

23 "His lord said to him, 'Well *done*, good and faithful slave! You were faithful over a few *things*; I will appoint you over many *things*. Enter into the joy of your lord!'

24 "And the one *who had received* the one talent also came to *him* and said, 'Lord, I knew that

> you are a hard man, harvesting where you did
> not sow, and gathering where you did not scat-
> ter out.
>
> 25 "'And I was afraid, and went away and hid
> your talent in the earth; see, you have what *is*
> yours.'
>
> 26 "But his lord answered and said to him, 'You
> evil and lazy slave—you knew that I harvest
> where I did not sow, and gather where I did
> not scatter out?
>
> 27 "'Therefore it was necessary for you to have
> put my money with the bankers, and when I
> came I *myself* would have received back what
> *is* mine with interest!
>
> 28 "'Therefore take the talent from him, and give
> *it* to the one who has the ten talents.
>
> 29 "'For to everyone who has will more be given,
> and he will have an abundance; but from the
> one who does not have, even what he has will
> be taken.
>
> 30 "'And cast out the worthless slave into the
> outer darkness; there, there will be weeping
> and gnashing of teeth.'

Christ then tells a third parable. If the second one focused on the state of preparedness for those waiting, this parable focuses on the need to work diligently while waiting. In this parable we have **a man leaving home** *who* **called his own slaves and delivered to them his possessions. To one** of his slaves **he gave five talents, to another two, and to another one.** That is, he parceled out all his wealth to his three slaves, giving different amounts to **each** one **according to his own power,** his differing ability and business acumen. After that, **he left home,** expecting his slaves to use his wealth as good stewards, trading and making a profit for their master.

Most of his faith was not misplaced. The first slave was zealous, and **immediately** after his master left, the slave **went and**

worked with the five talents **and gained five other *talents*.** A talent (a weight, not a coin) was worth about six thousand denarii, so that five talents would be worth 30,000 denarii. This was therefore an immense sum, for a denarius was a day's wage for the working man.

The second slave was just as zealous as the first, for he **likewise** went out immediately and did business with his two talents so that he **gained two other *talents*,** for a total gain of 12,000 denarii.

But he who received the one talent was different. He **went away and dug in the earth, and hid his lord's money.** (Hiding money in the earth was the usual way of safekeeping; compare the parable of the hidden treasure in 13:44.) This was a dereliction of duty and disobedience, for the slave was clearly supposed to trade with the talent and increase his master's money.

The lord of those slaves finally returns **after much time** (compare the delay of the master in the previous two parables), and summons his slaves to **settle accounts with them** and find out how they did. **The one who had received the five talents came to *him*** eagerly, carrying with him to show his lord the **five other talents** he had earned, and announced his good news: **"Lord, you delivered to me five talents; see, I have gained five other talents."** We can almost see the slave beaming as he anticipates his master's praise.

The master is indeed impressed. **"Well *done*, good and faithful slave! You were faithful over a few *things*; I will appoint you over many *things*. Enter into the joy of your lord!"** That is, he fulfilled well the simple order he was given, and will be rewarded with a promotion to greater responsibility and privilege. The **joy of** his **lord** was the greater prosperity his master could enjoy—and in which the slave could have his share. A large party seems to have been in view.

After such praise being showered on the first slave, the second slave is eager to recount his success. In words almost identical to the first slave, the second also **comes to *him*** eagerly, declaring, **"Lord, you delivered to me two talents; see, I have gained two other talents."** This slave also is praised, with the exact same words as the first one was. (It would seem that what the Lord values is not the amount produced, but the zeal manifested, for even though the second slave earned less than half as much as the first, he received the same praise. He worked just as hard, doubling his money, and so received the same reward.) This second slave also received promotion and his share in the new prosperity.

It was time for the third slave, **the one *who had received* the one talent**. If he had earned but one talent more, his reward would have been equal to his comrades'. But he was disobedient to his lord's parting orders, and now his disobedience must become known. (So must all our misdeeds finally appear before our Master.) He **also came to** his master, but (we think) not with the eagerness of his fellows, but hanging back until he had no choice but to step forward and report. He still clutched in his hand the original talent. His explanation for his disobedience was not so much an apology for himself as an accusation of his lord: **"I knew that you are a hard man, harvesting where you did not sow, and gathering where you did not scatter out. And I was afraid, and went away and hid your talent in the earth; see, you have what *is* yours."** And with this (we think), he held up the talent for his lord to take back.

It was an astonishing speech for a slave to make to his owner. He accuses him of unfairly demanding a high return, of giving them a task too difficult for them to fulfill. Because he was given such an impossible task, he says, he **was afraid**, and **went away and hid** the **talent in the earth** to keep it safe. Proffering his master the original sum of money, he says, **"See, you have what *is* yours."** In other words, "Take back your money; I have no responsibility for it any longer."

After such stellar performances from the first two slaves (which incidentally disprove the third slave's contention that his master's demands were unfair), the lord is floored at this. He explodes, **"So you knew that I harvest where I did not sow, and gather where I did not scatter out? Therefore it was necessary for you to have put my money with the bankers, and when I came I would have received back what is mine with interest!"** The slave had made a surly reference to **what *is* yours**. The master now quotes this, and says that if the slave had made even a little effort, the master could receive back that **what *is* yours** (called **what *is* mine** in v. 27) with interest. That is, even by the slave's own figuring of the matter, he could have done better! The truth was that the slave was simply **evil and lazy**.

By way of punishment, the master commands his attendants to **take the talent from him, and give *it* to the one who has the ten talents**. (In this way, Christ teaches that **everyone who has** God's blessing in this age for his obedience **will be given more** in the age to come, whereas **the one who does not have** God's blessing now will forfeit **what** little he has in the lake of fire; compare Mark 4:24–25.) The **worthless slave** will be **cast out** of the household, never to enjoy the joy and bounty of his lord again. Again the parable shades off into reality, for the slave finds himself in **the outer darkness**, where **there will be weeping and gnashing of teeth**.

In this third parable, Christ teaches His disciples in what the required preparedness (v. 10) consists: not in simply waiting in laziness for the Lord to return, but in zealous work. The **talents** and spiritual gifts given to us must be used to the full. Only so will we enter into the eternal **joy of** our **Lord** in the age to come.

§XIII.6. The Last Judgment: The Sheep and the Goats

The discourse ends, quite appropriately, with the Last Judgment. Though the image of dividing all men into two groups as a shepherd separates the sheep from the goats is parabolic, this is not so much a parable as it is a stylized description of the Last Judgment itself.

Christ's description of the Last Judgment cannot properly be understood apart from the Jewish conceptions of that Judgment which were common in His day. The *Book of Enoch* (a Jewish apocalyptic work, dating from just before Christ) contains one such conception of the messianic judgment. In chapters 62–63 of this work, we read the following:

> The kings and the mighty and those who hold the earth
> . . . shall be terrified when they see the Son of man sitting
> on the throne of his glory. And all the kings and the mighty

and those who rule the earth shall fall down before him on their faces and worship and set their hope upon the Son of man and petition him and supplicate for mercy at his hands. Nevertheless the Lord of Spirits will so press them that they shall hastily go forth from His presence and their faces shall be filled with shame. . . . And they shall say, "Light has vanished from before us, for we have not believed before Him, nor glorified the Name of the Lord of Spirits. . . ." After that they shall be driven from the presence of the Son of man.

This passage reveals what most Jews expected would happen at the Last Judgment: All the mighty rulers of the Gentile nations that had oppressed Israel would finally confess the supremacy of their God (the Lord of Spirits) and of His Messiah (the Son of man). They would regret not believing in Him and would be driven from His Presence into hell.

Jesus paints a very different picture of what the Judgment will be like, and like His other portrayals of that Judgment, it is one that contains surprises (compare 7:22–23; 8:11–12; 22:12; 25:11–12). The surprise here is who are the brothers of the Son of man, those whom He came to vindicate and avenge. Contemporary Jewish expectation said that these were His fellow-Jews, and that the nations would be judged on how they treated Israel and would be condemned for being pagan. Jesus, however, asserts that it is the poor of the earth who are His brothers, and that the nations will not be judged on how they treated Israel, but *on how they treated the poor.* (As St. Theophylact wrote concerning this passage, "Every poor man is Christ's brother because Christ too spent His life in poverty.")

This is the surprise in store for all at that Judgment—both the righteous and the unrighteous. The Last Judgment is thus not perceived in terms of national vindication for Israel, but in terms of a judgment of the hearts of all men—a judgment that cuts across the division of Jew and Gentile. The Jews who called Abraham their father had no immunity at this Judgment. They must bring forth the fruits of mercy for their fellowmen if they would be saved.

ॐ ॐ ॐ ॐ ॐ

31 "But when the Son of man comes in His glory, and all the angels with Him, then He will sit upon the throne of His glory.

32 "And all the nations will be gathered before Him; and He will separate them from one another, as the shepherd separates the sheep from the goats;

33 "and He will stand the sheep on His right, and the goats on the left.

34 "Then the King will say to those on His right, 'Come, you blessed of My Father, inherit the Kingdom prepared for you from the foundation of the world!

35 "'For I hungered, and you gave Me *something* to eat; I thirsted, and you gave Me *something* to drink; I was a stranger, and you gathered Me in;

36 "'naked, and you clothed Me; I was ailing, and you visited Me; I was in prison, and you came to Me.'

37 "Then the righteous will answer Him, saying, 'Lord, when did we see You hungering and nourish You, or thirsty and give You drink?

38 "'And when did we see You a stranger and gather *You* in, or naked and clothe *You*?

39 "'And when did we see You ailing, or in prison, and come to You?'

40 "And the King will answer and say to them, 'Amen I say to you, inasmuch as you did *it* to one of the least of these My brothers, you did *it* to Me.'

In His climactic description of the Last Judgment, Jesus says that when He will **come in His glory** at the world's end, **then He will sit**

upon the throne of His glory as supreme Judge over all. (We note in passing that in 16:27 He spoke of coming in *His Father's* glory, while here He speaks of His own glory. The glory of His Father is His glory also, for He has all the authority of the Father.) The image here is of a victorious King setting up his throne immediately after a battle, ready to reward His supporters and partisans and punish those who opposed Him (see Luke 19:27; Jer. 39:5–12). In this battle, it is the whole earth that is subdued before Christ. **All the nations will be gathered before Him** for judgment, and **He will separate them from one another as the shepherd separates the sheep from the goats.** (Shepherds did this, some say, because while goats need to be warm and enclosed, sheep prefer the open air.) In this separation, some were made to **stand** on **His right** as they awaited sentence, and others **on the left.**

The word rendered **nations** is the Greek *ethne*, sometimes rendered "Gentiles." It corresponds to the Hebrew *goyim* and means the nations of the world, as opposed to the Israel of God. Any Jew listening to this story thus far would have expected the nations to be **separated from one another** on the basis of their treatment of Israel. **The sheep** would have been those Gentiles who supported Israel, and **the goats**, those who oppressed them.

At length, the King speaks and renders judgment. **Those on His right** (the place of honor) are pronounced **blessed of** His **Father**, and told to **come** forward and **inherit the Kingdom** which God has **prepared** for them **from the foundation of the world.** And then comes the reason for this reward—when the King **hungered**, they **gave** Him *something* **to eat**; when He **thirsted**, they **gave** Him *something* **to drink**. When He was **a stranger** in a strange place and defenseless, they **gathered** Him **in** to give Him shelter; when He was **naked** and cold, they **clothed** Him to keep Him warm. When He was **ailing** and sick, they **visited** and tended Him; when He was languishing **in prison**, they **came** to Him to encourage Him.

The righteous, though happy to be so rewarded, are nonetheless puzzled, for **when** did they ever **see** Jesus their King in such straits and care for Him like that? (Each category is repeated one by one, for dramatic effect as the narrative builds.) Their puzzlement reflects that of all those listening to Jesus' words, for the disciples, like all Jews, expected a different set of criteria for the Judgment.

Then comes the surprise: **inasmuch as** they **did *it* to one of the least of these** suffering ones, His **brothers**, they **did *it*** to Him. The focus of the Last Judgment, therefore, has nothing to do with being Jewish. It has to do with being merciful to the helpless of the earth. As Christ has repeatedly taught, what God demands in the Law is mercy, not sacrifice (9:13; 12:7).

ॐ ॐ ॐ ॐ ॐ

41 "Then He will also say to those on the left, 'Go away from Me, you accursed ones, into the eternal fire prepared for the devil and his angels;

42 "'for I hungered, and you did not give Me *something* to eat; I thirsted, and you did not give Me *something* to drink;

43 "'I was a stranger, and you did not gather Me in; naked, and you did not clothe Me; sick, and in prison, and you did not visit Me.'

44 "Then they *themselves* also will answer, saying, 'Lord, when did we see You hungering, or thirsting, or a stranger, or naked, or sick, or in prison, and did not serve You?'

45 "Then He will answer them, saying, 'Amen I say to you, inasmuch as you did not do *it* to one of the least of these, neither did you do *it* to Me.'

46 "And these will go away into eternal punishment, but the righteous into eternal life."

Then the King turns to **those on the left** (who perhaps were not privy to His talk with those on the right). His judgment now is severe. If the righteous are invited to "come" (v. 34), the unrighteous are commanded to **go away**, and are banished from the King's Presence. They are sent **into the eternal fire**, one so terrible that it was **prepared** by God **for the devil and his angels**. Those on the right are blessed, but these are **accursed**, under the sentence of condemnation and wrath. And they deserve it, for when the King **hungered** and was in need, they treated Him like an enemy, and **did not give** Him *something* **to eat**. They let Him starve before their very eyes. Time after time, the King was in need—**thirsting, a stranger, naked, sick, in prison**—and time after time they left Him languishing in distress. When they were on top and He was on the bottom, they were content to leave Him there. How can they expect anything but His vengeance now that the roles are reversed?

Those on the left are stunned at this absurd accusation. They address Him as **Lord**, for they consider themselves righteous and His loyal partisans (compare 7:21–22). What is He talking about? When has He ever been in need of their help and they **did not serve** Him? The surprising criterion is revealed to them also: **inasmuch as** they **did not do** *it* **to one of the least of these, neither did** they **do** *it* **to** Him. As the Fathers will later affirm, when we see our neighbor, we see our God. Even the rabbis of Jesus' day had some inkling of this for, commenting on Deuteronomy 15:9, they said that when food is given to the poor, God counts it as given to Him.

Protests from those on the left are unavailing. They **go away into eternal punishment** where the King sends them, **but the righteous into eternal life**. For the disciples and all those listening, the message is clear: What God wants from all is compassion for one's suffering neighbor, and all who do this will be saved—whether Jew or Gentile. As St. Paul will later write, there will be glory and honor and peace to every one that does good, both Jew and Greek, for there is no partiality with God (Rom. 2:7–11).

§XIII.7. Conclusion

ॐ ॐ ॐ ॐ ॐ

26 1   And it happened that when Jesus had finished all these words, He said to His disciples,

> 2   "You know that after two days the Passover happens, and the Son of man is to be delivered *up* to be crucified."

This final discourse ends as the others did, with the formula that **Jesus finished all these words**. Matthew then focuses on the coming Passion, relating Jesus' saying during that final week that **after two days the Passover happens**, when **the Son of man is to be delivered *up*** by His people **to be crucified** by the Romans.

✵ XIV ✵

THE PASSION
(26:3—27:66)

§XIV.1. The Anointing at Bethany and the Plan to Betray Jesus

✺ ✺ ✺ ✺ ✺

26 3 Then the chief-priests and the elders of the people were gathered in the court of the high-priest, named Caiaphas;

4 and they counseled to seize Jesus by guile and kill *Him*.

5 But they were saying, "Not in the festal *crowd*, lest an uproar happen among the people."

6 Now when Jesus was in Bethany, in the house of Simon the leper,

7 a woman came to Him with an alabaster *flask* of expensive perfume, and she poured it on His head as He reclined.

8 But the disciples were indignant when they saw *it* and said, "Why this loss?

9 "For this might have been sold for much and given to the poor."

10 But Jesus, knowing this, said to them, "Why are you causing toil for the woman? For she has worked a good work for Me.

11 "For you always have the poor with you; but Me you do not always have.

12 "For when this *woman* put this perfume on My body, this *woman* did *it* to prepare Me for burial.

> 13 "Amen I say to you, wherever this Gospel is heralded in the whole world, what this *woman* has done will also be spoken of for a memorial of her."
>
> 14 Then one of the Twelve, named Judas Iscariot, went to the chief-priests,
>
> 15 and said, "What are you willing to give me to deliver Him up to you?" And they set *aside* for him thirty *pieces of* silver.
>
> 16 And from then on he was seeking for an opportune *time* to deliver Him up.

Matthew now relates how Christ's prediction of His imminent death (v. 2) is fulfilled. It was during this time that **the chief-priests and the elders of the people were gathered in the court** (that is, the palace) **of the high-priest, named Caiaphas**. These men had all been continually bested by Jesus in the Temple, and were determined to have Him arrested and destroyed. **They counseled** together that the only way to do this was to **seize Jesus by guile**. The population of Jerusalem had swollen from its usual 50,000 to about 250,000 for the Passover feast, and many of these were Galileans and supporters of Jesus. The Temple authorities could not simply move in and seize Him openly in the middle of **the festal *crowd***, for **an uproar** and a riot would **happen among the people**, and the officers attempting the arrest would be torn to pieces. Jesus' foes needed a way of arresting Him secretly.

Their break came soon enough, in the form of Judas Iscariot and his willingness to betray his Lord. To show the enormity of this betrayal of his lord, Matthew juxtaposes it with a scene of tender devotion (vv. 6–13) that occurred before that prediction (vv. 14–16).

This occurred **when Jesus was in Bethany, in the house of Simon the leper**. (That is, of Simon who was *formerly* a leper; it is inconceivable that he would host a gathering while still leprous.) This happened six days before the Passover, when Jesus was at a party held in His honor by Lazarus, Martha, and Mary (John 12:1–8). (It is possible this party was held in Simon's house because it was larger and needed to accommodate the large crowd invited.) It was during this feast that **a woman came to Him**. (From John 12:3, we learn that this was Mary, the sister of Lazarus.)

She had **an alabaster *flask* of expensive perfume**, probably one that had been preserved for generations as a family heirloom. These flasks had long necks that were broken to pour out their contents, and once broken, there was no way to stopper them again. All the contents must be used at one time. She **poured it on His head as He reclined** at table during the meal. (It would appear from the parallel in John 12:3 that there was too much perfume for it all to be poured on His head, and in an act of impulsive devotion, she knelt to pour out the rest on His feet, wiping off the excess with her hair.) It was an astonishing act of devotion, and especially so from a woman in public.

The disciples were indignant when they saw *it*, however, and protested, **"Why this loss? For this might have been sold for much and given to the poor."** (It was Judas who actually spoke up; John 12:4f.) It is estimated that the perfume was worth more than 300 denarii, almost a year's wages for a laborer (Mark 14:5)—a sizable gift for the poor, and one that could do much good. From the human perspective, the disciples had a point. They felt sure that Jesus, who had such concern for the poor, would share their view.

Jesus, though, looks at this act from the divine perspective, and does not share their view. **Knowing** by His supernatural insight what they are doing (did they take her aside to rebuke her privately?), He instantly springs to the woman's defense, saying, **"Why are you causing toil** and trouble **for the woman? For she has worked a good work for Me"**—a true *mitzvah*, worthy of divine reward. Are they so concerned to help the poor? Well, they **always have the poor with** them, and can help them any time they like. But it is otherwise with Him; the time for such deeds of love is quickly slipping away. Anointing a body for burial is a good work, and that is what **this *woman*** has just done—she has **put this perfume on** His **body to prepare** Him **for burial**. And she will have her just reward: **wherever this Gospel is heralded in the whole world, what** she **has done will also be spoken of for a memorial of her**.

It was an unexpected response. (And from the disciples' standpoint, an odd one, for surely Jesus would not need burial for some years to come.) A **memorial** (Gr. *mnemosunon*) was something done or offered as a memorial before God, so that He would remember the person thus commended and reward him. (In Lev. 2:2 LXX the word is used for a memorial sacrifice.) What Jesus meant was that the woman's act of devotion would function as her memorial before God on the last day. Every time the Gospel was preached, this act would be rehearsed along with it, so that the Gospel preachers would continually offer this memorial on her behalf.

If the disciples were amazed at this response, Judas was more than amazed. For him it was more than he could stand—to be publicly rebuked in favor of a woman. After they left the party, resentment burned within him, and when he had opportunity, he **went to the chief-priests and said, "What are you willing to give me to deliver Him up to you?"** This was the break the Temple authorities had been hoping for. **They set *aside* for him thirty *pieces of* silver**, promising to give it to him when the deed was done (Mark 14:11). Judas then began to look for his chance **to deliver Him up** to his new friends.

Matthew makes a point of identifying him as **one of the Twelve**, the inner circle, to stress how heinous the betrayal was, and of giving his full name, **Judas Iscariot**, to fix the blame on the right person.

The amount promised, **thirty *pieces of* silver**, was not a large amount, being the classic amount given to compensate for the loss of a slave in Exodus 21:32. It is possible that this paltry amount was chosen by the chief-priests as a way of showing their contempt for Jesus. And Judas does not bargain for more. He is not motivated solely by greed, but also by resentment of his Lord.

§XIV.2. The Last Supper

৩৭ ৩৭ ৩৭ ৩৭ ৩৭
17 Now on the first *day* of Unleavened *Bread*
the disciples came to Jesus, saying, "Where

do You want us to prepare for You to eat the Passover?"

18 And He said, "Go into the city to such a one, and say to him, 'The Teacher says, "My *appointed* time is near; with you I am doing the Passover with My disciples."'"

19 And the disciples did as Jesus had directed them; and they prepared the Passover.

20 Now when evening had come, He was reclining with the Twelve.

21 And as they were eating, He said, "Amen I say to you that one of you will deliver Me up."

22 And being extremely grieved, each one began to say to Him, "Surely I am not *the one*, Lord?"

23 And He answered and said, "He who dipped his hand with Me in the dish is the one who will deliver Me up.

24 "The Son of man indeed goes just as it is written about Him; but woe to that man by whom the Son of man is delivered up! *It would have been* good for him if that man had not been born."

25 And Judas, who was delivering Him up, answered and said, "Surely I am not *the one*, Rabbi?" He says to him, "You *yourself* have said it."

The scene now moves ahead to **the first *day* of Unleavened Bread** (popularly so-called—that is, the time when the Passover lambs were being slain for the Passover meal, which began the seven-day Feast of Unleavened Bread). **The disciples came to Jesus** inquiring where they were to **eat the Passover**. The Passover meal had to be eaten within Jerusalem, and the city was swarming with Jesus' foes. He was safe while in the public eye, but at risk of arrest when alone. The location of their Passover meal must be kept secret from His enemies.

Jesus therefore had prearranged for a secret location for their final meal. Mark 14:13f has a fuller account of how the disciples would recognize their contact. Matthew relates only Jesus' instruction that the disciples were to find **such a one** in the city and give him the password, **"The Teacher says, 'My *appointed* time is near; with you I am doing the Passover with My disciples,'"** and that **the disciples did as Jesus had directed them.**

When evening had come for the Paschal meal, Jesus **was reclining with the Twelve**. The Passover meal followed a prescribed ritual. The head of the house would chant a blessing over the first cup of wine (the cup of *Kiddush* or sanctification), giving thanks to God for the wine and for the feast. Each would then drink the cup that stood before him. A basin of water was brought in, and all washed their hands. Then the table of food was brought in, consisting of the Passover itself (i.e. the lamb offered that day in the Temple), unleavened bread, bitter herbs, greens, and a dish of stewed fruit. The host would then dip some of the bitter herbs and hand them to each, as a kind of preliminary appetizer. A second cup of wine was filled and blessed with a prayer (the cup of *Haggadah*, or storytelling), and the story of the Exodus was recounted.

It was as they were eating this preliminary appetizer that Jesus began to be upset. He solemnly affirmed that **one of** them would **deliver** Him **up** to His foes. That is, even in this atmosphere of cozy safety, a traitor lurked in their midst, throwing the joy of the meal into shadow. The disciples were stunned at this news. All were **extremely grieved**, and **began to say to Him, "Surely I am not *the one*, Lord?"** trusting Christ's words over their own self-confidence. Christ would only say that it was one **who dipped his hand with** Him **in the dish**—that is, one now enjoying table-fellowship. Such table-fellowship was sacred in those days, and to eat with someone and then to turn against him was the ultimate betrayal.

This betrayal, however, was part of God's plan. The Scriptures had predicted this, so that **the Son of man was indeed going just as it was written about Him** (see Is. 53; Ps. 41:9). But this did not lessen the guilt of the traitor. **Woe** to him! Such was the divine punishment awaiting his impenitence that *it would have been* **good for him if that man had not been born**.

In saying this, Christ was not angrily threatening the traitor Judas. Rather, He was revealing the judgment awaiting him if he did not repent afterwards. The other disciples cowered in fear before the threat of such wrath, but Judas did not. Rather, he hardened his heart against His loving Master. When all were asking if they were the one, he hypocritically joined in, saying, **"Surely I am not *the one*?"** in order not to stand out, even using the honorific term **Rabbi**. Christ knew the hearts of all, and under His breath, He answered his question (for Judas was seated close to Him), saying, **"You *yourself* have said it."**

It was after this that Judas went out from the group to find Christ's enemies and direct them to the place of prayer to which the Lord was accustomed to resort, the Garden of Gethsemane. The purpose of Judas' departure, however, was known to none but Jesus (John 13:26–30). It would seem that Judas was not present for the Passover meal itself, nor for the institution of the Eucharist within it.

---

৯৯ ৯৯ ৯৯ ৯৯ ৯৯

26 And while they were eating, Jesus took bread, and having blessed, He broke *it* and gave *it* to the disciples, and said, "Take, eat; this is My Body."

27 And having taken a cup and given thanks, He gave *it* to them, saying, "Drink from it, all of you;

28 "for this is My Blood of the covenant, which is poured out for many for forgiveness of sins.

29 "But I say to you, I will by no means drink of this fruit of the vine from now on until that day when I drink it new with you in the Kingdom of My Father."

30 And having sung *a hymn*, they went out into the Mountain of Olives.

St. Matthew presupposes the context of the Passover meal. The meal proper began after the second cup of wine was drunk—after the story of the Exodus and the singing of the first part of the Great Hallel, Psalms 113–114. It began with the head of the house taking the bread, chanting the usual blessing ("Blessed are You, O Lord our God, King of the universe, who brings forth bread from the earth"), breaking the bread, and eating. (The bread was also dipped into the dish of stewed fruit and eaten with bitter herbs, in memory of the bitterness of the Egyptian bondage.) The meal continued long into the night. It ended with the blessing of the third cup of wine (the cup of blessing) after the meal was done. There was also a fourth cup of wine, the cup of *Hallel*, or praise, over which was sung a hymn—the second part of the Great Hallel, Psalms 115–118.

All of this is presupposed by Matthew, who relates only two things Christ said during this meal. After **Jesus took** the **bread** with which the meal itself began, He **blessed** it by chanting the usual blessing, and **broke it, and gave it to the disciples**. This was all as per usual and was done at every Jewish meal. But as He gave them the bread, He uttered the cryptic and disquieting words, **"Take, eat; this is My Body."** The words were bewildering, and were no part of the normal distribution of bread, at Passover or any other time.

Then after the meal, **having taken a cup** (the third cup, after the meal itself was finished) and having **given thanks** with the usual thanksgiving, "Blessed are You, O Lord our God, King of the universe, who created the fruit of the vine," **He gave it to them, saying, "Drink from it, all of you; for this is My Blood of the covenant which is poured out for many for forgiveness of sins."** This too was unusual, for not only did they customarily drink each from his own cup, but the words were as chilling as those spoken as the meal began when He distributed the broken bread.

Their perplexity was not resolved when He refused to drink of the final cup of wine, the cup of *Hallel* or praise. This was to be a cup of rejoicing in joy and freedom, but Christ would not drink it. Instead, He said that He **would by no means drink of this fruit of the vine from now on until that day when** He **would drink it new with** them **in the Kingdom of** His **Father**. Though they could not know it, He was about to go forth not to joy and freedom, but to pain and death. Now was not the time for rejoicing, but for summoning up all His courage to do the will of the Father. Later would come the time of joy, when He would drink with them the new wine in the Kingdom of God.

The meal ended as every Passover did, when they had **sung *a hymn***, the rest of the Great Hallel, Psalms 115–118. They then left the room to go out **into the Mountain of Olives**, a fifteen-minute walk to their usual place of prayer.

What did the Lord's cryptic words over the bread and the cup mean? They meant that His coming death was no unwilling martyrdom, but a voluntary sacrifice sealing a covenant with God, the offering through which many (that is, all the people) would find forgiveness of sins. He would offer His Body and His Blood on the Cross, and that sacrifice would be recalled before God and present in their midst as a memorial through their future eucharistic meals together. By eating the bread and drinking the cup, they would also partake of His Body and Blood, and live forever as He had promised (John 6:58).

§XIV.3. Gethsemane and Jesus' Arrest

ॐ ॐ ॐ ॐ ॐ

31 Then Jesus says to them, "You *yourselves* will all stumble because of Me this night; for it is written, 'I will strike the shepherd, and the sheep of the flock will be scattered out.'

32 "But after I have been raised, I will go before you into Galilee."

33 But Peter answered and said to Him, "Though all stumble because of You, I *myself* will never stumble!"

34 Jesus said to him, "Amen I say to you that this night, before a rooster sounds, you will *completely* deny Me three times."

35 Peter says to Him, "Even if it is necessary for me

> to die with You, I will by no means *completely*
> deny You!" And all the disciples said likewise.

Christ then tries to prepare His disciples for the trials to follow. From John 13:36–38, we learn that this exchange took place at the Passover meal. The prediction of the disciples' failure is placed here, immediately before the story of the prediction's fulfillment, to show more clearly that Christ knew what was to befall Him. His arrest and death were therefore not involuntary, but voluntary.

He foretells that the disciples, even though His trusted comrades (the **you** is emphatic—"you and none other"), **will all stumble** and fall away that very **night**. As unlikely as it seems to them, this is inevitable, for **it was written** in Scripture, **"I will strike the shepherd, and the sheep of the flock will be scattered out"** (Zech. 13:7). This does not mean, of course, that the prophecy will *cause* the disciples' failure, only that such a failure was foreseen. God will allow men to **strike the shepherd**, and that one blow will **scatter out** all **the sheep of the flock** He has been guarding. The disciples will therefore flee when their Master is taken. But that scattering will not be final. **After** He has been **raised** up, He will **go before** them **into Galilee**—even as a shepherd goes before his flock when he leads them. Let them follow His lead and gather again as His flock in the safety of Galilee.

Peter, with his usual impatient zeal, instantly contradicts Him. Perhaps he feels the need to vindicate himself and prove that he should be first among the disciples (compare Luke 22:24). Certainly he is more loyal than the others! **Though** they may **all stumble** that night, he himself (the **I** is emphatic) will **never stumble!**

Christ strives to deflate Peter's egoism. He assures Peter that **this** very **night**, within a few short hours, and **before the rooster sounds** at its usual one or two in the morning, Peter will *completely deny* Christ **three times**. (The word rendered *completely deny* in vv. 34–35 is *aparneomai*, a more intensive form of the verb *arneomai*, "to deny.") Peter should cease his boasting, for he is soon to utterly deny his Lord, time and again. Peter is aghast at this further prediction, for it stings his already swollen ego. As if to convince Jesus that

He is wrong about him, he promises that **even if it were necessary** for him **to die with** Him, he would **by no means** *completely* **deny** Him like that. He would rather die! Not to be outdone, **all the disciples said likewise** too.

༄ ༄ ༄ ༄ ༄

36 Then Jesus comes with them to a place called Gethsemane, and says to His disciples, "Sit here until I go over there and pray."

37 And He took with Him Peter and the two sons of Zebedee, and began to be grieved and upset.

38 Then He says to them, "My soul is very sorrowful, *even* to death; remain here and keep alert with Me."

39 And He went *before* them a little, and fell on His face and prayed, saying, "My Father, if it is possible, let this cup pass from Me, yet not as I *Myself* will, but as You *Yourself will*."

Having revealed the apostles' pride and self-confidence, Matthew then narrates the fall that came after (Prov. 16:18). After the Passover meal, **Jesus comes with them to a place called Gethsemane** (or "oil press"), a garden olive orchard probably enclosed by a hedge or low wall. This was His usual place of retreat, where Judas knew He would go after the meal. The long shadows of the Cross now begin to fall over His heart, and He **began to be grieved and upset.** The inner turmoil of the Son of God will remain forever beyond our earthly knowledge, for we cannot know what it was for Him to absorb in Himself and take away the sins of the world. We can only observe His struggle from the outside, and rejoice with trembling (Ps. 2:11) that He did this for us.

He wanted some time for prayer before His arrest, and so **He took with Him Peter and the two sons of Zebedee** to post them as a guard for His solitude. He told them that His **soul** was **very sorrowful,** *even* **to death,** so that He needed to pray over such an unbearable burden. Let them **remain** there as watchmen and **keep alert with** Him while He prayed alone. Withdrawing a short space from them, He **fell on His face**. Standing was the usual posture for prayer. Prostrating oneself in prayer was only done in times of great distress.

The gist of His prayer (doubtless heard by Peter, James, and John before they dozed off) was that **if it** was **possible**, His **Father** would **let the cup** of suffering **pass from** Him. In the immense abyss of divine wisdom and creativity, perhaps there was yet some way the salvation of the world could be accomplished without Christ having to drink to the dregs that dread chalice of despair. Yet even if not, if that cup must be drunk, He was ready to do so, for He chose **not** His own **will** but the Father's. That is, Jesus aligned His human will with the divine will of the Father, choosing whatever the Father would decide. In this naked act of decision and courage, Christ gave an example to the martyrs who would follow Him and showed them the way home.

ॐ ॐ ॐ ॐ ॐ

40 And He comes to the disciples and finds them sleeping, and says to Peter, "So, are you not strong *enough* to keep alert with Me *for* one hour?

41 "Keep alert and pray that you may not enter into testing; the spirit indeed *is* ready, but the flesh *is* weak."

42 He went away again a second time and prayed, saying, "My Father, if it is not possible for this to pass from *Me* unless I drink it, Your will be done."

43 And again He came and found them sleeping, for their eyes were burdened.

44 And He left them again, and went away and prayed a third *time*, saying the same word again.

45 Then He comes to the disciples and says to

> them, "Are you still sleeping and taking your
> rest? Behold, the hour has drawn near and the
> Son of man is being delivered up into the hands
> of sinners.
>
> 46 "Arise, let us go; behold, the one who delivers
> Me *up* has drawn near!"

After these first minutes of prayer, **He comes to the disciples**
whom He left to guard His solitude, **and finds them sleeping**. (This
was not surprising, given the stress they were under, plus the wine
from the Passover meal, and the late hour.) As He gently shakes
them awake, He **says to Peter** words of reproof meant for all (for
the verbs are in the plural), **"Are you not strong *enough* to keep
alert with Me *for* one** mere **hour? Keep alert and pray that you
may not enter into testing."** Even in His own agony, the Good
Shepherd takes thought for the welfare of His sheep. For there was
a possibility that the trauma of the coming hours would cause them
to fall away from Him permanently, and it was against this **testing**
that they must **pray**.

The word rendered *testing* is the Greek *peirasmos*, sometimes
rendered "temptation." Christ does not mean that the disciples
should pray that they might be spared the psychological experience
of temptation, and remain untouched by any difficulty. Rather,
He means that they should pray to avoid Satan's fiery onslaught
(compare Luke 22:31), that they might not be overwhelmed by
the suffering it will cause. This testing was the special work of the
devil. The disciples' inner motivation, their **spirit**, was certainly
ready and willing to cling to the faith, but their **flesh** was **weak**
and fearful. They must pray to be strengthened and to emerge with
their faith intact.

After this, Christ **went away again a second time**, praying as
He did before. When He **again came and found them sleeping**,
they did not know how to answer Him when He again roused them
(Mark 14:40). Christ **left them again and went away and prayed
a third** *time*. The Lord thereby left His Church an example of
persevering prayer (even if His disciples did not!).

When He returned to the disciples the third time, He once more found them sleeping. In His compassion, He does not scold them for the weakness. He simply asks them, **"Are you still sleeping and taking your rest?"** Are they still taking thought only for their own comfort? The time for that is now past. **Behold**—they can see it for themselves! **The Son of man** is even now **being delivered up into the hands of sinners** and Gentiles. **Arise**—up now! **Behold**—the **one who is delivering** Him *up* has arrived! His arrest is no surprise to Jesus; He foreknew all that was about to happen.

ॐ ॐ ॐ ॐ ॐ

47 And while He *Himself* was speaking, behold! Judas, one of the Twelve, came up, and with him a great crowd with swords and wooden *clubs*, from the chief-priests and elders of the people.

48 Now he who was delivering Him *up* gave them a sign, saying, "Whomever I will kiss, He Himself is *the one*; seize Him."

49 And immediately he came to Jesus and said, "Hail, Rabbi!" and *fervently* kissed Him.

50 And Jesus said to him, "Comrade, *do what you have come for*." Then they came and laid hands on Jesus and seized Him.

51 And behold! one of those who were with Jesus stretched out his hand, drew out his sword, and having struck the slave of the high priest, took off his ear.

52 Then Jesus says to him, "Return your sword into its place; for all those who take the sword will perish by the sword.

53 "Or do you think that I am not able to entreat My Father and He will provide Me now with more than twelve legions of angels?

54 "How then will the Scriptures be fulfilled, that it must happen this way?"

> 55 At that time Jesus said to the crowds, "Have
>   you come out as against a thief, with swords
>   and wooden *clubs*, to take Me? Every day I was
>   sitting in the Temple teaching and you did not
>   seize Me.
> 56 "But all this has happened that the Scriptures
>   of the prophets may be fulfilled." Then all the
>   disciples left Him and fled.

It was **while** Jesus **was speaking** these words that **Judas came up, and with him a great crowd** armed with **swords and wooden clubs**. Though **one of the** trusted **Twelve**, Judas had now gone over to side with Christ's foes. This crowd had come **from the chief-priests and elders of the people** to arrest Jesus and return Him to the Sanhedrin for trial. (These **chief-priests and elders** were the very people mentioned in 26:3f as plotting to seize Jesus and kill Him.)

Why did they come with weapons? It seems they were taking no chances, for this was their one chance to arrest Jesus when He was alone, far from the protecting public. The weapons were to subdue His disciples, should they try to mount an armed defense.

The crowd, with their torches and weapons, held back, hiding in the shadows, waiting for the prearranged sign from Judas, their leader. For he **gave them a sign, saying, "Whomever I will kiss** in greeting, **He Himself is *the one*."** They could not risk arresting the wrong man in the darkness and letting Jesus Himself slip away in the confusion. They must be sure of their target. They therefore watched Judas from a distance in the flickering torchlight, as he **came to Jesus and said, "Hail, Rabbi!" and *fervently* kissed Him**. (The verb translated *fervently kiss* is the Gr. *kataphileo*—a more intensive form of the verb *phileo*, "to kiss"; compare its use in Luke 15:20.)

The kiss was a form of very respectful greeting, and the title **Rabbi** was also a mark of honor. (The word rendered *Hail*—Gr. *chaire*—simply means "hello"; compare its use in 28:9.) That Judas should use such deference in the very act of betrayal was stunning in its hypocrisy. In response, Jesus addresses him mildly as

comrade (Gr. *etaire*; compare its use in 20:13; 22:12), and simply tells him to do what he has come to do. That is, Jesus had no anger or resentment toward Judas, but neither was He taken in by this show of respect. Instead, He tells Judas to get on with it.

When **they came and laid hands on Jesus and seized Him**, **one of those who were with Jesus stretched out his hand, drew out his sword**, and **struck the slave of the high priest** so that he **took off his ear**. Though the swordsman is left unnamed by Matthew, we know from John 18:10 that this was Peter, who was determined to fulfill his boast of verses 33f. In the confusion and darkness, he was near to Jesus and tried to prevent his Master being taken. No doubt he was aiming to take off the *head* of the slave seizing Jesus, not just his *ear*, but he was a fisherman, and was better with the dragnet than the sword.

Jesus, however, replies that such resistance will not accomplish God's will. He has already aligned His will with the Father's, and will not refuse the cup of suffering thus put to His lips. Besides, Peter's resort to violence is not the way of the Kingdom, for **all those who take the sword** and choose the way of violent retaliation will find that it brings its own judgment. When He commands Peter to **return** his **sword into its place**, Christ forever disarms those who think to spread the Kingdom by force. Violent revolution will not bring the Kingdom of the heavens, but will only take the life of the revolutionaries.

Or do His disciples think He needs the help of twelve weak *men*? Do they not know that He is **able to entreat** His **Father** and receive at that very moment the provision of **twelve legions of angels?** (At 6000 to a legion, that would be 72,000 angels.) But that would be to resist the will of God. **The Scriptures** foretold all this must **happen this way**, and He will not resist what God there foretold.

Jesus does, however, point out to the crowd the injustice of the arrest. Have they **come out as against a thief**, that they need **swords and wooden *clubs* to take** Him into custody? For **every day** He **was sitting in the Temple teaching**, and they **did not seize** Him then. If He were truly a criminal, why did they not arrest Him then, when such elaborate arrangements were unnecessary? Obviously because He is *not* a criminal, and their arrest is unjust. The secrecy of the arrest proves it is unjust, for they dare not do it publicly, where all can see. Seeing that He would offer no resistance, they seized Him. **All the disciples**, however, **left Him and fled**, even those who had pledged their very lives to defend Him just a few hours before. All that Christ had foretold was being fulfilled.

§XIV.4. Jesus' Trial

ॐ ॐ ॐ ॐ ॐ

57 And those who had seized Jesus led *Him* away to Caiaphas, the chief-priest, where the scribes and the elders were gathered together.

58 But Peter also was following Him from a distance as far as the courtyard of the chief-priest, and entered inside, and sat down with the attendants to see the end.

59 Now the chief-priests and the whole council were seeking false-witnessing against Jesus, so that they might put Him to death;

60 and they did not find *it, even though* many false-witnesses came forward. But later two came forward,

61 *and* said, "This *man* said, 'I am able to tear down the sanctuary of God and to build *it* in three days.'"

62 And the chief-priest stood up and said to Him, "Do You make no answer *to* what these *men* witness against You?"

63 But Jesus was silent. And the chief-priest said to Him, "I adjure You by the living God that You tell us whether You *Yourself* are the Christ, the Son of God."

64 Jesus says to him, "You *yourself* have said it; but I tell you, from now on you will see the

> Son of man sitting at the right of the Power, and coming on the clouds of heaven."
>
> 65 Then the chief-priest tore his garments, saying, "He has blasphemed! What further need do we have of witnesses? Behold, now you have heard the blasphemy.
>
> 66 "What do you think?" They answered and said, "He is liable of death!"
>
> 67 Then they spat into His face and buffeted Him with their fists, and some slapped *Him,*
>
> 68 and said, "Prophesy to us, Christ! Who is the one who hit You?"

Jesus was then **led away** under guard **to Caiaphas, the chief-priest** and head of the Great Sanhedrin or council, in order that He might be tried and condemned. (Matthew omits the quick visit to Caiaphas' father-in-law Annas, narrated in John 18:13, 19–24, since this private interview by the former high-priest had no legal status.) Technically speaking, the Sanhedrin did not meet at night to try capital offenses, but it was necessary for Jesus to be brought before Pilate the governor at daybreak if He was to be condemned and executed by the Romans that day, before Jesus' followers had time to mobilize in His defense. And that meant Jesus must be tried and found guilty by a Jewish court *before* daybreak. Hence the necessity of a night trial before the Sanhedrin.

Assuming Jesus was arrested after 11:00 P.M., it would have been almost midnight when He was brought to trial at the house of Caiaphas, **where the scribes and the elders were gathered together**. True to his word, **Peter also was following** Jesus **from a distance as far as the courtyard**. He had no access to the plenary proceedings of the trial itself, since he was not a member of the Sanhedrin, nor called to be a witness for them. But, having recovered from the panic of his initial flight, he followed as closely as he could. Sick with dread, he **sat down with the attendants** of Caiaphas' house **to see the end** and outcome of the whole affair, wondering how he could be of use to his Lord.

Meanwhile, at the trial itself, **the chief-priests** (the Temple executive officers) **and the whole council** present **were seeking false-witnessing against Jesus, so that they might put Him to death**. This was not a trial to determine guilt or innocence, but to reach a predetermined end. Even so, such a goal was not easy to attain. Those present would have to give an account of their actions to the rest of the Jewish nation the next day, so that due process must be observed. Witnesses must give their testimony showing Jesus to be guilty of a capital offense, even if those witnesses were in fact lying. This proved to be difficult, *even though* many **false-witnesses came forward**, for their testimony did not agree, and due process was insistent that such testimony be consistent.

At length two came forward with their testimony that **"This man said, 'I am able to tear down the sanctuary of God and to build *it* in three days.'"** This indeed was a serious charge and the best piece of evidence they had. To threaten to destroy the Temple was sacrilege and a capital offense. Both the men agreed that Jesus had said it. (In fact, Jesus had *not* said that He was able to tear down the Temple and rebuild it in three days. Rather, He once said that if His foes would tear down "this Temple"—that is, His body—He would raise that up in three days. This was said early in His ministry, and He was being misquoted; compare John 2:18–21.)

Jesus' foes wanted to goad Him into repeating the saying then and there—or at least into saying something they could use against Him. For although the two men had agreed that Jesus had said this, their witness was not identical, but differed in crucial details (Mark 14:59), and therefore was not legally admissible. The **chief-priest** therefore **stood up** and asked Him to **make** an **answer** to the accusation just brought against Him, hoping that He would repeat what He once said about destroying the sanctuary. This Jesus refused to do. The time for teaching was past, and it was no part of His purpose to be acquitted and released.

This was getting serious for His foes, for the night was wearing on, and they were no closer to condemning Jesus of a capital offense. If Jesus continued remaining silent, this unique opportunity of handing Him over to Pilate would slip away. They were desperate for

Jesus to say something incriminating, and so finally **the chief-priest said to Him, "I adjure You by the living God that You tell us whether You *Yourself* are the Christ, the Son of God."** Many had been saying this secretly, claiming that He was indeed the designated Messiah (compare John 7:31)—what did *He* say?

Jesus could not remain silent about this, lest His silence be taken for denial (especially when being adjured in the Name of His Father). He therefore replied, **"You *yourself* have said it** (that is, you have answered your own question), **but I tell you, from now on you will see the Son of man sitting at the right of the Power, and coming on the clouds of heaven."**

In this affirmation, Jesus was alluding to Psalm 110:1 (where the Messiah is given a throne at the right hand of God) and to Daniel 7:13 (where the Messiah comes on the clouds to the Ancient of Days to receive the Kingdom from Him). Jesus was not only claiming to be the Messiah, but was contrasting His present lowly position with the glory He would soon receive from God. His foes might think they had a mere mortal in their clutches, but they were dealing with the exalted Christ of God. Now He was standing before them as their helpless prisoner; soon He would be sitting by the Throne of the Power as their Judge. (In classic Jewish fashion, Jesus uses the term **the Power** as a circumlocution for the Name of God.)

Jesus' judges, however, remained blind to His true dignity. All they saw was that now they had what they wanted. **The chief-priest tore his garments**, as if in mourning for hearing such a sacrilegious outrage. For a man like Jesus to impersonate the exalted Christ! Caiaphas cried out, **"He has blasphemed! What further need do we have of witnesses? Behold, now you have heard the blasphemy** for yourselves!" They now had all the evidence they needed, and he instantly called on them for their verdict. The council was stacked (we may think that such men as Joseph of Arimathea, a member of the council who supported Jesus, were not invited to this night session), and **they answered, "He is liable of death!"**

This verdict allowed the arresting officers to vent their fury on the condemned prisoner, even though such treatment was no part of the legal procedure. **They spat into His face and buffeted Him** with their fists. Some slapped *Him* (apparently having blindfolded Him), challenging Him to **prophesy**. Since He was the **Christ**, and therefore possessed supernatural knowledge as the prophets did, He could tell **who** was **the one who hit** Him!

ॐ ॐ ॐ ॐ ॐ

69 Now Peter was sitting outside in the courtyard, and one servant-girl came to him and said, "You *yourself* also were with Jesus of Galilee."

70 But he denied before everyone, saying, "I do not know what you say."

71 But when he had gone out to the door another *servant-girl* saw him and says to those who were there, "This *man* was with Jesus of Nazareth."

72 And again he denied with an oath, "I do not know the man."

73 After a little, the bystanders came up and said to Peter, "Truly you *yourself* also are one of them, for even your speaking makes you plain."

74 Then he began to curse and swear, "I do not know the man!" And immediately a rooster sounded.

75 And Peter remembered the word which Jesus had said, "Before a rooster sounds, you will *completely* deny Me three times." And he went outside and wept bitterly.

Meanwhile, the trial was dragging on through the night. At perhaps about 1:00 A.M. **Peter was sitting outside in the courtyard**, warming himself by the light of a fire. The light from this fire allowed **one servant-girl** to see his face, and she **came to him and said, "You *yourself* also were with Jesus of Galilee."** That is, he was one of them and should be arrested too. By specifying the witness as **one servant-girl**, Matthew invites us to appreciate the irony: Peter promised he would be true no matter what the odds, and here he was cowed by a mere servant-girl. Peter, for his part, was determined not to be arrested, for all hope of helping Jesus depended on him remaining free. He therefore **denied** Jesus **before everyone, saying, "I do not know what you say."**

Feeling his location by the fire to be unsafe, he moves to a place by the door or entranceway. There he is later met by **another** *servant-girl*, who challenges him, saying to those around her, **"This man was with Jesus of Nazareth."** Others join in the accusation (a man is mentioned in Luke 22:58), and Peter is again forced to say, **"I do not** even **know the man** you are talking about." For emphasis, he adds an oath, which Christ had forbidden His disciples to use (see 5:34f)—Peter was falling away more and more from the ways of the Master.

After a little, Peter returns to the charcoal fire burning in the courtyard, trying to blend in. One of **the bystanders** around the fire came up and said to Peter, **"Truly you *yourself* also are one of them, for even your speaking makes you plain."** When Peter had been speaking to them, he of course spoke with the accent characteristic of all Galileans (Galileans pronounced their gutturals differently than the Judeans did), and thus marked himself as a Galilean. Surely a Galilean would be a disciple of Jesus! The chorus of accusers grew louder, with all present (including the relative of the man whose ear Peter cut off in the garden; see John 18:26) identifying Peter as one of Jesus' disciples. Peter was desperate and **began to curse and swear.** That is, he began invoking oaths and curses upon himself if he even knew the man. (In pretending not to be one of His disciples, Peter will not even use the Name "Jesus"—he calls him simply **the man.**)

While Peter is in full swing, about 1:30 A.M., **a rooster sounded.** Something about this morning sound moved in his subconscious, and then he **remembered**—in **the word which Jesus had said** just a few short hours ago, He had predicted that **before a rooster sounds,** Peter would *completely* deny Him **three times.** The sound of the rooster brought home the significance of his actions. Peter had thought he was remaining free so that as a loyal disciple he could help his Lord. In actuality, he had spent the night denying his Master, just as the Master foretold. Crushed with this self-knowledge, he rushed **outside** and **wept bitterly**.

ॐ ॐ ॐ ॐ ॐ

27 1 Now when morning had come, all the chief-priests and the elders of the people took counsel against Jesus to put Him to death;

2 and they bound Him, and led *Him* away and delivered Him up to Pilate the governor.

When morning had come, as dawn was just breaking, the council held another hasty consultation. They met together to decide what charges they would bring against Jesus when they brought Him before Pilate in order **to put Him to death**. For falsely claiming to be the Messiah might be a capital charge in their eyes, but not in the eyes of the Romans; and the Jews, as a conquered country, did not have the legal authority to execute criminals. That right the Romans reserved to themselves. They therefore had to come up with a charge that would justify execution in the eyes of the Romans. It was decided that they would accuse Jesus of being a military Messiah and a revolutionary, of setting Himself up as a rival king against Caesar. That was a charge for which the Romans would execute the guilty party. Having decided on their strategy, **they bound** Jesus, and **delivered Him up to Pilate the governor** to be judged by him.

ॐ ॐ ॐ ॐ ॐ

3 Then when Judas, who had delivered Him up, saw that He had been condemned, he regretted *it* and returned the thirty *pieces* of silver to the chief-priests and elders,

4 saying, "I have sinned by delivering up inno-cent blood." But they said, "What *is that* to us? See *to it* yourself."

5 And he threw the *pieces* of silver into the

> sanctuary and departed, and he withdrew and hanged himself.
>
> 6 And the chief-priests took the *pieces* of silver and said, "It is not permitted to put them into the *Temple* treasury, since it is the price of blood."
>
> 7 And they took counsel and with them bought the potter's field as a burial *place* for strangers.
>
> 8 Therefore that field has been called the Field of Blood until today.
>
> 9 Then that which was spoken through Jeremiah the prophet was fulfilled, saying, "And they took the thirty *pieces* of silver, the price of the one who was priced by the sons of Israel;
>
> 10 "and they gave them for the potter's field, as the Lord directed me."

Matthew then relates the fate of **Judas, who delivered** Jesus **up** to His foes. When he **saw that** Jesus **had been condemned, he regretted** his actions, **and returned the thirty *pieces* of silver to the chief-priests and elders**. The word rendered *regretted* is the Greek *metamelomai*, a different word from that usually used for repentance (*metanoeo*). Judas thus did not repent in the sense of turning his life around. Rather, he was simply overcome by remorse as he continued his downward spiral.

What was it that caused this remorse? Certainly not surprise at the outcome of his betrayal of Jesus, for Jesus' destruction had all along been the plan of His foes. That was why the location of the Paschal supper had been kept secret. It seems that Judas' resentment of Jesus, which had been burning hot since He rebuked him at the anointing at Bethany (26:6f), now was sated by seeing that Jesus **had been condemned**.

This is the nature of such sinful appetites. Amnon burned with lust for his sister Tamar, yet after his lust was sated, he would have none of her, and could not bear even the sight of her (2 Sam. 13). It seems to have been the same with the hatred of Judas—after his lust for doing Jesus injury had been sated, his conscience smote him mightily, for he knew that Jesus had done nothing to warrant this.

He therefore found **the chief-priests and elders,** whose tool he had become short days ago, and tried to return **the thirty *pieces* of silver**. Though he could not undo his deed, he felt compelled to distance himself from it as much as he could. He found them in the Temple courts that morning, perhaps while Jesus was being examined by Herod (Luke 23:7f). We can almost see them as they stood in a huddle, intent on planning their next move. Judas drew near to them, clutching the money with shaking hands, and gasping out the words that filled his mind like fire, **"I have sinned by delivering up innocent blood."** The Law laid a curse on any who took a bribe to shed innocent blood (Deut. 27:25), and Judas felt that curse weighing upon him now. Let them take back the money, that he might shake himself free of this curse!

If he thought he would find a sympathetic response, he was mistaken. Having used him for their low purpose, they despised him, as men always despise the traitors they use. Perhaps they turned from their deliberations just long enough to say, **"What is *that* to us? See *to it* yourself."**

Judas' despair was now complete, and he found himself trapped in a world that held only doom for him. Running through the Temple courts to the Court of the Priests (the place where sacrifice was made), **he threw the *pieces* of silver into the sanctuary** there in a final act of desperation. If the priests would not willingly take back the silver that stained his hands, let their Temple receive it! Having hurled the coins as far from him as possible, **he withdrew** from the Temple courts **and hanged himself**.

Comparing this account with that in Acts 1:18f, it would seem that Judas crossed the Kidron Valley to a place where the Kidron and Hinnom valleys converge, the potter's field of Jeremiah 19:1–2. There he climbed a tree and hanged himself, possibly with the belt which girded him and had carried the thirty coins. This belt tore or otherwise gave way, so that Judas fell from the tree onto the rocks below and suffered mutilation.

The chief-priests found the coins, which fell onto the floor of the Court of the Priests. The normal thing would be to put offerings **into the *Temple* treasury**, but this was clearly inappropriate, since it was **the price of blood**. They therefore decided to put the money to a charitable purpose. With the money they **bought the potter's field** in which Judas fell (in Judas' name, since the money was still technically his; Acts 1:18). This land had a horrible history, being the Topheth of Jeremiah 7:31; 19:6, the place where child sacrifice was carried out in the days of old. It was clearly unsuitable for burying Jews in, but an acceptable **burial *place* for strangers**. Gentiles dying in Jerusalem might be buried there, since such Gentiles were already unclean. Formerly the land was called "the potter's field," since it still had a clay soil used by potters for their craft. Now, however, it began to be **called the Field of Blood,** since it was a graveyard for the unclean, bought with the money of a suicide.

Matthew concludes his narrative of Judas' end by showing how this last detail **fulfilled** the prophecy of **Jeremiah**. Jeremiah had spoken of the potter's field as a place of judgment (Jer. 19:1f). Zechariah had spoken of being devalued by the sons of Israel, of being paid a mere **thirty *pieces* of silver** for his work as their shepherd, and of taking that money to the potter (Zech. 11:12–13). Matthew conflates the two prophecies, ascribing them both to Jeremiah as the more major of the two. (A common practice in such multiple citations; compare Mark quoting both Mal. 3:1 and Is. 40:3 and ascribing both to Isaiah in Mark 1:2–3.)

The substance of these prophecies is not predictive in the strict sense; rather they give details from the lives of the prophets. As with Hosea 11:1 (quoted in Matt. 2:15), these words from Jeremiah and Zechariah are significant for their foreshadowing of these Gospel events. For Matthew, it cannot be a coincidence that the prophets speak of that same potter's field, of a shepherd being valued at thirty pieces of silver, and of that money being given for the potter's field. These details of Judas' end therefore confirm Jesus' identity as the Messiah at the time of His death, just as do the details of His leaving Egypt after His birth.

ॐ ॐ ॐ ॐ ॐ

11 Now Jesus stood before the governor, and the governor asked Him, saying, "Are You *Yourself* the King of the Jews?" And Jesus said to him, "You *yourself* say."

12 And while He was being accused by the chief-priests and elders, He answered nothing.

13 Then Pilate says to Him, "Do You not hear how many things they witness against You?"

14 And He did not answer him with regard to even one word, so that the governor marveled much.

15 Now at the feast the governor was accustomed to release for the crowd one prisoner, whomever they wanted.

16 And they were holding at that time a notable prisoner called Barabbas.

17 When therefore they were gathered together, Pilate said to them, "Whom do you want me to release for you? Barabbas, or Jesus who is called Christ?"

18 For he knew that because of envy they had delivered Him *up*.

19 And while he was sitting on the judgment-seat, his wife sent to him, saying, "*Have* nothing *to do with* that righteous man, for today I suffered much in a dream because of Him."

20 But the chief-priests and the elders persuaded the crowds to ask for Barabbas, and to destroy Jesus.

21 But the governor answered and said to them, "Which of the two do you want me to release for you?" And they said, "Barabbas!"

22 Pilate says to them, "What therefore will I do

> with Jesus who is called Christ?" They all say,
> "Let *Him* be crucified!"
>
> 23 And he said, "Why? What wickedness has
> He done?" But they were crying all the more,
> saying, "Let *Him* be crucified!"
>
> 24 And when Pilate saw that he was profiting
> nothing, but rather that an uproar was hap-
> pening, he took water and washed his hands
> before the crowd, saying, "I am innocent of the
> blood of this *man*; see *to it* yourselves."
>
> 25 And all the people answered and said, "His
> blood *be* upon us and upon our children!"

Matthew then returns to the story of Jesus' trial before Pilate. Jesus **stood before the governor** Pilate as one accused of being "the King of the Jews"—that is, one who was setting himself up as a rival king to Caesar. Pilate asks Jesus if this charge is true, saying, **"Are You *Yourself* the King of the Jews?"** The **You** is emphatic in the Greek, as if Pilate can scarcely believe that this person could be the formidable and dangerous rebel. Jesus, as the true Messiah and King of Israel, does not deny the charge, but affirms, **"You *yourself* say"**—the words are yours, and you have answered your own ques-tion. (From John 18:34, we learn that Jesus asked a counter ques-tion to clarify in what sense the title was intended—as a political revolutionary, or as a transcendent revealer of truth.)

The chief-priests and elders were there as His accusers, and they bombarded Pilate with accusations of every kind against Jesus—including some false ones, such as that He counseled men to refuse payment of taxes to Rome (Luke 23:2). To all of these accusations, Jesus **answered nothing**, for He would not fight against the will of His Father. Pilate was used to the accused vigorously defending themselves, reacting with fear and anger, but here was One who maintained a serene peace in the face of this angry barrage. **The governor** could only **marvel much** at such serene refusal to defend oneself against **even one word** or charge.

Pilate was a man of many years' experience, and he could tell at once that Jesus, deluded visionary though He seemed to him, was no threat to Rome. He was also knowledgeable enough about the local Jewish politics to see that it was **because of envy** of Jesus' popularity that **they had delivered Him *up*** to him.

Moreover, **while he was sitting on the judgment-seat** and trying the case, **his wife sent to him, saying, "*Have* nothing *to do with* that righteous man, for today** (i.e. the previous night) **I suffered much in a dream because of Him."** We cannot know what her nightmare was (was it a premonition that later ages would execrate the name of her husband as the one who presided over a miscarriage of justice? For so it is: we all confess that Christ "suffered under Pontius Pilate"), but she was adamant that he should avoid trying that case. It would seem that God, who sent a dream to the pagan Magi (2:12), sent a dream to Pilate's wife also. The irony is stunning—even a pagan can see that Jesus is **righteous** and innocent!

For all these reasons, Pilate was determined to release Jesus. He was a brutal and cynical man, but he was still a Roman, with a Roman's sense of justice, and took no delight in condemning the innocent for the sake of a Jewish lobby.

There seemed to be a way out: He could find Jesus guilty (as the chief-priests demanded), and yet set Him free as part of the customary Passover amnesty (as Roman justice demanded). As an investment in good community relations, Rome **was accustomed to release for the crowd one** condemned **prisoner, whomever they wanted**, as a demonstration of Rome's generosity. This happened during the Passover **feast**.

The Romans **were holding at that time a notable prisoner called Barabbas**. He is described in Mark 15:7 as one who had committed murder during a riot; he was probably a Zealot, or at least one with Zealot sympathies. Pilate offered them the choice of **Barabbas, or Jesus who is called Christ**. Knowing Jesus' great popularity with the crowd, doubtless he was confident they would choose Jesus.

Pilate, however, had underestimated the determination of **the chief-priests and the elders**. They **persuaded the crowds to ask**

for Barabbas and to destroy Jesus. This was perhaps not that hard a thing, for Jesus' famous popularity was based on the crowd's confidence that He was about to destroy Roman sovereignty in Israel, and His trial by the Romans proved that confidence had been misplaced. Barabbas, on the other hand, was a true revolutionary who hated Rome, and could have appeared to them as a patriot. When Pilate therefore turned to the crowd and shouted, **"Which of the two do you want me to release for you?"** they shouted back, **"Barabbas!"**

This was not what Pilate expected, and it constituted a miscarriage of the famous Roman justice. Did they think if they demanded Barabbas that he would release Jesus also? He therefore shouted again, **"What therefore will I do with Jesus who is called Christ?"** He doubtless expected the answer, "Release Him too!" and was stunned to hear them **all say, "Let *Him* be crucified!"**

Pilate's further attempts to reason with the crowd and discover a reason for their unexpected hatred of one of their own race produced no results, other than further **uproar** and the beginnings of a riot. He had no intention of risking such a riot in Jerusalem when it was overflowing with pilgrims, and in the end, he was prepared to sacrifice principle to expediency.

He therefore **took water and washed his hands** before the crowd in the universal gesture of innocence, saying, **"I am innocent of the blood of this *man*; see *to it* yourselves."** That is, he will do what they want, but declares that he believes it unjust. **All the people** in the mob shouted back their acquiescence in his decision to crucify Jesus. They were confident that Jesus was worthy of death for pretending to be the Messiah, and were sure that this was no miscarriage of justice, as Pilate said it was. They therefore said they were ready to bear the responsibility for His execution, for they felt it was just. They shouted back, **"His blood *be* upon us and upon our children!"**

For St. Matthew, there is heavy irony in this exchange. In telling the crowd to see to the man's innocent blood themselves (27:24), Pilate is unconsciously echoing the words of the chief-priests to

Judas about that innocent blood (27:4). The crowd therefore fulfills the role of Judas—and may expect to share his doom also.

Furthermore, Matthew means us to connect this with the Lord's words in 23:35–36. In that passage, Christ declared that "all the righteous blood" shed through Israel's history would finally be required of "this generation"—that is, of the men then present and their children. The prophecy of 23:35–36 finds fulfillment in the destruction of Jerusalem by the Romans in AD 70. The blood of all those righteous men—including now the blood of the Son of God—would be required of the howling mob and their children, for it is they who would be alive when the Romans destroyed their city within one generation. In accepting the responsibility for the death of Jesus, the Jerusalem crowd sealed the fate of the doomed city.

ॐ ॐ ॐ ॐ ॐ

26 Then he released Barabbas to them, but having Jesus scourged, he delivered Him *up* to be crucified.

27 Then the soldiers of the governor took Jesus into the Praetorium and gathered the whole cohort around Him.

28 And they stripped Him and put around Him a scarlet cloak.

29 And after weaving a crown of thorns, they put *it* around His head, and a reed in His right *hand*, and they kneeled down before Him and mocked Him, saying, "Hail, King of the Jews!"

30 And they spat at Him, and took the reed and were striking Him on the head.

31 And after they had mocked Him, they stripped Him of the scarlet *cloak* and clothed Him in His garments, and led Him away to crucify *Him*.

The final result is that Pilate **released Barabbas to them**, and after having **Jesus scourged, he delivered Him *up* to be crucified**. Matthew then relates the abuse Jesus suffered prior to this crucifixion. (He relates this in summary form; see John 19:1–16 for a more chronological account, in which the mocking occurred before His final condemnation.)

Part of this abuse was His being mocked by the soldiers. They **took Jesus into the Praetorium** (that is, the place used by the governor while in temporary residence there; probably Herod's palace). The **whole cohort** was there for the spectacle—not the entire 600 soldiers that made up a cohort, but the entire detachment of the cohort then present. There were none present who did not join in the mockery.

The soldiers had nothing but contempt for Jewish revolutionary aspirations, and here was one who was the focus of those aspirations. They had no idea that Jesus was not a revolutionary, and they delighted to heap abuse on the one who, they thought, aspired to political kingship. If He was a king, He should be clothed in the imperial purple! They therefore **stripped Him** of His own robes and **put around Him a scarlet cloak**, possibly the short cloak worn by soldiers. (The term "purple" was a loose one, denoting colors from rose to true purple, and the scarlet cloak of soldiers would qualify as a substitute for the imperial purple they were aping.)

The Jewish king needed a crown too. **After weaving a crown of thorns** from the thorn bushes growing nearby, **they put *it* around His head**, its sharp spikes piercing His scalp. And what was a king without his scepter? They found **a reed** and put it **in His right *hand***, seated Him in a chair, and in hideous pantomime, **kneeled down before Him** in mock allegiance, saying, **"Hail, King of the Jews!"** Instead of the customary kiss of allegiance, however, **they spat at Him**, and took the reed and began **striking Him on the head**. After their brutal horseplay, **they stripped Him of the scarlet *cloak* and clothed Him in His** own **garments** before leading Him away to the place of execution. St. Matthew narrates this brutal mocking not so much to win sympathy for Jesus as to show how His predictions were all fulfilled (20:17–19).

§XIV.5. Jesus' Crucifixion

ॐ ॐ ॐ ॐ ॐ

32 And as they were coming out, they found a man of Cyrene named Simon; this *man* they conscripted to bear His Cross.

33 And when they had come to a place called Golgotha (which is called "Place of a Skull"),

34 they gave Him wine to drink mixed with gall; and *after* tasting *it*, He was not willing to drink.

35 And when they had crucified Him, they divided up His garments, casting lots;

36 and sitting down, they were guarding Him there.

37 And they put up above His head His charge, which was written, "This is Jesus, the King of the Jews."

38 Then two thieves were crucified with Him, one on the right and one on the left.

39 And the ones going by were slandering Him, wagging their heads,

40 and saying, "You who would tear down the sanctuary and build *it* in three days, save Yourself! If You are the Son of God, come down from the cross!"

41 Likewise the chief-priests also, with the scribes and elders, were mocking and saying,

42 "He saved others; Himself He is not able to save! He is the King of Israel—let *Him* now come down from the cross and we will have faith in Him!

43 "He trusts in God; let Him rescue *Him* now, if He wants Him, for He said, 'I am the Son of God.'"

44 And the thieves who had been crucified

> with Him also were reproaching Him in the
> same *way*.

As they were coming out of the city, Jesus was unable to carry His own crossbeam all the way to the place of execution, having been weakened from the scourging. The soldiers therefore **found a man of Cyrene named Simon**. He was evidently a Jew from the Diaspora, now coming into Jerusalem, perhaps for the services of Passover week. Roman soldiers had the right to **conscript** locals to carry burdens for them, and they made use of this right, forcing Simon **to bear His Cross**.

Their destination was **a place** just outside the city **called Golgotha**, translated as **"Place of a Skull."** It is possible that the hill looked something like a skull, as well as being the place where crucifixions were carried out. Upon reaching the site, some people (probably pious Jewish women, who provided this service to their condemned countrymen) **gave Him wine to drink mixed with gall**. The word rendered *gall* indicates a bitter-tasting substance, in this case myrrh (Mark 15:23). It was offered as a narcotic to dull the pain, but *after* **tasting it** and discovering its contents, **He was not willing to drink** it. In Gethsemane Christ had determined to drink the cup of suffering the Father would give Him, and He would not reduce that suffering by drinking this other cup.

After this they **crucified Him**. This was done by nailing His hands to each end of the crossbeam carried to the site, hoisting Him up, securing this beam to a vertical one planted in the earth, and nailing His feet to this latter beam. When this was done, they sat down to begin **guarding Him** (lest His supporters should attempt a rescue), waiting for Him to die. To pass the time, **they divided up His garments, casting lots** to see who should take what. His garments included His inner and outer garments, His belt, sandals, and head-covering. Some were worth more than others, which is perhaps why the lot was used. When Jesus died, He was despoiled of everything—even His clothing. Though Matthew does not mention Psalm 22:18, which says, "They divide my garments among them, and for my raiment they cast lots," it seems likely that he intends his readers to see how this detail of Christ's execution fulfills this prophetic psalm.

St. Matthew also calls attention to the **charge** which **they put up above His head**, specifying the crime for which He was being killed. The charge said, **"This is Jesus, the King of the Jews."** All those executed had their crimes thus prominently displayed as a deterrent lest any should imitate them. The charge was written on a board whitened with chalk and hung around the neck of the condemned, or, in this case, nailed to the cross above the condemned man's head. The Romans meant the inscription to identify Jesus as an insurgent. For Christians, however, this had a deeper significance, one the Romans did not intend: Jesus was indeed the King of the Jews, and it was as the Messiah that He was dying.

Matthew then relates the mockery that attended Christ's final suffering. At the time He was executed, **two thieves were crucified with Him, one on the right and one on the left**, so that Jesus was in the middle of them, classed as just another criminal.

All His foes were there to jeer at Him. Once He was hoisted up on the cross, they considered their victory to be complete. Here was the unanswerable proof that He was a liar, and was not the Messiah! The passersby began **wagging their heads** in derision, crowing, **"You who would tear down the sanctuary and build *it* in three days, save Yourself! If You are the Son of God** as You claimed, **come down from the cross!"** He claimed to be greater even than the Temple—surely He could do this?

The **chief-priests** and **scribes** and **elders**, those He had bested throughout the last week, were also there to savor their victory. Some Savior Jesus was! **He saved others** by healing them, but **Himself He is not able to save!** They ironically called out, **"He is the King of Israel** all right—just look how royally triumphant He looks! **Let *Him* now come down from the cross and we will have faith in Him!** We'll become His disciples right now! **He trusts in God** as His Father—**let Him rescue *Him* now, if He wants Him** and delights in Him. After, all, He is '**the Son of God**'!"

In quoting these taunts about "letting God rescue Him if He wants Him," it seems as if Matthew intends his readers again to identify the connection with Psalm 22:8 ("let God rescue him, for He delights in him"), even as the reference in verse 39 to His foes "wagging their heads" is meant to connect with Psalm 22:7. Without saying it directly, Matthew invites us to find in this also the fulfillment of prophecy.

As the crowning indignity, even **the thieves who had been crucified with Him** joined in with the others in **reproaching Him**. (St. Luke records that one of the thieves repented and told his fellow to cut it out; Luke 23:39–42.)

ॐ ॐ ॐ ॐ ॐ

45 Now from the sixth hour darkness occurred over all the land until the ninth hour.

46 And about the ninth hour Jesus shouted out with a great voice, saying, "Eli, Eli, lama sabachthani?"—that is, "My God, My God, why have You abandoned Me?"

47 And some of those who were standing there, when they heard *it*, were saying, "This *man* is calling Elijah."

48 And immediately one of them ran, and taking a sponge he filled *it* with vinegar and put *it* on a reed, and gave a drink to Him.

49 But the rest said, "Let *Him be*; let us see if Elijah comes to save Him."

The final sufferings of Christ are briefly related. **From the sixth hour** (i.e. noon) **darkness occurred over all the land until the ninth hour** (i.e. about 3:00 P.M.). This was no ordinary darkness, but a sign of apocalyptic horror. The prophets had spoken of cataclysmic judgment in terms of "the sun going down at noon" (Amos 8:9), and "the sun setting while it is yet day" (Jer. 15:9). This was such a cataclysm, for the Creator was being outraged by His creation. Like one hiding his face from a terrible sight, the sun hid its face from the sight of the Son of God being crucified.

At **about the ninth hour Jesus shouted out with a great voice, saying, "Eli, Eli, lama sabachthani?"** translated from the Hebrew as, **"My God, My God, why have You abandoned Me?"** These words are found at the beginning of Psalm 22. But here Jesus is not quoting Scripture. Rather, the Scripture is quoting *Him*, prophesying His agony and dereliction. In speaking of His being forsaken by God, we come upon a subject the reality of which is largely hidden from us in this world. It is not for us to attempt to pry into the mystery of those hours when the Lamb of God bore away the sins of the world and became a curse for us (John 1:29; Gal. 3:13). It is for us simply to tremble in gratitude that Christ drank that cup so that we might never have to.

Those **who were standing there,** however, could not understand the Hebrew, and thought that the word "Eli" (Hebrew for "My God") meant that He was **calling Elijah.** There was a belief that Elijah would come to rescue the innocent sufferer, and they concluded that Jesus was calling for Elijah to come and save Him from the cross. Jesus called for a drink so that His parched throat could speak (John 19:28–30), and **one of them ran** to fulfill this request. He **took a sponge** and **filled** *it* **with vinegar** (meaning in that day a sour wine drunk by laborers; Ruth 2:14), and **gave a drink to Him** so that He could speak. The crowd, however, was more interested in seeing **if Elijah** would **come to save Him.** This incomprehension of the crowd shows how isolated Christ was. He was dying for the sins of the world, and they remained callous and clueless.

ॐ ॐ ॐ ॐ ॐ

50 And Jesus cried out again with a great voice, and yielded *His* spirit.

51 And behold! the curtain of the sanctuary was torn in two from top to bottom, and the earth was shaken, and the rocks were torn,

52 and the tombs were opened, and many bodies of the saints who had fallen asleep were raised,

53 and coming out of the tombs after His

> rising they entered into the holy city and were
> revealed to many.

When Christ received the vinegar and had moistened His throat, He lifted up His voice in one final cry of triumph, **crying out again with a great voice**. (From John 19:30, we learn that He cried, "It is finished!" and then **yielded *His* spirit**, saying, "Father, into Your hands I commit My spirit"; Luke 23:46.) It was as if this final cry were the signal for the world to end: **the curtain of the sanctuary was torn in two, the earth was shaken, the rocks were torn, and the tombs were opened, and many bodies of the saints were raised**. (The passive mood of these verbs testifies to the divine power.) It was as if a shudder ran through all the earth.

Common Jewish expectation held that such phenomena as earthquakes and the sun being darkened would attend the last days, which would culminate in the resurrection of the dead. St. Matthew relates these phenomena here as attending the death of Christ to show that He is the Messiah, and His death inaugurates the last days.

The rending of **the curtain of the sanctuary**, however, was not a part of that common expectation. The curtain spoken of was probably the large curtain separating the sanctuary from the forecourt, which was visible to all in the Temple, and not the inner curtain separating the Holy Place from the Holy of Holies. This rending was a sign of catastrophe, as if God Himself were rending His garments, desecrating His own Temple over the outrage of the death of His Son. The supernatural aspect of this rending is stressed in saying that it **was torn in two from top to bottom**. Men might be able to tear the curtain from the bottom to the top, but no man was tall enough to seize it from the top and rip it from there—only God could do that.

Much has been written on the raising of the **bodies of the saints who had fallen asleep** and who **came out of the tombs after** Christ's **rising** and **entered into the holy city and were revealed to many**. Matthew's brief description does not allow complete certainty about the nature of this event. By the term **saint**, it seems as if St. Matthew refers to the recent Christian dead, those disciples of Jesus who had recently died and were buried in the Jerusalem area. We would suggest the following:

The great earthquake that attended the death of Christ and caused the rocks to be split also shook the stones from the doors of the rock-tombs in the area. After Christ's rising, many bodies of the saints (i.e. the Christian dead in those tombs) also were raised. (The phrase **after His rising** could describe either the time they were raised or the time they entered the holy city; we prefer the first alternative, since this connects their resurrection with that of Christ, the First-fruit; 1 Cor. 15:23.) This resurrection was not a simple resuscitation like that of Lazarus. These saints were raised to the new order of the age to come and were not to die again. After Jesus' resurrection they also entered Jerusalem and were revealed to many there in brief visions, even as Jesus appeared to two disciples on the road to Emmaus and then vanished from their sight (Luke 24:31). They thus constituted additional proof that Christ had been raised, harrowing hell and bestowing resurrection on the fallen (Paschal kontakion). The final resurrection had begun.

We can imagine how Matthew and his fellow disciples heard of this event. The earthquake that occurred at Jesus' death disturbed any number of graves, dislodging the stones that closed their doors. Word got around after Jesus' resurrection that the families of those disciples of His who had recently died had seen visions of their recently departed—some of the very ones whose tombs had been affected, and whose bodies were now missing. Most would put down the absence of the bodies to grave robbers, but the Christians would connect it to the visions seen. They would conclude that these dead had been raised to resurrection with Jesus, and had ascended to heaven after appearing to them.

ॐ ॐ ॐ ॐ ॐ

54 Now the centurion, and those with him guarding Jesus, when they saw the earthquake and the things happening, were extremely frightened and said, "Truly this was the Son of God!"
55 And many women were there observing from

> a distance, who had followed Jesus from Gali-
> lee, serving Him,
> 56 among whom were Mary Magdalene, Mary the
> mother of James and Joseph, and the mother
> of the sons of Zebedee.

The centurion and his fellow-soldiers who presided over the executions saw the darkening of the sun and the earthquake and **were extremely frightened**. They knew from local reports that Jesus had claimed to be the Son of God (though they did not understand all that was meant by that), and these things appeared to confirm it. Jesus had died triumphantly and seemingly voluntarily (v. 50), and His death was evidently the signal for an earthquake. No wonder they concluded that His claims were true after all, and confessed, **"Truly this was the Son of God!"** For Matthew, this confession from pagans shows the blindness of his own people, the Jews, to be all the more culpable. Even Gentiles can see that Jesus is the Messiah—why cannot Israel see this?

St. Matthew then mentions the **many women** who were **there observing from a distance**, the women **who had followed Jesus from Galilee, serving Him** and attending to the needs of Him and the Twelve. Some of them were listed as **Mary Magdalene, Mary the mother of James and Joseph** (almost certainly the same James and Joseph already mentioned in 13:55, the kinsmen of the Lord), and **the mother of the sons of Zebedee** (probably the Salome mentioned in Mark 15:40). These are singled out here because they would have a role as witnesses of Christ's resurrection later. Matthew is careful to show how they witnessed Christ's death and the place of His burial (v. 61)—there was no chance they would later go to the wrong tomb.

§XIV.6. Jesus' Burial

> ৺ৡ ৺ৡ ৺ৡ ৺ৡ ৺ৡ
> 57 And when it was evening, there came a rich
> man from Arimathea, Joseph by name, who

> himself had also become a disciple of Jesus.
>
> 58 This *man* came to Pilate and asked for the body of Jesus. Then Pilate ordered *it* to be given to him.
>
> 59 And Joseph took the body and wrapped it up in a clean linen *cloth*,
>
> 60 and laid it in his new tomb, which he had hewn in the rock, and he rolled a great stone to the door of the tomb and went away.
>
> 61 And Mary Magdalene was there, and the other Mary, sitting opposite the grave.

As the **evening** was coming, **a rich man from Arimathea** (that is, whose ancestral home was Ramathaim-Zophim, about twenty miles northwest of Jerusalem), **Joseph by name**, took matters into his own hands. (The Lord's Mother, we may think, was too prostrate with grief to make such a request.) Though a member of the Sanhedrin (Mark 15:43), he **had also become a disciple of Jesus**. Because of the hostility of his fellows, however, he had been quiet about his faith (John 19:38). Joseph **came to Pilate and asked for the body of Jesus**. This took some courage, for those crucified for sedition were not usually given back to family or friends. Pilate, who had contempt for Jesus' foes and who had thought Him innocent, was willing to make an exception, and **ordered** the corpse **to be given to him**. Also, to give Jesus' body honorable burial would be for Joseph to publicly align himself with the disgraced Nazarene, to his great personal cost.

Assisted by his fellow Sanhedrinist Nicodemus (John 19:39), Joseph **took the body and wrapped it up in a clean linen *cloth*, and laid it in his new tomb,** for it was close to the place of execution. This tomb was located in a garden and had been **hewn in the rock** with **a great stone** which could be **rolled** in front of the open **door**. Matthew stresses that Joseph's tomb was **new**—that is, that it had never been used. Tombs had interior places for the burial of several corpses, but this tomb was entirely empty, so that there was no possibility later of mixing up the corpses inside, or of mistakenly thinking that Jesus' body was gone when it was still lying within.

Though excluded from the hasty burial rites done by the important Sanhedrinists, **Mary Magdalene was there**, and **the other Mary** also (the mother of James and Joseph), observing everything from a short distance. From their place **opposite the grave**, they could know the exact location when they went back later themselves to anoint the body. There was no chance they would go to the wrong tomb.

ॐ ॐ ॐ ॐ ॐ

62 Now on the next day, which is *the day* after *the* Preparation *day*, the chief-priests and the Pharisees gathered together with Pilate,

63 and said, "Lord, we remember that while living that deceiver said, 'After three days I am to arise.'

64 "Therefore, order that the grave be made secure until the third day, lest His disciples come and steal it and say to the people, 'He has been raised from the dead!' and the last deception will be worse than the first."

65 Pilate said to them, "You have a guard; go away, make *it as* secure as you know *how*."

66 And they went and made the grave secure, and with the guard they sealed the stone.

Consistent with his polemical purposes, St. Matthew also relates the part that Jesus' foes played in His burial. They acted **the next day** (that is, the Sabbath, here called *the day* **after** *the* **Preparation** *day* or the Friday Jesus died, to show that they lost no time). The delegation to Pilate consisted of **the chief-priests** (who were mostly Sadducees) and some **Pharisees**. The two groups were usually hostile, but they were united by their common and overriding hostility to Jesus.

They approached Pilate and said, **"Lord** (Gr. *Kyrie*, in this case, "sir"), **we remember that while living that deceiver said, 'After**

three days I am to arise.'" They therefore requested that Pilate post a guard so that **the grave be made secure until the third day**. They had their own Temple officers at their disposal, but it seems they wanted the added authority of Rome. Perhaps they wanted to preemptively ensure that Jesus' supporters would not appeal to Pilate themselves and take away the body, overthrowing the chief-priests' own guarding precautions.

How Jesus' foes knew about His claim that He would rise after three days is disputed. Some say that they inferred this from Jesus' words about building again the Temple of His body after three days (compare John 2:19). This seems unlikely, given that up to His trial and crucifixion, they still held to the popular misunderstanding of this saying, which said that Jesus was going to raise up the actual Temple (26:61; 27:40).

I suggest that Judas, one of the Twelve who was privy to these private predictions (16:21; 17:22; 20:19), mentioned them to Jesus' foes during his secret collaborations with them during that final week. There is no reason to think that the meeting mentioned in 26:14f was the only one held. Judas perhaps mentioned this prediction as scornful evidence of how deluded his former Master had become, and the chief-priests and Pharisees now remember it and take these precautions lest the disciples try to steal the body in fraudulent fulfillment of the words.

Though no friend of the Jewish delegation, Pilate is moved by their argument that **the last deception** may become **worse than the first**, and that Jesus' supporters may gather fresh support in their opposition of Rome. He therefore tells them, **"You have a guard** (Gr. *koustodia*, a loan-word from the Latin *custodia*); **go away, make it *as* secure as you know *how.*"** They therefore went on Saturday morning and **made the grave secure, and with the guard they sealed the stone**. By affixing seals to the stone (presumably after making sure the body had not been stolen Friday night), they were making sure the body could not be moved without their knowledge, for if the stone were moved, the broken seals would attest to it. Those seals were affixed **with the** Roman **guard**, and to break them was to challenge the might of Rome. Jesus' foes were taking no chances. A note of Christian irony, however, runs throughout this passage. They might make it as secure as they knew how, and even use Roman guards, but this would be no match for the power of God!

❧ XV ❧

THE RESURRECTION
(28:1–20)

§XV.1. The Empty Tomb and the Appearance to the Women

❧ ❧ ❧ ❧ ❧

28 1 Now after the Sabbath, in the dawning towards the first *day* of the week, Mary Magdalene and the other Mary came to observe the grave.

2 And behold! a great earthquake happened, for an angel of the Lord descended from heaven and came and rolled away the stone and sat upon it.

3 And his appearance was as lightning and his clothing as white as snow;

4 and for fear of him those guarding were shaken and became as dead *men*.

5 And the angel answered and said to the women, "You, do not be afraid, for I know that you are seeking Jesus who has been crucified.

6 "He is not here, for He was raised, just as He said. Come, see the place where He was lying.

7 "And quickly go, tell His disciples that He was raised from the dead; and behold, He is going before you into Galilee; there you will see Him. Behold, I have told you."

8 And they departed quickly from the tomb with

> fear and great joy, and ran to declare *it* to His
> disciples.
> 9 And behold! Jesus met them, saying, "Hail!"
>   And they came up and seized His feet and
>   worshipped Him.
> 10 Then Jesus says to them, "Do not be afraid;
>   go away and declare to My brothers to go into
>   Galilee; there they will see Me."

St. Matthew relates two resurrection appearances, one to the women and one at the appointed rendezvous in Galilee, along with the story spread among the Jews to counteract this Christian witness.

The first story of the appearance to the women happens **after the Sabbath, in the dawning towards the first *day* of the week.** The women mentioned earlier in 27:56 planned to meet early on the first day of the week at the tomb of Christ to try to anoint the body of Jesus. Leaving from their separate locations in Jerusalem, **Mary Magdalene and the other Mary** came to the burial site **to observe the grave,** and to decide how best to have the stone moved (Mark 16:3). Much to their surprise (Matthew uses his characteristic **behold!**), they saw that **a great earthquake happened** earlier that day, and that the stone sealing the door of the tomb had been moved aside.

As the spiritual cause of this earthquake, **an angel of the Lord descended from heaven and came and rolled away the stone and sat upon it** in triumph. This was not to allow the Lord to leave—He who could pass through closed doors (John 20:19)—but to allow the women later to see that the tomb was empty. It was the blinding and unexpected appearance of the angel (like **lightning**) that caused **those guarding** Jesus to be **shaken and become as dead *men***—that is, to faint away. They evidently remained unconscious throughout the visit of the women. The irony of this is not to be missed—Christ, whom all supposed dead, is alive and has gone. Those guarding Him, however, were lying somewhere on the site **as dead *men.***

The women then entered the tomb and met this angel (with another one; compare Luke 24:4; John 20:12). Startled by this, they prostrated themselves in fear (Luke 24:5). **The angel answered** their unspoken question, saying, **"You, do not be afraid, for I know that you are seeking Jesus who has been crucified. He is not here, for He was raised, just as He said. Come, see the place where He was lying."** The absence of the body would confirm His words. Then the angel gave them a directive: they must **quickly go** and **tell His disciples that He was raised from the dead** and was **going before** them **into Galilee** for His prearranged rendezvous with all of them (26:32). The angel was charged to give them this message, and in the absence of any response from them, he concludes, **"Behold, I have told you,"** even as he was commanded.

Once the women picked themselves up off the ground, **they departed quickly from the tomb with fear and great joy, and ran to declare** this **to His disciples**, telling no one on the way (Mark 16:8). It was while they were going that **Jesus met them**, greeting them with the customary greeting **"Hail!"** (or "hello"). Knowing Him to be the Lord, they **came up and seized His feet** with joy and homage **and worshipped Him**. The fear with which they fled from the tomb (v. 8) still gripped their hearts, and so Jesus said, **"Do not be afraid. Go away and declare to My brothers to go into Galilee; there they will see Me."** (We note that though they all forsook Him, He yet regards them as His **brothers**.) The Lord would yet reveal Himself to the Twelve in Jerusalem and its environs (Luke 24:13f; John 20:19f), but the great meeting with the majority of His disciples was to occur in the safety of Galilee. (It seems as if this is where the "more than 500 brothers" saw Him "at once"; 1 Cor. 15:6.) In His love for His own, Christ sets His heart on this reunion.

§XV.2. The Story Spread among the Jews

ॐ ॐ ॐ ॐ ॐ

11 Now while they were on their way, behold, some of the guard came into the city and

> declared to the chief-priests all the things that happened.
>
> 12 And when they had assembled with the elders and taken counsel, they gave sufficient money to the soldiers,
>
> 13 and said, "You are to say, 'His disciples came by night and stole Him away while we *ourselves* were sleeping.'
>
> 14 "And if this is heard before the governor, we *ourselves* will persuade him and make you worry-free."
>
> 15 And they took the money and did as they were taught; and this word was spread among the Jews, up to today.

Matthew then relates a story about how these resurrection appearances were denied by the Jewish community at large. It was while the women **were on their way** to the disciples that the guards revived. They found the tomb empty, and knew that they were in trouble. (The penalty for a Roman soldier for falling asleep on guard duty was death.) They **declared** the story about the vision of the angel and the empty tomb first of all **to the chief-priests**. (To report it to their Roman superiors would have resulted in their being instantly punished.)

The Jewish authorities then **assembled with the elders** to decide the best way to proceed. It is interesting to speculate on what they thought had actually happened. Perhaps they assumed that all the guards had fallen asleep (rather unlikely, given the stiff Roman penalty for such action), and that the disciples had indeed stolen the body during this time. How else could they account for its absence? They therefore **gave sufficient money to the soldiers** (that is, a lot of money) and told them to stick to this story.

The bribe was necessary to ensure their compliance. In addition, they assured the soldiers that **if this** story of their sleeping on duty was **heard before the governor** Pilate, they themselves, the chief-priests, could be counted on (the **we** is emphatic) to **persuade him and make** the soldiers **worry-free** (possibly through saying they were abundantly satisfied with the soldiers' performance). The soldiers **took the money** (and the deal) and **did as they were taught**. (Indeed, what else could they do?) Accordingly, St. Matthew reports, **this** story **was spread among the Jews up to** his day, as the usual Jewish explanation of the empty tomb.

It is significant that the Jews of Jerusalem never tried to deny the story of the empty tomb. Rather, they were forced to come up with an alternative explanation for it—even one so unlikely as a watch of Roman guards all falling asleep simultaneously and sleeping through some terrified disciples moving the stone and stealing the body. The story was not even self-consistent, for if the soldiers were asleep, how could they know that it was the disciples who stole the body? Matthew records the Jewish version to highlight how flimsy is their case.

§XV.3. Appearance in Galilee and the Final Commission

꙰ ꙰ ꙰ ꙰ ꙰

16 But the eleven disciples went into Galilee, to the mountain which Jesus had appointed.

17 And when they saw Him, they worshipped, but some hesitated.

18 And Jesus came and spoke to them, saying, "All authority has been given to Me in heaven and on earth.

19 "Go therefore and make disciples of all the nations, baptizing them in the Name of the Father and of the Son and of the Holy Spirit,

20 "teaching them to keep all things, whatsoever I commanded you; and behold, I *Myself* am with you all the days, even to the consummation of the age."

St. Matthew concludes his Gospel with Christ's final appearance to His own in Galilee and His commission to spread His Word to all the world.

At length **the eleven disciples went into Galilee, to the mountain which Jesus had appointed**. (Which mountain is not here specified; one wonders if the Mountain of Transfiguration is meant.) **When they** first **saw Him** on the mountain, **they worshipped** and bowed down as the women had, **but some hesitated**, wondering if it was truly the Lord.

What was the cause of this hesitation? (The word used is *distazo*, used also in 14:31 for the hesitation of Peter as he walked on the water.) It would seem that the Lord's outward form was not immediately recognizable to all as the Lord, and they were at first not sure that this stranger was He. (Thus those on the road to Emmaus did not recognize Him at first, Luke 24:16; nor did the apostles on the Sea of Tiberias, John 21:12). It was not until He **came** near **and spoke to them** that they knew it was the Lord. Matthew mentions this hesitation to show how their initial doubt was overcome when Christ spoke and confirmed to them by His word that He was truly risen from the dead—and to show that their task was to overcome the doubts of the rest of their countrymen also.

In His words to them, Jesus declared that as the risen Messiah, **all authority** had **been given** to Him by His Father **in heaven and on earth**. That is, in fulfillment of the ancient prophecies, the nations to the ends of the earth were given to Him as His inheritance also (Ps. 2:8; 72:8). The apostles' mission, which once was confined to Israel (10:5–6), was now to extend to all the earth. They must **go therefore and make disciples of all the nations, baptizing them in the Name of the Father and of the Son and of the Holy Spirit**, **teaching them to keep** all His commands (for example, those contained in chapters 5–7). Discipleship is thus not just a matter of being baptized, but also of **keeping all things**, **whatsoever** He **commanded** (compare John 14:15, 21; 15:10).

Though not mentioned much in this Gospel (lest later Christians anachronistically project back a full post-Pentecostal baptism into the early ministry of Jesus), the normal way of becoming Jesus' disciple even during His ministry was by accepting baptism (see John 3:22; 4:1–2). This baptism was now to be extended to all, even to Gentiles. (The question of whether these Gentiles must first accept circumcision was not yet asked.)

By saying that this baptism was **in the Name of the Father and of the Son and of the Holy Spirit** (literally "*into* the Name," Gr. *eis to onoma*), Matthew means that those baptized were brought into relationship with the power of the Holy Trinity. This is what the phrase to be baptized *eis*, "into," someone meant. (Hence to be baptized "*eis*, into, Moses" [1 Cor. 10:2] meant to be in a relationship with Moses, as his disciple.) The disciples of Jesus thus come to know all the fullness of God. And this God was a Trinitarian God, for **the Son** and **the Holy Spirit** are mentioned with **the Father** as being all in one single **Name**. The Father sent the Son, who Himself pours out the Holy Spirit upon His disciples.

Though there is no other mention of this Trinitarian phrase in the New Testament, there is no reason to question its authenticity. The *Didache*, a document dating from about AD 100, mentions this as the usual baptismal formula, and there is no trace in church history of any other. The phrase in Acts 19:5 about being baptized "in the Name of the Lord Jesus" clearly means accepting Christian baptism, just as the phrase about being baptized "into John's baptism" in Acts 19:3 means accepting Johannine baptism.

The Lord's words conclude with His promise to be with His disciples **all the days** of this age, even to its **consummation** and end. Jesus had promised to be in the midst of His disciples, even if the assembly were but two or three (18:20). That promise is repeated here. In the apostolic mission to all the nations, the Church need not fear. Whatever persecution and suffering may come, Jesus Himself (the **I** is emphatic) will never depart from them, but will be with them to sustain and strengthen them. As long as the age endures, He will be in the midst of His people.

About the Author

Archpriest Lawrence Farley currently pastors St. Herman of Alaska Orthodox Mission (OCA) in Surrey, B.C., Canada. He received his B.A. from Trinity College, Toronto, and his M.Div. from Wycliffe College, Toronto. A former Anglican priest, he converted to Orthodoxy in 1985 and studied for two years at St. Tikhon's Orthodox Seminary in Pennsylvania. He has also published *Let Us Attend: A Journey Through the Orthodox Divine Liturgy.*

ANCIENT FAITH RADIO
www.ancientfaithradio.com

Visit www.ancientfaithradio.com to listen to Fr. Lawrence Farley's regular podcast, "The Coffee Cup Commentaries."

Also in the *Orthodox Bible Study Companion Series*

Universal Truth: The Catholic Epistles of James, Peter, Jude and John
> Paperback, 232 pages (ISBN 978-1-888212-60-0)
> CP Order No. 007611—$15.95*

Shepherding the Flock: The Pastoral Epistles of Saint Paul the Apostle to Timothy and Titus
> Paperback, 144 pages (ISBN 978-1-888212-56-3)
> CP Order No. 007516—$13.95*

The Gospel of John: Beholding the Glory
> Paperback, 376 pages (ISBN 978-1-888212-55-6)
> CP Order No. 007110—$19.95*

The Gospel of Mark: The Suffering Servant
> Paperback, 224 pages (ISBN 978-1-888212-54-9)
> CP Order No. 006035—$16.95*

First and Second Corinthians: Straight from the Heart
> Paperback, 319 pages (ISBN 9781-888212-53-2)
> CP Order No. 006129—$17.95*

The Prison Epistles:
Philippians – Ephesians – Colossians – Philemon
> Paperback, 224 pages (ISBN 978-1-888212-52-5)
> CP Order No. 006034—$15.95*

The Epistle to the Romans: A Gospel for All
> Paperback, 208 pages (ISBN 978-1-888212-51-8)
> CP Order No. 005675—$15.95*

*plus applicable tax and postage & handling charges. Prices current as of 7/09. Please call Conciliar Press at 800-967-7377 for complete ordering information.

Check the Conciliar Press website (www.conciliarpress.com) for announcements of future releases in this series.

Other Books of Interest

The Orthodox Study Bible: Old and New Testaments

Featuring a Septuagint text of the Old Testament developed by outstanding Orthodox scholars, this Bible also includes the complete Orthodox canon of the Old Testament, including the Deuterocanon; insightful commentary drawn from the Christian writers of the first ten centuries; helpful notes relating Scripture to seasons of Christian feasting and fasting; a lectionary to guide your Bible reading through the Church year; supplemental Bible study articles on a variety of subjects; a subject index to the study notes to help facilitate Bible study; and more.

Available in hardcover, bonded leather, and genuine leather editions.

Visit www.orthodoxstudybible.com for more detailed information.

Wise Lives, *by Patrick Henry Reardon*

Although it is found in every major extant Christian manuscript of the Old Testament, the later exclusion of the Wisdom of Sirach (also known as Ecclesiasticus) from the Protestant canon has made it one of the little-known gems of Holy Scripture. Composed in Hebrew and translated into Greek in the second century before Christ, it is among the last books of the Old Testament.

Sirach represents the more primitive and conservative aspect of Israel's Wisdom tradition—the practical application of the fear of God to daily life—but he enhances that tradition by a singular attention to biography and historical literature in the shaping of the soul. In short, *Wise Lives.*

Sirach's social context—the struggle to preserve the Jewish religion and culture against the corrosive influence of Hellenic paganism—will resonate with Christians living in the secular world today. In this commentary, Fr. Patrick Reardon illustrates for contemporary readers the riches of this often-neglected jewel of the Bible.

Paperback, 180 pages (ISBN 978-0-9822770-3-4)

CP Order No. 007720—$16.95*

Christ in the Psalms, *by Patrick Henry Reardon*

A highly inspirational book of meditations on the Psalms by one of the most insightful and challenging Orthodox writers of our day. Avoiding both syrupy sentimentality and arid scholasticism, *Christ in the Psalms* takes the reader on a thought-provoking and enlightening pilgrimage through this beloved "Prayer Book" of the Church. Which psalms were quoted most frequently in the New Testament, and how were they interpreted? How has the Church historically understood and utilized the various psalms in her liturgical life? How can we perceive the image of Christ shining through the psalms? Lively and highly devotional, thought-provoking yet warm and practical, *Christ in the Psalms* sheds a world of insight upon each psalm, and offers practical advice for how to make the Psalter a part of our daily lives.

Paperback, 328 pages (ISBN 978-1-888212-21-7)
CP Order No. 004927—$17.95*

Christ in His Saints
by Patrick Henry Reardon

In this sequel to *Christ in the Psalms,* Patrick Henry Reardon once again applies his keen intellect to a topic he loves most dearly. Here he examines the lives of almost one hundred and fifty saints and heroes from the Scriptures— everyone from Abigail to Zephaniah, Adam to St. John the Theologian. This well-researched work is a veritable cornucopia of Bible personalities: Old Testament saints, New Testament saints, "Repentant saints," "Zealous saints," "Saints under pressure" . . . they're all here, and their stories are both fascinating and uplifting. But *Christ in His Saints* is far more than just a biblical who's who. These men and women represent that ancient family into which, by baptism, all believers have been incorporated. Together they compose that great "cloud of witnesses" cheering us on and inspiring us through word and deed.

Paperback, 320 pages (ISBN 978-1-888212-68-6)
CP Order No. 006538—$17.95*

Creation and the Patriarchal Histories:
Orthodox Christian Reflections on the Book of Genesis
by Patrick Henry Reardon

The Book of Genesis is foundational reading for the Christian, concerned as it is with the origins of our race and the beginnings of salvation history. Its opening pages provide the theological suppositions of the entire biblical story: Creation, especially that of man in God's image, the structure of time, man's relationship to God, the entrance of sin into the world, and God's selection of a specific line of revelation that will give structure to history. Early Christian writers such as St. Paul saw no dichotomy between the writings of the Law, of which Genesis is the beginning, and the Gospel. Rather, the Gospel is the key to understanding the Law. In *Creation and the Patriarchal Histories,* Fr. Reardon shows clearly how the proper understanding of Creation and the Fall informs all of Christian doctrine, and how the narratives of the patriarchs from Noah to Joseph pave the way for the salvation history that continues in Exodus.

Paperback, 160 pages (ISBN: 978-1-888212-96-9)
CP Order No. 007605—$13.95*

The Trial of Job:
Orthodox Christian Reflections on the Book of Job
by Patrick Henry Reardon

"The Book of Job always constituted essential and formative reading about the ways of the soul. This has always been the conviction of the spiritual classics through the centuries. Yet, for some reason, the figure of Job is elusive to us—possibly because he seems so comfortably distant; or perhaps because he seems so frightfully close. What Fr. Patrick Reardon achieves with this book is to render Job comprehensible (to those of us who are still lay readers of Scripture), tangible (to those who have not yet tasted the way of darkness and despair), and accessible (to those who have already experienced any form of brokenness and broken-heartedness). Ultimately, all of us identify with one or another aspect of Job's life. As life inevitably informs and as this book intuitively confirms, one cannot sing Psalms without having read Job!"—Fr. John Chryssavgis, author of *Light Through Darkness* and *Soul Mending*

Paperback, 112 pages (ISBN: 978-1-888212-72-3)
CP Order No. 006812—$10.95*

Chronicles of History and Worship:
Orthodox Christian Reflections on the Books of Chronicles
by Patrick Henry Reardon

The Old Testament Books of Chronicles contain some of the most neglected passages in all of Scripture. Understanding their message can be a difficult and daunting task for the modern reader. Patrick Reardon brings these important books to life, unfolding their powerful message for our own day and age. Like any family history, the story of Chronicles is told with a distinct purpose in mind. It asks the question: "What was the real and lasting significance of King David and his house?" Beginning with the long list of names of the first chapter, this heritage is revealed in cosmic significance. It has in fact become the family tree of every true believer. The centrality of worship is also clearly revealed in these pages. Far from being irrelevant or antiquated, these truths are alive today, reflected in the liturgy and life of the Church.

Paperback, 188 pages (ISBN: 978-1-888212-83-9)
CP Order No. 007109—$14.95*

*plus applicable tax and postage & handling charges. Prices current as of 7/09. Please call Conciliar Press at 800-967-7377 for complete ordering information, or order online at www.conciliarpress.com.

Conciliar Media Ministries hopes you have enjoyed and benefited from this book. The proceeds from the sales of our books only partially cover the costs of operating our nonprofit ministry. We are committed to publishing high-quality books in a variety of formats with an Orthodox Christian worldview. Your financial support makes it possible to continue this ministry both in print and online. Donations are tax-deductible and can be made at www.conciliarmedia. com <http://www.conciliarmedia.com/>.